MICROSOFT® OFFICE WORD 2010

QuickSteps

About the Author

Marty Matthews has used computers for more than 40 years, from some of the early mainframe computers to recent personal computers. He has done this as a programmer, systems analyst, manager, and company executive. As a result, he has firsthand knowledge of not only how to program and use a computer, but also how to make the best use of all that can be done with one.

Over 25 years ago, Marty wrote his first computer book on how to buy mini-computers. In the intervening years, he has written more than 70 books, including ones on desktop publishing, Web publishing, Microsoft Office, and Microsoft operating systems from MS-DOS through Windows 7. Recent books published by McGraw-Hill include *Windows 7 QuickSteps, Microsoft Office Word 2007 QuickSteps*, and *Dynamic Web Programming: A Beginner's Guide*.

Marty lives with his wife Carole on an island in Puget Sound in Washington State.

MICROSOFT® OFFICE WORD 2010
QuickSteps

MARTY MATTHEWS

New York Chicago San Francisco
Lisbon London Madrid Mexico City
Milan New Delhi San Juan
Seoul Singapore Sydney Toronto

The McGraw·Hill Companies

Library of Congress Cataloging-in-Publication Data

Matthews, Martin S.
  Microsoft Office Word 2010 quicksteps / Marty Matthews.
    p. cm.
  Includes index.
  ISBN 978-0-07-163487-8 (pbk.)
  1. Microsoft Word. 2. Word processing. I. Title.
  Z52.5.M52M3892 2010
  005.52—dc22

                                             2010010352

McGraw-Hill books are available at special quantity discounts to
use as premiums and sales promotions, or for use in corporate
training programs. To contact a representative, please e-mail us at
bulksales@mcgraw-hill.com.

ISBN   978-0-07-163487-8
MHID   0-07-163487-8

SPONSORING EDITOR / Roger Stewart

EDITORIAL SUPERVISOR / Patty Mon

PROJECT MANAGER / Rajni Pisharody, Glyph International

ACQUISITIONS COORDINATOR / Joya Anthony

TECHNICAL EDITOR / Carole Matthews

COPY EDITOR / Lisa McCoy

PROOFREADER / Claire Splan

INDEXER / Jack Lewis

PRODUCTION SUPERVISOR / Jim Kussow

COMPOSITION / Glyph International

ILLUSTRATION / Glyph International

ART DIRECTOR, COVER / Jeff Weeks

COVER DESIGNER / Pattie Lee

SERIES CREATORS / Marty and Carole Matthews

SERIES DESIGN / Bailey Cunningham

Roger Stewart

My sponsoring editor for approaching 20 years who can prod me when I need prodding, appreciate both the trials and successes of an author, have faith in me when few others did, and through it all become someone I very much appreciate calling my friend. Thanks for it all, Roger.

—Marty

Contents at a Glance

Contents

Chapter 7 · Working with Illustrations 165

Chapter 8 · Using Special Features 191

Acknowledgments

This book is a team effort of truly talented people. Among them are:

Lisa McCoy, copy editor, added greatly to the readability and understandability of the book while always being a joy to work with. Thanks, Lisa!

Joya Anthony, acquisitions coordinator, keeps all the chapters flowing and the participants close to schedule with gentle reminders, and does so with kindness. Thanks Joya!

Patty Mon and **Rajni Pisharody**, project editors, greased the wheels and straightened the track to make a very smooth production process. Thanks, Patty and Rajni!

Roger Stewart, sponsoring editor, believed in us enough to sell the series, and continues to stand behind us as we go through the third edition. Thanks, Roger!

Carole Matthews, writing partner, parenting partner, life partner, and, oh, by the way, technical editor, shares all that is my life and gives meaning and substance to it all, for over 38 years! Thank you, I love you Carole!

Introduction

QuickSteps books are recipe books for computer users. They answer the question "How do I..." by providing a quick set of steps to accomplish the most common tasks with a particular operating system or application.

The sets of steps are the central focus of the book. QuickSteps sidebars show how to quickly perform many small functions or tasks that support the primary functions. QuickFacts sidebars supply information that you need to know about a subject. Notes, Tips, and Cautions augment the steps; they are presented in a separate column so as not to interrupt the flow of the steps. The introductions are minimal rather than narrative, and numerous illustrations and figures, many with callouts, support the steps.

QuickSteps books are organized by function and the tasks needed to perform that function. Each function is a chapter. Each task, or "How To," contains the steps needed for accomplishing the function, along with the relevant Notes, Tips, Cautions, and screenshots. You can easily find the tasks you need through:

- The table of contents, which lists the functional areas (chapters) and tasks in the order they are presented

- A How To list of tasks on the opening page of each chapter

- The index, which provides an alphabetical list of the terms that are used to describe the functions and tasks

- Color-coded tabs for each chapter, or functional area, with an index to the tabs in the Contents at a Glance section (just before the table of contents)

Conventions Used in This Book

Microsoft Office Word 2010 QuickSteps uses several conventions designed to make the book easier for you to follow:

- A in the table of contents and in the How To list in each chapter references a QuickSteps sidebar in a chapter, and a references a QuickFacts sidebar.

- **Bold type** is used for words or objects on the screen that you are to do something with—for example, "click **Start** and click **Computer**."

- *Italic type* is used for a word or phrase that is being defined or otherwise deserves special emphasis.

- <u>Underlined type</u> is used for text that you are to type from the keyboard.

- SMALL CAPITAL LETTERS are used for keys on the keyboard, such as **ENTER** and **SHIFT**.

- When you are expected to enter a command, you are told to press the key(s). If you are to enter text or numbers, you are told to type them.

How to...

- Use the Start Menu to Start Word
- Start Word in Other Ways
- Reviewing Versions of Office 2010
- Exiting Word
- Explore the Word Window
- Familiarize Yourself with the Ribbon
- Use the Mouse
- Use Tabs and Menus
- Using the Mini Toolbar
- Use Views
- Work with File View
- Customize the Ribbon
- Customize the Quick Access Toolbar
- Show or Hide ScreenTips
- Changing the Window Color
- Add Identifying Information to Documents
- Setting Preferences
- Open Help
- Using the Help Toolbar
- Conduct Research
- Use the Thesaurus
- Translate a Document
- Accessing Microsoft Office Resources
- Update Word

Chapter 1
Stepping into Word

Microsoft Word is the most widely used of all word-processing programs, and Word 2010 is the latest version in that line. While maintaining the core features and functionality of Word from years past, this version continues the evolution of Microsoft Office products from a menu-driven user interface (the collection of screen elements that allows you to use and navigate the program) to that of a customizable *ribbon*, an organizational scheme to better connect tools to tasks. Along with these and other infrastructure enhancements, Word 2010 adds several new ease-of-use features, such as a *paste preview* so you can see the results of a change before you make it, and this version improves on many functional features such as the new *File* view, also called the *Backstage view*, which provides a single location for essential information about your document. While preserving the simple elegance of producing a professional-looking document, Microsoft continues to find ways to make that task less onerous and adds features that allow you to use and distribute information in more meaningful ways.

In this chapter you will become familiar with Word; see how to start and exit it; use Word's windows, panes, ribbon, toolbars, and menus; learn how to get help; and find out how to customize Word and the ribbon.

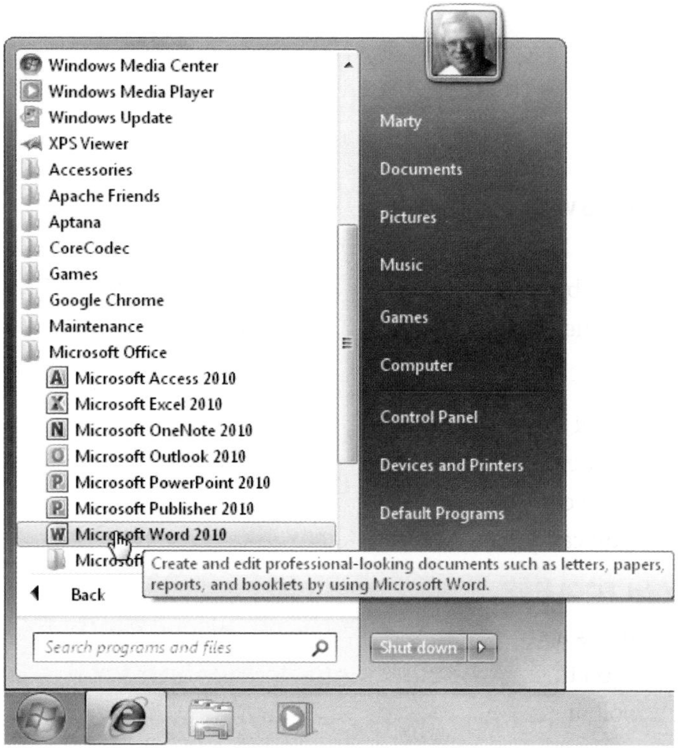

Start and Exit Word

How you start Word depends on how Word was installed and what has happened to it since its installation. In this section you'll see a surefire way to start Word and some alternatives. You'll also see how to exit Word.

Use the Start Menu to Start Word

If no other icons for or shortcuts to Word are available on your desktop, you can always start Word using the Start menu.

1. Start your computer if it is not already running, and log on to Windows if necessary.
2. Click **Start**. The Start menu opens.
3. Click **All Programs**, scroll down the menu if needed by clicking the bar on the right, click **Microsoft Office**, and click **Microsoft Word 2010**, as shown in Figure 1-1.

Start Word in Other Ways

In addition to using All Programs on the Start menu, you can create several other ways in which Word can be started.

USE THE START MENU ITSELF

The icons of the programs you use most often are displayed on the left side of the Start menu. If you frequently use Word, its icon and name will appear there. To use that option to start Word:

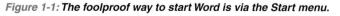

Figure 1-1: *The foolproof way to start Word is via the Start menu.*

1. Click **Start**. The Start menu opens.

2. Click the **Word** icon on the left of the Start menu.

PIN WORD TO THE START MENU

The Start menu's contents and sequence of items will differ based on how often you use the various programs. If you think that you may use other programs more frequently, you can keep Word on the Start menu by "pinning" it there.

1. Click **Start** to open the Start menu, click **All Programs**, scroll down (if needed), and click **Microsoft Office**.

2. Right-click (click the right mouse button) **Microsoft Word 2010**, and click **Pin To Start Menu**.

Word can then be started using the previous set of steps.

CREATE A DESKTOP SHORTCUT

An easy way to start Word is to create a shortcut icon on the desktop and use it to start the program.

1. Click **Start**, click **All Programs**, and click **Microsoft Office.**

2. Right-click **Microsoft Office Word 2010**, click **Send To**, and click **Desktop (Create Shortcut)**.

In this case, Word is started by double-clicking (pressing the mouse button twice in rapid succession) the shortcut icon.

USE THE TASKBAR

Depending on the version of Windows that you have, you can place a Word shortcut on the taskbar at the bottom of your screen in two different ways. In Windows XP and Vista, you can place the Word shortcut in the Quick Launch toolbar; in Windows 7, you can pin the shortcut to the taskbar itself.

USE THE QUICK LAUNCH TOOLBAR

The Quick Launch toolbar is a small area on the taskbar next to the Start button. You can put a Word icon on the Quick Launch toolbar and use it to start Word. If your Quick Launch toolbar is not visible, open it and put a Word icon there.

1. If you don't see a Quick Launch toolbar, right-click a blank area of the taskbar, click **Toolbars**, and click **Quick Launch**. The Quick Launch toolbar is displayed.

2. Click **Start**, click **All Programs**, click **Microsoft Office**, and drag the **Microsoft Office Word 2010** icon to where you want it on the Quick Launch toolbar.

To start Word, click the icon on the Quick Launch toolbar.

PIN WORD TO THE TASKBAR

In Windows 7 you can pin a Word icon to the taskbar, where it will remain to be restarted after you have shut it down (in prior versions of Windows, icons only showed up on the taskbar if they were running). You may have noticed in pinning Word to the Start menu that you could also choose to pin it to the taskbar. Another way to accomplish this is after you have started Word.

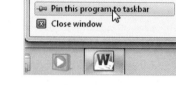

1. Start Word in any of the ways already described. Once Word is running, its icon will appear on the taskbar.

2. Right-click the Word icon on the taskbar and click **Pin This Program To Taskbar**.

Word now can be started by clicking the icon on the taskbar.

Exit Word

To exit Word when you are done using it:

- Click the **File** tab in the upper-left corner of the Word window, shown in Figure 1-2, and click **Exit.**

  –Or–

- Click the **Close** icon on the right of the title bar. ▄▄x▄▄

Explore Word

Word uses a wide assortment of windows, ribbon tabs, toolbars, menus, and special features to accomplish its functions. Much of this book explores how to find and use all of those items. In this section you'll learn to use the most common features of the default Word window, including the parts of the window, the tabs on the ribbon, and the task pane.

QUICKFACTS

REVIEWING VERSIONS OF OFFICE 2010 *(Continued)*

Office 2010 on the desktop platform is available in four versions:

- **Office Starter 2010** is only available preinstalled on a new computer, has reduced functionality, and is paid for with advertising. It can be directly upgraded to one of the following three full versions of Office 2010 through a product key card purchased from a retail outlet.

- **Office Home & Student 2010** is available to be installed from a DVD or via Click-To-Run over the Internet, and contains the full version of Word, Excel, PowerPoint, and OneNote.

- **Office Home & Business 2010** is available to be installed from a DVD or via Click-To-Run over the Internet, contains all the features of Office Home & Student, and adds Outlook.

- **Office Professional 2010** is available to be installed from a DVD or via Click-To-Run over the Internet, contains all the features of Office Home & Business, and adds Access and Publisher.

There are also two enterprise editions available only through a volume license. Office Standard adds Publisher to Office Home & Business, and Office Professional Plus adds SharePoint Workspace and InfoPath to Office Professional.

This book, which covers the full version of Word 2010, is applicable to all the editions with a full version of Word and, to a limited extent, those features that are included in Office Starter and Office Web Apps.

Explore the Word Window

The Word window has many features to aid you in creating and editing documents. The view presented to you when you first start Word is shown in Figure 1-2. You can see the primary parts of the ribbon in Figure 1-3. The principal features of the Word window, including the various ribbon tabs, are described further in this and other chapters of this book.

Familiarize Yourself with the Ribbon

The familiar toolbars and menus from versions of Word prior to 2007 are gone. The original menu structure used in earlier Office products (File, Edit, Format, Window, Help, and other menus) was designed to accommodate fewer tasks and features. That menu structure has simply outgrown its usefulness. Microsoft's solution to the increased number of features is the *ribbon*, the container at the top of all Office program windows that holds the tools and features you are most likely to use (see Figure 1-3). The ribbon collects tools for a given function into *groups*—for example, the Font group provides the tools to work with text. Groups are then organized into tabs for working on likely tasks. For example, the Insert tab contains groups for adding components, such as tables, links, and charts to your document (or spreadsheet or slide presentation). Each Office program has a default set of tabs, with additional *contextual* tabs that appear as the context of your work changes. For instance, when you select a picture, a Format tab containing shapes and drawing tools that you can use with the particular object appears beneath the defining tools tab (such as the Picture Tools tab shown in Figure 1-3); when the object is unselected, the Format tab disappears.

The ribbon contains labeled buttons you can click to use a given command or tool. Depending on the tool, you are then presented with additional options in the form of a list of commands, a dialog box or task pane, or galleries of choices that reflect what you'll see in your work. Groups that contain several more tools than can be displayed in the ribbon include a *Dialog Box Launcher* icon that takes you directly

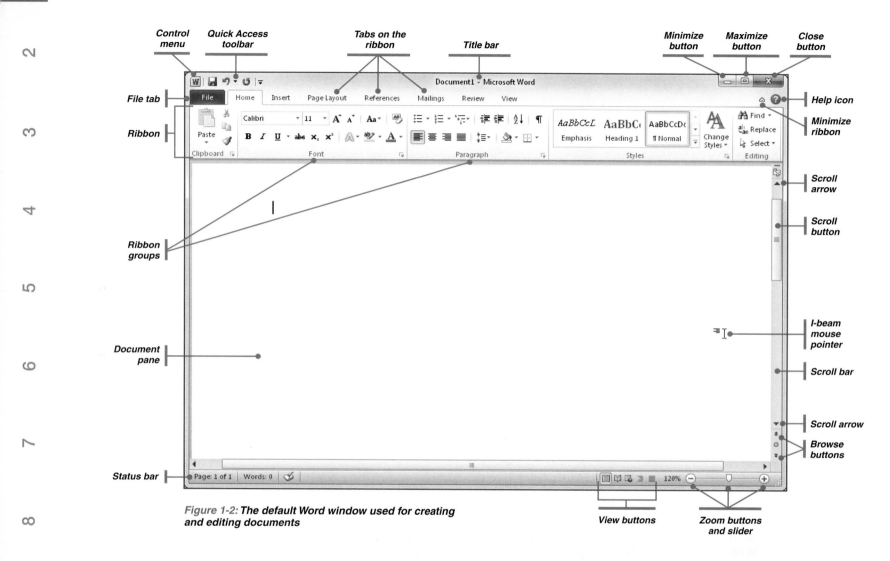

Figure 1-2: **The default Word window used for creating and editing documents**

to these other choices. The ribbon also takes advantage of Office features, including a live preview of many potential changes (for example, you can select text and see it change color as you point to various colors in the Font Color gallery). See the accompanying sections and figures for more information on the ribbon and other elements of the Word window.

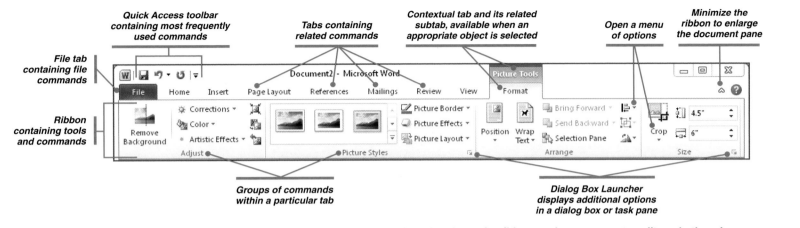

Quick Access toolbar containing most frequently used commands

Tabs containing related commands

Contextual tab and its related subtab, available when an appropriate object is selected

Open a menu of options

Minimize the ribbon to enlarge the document pane

File tab containing file commands

Ribbon containing tools and commands

Groups of commands within a particular tab

Dialog Box Launcher displays additional options in a dialog box or task pane

Figure 1-3: Organized into tabs and groups, the commands and tools on the ribbon are how you create, edit, and otherwise work with documents.

TIP

The ribbon adapts to the size of your Word window and your screen resolution, changing the size and shape of buttons and labels. You can see the difference yourself by increasing or decreasing the size of the window. For instance, if your Word window is initially not maximized, maximize it and notice how the ribbon appears, and then click the Restore button on the title bar and again notice the ribbon. Drag the right border of the Word window toward the left, and see how the ribbon changes to reflect its decreasing real estate.

At the left end of the ribbon is the File tab and above the left end of the ribbon is the Quick Access toolbar. The File tab provides access to the File view, which lets you work *with* your document (such as saving it), as opposed to the ribbon, which centers on working *in* your document (such as editing and formatting). The Quick Access toolbar provides an always-available location for your favorite tools. It starts out with a small default set of tools, but you can add to it. See the accompanying sections and figures for more information on the ribbon and the other elements of the Word window.

Use the Mouse

A *mouse* is any pointing device—including trackballs, pointing sticks, and graphic tablets—with two or more buttons. This book assumes you are using a two-button mouse. Moving the mouse moves the pointer on the screen. You *select* an object on the screen by moving the pointer so that it is on top of the object and then pressing the left button on the mouse.

You may control the mouse with either your left or right hand; therefore, the buttons may be switched. (See *Windows 7 QuickSteps*, published by McGraw-Hill,

TIP

To gain working space in the document pane, you can minimize the size of the ribbon. To do this, click the **Minimize The Ribbon** button to the left of the Help button ⌃ ❓ in the upper-right corner of the ribbon's tab bar, or press **CTRL+F1** to toggle the size of the ribbon. You can also double-click the active tab name. Double-click it again to restore the size of the ribbon.

for how to switch the buttons.) This book assumes the right hand controls the mouse and the left mouse button is *"the* mouse button." The right button is always called the "right mouse button." If you switch the buttons, you must change your interpretation of these phrases.

Five actions can be accomplished with the mouse:

- **Point** at an *object* on the screen (a button, an icon, a menu or one of its options, or a border) to highlight it. To *point* means to move the mouse so that the tip of the pointer is on top of the object.

- **Click** an object on the screen to *select* it, making that object the item that your next actions will affect. Clicking will also open a menu, select a menu option, or activate a button or "tool" on a toolbar or the ribbon. *Click* means to point at an object you want to select and quickly press and release the left mouse button.

- **Double-click** an object to open or activate it. *Double-click* means to point at an object you want to select, and then press and release the left mouse button twice in rapid succession.

- **Right-click** an object to open a context menu containing commands used to manipulate that object. *Right-click* means to point at an object that you want to select, and then quickly press and release the right mouse button. For example, right-clicking text opens the context menu shown on the left.

- **Drag** an object to move it on the screen to where you want it moved within the document. *Drag* means to point at an object you want to move and then hold down the left mouse button while moving the mouse. The object is dragged as you move the mouse. When the object is where you want it, release the mouse button.

Use Tabs and Menus

Command tabs are displayed at the top of the ribbon or in a dialog box. Menus are displayed when you click a down arrow on a button on the ribbon, a dialog box, or a toolbar. You can use tabs and menus in the following ways:

- To open a tab or menu with the mouse, click the tab or menu.

- To open a tab or menu with the keyboard, press **ALT** and the letter that appears in a small box for the object, tab, or menu name. For example, press **ALT+F** to open the File tab menu.

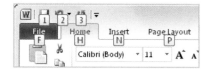

- To select an option on a tab or menu, click the tab or menu to open it, and then click the option.

- A number of menu options have a right-pointing arrow on their right to indicate that a submenu is associated with that option. To open the submenu, move the mouse pointer to the menu option with a submenu. After the submenu appears, move the mouse pointer to the submenu, and click the desired option.

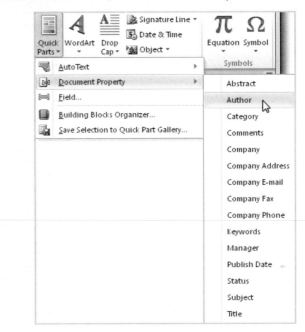

Use Views

Word presents text in several views, allowing you to choose which one facilitates the task you are doing. To access a view, click the **View** tab, and then click one of the following Document Views group buttons:

- **Print Layout** displays the text as it looks on a printed page.
- **Full Screen Reading** replaces the ribbon with a Full Screen toolbar. Click **View Options** to select options for displaying and using this screen view, such as whether to allow typing, tracking changes, displaying one or two pages, enlarging text, showing comments, and so on. Click **Close** to return to Normal view.

🖫 🖨 ⚒ Tools ▾ 🔖 ᵃᵇ⁄ ▾ 🗔   ◀ Page 1 of 1 ▾ ▶   🖳 View Options ▾ ⊠ Close

- **Web Layout** shows how the text will look as a Web page. Creating Web layout pages is discussed in Chapter 9.
- **Outline** displays the text in outline form, with a contextual Outlining tab on the ribbon, shown in Figure 1-4. You can use this view to promote and demote levels of text and rearrange levels, as shown in the Outline Tools group. With the Show Document button, you can toggle commands to extend your ability to create, insert, link, merge, split, and lock the document. Click **Close Outline View** to return to Normal view. Outlining is discussed further in Chapter 4.
- **Draft** displays the text of the document in draft status for quick and easy editing. Headings and footings may not be visible.

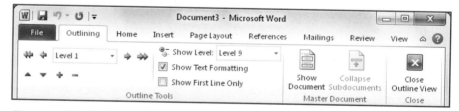

Figure 1-4: *The Outline view allows you to rearrange and manipulate the document in various ways using a special Outlining tab.*

Personalize and Customize Word

You can personalize Word, or make it your own, by changing the settings Word has for options such as the layout and contents of the ribbon, the tools available on the Quick Access toolbar, or your user name and initials. You can customize Word by changing the general default settings with regard to editing, proofing, display, and other options. Many of these options are discussed in the other chapters.

Here we will look at customizing the ribbon, the Quick Access toolbar, the display, and other options. We'll begin by looking at Office 2010's new File view.

Work with File View

Word 2010 shares with the other Office 2010 programs an improved way to easily do many of the customization tasks, as well as access tasks that affect a total document, such as opening, closing, printing, and saving from one screen, avoiding the need to open several dialog boxes. This all-encompassing view is called the File view (it is also called the "Backstage view") since it handles many file-related tasks, like saving or opening a file, an example of which is shown in Figure 1-5.

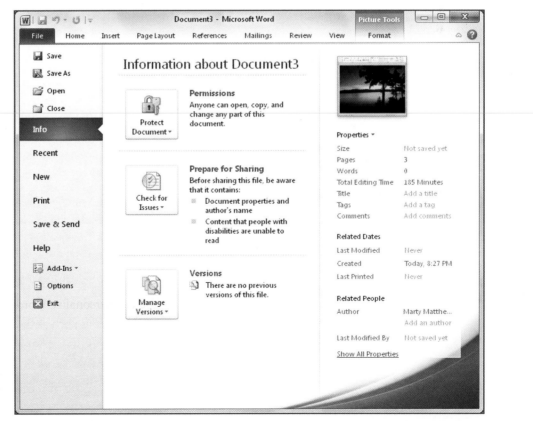

Figure 1-5: **File view provides information about the document and handles many file-related tasks.**

To display the File view:

1. Open Word using one of the methods described in "Start and Exit Word" earlier in this chapter.

2. Click the **File** tab, and then click one of the areas of interest on the left of the window. For example, clicking Print provides a document preview and options for printing your work.

3. When finished, click the **File** tab again (or any other tab) to return to the Word window.

Customize the Ribbon

The default ribbon consists of eight tabs, including File (see Figure 1-2), each tab containing several groups and sub-groups that combine related tasks. While Word strives to provide a logical hierarchy to all the tasks available to you, it also recognizes that not everyone finds their way of thinking to be the most convenient and offers you the ability to change how things are organized. You can remove groups from the existing Main tabs, create new tabs and groups, and populate your new groups from a plethora of available commands/tasks.

To customize the ribbon:

Click the **File** tab, and in the left pane, click **Options**. In the Word Options dialog box, also in the left pane, click **Customize Ribbon**.

–Or–

Right-click any tool on the ribbon, and click **Customize The Ribbon**.

In either case, the Customize The Ribbon And Keyboard Shortcuts view, shown in Figure 1-6, displays the list of available commands/tasks/tools on the left and a hierarchy of tabs and groups on the right.

REARRANGE TABS AND GROUPS

You can easily change the order in which your tabs and groups appear on the ribbon.

1. On the Customize The Ribbon And Keyboard Shortcuts view, click the **Customize The Ribbon** down arrow on the right, and select the type of tabs that contain the groups you want to work with.

NOTE

You'll see two types of tabs on the ribbon. The Main tabs appear when you open a document and contain a generalized set of tools. Tool tabs appear when you are working with certain Word features, such as pictures, and contain specific tools for working with these features (see Figure 1-3).

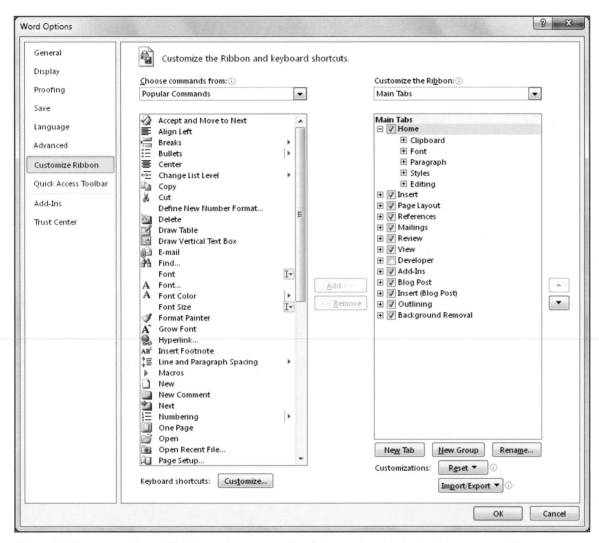

Figure 1-6: *You can easily modify tabs and groups on the ribbon and assign tools where you want them.*

2. To rearrange tabs, select the tab whose position on the ribbon you want to change, and click the **Move Up** and **Move Down** arrows on the right side of the tabs list to reposition the tab. (The topmost items in the list appear as the leftmost on the ribbon.)

3. To rearrange groups, click the plus sign next to the tab name to display its groups, and then click the **Move Up** and **Move Down** arrows to the side of the tabs list to reposition the group.

4. When finished, click **OK** to close the Word Options dialog box.

CREATE NEW TABS AND GROUPS

You can create new tabs and groups to collect your most often used tools.

To add a new tab from within the Word Options dialog box, Customize Ribbon option:

1. Click **New Tab** at the bottom of the tabs list. A new custom tab and group is added to the list.

2. Move the tab where you want it (click the up and down arrows on the right as described in the previous section, "Rearrange Tabs and Groups").

3. Rename the new tab and new group by selecting the item and clicking **Rename** at the bottom of the tabs list.

–Or–

Right-click the tab or group, and click Rename.

In either case, type a new name, and click OK.

To add a new group:

1. Select the tab where you want to add a new group, and then click **New Group** at the bottom of the tabs list. The list of all groups in that tab appears with a new custom group at its bottom.

2. Rename and rearrange the group within the tab as previously described.

3. If finished, click **OK** to close the Word Options dialog box.

ADD OR REMOVE COMMANDS/TOOLS

Once you have the tabs and groups created, named, and organized, you can add the tools you want to your custom groups. You can't add tools to an existing group.

1. On the Customize The Ribbon And Keyboard Shortcuts view, click the **Choose Commands From** down arrow. You will see a menu of categories of commands and tabs, such as Commands Not In The Ribbon or Tool Tabs. Choose a category of commands or tabs, or choose All Commands to see the full list. Select (highlight the tool by clicking it) the first tool you want to add to a custom group.

2. In the tabs list on the right, select the custom group to which you want to add the tool.

3. Click **Add** between the lists of commands and tabs. The command/tool is added under your group.

4. Repeat steps 1 through 3 to populate your groups with all the tools you want.

5. If you make a mistake, remove a tool from a custom group by selecting the tool and clicking **Remove**.

6. Use **the Move Up** and **Move Down** arrows to the right of the tabs list to organize the added tools within your groups, and click **OK** when finished.

Customize the Quick Access Toolbar

The Quick Access toolbar can become a "best friend" if you modify it so that it fits your personal way of working.

TIP

Don't be afraid to experiment with your ribbon by adding tabs and groups. You can always revert back to the default Word ribbon layout by clicking **Reset** under the tabs list and then choosing to restore either a selected tab or all tabs.

TIP

You can create a file that captures your customizations to the ribbon and the Quick Access toolbar so that you can use them on other computers running Word 2010. In the Word Options dialog box, click either **Customize Ribbon** or **Quick Access Toolbar**, click **Import/Export** in either view, and then click **Export All Ribbon And Quick Access Toolbar Customizations**. To use a previously created customization file, click **Import/Export** and then click **Import Customization File**. Depending on whether you're exporting or importing a customization file, a File Save or File Open dialog box appears that allows you to either store a new file or find an existing one, respectively.

ADD TO THE QUICK ACCESS TOOLBAR

The Quick Access toolbar should contain the commands you most commonly use. The default tools are Save, Undo, and Redo. You can add commands to it if you want.

1. Click the down arrow to the right of the Quick Access toolbar, and select one of the commands on the drop-down menu to add it to the toolbar.

–Or–

Click the Quick Access toolbar down arrow, and click **More Commands** to view a more expansive list of Word tools.

–Or–

Click the **File** tab, click **Options**, and click **Quick Access Toolbar**.

In either of the last two cases, the Word Options dialog box appears with the Quick Access toolbar customization options, as displayed in Figure 1-7.

2. Open the **Choose Commands From** drop-down list, and select the source of the commands you want from the available options.

3. In the leftmost list box, find and click the command you want to add to the toolbar, and then click **Add** to move its name to the list box on the right. Repeat this for all the commands you want in the toolbar.

4. Click **OK** when you are finished.

MOVE THE QUICK ACCESS TOOLBAR

You can display the Quick Access toolbar at its default position (above the ribbon) or directly below the ribbon using one of the following methods:

Right-click a tool on the Quick Access toolbar or on the ribbon, and click **Show Quick Access Toolbar Below The Ribbon** (once located below the ribbon, you can move it above the ribbon in the same manner).

> **NOTE**
> You can add a command to the Quick Access toolbar from the ribbon by right-clicking the button and choosing **Add To Quick Access Toolbar**.

Remove from Quick Access Toolbar
Customize Quick Access Toolbar...
Show Quick Access Toolbar Below the Ribbon
Customize the Ribbon
Minimize the Ribbon

Select tools from
tabs and lists

Available tools in
a selected list or tab

Add and
remove tools

Customize for all
documents or just
the current one

Change a tool's position
on the toolbar

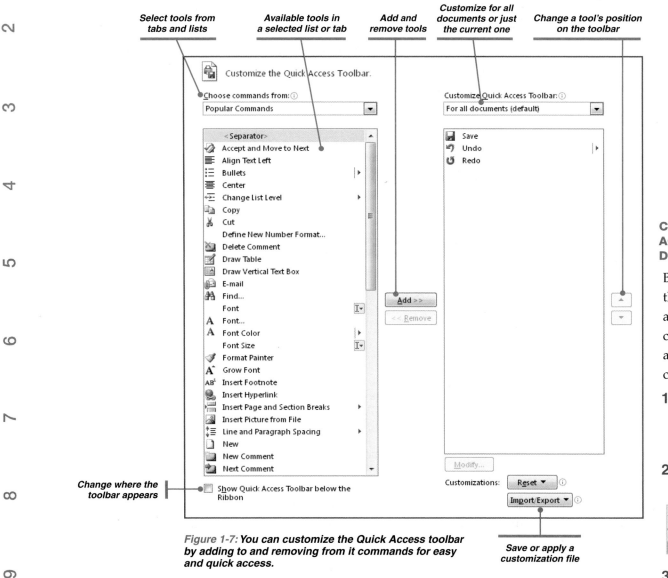

Figure 1-7: **You can customize the Quick Access toolbar by adding to and removing from it commands for easy and quick access.**

Change where the
toolbar appears

Save or apply a
customization file

–Or–

Right-click a tool on the Quick Access toolbar, and click **Customize Quick Access Toolbar** to open the Customize The Quick Access Toolbar pane. Click the **Show Quick Access Toolbar Below The Ribbon** check box in the lower-left corner, and click **OK** (to return the toolbar above the ribbon, open the pane and clear the check box).

CUSTOMIZE THE QUICK ACCESS TOOLBAR FOR A DOCUMENT

By default, changes made to the Quick Access toolbar are applicable to all documents. You can create a toolbar that only applies to the document you currently have open.

1. In the Customize The Quick Access Toolbar pane, click the **Customize Quick Access Toolbar** down arrow.

2. Click the option that identifies the document the toolbar will apply to.

3. Click **OK** when finished.

REARRANGE TOOLS ON THE QUICK ACCESS TOOLBAR

You can change the order in which tools appear on the Quick Access toolbar.

1. In the Customize The Quick Access Toolbar pane, select the tool in the list on the right whose position you want to change.

2. Click the **Move Up** or **Move Down** arrow to the right of the list to move the tool. Moving the tool up moves it to the left in the on-screen toolbar; moving it down the list moves it to the right in the on-screen toolbar.

3. Click **OK** when finished.

Show or Hide ScreenTips

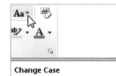

Change Case

Change all the selected text to UPPERCASE, lowercase, or other common capitalizations.

(?) Press F1 for more help.

When you hold the mouse pointer over a command or tool, a ScreenTip is displayed. The tip may be just the name of the tool or command, or it may be enhanced with a small description. You can hide the tips or change whether they are enhanced or not.

1. Click the **File** tab, and click **Options.**

2. Click the General option.

3. Open the ScreenTip Style drop-down list, and choose the option you want.

4. Click **OK** to confirm the choice.

Add Identifying Information to Documents

You can add identifying information to a document to make it easier to organize your documents and to find them quickly during searches, especially in a shared environment (see Chapter 9 for more on removing this document information).

1. Click the **File** tab, click **Info** on the left, click **Properties** in the far-right pane, and click **Show Document Panel.** A Document Information panel containing standard identifiers displays under the ribbon, as shown in Figure 1-8.

CHANGING THE WINDOW COLOR

You can change the background color of the Word window, which is set to silver by default, to black or blue instead.

1. Click the **File** tab, and click **Options**.

2. Click the **General** tab.

3. Click the **Color Scheme** down arrow, and click the color you want.

4. Click **OK** to save the change.

To change keyboard shortcuts for a specific command, click **File**, click **Options**, and click **Customize Ribbon**, which opens the Word Options dialog box. On the bottom-left area, next to Keyboard Shortcuts, click **Customize**. Under Categories, click a tab. The commands on that tab will be displayed under Commands. Click the command for which you want to change or specify a shortcut key. Under Current Keys, you'll see the shortcut key currently in use, if any. To add a new shortcut key, click in the **Press New Shortcut Key** box and then press the key combination you want and click **Assign**. To remove a shortcut key combination, click it under Current Keys and click **Remove**. Click **Reset All** to restore the original shortcuts. Click **Close** when you're through.

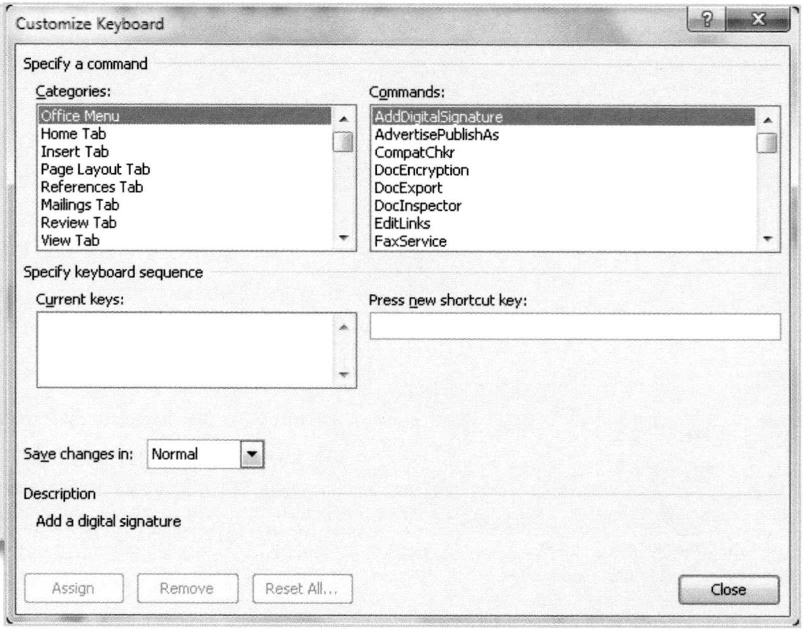

Customize Keyboard

Specify a command

Categories: Commands:

Office Menu   AddDigitalSignature
Home Tab   AdvertisePublishAs
Insert Tab   CompatChkr
Page Layout Tab   DocEncryption
References Tab   DocExport
Mailings Tab   DocInspector
Review Tab   EditLinks
View Tab   FaxService

Specify keyboard sequence

Current keys: Press new shortcut key:

Save changes in: Normal

Description

Add a digital signature

Assign   Remove   Reset All...   Close

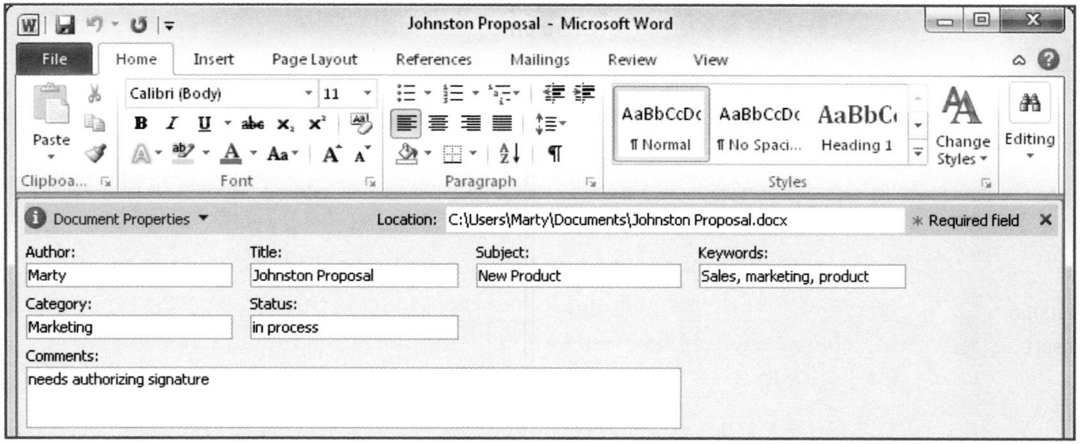

2. Type identifying information, such as title, subject, and keywords (words or phrases that are associated with the document).

3. To view more information about the document, click the **Document Properties** down arrow in the panel's title bar, and click **Advanced Properties**. Review each tab in the Properties dialog box to see the information available and make any changes or additions. Close the Properties dialog box when you are finished.

Document Properties ▼
Aut   Advanced Properties...

Johnston Proposal - Microsoft Word

File   Home   Insert   Page Layout   References   Mailings   Review   View

Calibri (Body)   11

Paste

Clipboa...   Font   Paragraph   Styles

AaBbCcDc   AaBbCcDc   AaBbC(Change Styles   Editing
¶ Normal   ¶ No Spaci...   Heading 1

ℹ️ Document Properties ▼   Location: C:\Users\Marty\Documents\Johnston Proposal.docx   ✷ Required field   ✕

Author: Title: Subject: Keywords:
Marty   Johnston Proposal   New Product   Sales, marketing, product

Category: Status:
Marketing   in process

Comments:
needs authorizing signature

Figure 1-8: A Document Information panel beneath the ribbon allows you to more easily locate a document by searching for identifying data.

4. When you are finished with the Document Information panel, click the **X** at the rightmost end of the panel's title bar to close it.

QUICKSTEPS

SETTING PREFERENCES

Setting preferences allows you to adapt Word to your needs and inclinations. The Word Options dialog box provides access to these settings.

Click the **File** tab, and then click **Options**.

SELECT THE DISPLAY ELEMENTS THAT YOU WANT TO APPEAR

Click the **Display** option, as shown in Figure 1-9, then:

- Click the options in the Page Display Options area that you want to display.

- Click the formatting marks you want to see—Show All Formatting Marks is a good choice.

- Click the options that you want in the Printing Options area.

SET GENERAL OPTIONS

1. Click the **General** option (see Figure 1-10), then:

   - Review and click the check marks that are relevant for your situation. Earlier in this chapter, you saw how to disable the mini toolbar, show and hide ScreenTips, and change the color scheme of the Word window. If you are unsure about other options, keep the default settings and see how well these work for you.

   - Type the user name you want displayed in documents revised using the Track Changes feature.

   - Type the initials associated with the user name that will be displayed in comments you insert into a document.

   Continued . . .

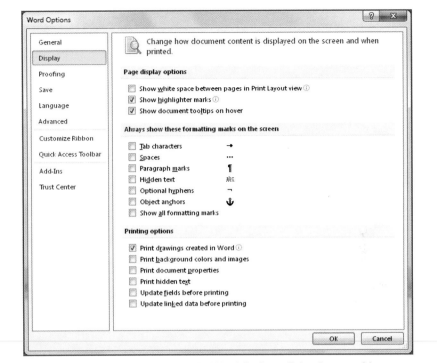

Figure 1-9: *The Display options in the Word Options dialog box provides page display, formatting, and printing preferences.*

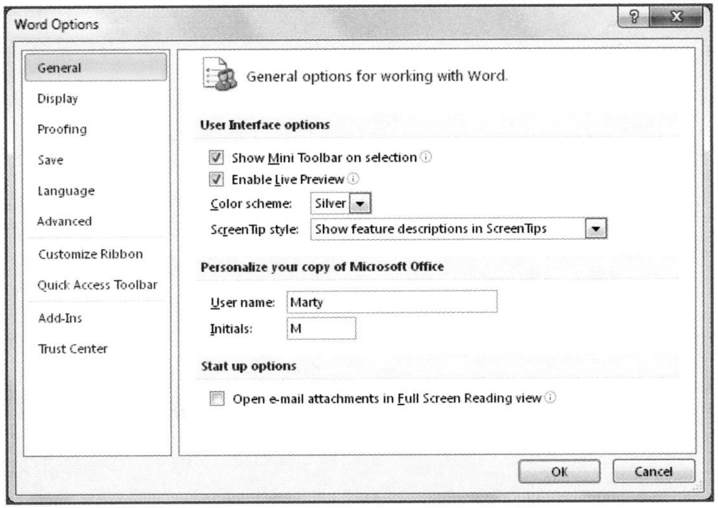

Figure 1-10: *Many basic preferences used in Word are set in the Display options of the Word Options dialog box.*

Get Help

Help can be accessed both locally and online from Microsoft servers. A different kind of help, which provides the Thesaurus and Research features, is also available.

Open Help

The online Word Help system is maintained online at Microsoft. It is easily accessed.

Click the **Help** icon ❓ , and the Word Help window will open, shown in Figure 1-11.

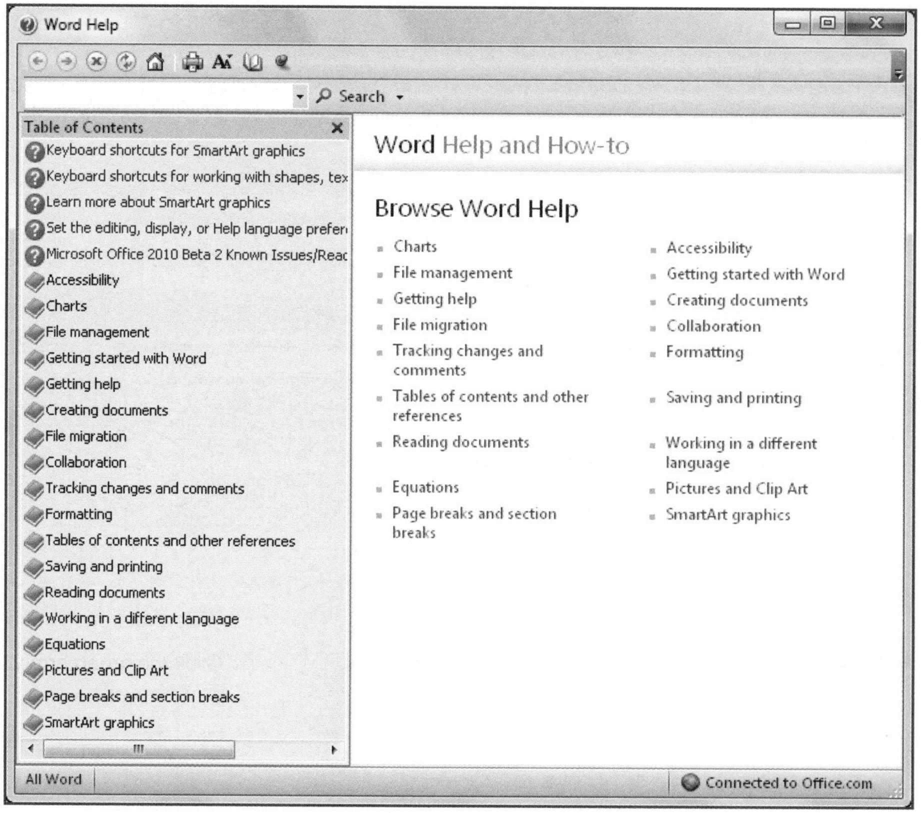

Figure 1-11: When you click the Help icon, the Word Help dialog box appears, where you can click the topic you want or search for specific keywords.

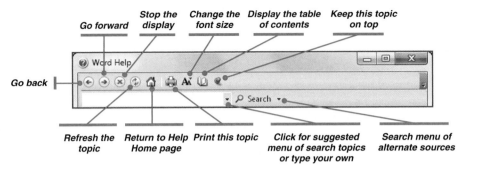

Figure 1-12: *Use the Help toolbar to navigate through the topics and print them out.*

QUICKSTEPS

USING THE HELP TOOLBAR

On the toolbar at the top of the Word Help window are several options for navigating through the topics and printing one out (possibly for later reference), as seen in Figure 1-12.

- Find the topic you want, and click it.

  –Or–

- Type keywords in the Search text box, and click **Search**.

Conduct Research

You can conduct research on the Internet using Word's Research command. Clicking this command displays a Research task pane that allows you to enter your search criteria and specify references to search.

1. Click the **Review** tab, and in the Proofing group, click **Research**. You may be asked for the language you are using. Click it, and the Research task pane will appear on the right of the document pane, as shown in the example in Figure 1-13.

2. Type your search criteria in the Search For text box.

3. To change the default reference, click the down arrow to open the drop-down list, and click a reference to be searched.

4. Click the green arrow to the right of the Search For box to start the search. The results will be displayed in the task pane.

5. Click **Close** to close the task pane.

TIP

You can translate a phrase from one language into another in the Research task pane.

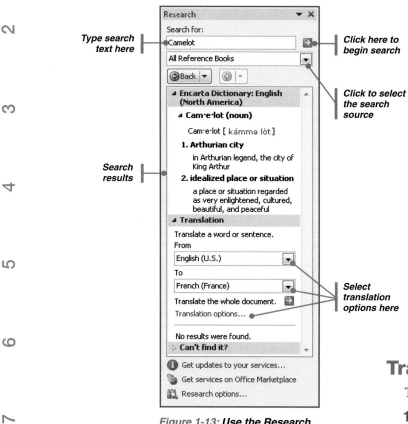

Type search text here

Click here to begin search

Click to select the search source

Search results

Select translation options here

Figure 1-13: Use the Research feature to search a dictionary, a thesaurus, an encyclopedia, and several other sources.

TIP

You can also access the Thesaurus by pressing **SHIFT+F7**.

Use the Thesaurus

You can find synonyms for words using the Thesaurus feature.

1. To use the Thesaurus, first select the word that you want a synonym for.

2. Click the **Review** tab, and in the Proofing group, click **Thesaurus**. The Research task pane will appear with the most likely synonyms listed.

- Click a listed word to search for its synonyms.

- Click the word down arrow to insert, copy, or look up the word.

3. Click **Close** to close the task pane.

Translate a Document

To translate a whole document from one language to another:

1. Click the **Review** tab, and in the Language group, click **Translate**, and click **Translate Document**. The Search task pane will appear with the translation as its source reference.

2. Click the **From** and **To** down arrows, and click the relevant languages.

3. Click **OK** to begin the translation. A Translate Whole Document message will appear, informing you that your document will be sent over the Internet to be translated.

4. Click **Send** to start the translation. Your translated document will appear in a browser window, as shown in Chapter 8.

pères a exposé sur ce continent, 1

elle tous les hommes sont égaux.

pères a exposé sur ce
lle all men are equal.

QUICKFACTS

ACCESSING MICROSOFT OFFICE RESOURCES

Microsoft maintains a resource center online that you can easily access. This resource center allows you to communicate with Microsoft about Office and Word subjects.

Click the **File** tab, and click **Help**. The Support page will open with the following options, as shown in Figure 1-14:

- **Microsoft Office Help** opens the Word Help window where you can search for information.

- **Getting Started** opens a Microsoft Office Web site that has a number of links to in-depth articles about Word 2010.

- **Contact Us** lets you send a message to Microsoft experts. You may be seeking advice for a problem or making suggestions for improvements to the product.

- **Options** opens the Word Options window, discussed in several sections in this chapter.

- **Check For Updates** finds out if updates are available for Microsoft Office and, if so, downloads them. (See "Update Word".)

- **About Microsoft Word** provides version, copyright, and product information, as well as access to licensing terms and further copyright information.

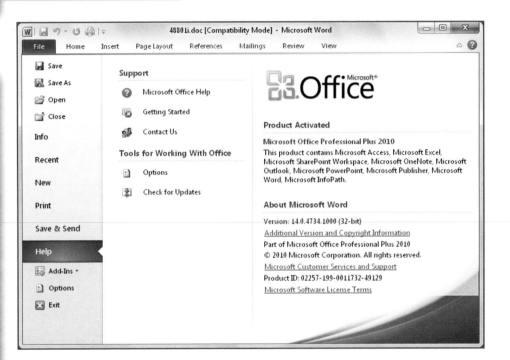

Figure 1-14: *The Support page in the File view facilitates communication with Microsoft.*

Update Word

Microsoft periodically releases updates for Office and Word (these are almost always problem fixes and not enhancements). You can check on available updates, download them, and install them from Word.

1. Click the **File** tab, and click **Help**.

2. On the Support page, click **Check For Updates**. Your Web browser may open and connect to the Microsoft Online Web site. Then the Windows Control Panel will open to Windows Update, as shown in Figure 1-15. This will update both Windows and Office.

3. Click **Check For Updates**. Your system will be checked for any necessary updates, and you will be given the opportunity to download and install them if you choose. When you have downloaded the updates you want, close your Web browser.

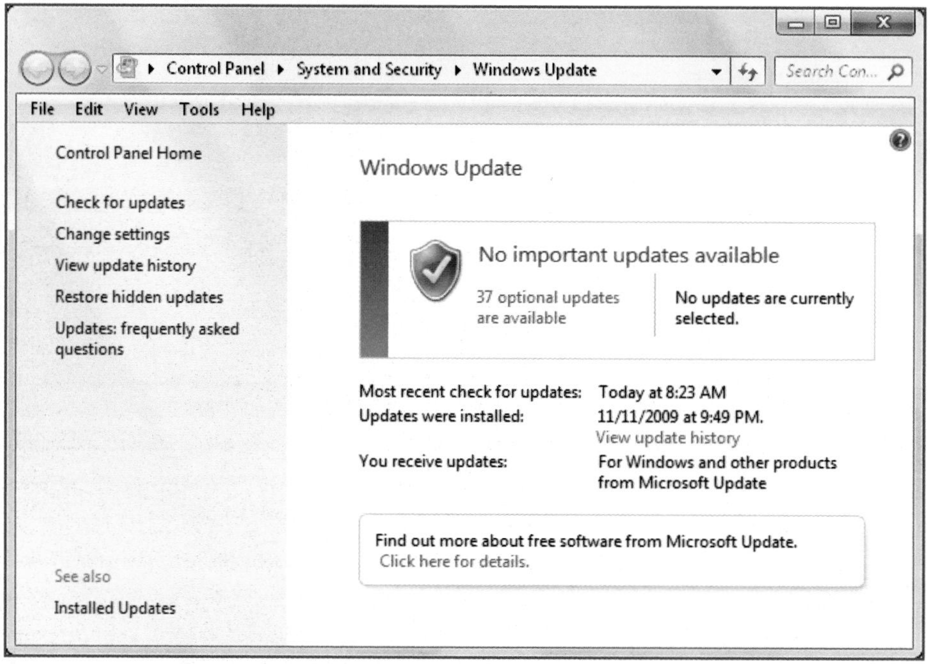

Figure 1-15: *One of the primary reasons to check for and download Office and Windows updates is to get needed security patches.*

Chapter 2
Working with Documents

Microsoft Office Word 2010 allows you to create and edit documents, such as letters, reports, invoices, plays, and books. The book you are reading now was written in Word. Documents are printed on one or more pages, and are probably bound by anything from a paper clip to stitch binding. In the computer, a document is a called a file, an object that has been given a name and is stored on a disk drive. For example, the name given to the file for this chapter is Chap02.docx. "Chap02" is the file name, and ".docx" is the file extension. You may or may not see the file extension, depending on how Windows is configured. Most files produced by editions of Word prior to 2007 used the .doc extension. Documents saved with Word 2007 and 2010 are, by default, saved with the .docx extension.

In this chapter you'll see how to create new documents and edit existing ones. This includes ways to enter, change, and delete text, as well as ways to find, select, copy, and move text.

Create a New Document

In the days before computers, creating a new document was known as "starting with a clean sheet of paper." Today, it is "starting with a blank screen"—actually, a blank area within a window on the screen, as shown in Figure 2-1. You can create a new document in two ways: using the default (or "normal") document template or using a unique template.

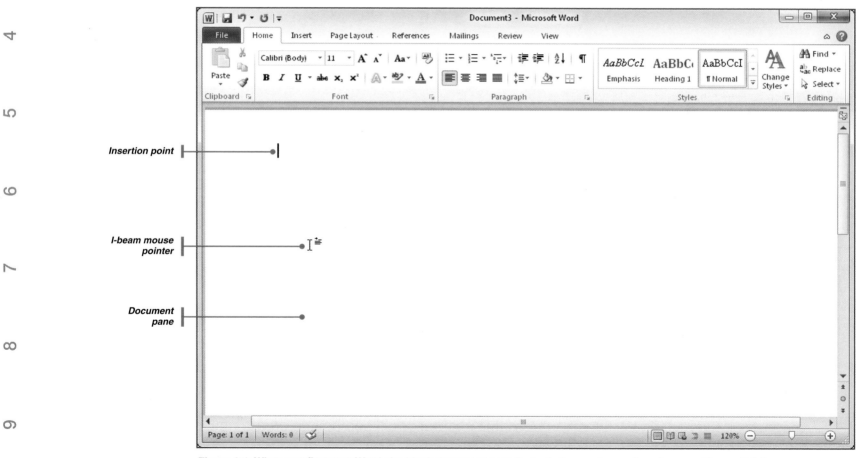

Figure 2-1: When you first start Word, the blank document pane is ready for you to create a document immediately.

Start a Document

Simply starting Word opens up a blank document pane into which you can start typing a new document immediately. The blinking bar in the upper-left corner of the document pane, called the *insertion point*, indicates where the text you type will appear.

To start Word, use one of the ways described at the beginning of Chapter 1.

Use a Unique Template

A template is a special kind of document that is used as a pattern or the basis for other documents you create. The template is said to be "attached" to the document, and every Word document must have a template attached to it. The template acts as the framework around which you create your document. The document that is opened automatically when you start Word 2010 uses a default template called Normal.dotm (versions prior to 2007 used Normal.dot). This is referred to as "the Normal template" and contains standard formatting settings. Other templates can contain boilerplate text, formatting options for the types of documents they create, and even automating procedures. Word is installed on your computer with a number of templates that you can use, and you can access other templates, both on your computer and through Office Online.

USE A TEMPLATE ON YOUR COMPUTER

With Word open on your computer:

1. Click the **File** tab, and then click New. The **New** Document dialog box appears, as shown in Figure 2-2.

2. Under Available Templates, you have the following options:
   - **Blank Document:** To use a new blank template
   - **Blog Post:** To create a simple blog post
   - **Recent Templates:** Templates you have used recently
   - **Sample Templates:** To use templates stored on your computer
   - **My Templates:** To use custom templates you have created

Figure 2-2: The New Document dialog box gives you choices for how to start a document.

- **New From Existing:** To use templates you can copy from existing documents
- **Office.com Templates:** To use templates from Microsoft's online resources

3. Click **Sample Templates**. The window shown in Figure 2-3 appears. Click the template you want, and then, on the bottom of the right pane, above the Create button, click **Document**, and then click **Create**. A document with the selected template will open.

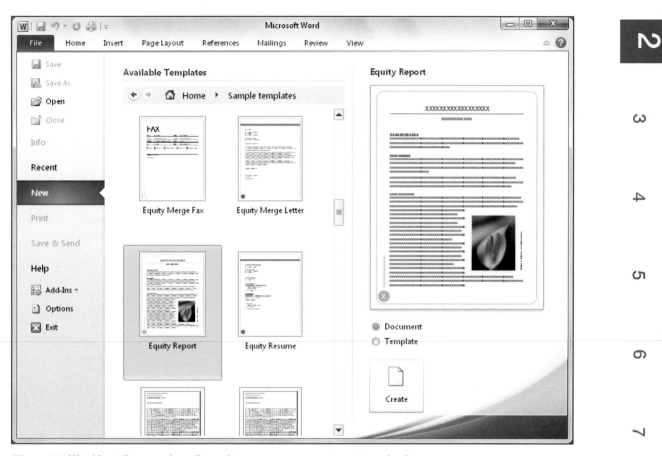

Figure 2-3: **Word installs a number of templates on your computer automatically.**

USE AN OFFICE ONLINE TEMPLATE

With Word open on your computer and a connection to the Internet:

1. Click the **File** tab, and then click **New**. The New Document dialog box will appear.

2. In the Templates pane, located beneath Office Online Templates, is a list of categories of templates. Click the category you want, and you'll see the possibilities related to it, as seen in Figure 2-4.

3. Find the template you want, and click Download in the right pane. A new document is opened with the template attached.

*Figure 2-4: **Microsoft offers many templates online, both for Word and its other Office products.***

Open an Existing Document

After creating and saving a document, you may want to come back and work on it later. You may also want to open and work on a Word document created by someone else or created in a different program. To do this, you must first

NOTE

Not all documents created in other programs can be opened by Word, although many can. See "Import a Document."

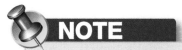

locate the document and then open it in Word. You can either locate the document directly from Word or search for it in Word or Windows.

Locate an Existing Document

With Word open on your screen:

1. Click the **File** tab, and click **Open**. The Open dialog box appears.
2. Double-click the drive, folder, and sequence of folders you need to open in order to find the document.
3. When you have found the document you want to open (see Figure 2-5), double-click it. It will appear in Word, ready for you to begin your work.

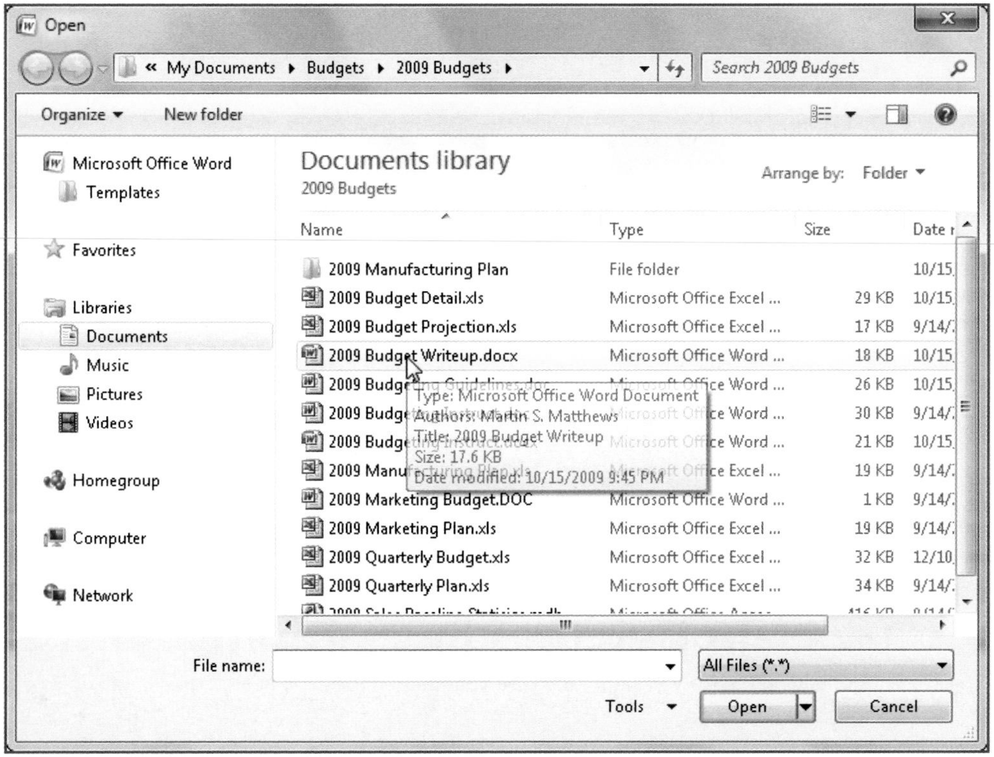

Figure 2-5: ***When you hold the mouse pointer over a document name, you see additional information about the document.***

If you have a hard time finding a document using the direct approach just described, you can search for it either in Word or in Windows.

SEARCH FOR A DOCUMENT IN WORD

A document search performed in Word looks for a piece of text that is contained within the document or within some property of the document, such as the name of the author, the creation date, or the name of the file. The basic search looks for text within the document.

1. Click the **File** tab, and click **Open**. The Open dialog box appears. Locate the folder or drive that you want to search.
2. In the Search text box on the upper-right area of the dialog box, begin to enter the text you want to search for (see Figure 2-6). As you type, the search will begin. The results are listed in the right pane of the dialog box, beneath the search text.
3. Double-click the file you want, or select it and click **Open** to open it in Word.

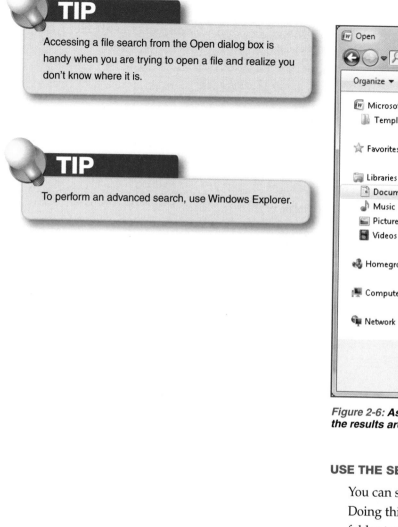

TIP

Accessing a file search from the Open dialog box is handy when you are trying to open a file and realize you don't know where it is.

TIP

To perform an advanced search, use Windows Explorer.

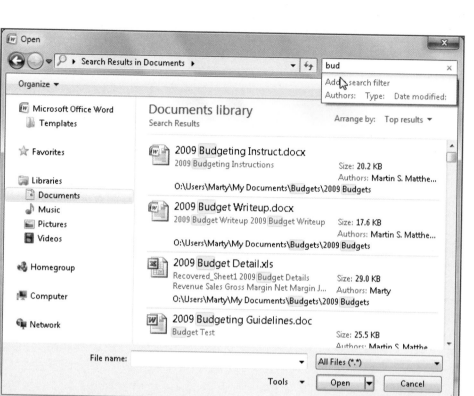

Figure 2-6: *As you type the text you want to search for, the search automatically begins and the results are listed beneath the search text.*

USE THE SEARCH AND SORT FEATURES

You can sort the files within the search results list using the column headings. Doing this allows you to sort files by some special property, such as name, date, folder type, author, or tag.

1. Display the Open dialog box (see the preceding set of steps), locate the drive or folder containing the file you want, and type your search text. The search results will be listed below as you type.

2. Click the **Change Your View** button on the right in the toolbar at left, and click **Details** if it is not already selected.

Documents library
Search Results

Arrange by: Top results ▼

Name	Type	Size	Date mo
2009 Budgeting Instruct...	Microsoft Office Word ...	21 KB	10/15/20
2009 Budget Writeup.d...	Microsoft Office Word ...	18 KB	10/15/20
2009 Budget Detail.xls	Microsoft Office Excel ...	29 KB	10/15/20
2009 Budgeting Guideli...	Microsoft Office Word ...	26 KB	10/15/20
2010 Budgets	File folder		10/15/20
Budgets	File folder		10/15/20
2009 Quarterly Budget.xls	Microsoft Office Excel ...	32 KB	12/10/20
2010 Quarterly Budget.xls	Microsoft Office Excel ...	32 KB	12/10/20

All Files (*.*)

[Open ▼] [Cancel]

---

3. Point to a column heading on which you want to sort the results, and click. The files and folders will be sorted on that column.

4. Click the column heading again, and the files and folders will be resorted into their original order.

Import a Document

If you have a word-processing document created in a program other than Word, you can most likely open it and edit it in Word.

1. Click the **File** tab, and click **Open**. The Open dialog box appears.

2. Find the folder or sequence of folders you need to open in order to find the document.

3. Click the down arrow on the right of the file type drop-down list box to display the list of files that you can open directly in Word (see Table 2-1 for a complete list).

4. Click the file type that you want to open. The Open dialog box will list only files of that type.

5. Double-click the file that you want to open.

TIP

To quickly find a folder that you have used previously, click the **Recent Pages** down arrow to the left of the folder name.

FILE TYPE	EXTENSION
OpenDocument text files	.odt
Plain text files	.txt
Rich text format files	.rtf
Text in any file	.*
Web page files	.htm, .html, .mht, .mhtml
Word 97 to 2003 files	.doc
Word 97 to 2003 template files	.dot
Word 2007 to 2010 document files (macro-enabled)	.docx (.docm)
Word 2007 to 2010 template files (macro enabled)	.dotx (.dotm)
WordPerfect 5.x and 6.x files	.doc, .wpd
Works 6.0 to 9.0 files	.wps
XML files	.xm

*Table 2-1: **File Types That Word Can Open Directly***

ENTERING SPECIAL CHARACTERS

Entering a character that is on the keyboard takes only a keystroke, but many other characters and symbols exist beyond those that appear on the keyboard, for example: ©, £, Ã, Ω, ♩, and •. You can enter these characters using either the Symbol dialog box or a sequence of keys (also called a keyboard shortcut).

SELECT SPECIAL CHARACTERS FROM THE SYMBOL DIALOG BOX

- Move the insertion point to where you want to insert the special character(s).

- Click the **Insert** tab, and then click **Symbol** in the Symbols group. A Symbol menu will open containing the symbols you most commonly use. If the symbol you want is on the list, click it, and the symbol will be inserted in the document.

- If the symbol you want is not on the menu, click **More Symbols**. The Symbol dialog box will appear.

  - Click the **Symbols** tab for characters within font styles.

  - Click the **Special Characters** tab for common standard characters.

- Click the character you want, as shown in Figure 2-7, click **Insert**, and then click **Close**. You should see the special character or symbol where the insertion point was.

Continued . . .

Write a Document

Whether you create a new document or open an existing one, you will likely want to enter and edit text. Editing, in this case, includes adding and deleting text, as well as selecting, moving, and copying it.

Enter Text

To enter text in a document that you have newly created or opened, simply start typing. The characters you type will appear in the document pane at the insertion point and in the order that you type them.

Determine Where Text Will Appear

The *insertion point*, the blinking vertical bar shown earlier in Figure 2-1, determines where text that you type will appear. In a new document, the insertion point is obviously in the upper-leftmost corner of the document pane. It is also placed there by default when you open an existing document. You can move the insertion point within or to the end of existing text using either the keyboard or the mouse.

MOVE THE INSERTION POINT WITH THE KEYBOARD

When Word is open and active, the insertion point moves every time you press a character or directional key on the keyboard (unless a menu or dialog box is open or the task pane is active). The directional keys include **TAB**, **BACKSPACE**, and **ENTER**, as well as the four arrow keys, and **HOME**, **END**, **PAGE UP**, and **PAGE DOWN**.

MOVE THE INSERTION POINT WITH THE MOUSE

When the mouse pointer is in the document pane, it appears as an I-beam, as you saw in Figure 2-1. The reason for the I-beam is that it fits between characters on

QUICKSTEPS

ENTERING SPECIAL CHARACTERS
(Continued)

ENTER SPECIAL CHARACTERS FROM THE KEYBOARD

You can use keyboard shortcuts to enter symbols and special characters. The numeric part of the shortcut must be entered on the numeric keypad.

1. Move the insertion point to where you want to insert the special characters.

2. Press **NUM LOCK** to put the numeric keypad into numeric mode.

3. Hold down **ALT** while pressing all four digits (including the leading zero) on the numeric keypad.

4. Release **ALT**. The special character will appear where the insertion point was.

The shortcut keys for some of the more common special characters are shown in Table 2-2.

NOTE

In Table 2-2, the comma (,) means to release the previous keys and then press the following key(s). For example, for a ¢, press and hold **CTRL** while pressing /, then release **CTRL** and press **C**. In addition, "NUM" means to press the following key on the numeric keypad. So, "NUM-" means to press "-" in the upper-right corner of the numeric keypad.

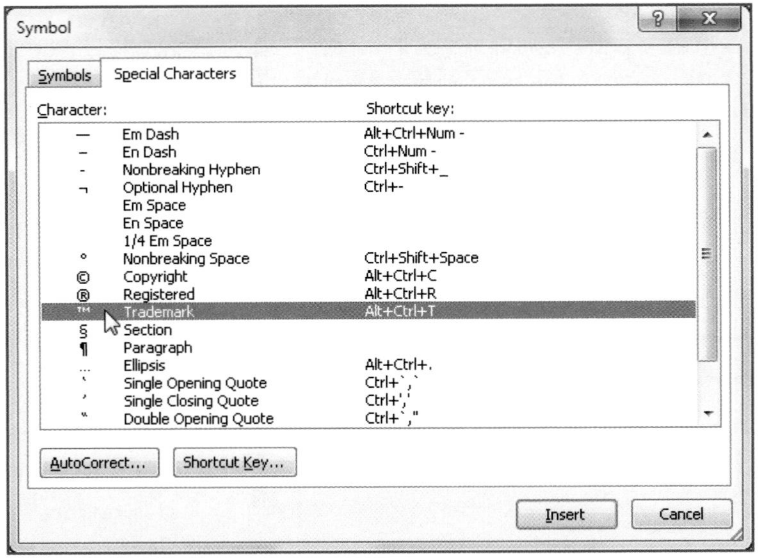

Figure 2-7: **The Symbol dialog box contains special characters, as well as several complete alphabets and symbol sets.**

CHARACTER	NAME	SHORTCUT KEYS
•	Bullet	**ALT+0149**
©	Copyright	**ALT+CTRL+C**
TM	Trademark	**ALT+CTRL+T**
®	Registered	**ALT+CTRL+R**
¢	Cent	**CTRL+/ , C**
£	Pound	**ALT+0163**
€	Euro	**ALT+CTRL+E**
–	En dash	**CTRL+NUM-**
—	Em dash	**ALT+CTRL+NUM-**

Table 2-2: **Shortcut Keys for Common Characters (see accompanying Notes)**

NOTE

When you click a common symbol or special character in the Symbol dialog box, you'll see the shortcut keys for the character.

€ | ¥ | © | ™ | ± | ≠

Character code: 00A9

Shortcut key: Alt+0169

TIP

You can insert multiple special characters in sequence by selecting one after another in the Symbol dialog box.

TIP

The AutoCorrect As You Type feature, which is discussed in Chapter 4, also provides a quick way of entering commonly used special characters, such as copyright, trademark, and registered symbols and en and em dashes.

CAUTION

In Word 2010, there is no "OVR" in the status bar to indicate that you are in overtype mode.

NOTE

In both insert and overtype modes, the directional keys move the insertion point without regard to which mode is enabled.

the screen. You can move the insertion point by moving the I-beam mouse pointer to where you want the insertion point and then clicking.

Insertion|Point

Insert Text or Type Over It

When you press a letter or a number key with Word in its default mode (as it is when you first start it), the insertion point and any existing text to the right of the insertion point is pushed to the right and down on a page. This is also true when you press the **TAB** or **ENTER** key. This is called *insert mode: New text pushes existing text to the right*.

In versions of Word prior to 2007, if you press the **INSERT** (or **INS**) key, Word is switched to *overtype* mode, and the OVR indicator is enabled in the status bar. In Word 2010, this capability is turned off by default, and the **INSERT** (or **INS**) key does nothing. The reason is that more often than not, the **INSERT** (or **INS**) key gets pressed by mistake, and you don't find out about this until after you have typed over a lot of text you didn't want to replace existing text. You can turn on this capability by clicking the **File** tab, clicking **Options**, clicking **Advanced**, and clicking **Use The Insert Key To Control Overtype Mode.**

In overtype mode, any character key you press types over (replaces) the existing character to the right of the insertion point. Overtype mode does not affect the **ENTER** key, which continues to push existing characters to the right of the insertion point and down. The **TAB** key in overtype mode does replace characters to the right, *unless* it is pressed at the beginning of the line—in which case, it is treated as an indent and pushes the rest of the line to the right.

Insert Line or Page Breaks

If you are used to typing on a typewriter, you have learned to press **RETURN** at the end of each line to go to the next line. In Word, as in all word-processing programs, you simply keep typing and the text will automatically wrap around to the next line. Only when you want to break a line before it would otherwise

end must you manually intervene. There are four instances where manual line breaks are required:

- At the **end of a paragraph**—to start a new paragraph, press **ENTER**.
- At the **end of a short line** within a paragraph—to start a new line, press **SHIFT+ENTER**.
- At the **end of a page**—to force the start of a new page, press **CTRL+ENTER**.
- At the **end of a section**—to start a new section, press **CTRL+SHIFT+ENTER**.

You can also enter a page break using the mouse:

With the insertion point placed where you want the break, click the **Insert** tab, and click **Page Break** in the Pages group. A page break will be inserted in the text. ⎘ Page Break

Select Text

In order to copy, move, or delete text, you first need to select it. *Selecting text* means to identify it as a separate block from the remaining text in a document. You can select any amount of text, from a single character up to an entire document. As text is selected, it is highlighted with a colored background, as you can see in Figure 2-8. You can select text with either the mouse or the keyboard.

SELECT TEXT WITH THE MOUSE

You can select varying amounts of text with the mouse.

- **Select a single word** by double-clicking it.
- **Select a single line** by clicking on the far left of the line when the I-beam mouse pointer becomes an arrow (this area on the left where the mouse pointer becomes an arrow is called the *selection bar*).
- **Select a single sentence** by holding down **CTRL** while clicking in the sentence.
- **Select a single paragraph** by double-clicking in the selection bar opposite the paragraph.
- **Select an entire document** by holding **CTRL+SHIFT** while clicking in the selection bar anywhere in the document.

⇖ **conceived in Liberty,**

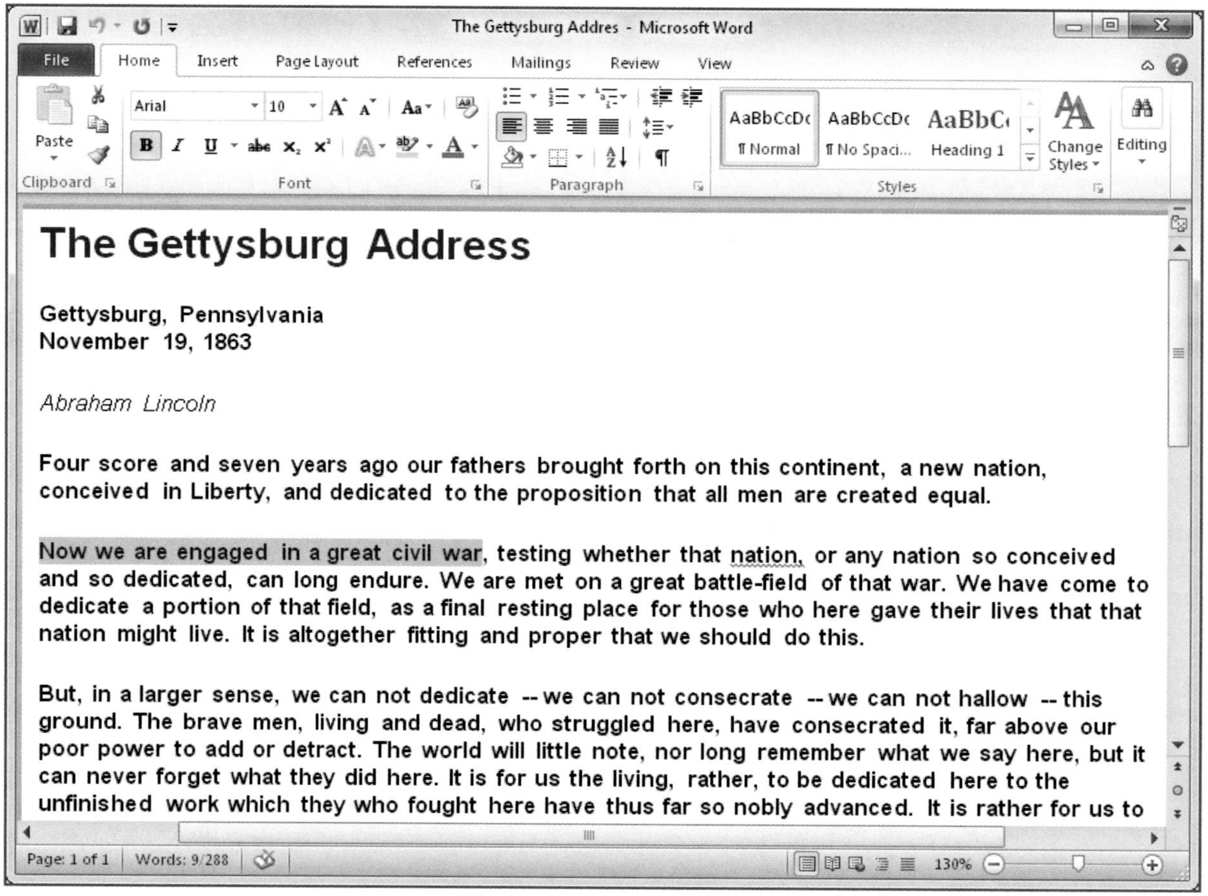

*Figure 2-8: **You will always know what you are moving, copying, or deleting because it is highlighted on the screen.***

- **Select one or more characters** in a word, or select two or more words by doing the following:

  1. Click to place the insertion point to the left of the first character.

  2. Hold **SHIFT** while clicking to the right of the last character. The selected text will be highlighted.

- **Select one or more characters** in a word, or to select two or more words by dragging:
  1. Move the mouse pointer to the left of the first character.
  2. Hold down the mouse button while dragging the mouse pointer to the right of the last character. The selected text will be highlighted.

SELECT TEXT WITH THE KEYBOARD

Use the arrow keys to move the insertion point to the left of the first character you want to select. For example:

- Hold down **SHIFT** while using the arrow keys to move the insertion point to the right of the last character you want to select.
- To select a line, place the pointer at the beginning of a line. Hold **SHIFT** and press **END**.
- To select the entire document using the keyboard, press **CTRL+A**.

Copy and Move Text

Copying and moving text are similar actions. Think of copying text as moving it and leaving a copy behind. Both copying and moving are done in two steps.

1. Selected text is copied or cut from its current location to the Clipboard.
2. The contents of the Clipboard are pasted to a new location, as identified by the insertion point.

USE THE CLIPBOARD

The *Clipboard* is a location in the computer's memory that is used to store information temporarily. Two Clipboards can actually be used:

- The **Windows Clipboard** can store one object, either text or a picture, and pass that object within or among other Windows programs. Once an object is cut or copied to the Windows Clipboard, it stays there until another object is cut or copied to the Clipboard or until the computer is turned off. The Windows Clipboard is used by default.
- The **Office Clipboard** can store up to 24 objects, both text and pictures, and pass those objects within or among other Office programs. Once the Office Clipboard is enabled, all objects that are cut or copied to it are kept on the Office Clipboard until the 25th object is cut or copied, which will replace the first object. All objects on the Office Clipboard are lost from the Clipboard when the computer is turned off.

QUICKSTEPS

USING THE OFFICE CLIPBOARD

As mentioned, the Office Clipboard is shared by all Office products. You can copy objects and text from any Office application and paste them in another application. The Office Clipboard contains up to 24 items. The 25th item will overwrite the first one.

OPEN THE CLIPBOARD

To display the Office Clipboard, click the **Home** tab, and then click the **Clipboard Dialog Box Launcher** in the Clipboard group. The Clipboard task pane Clipboard will open.

Continued . . .

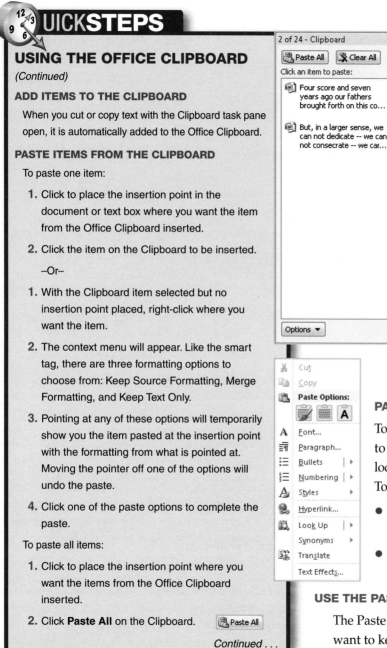

USING THE OFFICE CLIPBOARD
(Continued)

ADD ITEMS TO THE CLIPBOARD

When you cut or copy text with the Clipboard task pane open, it is automatically added to the Office Clipboard.

PASTE ITEMS FROM THE CLIPBOARD

To paste one item:

1. Click to place the insertion point in the document or text box where you want the item from the Office Clipboard inserted.

2. Click the item on the Clipboard to be inserted.

   –Or–

1. With the Clipboard item selected but no insertion point placed, right-click where you want the item.

2. The context menu will appear. Like the smart tag, there are three formatting options to choose from: Keep Source Formatting, Merge Formatting, and Keep Text Only.

3. Pointing at any of these options will temporarily show you the item pasted at the insertion point with the formatting from what is pointed at. Moving the pointer off one of the options will undo the paste.

4. Click one of the paste options to complete the paste.

To paste all items:

1. Click to place the insertion point where you want the items from the Office Clipboard inserted.

2. Click **Paste All** on the Clipboard.

Continued . . .

CUT TEXT

When you *cut text*, you place it on the Clipboard and delete it from its current location. When the Clipboard contents are pasted to the new location, the text has been *moved* and no longer exists in its original location. To cut and place text on the Clipboard, first select it and then:

● Press **CTRL+X**.

   –Or–

● Click the **Home** tab, and then click **Cut** in the Clipboard group.

COPY TEXT

When you *copy* text to the Clipboard, you leave it in its original location. Once the Clipboard contents are pasted to the new location, you have the same text in two places in the document. To copy text to the Clipboard, first select it and then:

● Press **CTRL+C**.

   –Or–

● Click the **Home** tab, and then click **Copy** in the Clipboard group.

PASTE TEXT

To complete a copy or a move, you must *paste* the text from the Clipboard to either the same or another document where the insertion point is located. A copy of the text stays on the Clipboard and can be pasted again. To paste the contents of the Clipboard:

● Press **CTRL+V**.

   –Or–

● Click the **Home** tab, and then click **Paste** (in the upper Clipboard area) in the Clipboard group.

USE THE PASTE OPTIONS SMART TAG

The Paste Options smart tag appears when you paste text. It asks you if you want to keep source formatting (the original formatting of the text—the leftmost

USING THE OFFICE CLIPBOARD

(Continued)

DELETE ITEMS ON THE CLIPBOARD

To delete all items, click **Clear All** on the Clipboard task pane. 🗙 Clear All

To delete a single item, move the pointer to the item, click the down arrow to the right of the item, and click **Delete**.

SET CLIPBOARD OPTIONS

1. On the Clipboard task pane, click **Options** on the bottom. A context menu is displayed.

2. Click one of the following options to select or clear it:

   - **Show Office Clipboard Automatically** always shows the Office Clipboard when copying.

   - **Show Office Clipboard When CTRL+C Pressed Twice** shows the Office Clipboard when you press **CTRL+C** twice rapidly on the same item.

   - **Collect Without Showing Office Clipboard** copies items to the Clipboard without displaying it.

   - **Show Office Clipboard Icon On Taskbar** displays the icon 🗐 on the right of the Windows taskbar when the Clipboard is being used (this may be hidden, in which case you can click the up arrow to see it).

   - **Show Status Near Taskbar When Copying** displays a momentary message about the items being added to the Clipboard as copies are made.

icon), merge with destination formatting (change the formatting to that of the surrounding text—the middle icon), or keep text only (remove all formatting from the text—the rightmost icon). The Set Default Paste option displays the Word Options dialog box so that you can set defaults for pasting text during a cut or copy action. The Paste Options smart tag is most valuable when you can see that the paste operation has resulted in formatting that you don't want.

The Paste Options smart tag allows you to preview the result of a paste with its selected formatting before you complete it. Simply point at one of the three formatting options in the smart tag menu, and the formatting of the pasted text will temporarily change to reflect that option. If you move the pointer to another option, the formatting will immediately change to the other option. Even after you make a decision and click an option, so long as the smart tag is still visible, you can reopen it, preview another choice, and make the change if you want.

UNDO A MOVE OR PASTE ACTION

You can undo a move or paste action by:

- Pressing **CTRL+Z**

  –Or–

- Clicking **Undo** on the Quick Access toolbar ↜

REDO AN UNDO ACTION

You can redo many actions you have undone by:

- Pressing **CTRL+Y**

  –Or–

- Clicking **Redo** on the Quick Access toolbar ↝

NOTE

To close the Office Clipboard and revert to the Windows Clipboard, click **Close** at the top of the task pane. The items you placed on the Office Clipboard while it was open will stay there until you shut down Word, but only the last item you cut or copied to the Office Clipboard can be pasted without reopening the Office Clipboard.

TIP

Place your pointer over the Office Clipboard icon in the taskbar to see how many items are currently on it.

TIP

You can generally undo the last several operations by repeating an Undo command.

NOTE

Under certain circumstances, especially while formatting, the Redo option becomes the Repeat option.

NOTE

You can recover deleted text using the Undo command in the same way that you can reverse a cut or paste action.

Delete Text

Deleting text removes it from its current location *without* putting it in the Clipboard. To delete a selected piece of text:

- Press **DELETE** or **DEL**.

  –Or–

- On the Home tab, click **Cut** in the Clipboard group.

Edit a Document

After entering all the text into a document, most people want to edit it and, possibly, revise it at a later date. You'll want to be able to move around the document, quickly moving from location to location, to do this.

Move Around in a Document

Word provides a number of ways to move around in a document using the mouse and the keyboard.

USE THE MOUSE

You can easily move the insertion point by clicking in your text anywhere on the screen, but how do you move to some place you cannot see? You have to change what you are looking at. Word provides two sets of tools for use with the mouse to do just that: the scroll bars and the browse buttons, as shown in Figure 2-9.

USE THE SCROLL BARS

There are two scroll bars: one for moving vertically within the document and one for moving horizontally. These are only displayed when your document is too wide or too long to be completely displayed within it's window. Each scroll bar contains four controls for getting you where you want to go. Using the vertical scroll bar, you can:

- **Move upward one line** by clicking the upward-pointing *scroll arrow*
- **Move upward or downward** by dragging the *scroll button* in the corresponding direction

- **Move up or down the screen's height** by clicking in the *scroll bar* above the scroll button to move towards the beginning of the document or by clicking below the scroll button to move towards the end of the document

- **Move downward by one line** by clicking the downward-pointing *scroll arrow*

The horizontal scroll bar has similar controls, only these are used for moving in a horizontal fashion.

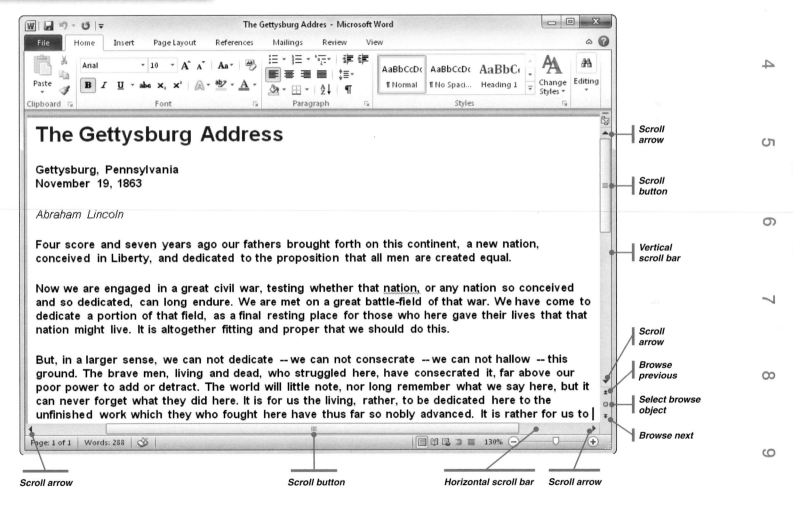

Figure 2-9: The scroll bars and browse buttons allow you to move easily to different locations within your document.

USE THE BROWSE BUTTONS

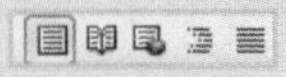

The browse buttons allow you to specify the type of object by which you want to browse through the document. The most obvious browse object—and the default one—is a page. With that as the object, you can browse through a document going forward or backward a page at a time.

Clicking the **Select Browse Object** button in the center opens a menu of objects from which you can select. By selecting one of these objects—such as a page, a heading, a comment, or an edit—you can move through the document, going from one chosen object to the next. Often overlooked, this feature can be quite handy. Place the pointer over the options to find out what the picture or icon represents.

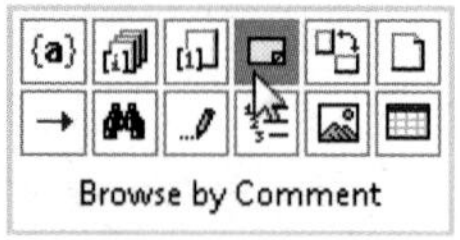

Browse by Comment

USE THE KEYBOARD

The following keyboard commands, used for moving around in your document, also move the insertion point:

- Press the **LEFT** or **RIGHT ARROW** key to move one character to the left or right.
- Press the **UP** or **DOWN ARROW** key to move one line up or down.
- Press **CTRL+LEFT ARROW** or **CTRL+RIGHT ARROW** to move one word to the left or right.
- Press **CTRL+UP ARROW** or **CTRL+DOWN ARROW** to move one paragraph up or down.
- Press **HOME** or **END** to move to the beginning or end of a line.
- Press **CTRL+HOME** or **CTRL+END** to move to the beginning or end of a document.
- Press **PAGE UP** or **PAGE DOWN** to move one screen up or down.
- Press **CTRL+PAGE UP** or **CTRL+PAGE DOWN** to move to the previous or next instance of the current browse object.
- Press **CTRL+ALT+PAGE UP** or **CTRL+ALT+PAGE DOWN** to move to the top or bottom of the window.

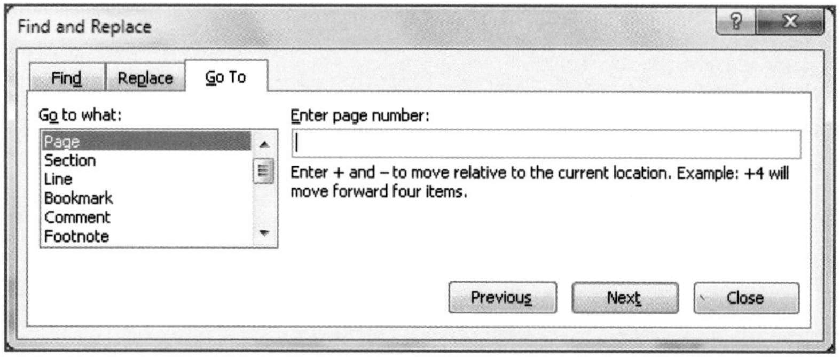

GO TO A PARTICULAR LOCATION

The Go To command opens the Go To tab in the Find And Replace dialog box, shown in Figure 2-10. This allows you

Find and Replace

Find | Replace | Go To

Go to what:
Page
Section
Line
Bookmark
Comment
Footnote

Enter page number:

Enter + and – to move relative to the current location. Example: +4 will move forward four items.

Previous | Next | Close

Figure 2-10: **The Go To command allows you to go to a particular page, as well as to locate other items within a document.**

> **NOTE**
>
> You can also move a certain number of items relative to your current position by typing a plus sign (+) or a minus sign (−) and a number. For example, if Page is selected and you type -3, you will be moved backwards three pages.

to go immediately to the location of some object, such as a page, a footnote, or a table. You can open the dialog box by:

- Pressing the **F5** key
- Pressing **CTRL+G**
- Clicking the **Home** tab, clicking the **Find** down arrow in the Editing group, and clicking **Go To**
- Clicking **Select Browse Object** beneath the vertical scroll bar, and then clicking **Go To**
- Clicking the left end of the status bar in the Page X Of Y area.

After opening the dialog box, select the object you want to go to from the list on the left, and then enter the number or name of the object in the text box on the right. For example, click **Page** on the left and type 5 on the right to go to page 5 in your document.

Find and Replace Text

Often, you may want to find something that you know is in a document, but you are not sure where, or even how many times, that item occurs. This is especially true when you want to locate names or words that are sprinkled throughout a document. For example, if you had repeatedly referred to a table on page 4 and the table was subsequently moved to page 5, you would need to search for all occurrences of "page 4" and change them to "page 5." In this example, you not only want to *find* "page 4," but you also want to *replace* it with "page 5."

Word allows you to do a simple search for a word or phrase, as well as to conduct an advanced search for parts of words, particular capitalization, and words that sound alike.

FIND TEXT WITH THE NAVIGATION PANE

If you just want to search for a word or phrase:

1. Click the **Home** tab, and click **Find** in the Editing group on the right. The navigation pane appears on the left of the Word window with the insertion point in a text box at the top of the pane.

2. Type the word or phrase for which you want to search in the text box. The results are displayed as you type. All occurrences of the word or phrase will be highlighted in the document and listed in the navigation pane, as you can see in Figure 2-11.

3. The results will be highlighted in the text. To select a result, click it in the navigation pane and the border will be highlighted. The word in the text will be highlighted with a different color, letting you know which result you have selected. To advance through the selections in the navigation pane, you can select the next occurrence by clicking the down arrow at the top of the navigation pane or clicking the occurrence in the navigation pane. You can also press **SHIFT+F4** to work your way through the occurrences in the document. When you are done, click **Close** in the navigation pane.

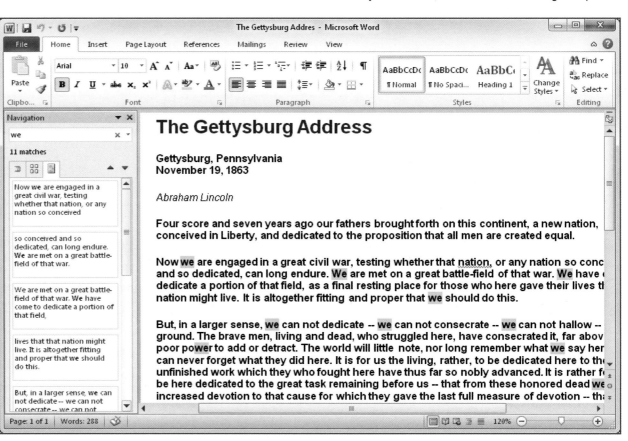

Figure 2-11: When you search for a word or phrase with the Find command, all occurrences of the word or phrase will be highlighted in the document.

Format	Special
Font...	
Paragraph...	
Tabs...	
Language...	
Frame...	
Style...	
Highlight	

FIND TEXT WITH FIND AND REPLACE

In prior versions of Microsoft Word, finding text was done using the Find And Replace dialog box, which is still available and allows for advanced searches. To open the Find And Replace dialog box:

Click **Find** in the Home tab's Editing group. In the navigation pane, click the down arrow on the right of the Search Document text box, and click **Advanced Find**.

–Or–

Click the **Find** down arrow in the Home tab's Editing group, click **Advanced Find**.

By clicking **More** in the Find And Replace dialog box, you will find that Word provides a number of features to make your search more sophisticated (see Figure 2-12). These include specifying the direction of the search, as well as the following additional search options:

- **Match Case:** Find a specific capitalization of a word or phrase.

- **Find Whole Words Only:** Find whole words only, so when searching for "equip," for example, you don't get "equipment."

- **Use Wildcards:** Find words or phrases that contain a set of characters by using wildcards to represent the unknown part of the word or phrase (see the "Using Wildcards" QuickFacts).

- **Sounds Like:** Find words that sound alike but are spelled differently (homonyms).

- **Find All Word Forms:** Find a word in all its forms—noun, adjective, verb, or adverb (for example, ski, skier, and skiing).

- **Match Prefix Or Match Suffix:** Find words containing a common prefix or suffix.

- **Ignore Punctuation Characters:** Find words, regardless of punctuation. This is especially useful when a word might be followed by a comma or period.

- **Ignore White-Space Characters:** Find characters regardless of spaces, tabs, and indents.

- **Format:** Find specific types of formatting, such as for fonts, paragraphs, etc.

- **Special:** Find special characters, such as paragraph marks, em dashes (—), or nonbreaking spaces (can't be the first or last character in a line).

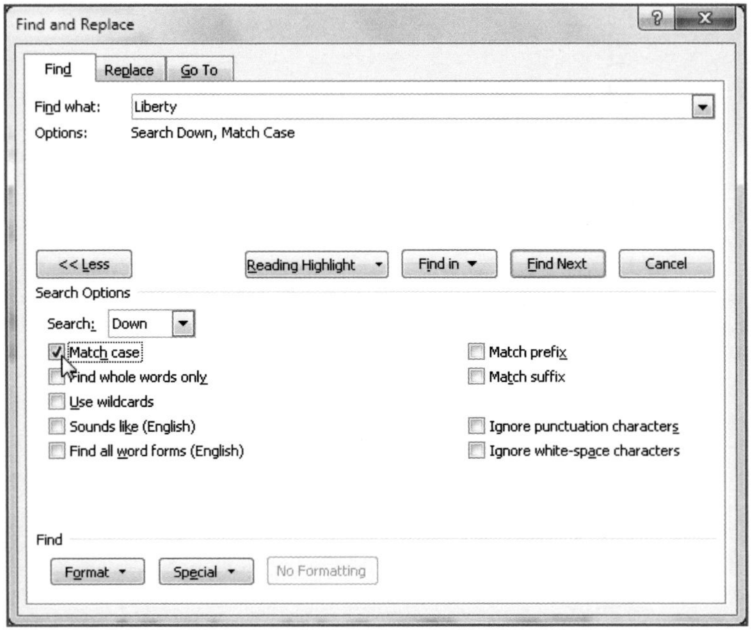

Figure 2-12: *Word offers a number of advanced ways to search a document.*

REPLACE TEXT

Sometimes, when searching for a word or phrase, you might want to replace it with something else. Word lets you use all the features of Find and then replace what is found.

1. Click the **Home** tab, and click **Replace** in the Editing group. The Find And Replace dialog box appears with the Replace tab displayed.

2. Enter the word or phrase for which you want to search in the Find What text box.

3. Enter the word or phrase you want to replace the found item(s) with in the Replace With text box, as shown in Figure 2-13.

4. Click **Find Next**. The first occurrence in the document below the current insertion point will be highlighted.

5. Choose one of the following options:

   - Click **Replace** if you want to replace the current instance that was found with the text you entered. Word replaces this instance and automatically finds the next one.

   - Click **Find Next** if you don't want to replace the text that was found and want to find the next occurrence.

   - Click **Replace All** if you want to replace all occurrences of the word that are found in the document.

6. When you are done, click **Close**.

Figure 2-13: *You can replace words and phrases either individually or all at once.*

QUICK**FACTS**

USING WILDCARDS

Wildcards are characters that are used to represent one or more characters in a word or phrase when searching for items with similar or unknown parts. You must select the **Use Wildcards** check box in the Find And Replace dialog box, and then type the wildcard characters, along with the known characters, in the Find What text box. For example, typing page ? will find both "page 4" and "page 5." The "?" stands for any single character.

Find what:	page ?
Options:	Use Wildcards

Word has defined the characters shown in Table 2-3 as wildcard characters when used with the Find command to replace one or more characters.

NOTE

When searching using wildcards, both Find Whole Words Only and Match Case are turned on automatically and cannot be turned off.

CHARACTER	USED TO REPLACE	EXAMPLE	WILL FIND	WON'T FIND
?	A single character	Page ?	Page 4 or Page 5	Page1
*	Any number of characters	Page *	Page 4 and Page 5	Pages1-5
<	The beginning of a word	<(corp)	Corporate	Incorporate
>	The end of a word	(ton)>	Washington	Toner
\	A wildcard character	What\?	What?	What is
[cc]	One of a list of characters	B[io]b	Bib or Bob	Babe
[c-c]	One in a range of characters	[l-t]ook	look or took	Book
[!c-c]	Any character except one in the range	[!k-n]ook	book or took	Look
{n}	n copies of the previous character	Lo{2}	Loo or Look	Lot
{n,}	n or more copies of the previous character	Lo{1,}	Lot or Look	Late
{n,m}	n to m copies of the previous character	150{1,3}	150 to 15000	15
@	Any number of copies of the previous character	150@	15, 150, or 1500	1400

*Table 2-3: **Wildcard Characters Used with the Find Command***

Complete and Save a Document

When you have completed working in a document, or if you feel that you have done enough to warrant saving it and putting it aside for a while, you should go though a completion procedure that includes checking the spelling and grammar, determining where to save the document, and then actually saving it.

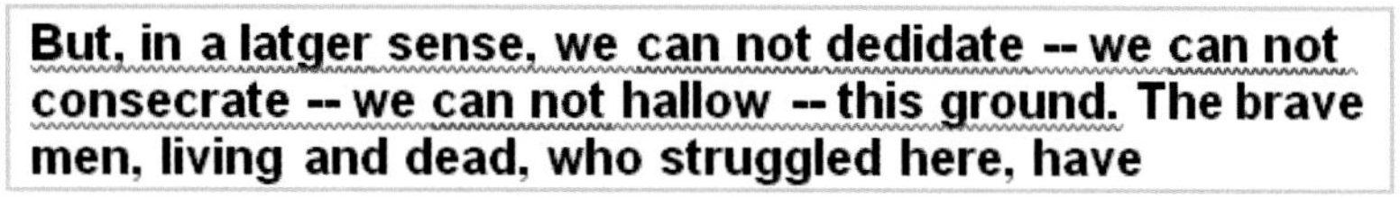

But, in a latger sense, we can not dedidate -- we can not consecrate -- we can not hallow -- this ground. The brave men, living and dead, who struggled here, have

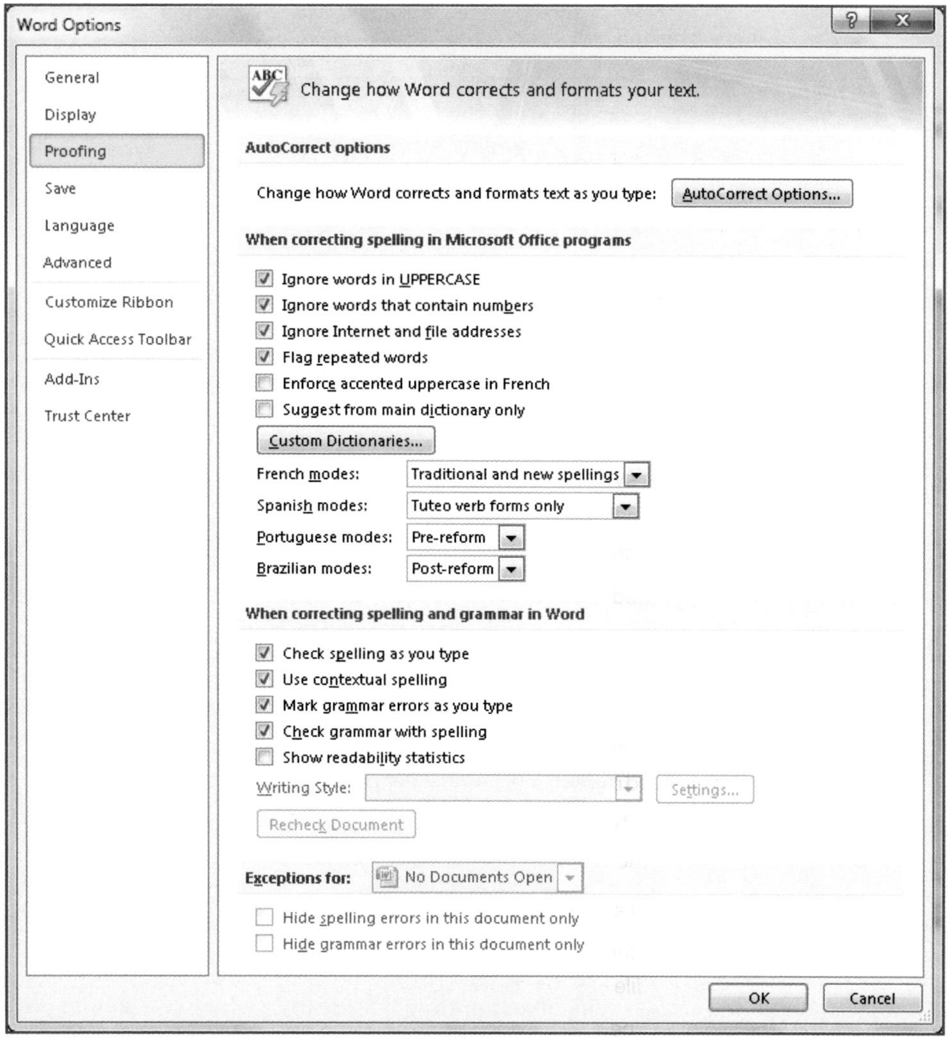

Check Spelling and Grammar

By default, Word checks spelling and grammar as you type, so it might be that these functions have already been performed. You can tell if Word is checking the spelling and grammar by noticing if Word automatically places a wavy red line under words it thinks are misspelled, a wavy blue line under two or more words that are contextually wrong, and a wavy green line beneath words and phrases whose grammar is questioned. You can turn off the automatic spelling and grammar checker. You can also have these features run using an array of options. You can ask Word to perform a spelling and/or grammar check whenever you want—most importantly, when you are completing a document.

CONTROL THE SPELLING AND GRAMMAR CHECKER

Word provides a number of settings that allow you to control how the spelling and grammar check is performed.

1. Click the **File** tab, click **Options**, and click the **Proofing** option on the left. The dialog box shown in Figure 2-14 will appear.

2. If you wish to turn off the automatic spelling checker, clear **Check Spelling As You Type**.

3. If you wish to turn off the automatic grammar checker, clear **Mark Grammar Errors As You Type**.

4. Click **Settings** to the right of Writing Style: Grammar Only to set the rules by which the grammar check is done.

5. Click **OK** twice to close both the Grammar Settings and Options dialog boxes.

Figure 2-14: *By default, Word checks spelling and grammar as you type, but you can disable those utilities in the Word Options dialog box.*

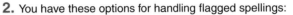

INITIATE SPELLING AND GRAMMAR CHECK

To manually initiate the spelling and grammar check:

1. Click the **Review** tab, and click **Spelling And Grammar** in the Proofing group. The Spelling And Grammar dialog box will appear and begin checking your document. When a word is found that Word believes might not be correct, the dialog box will display both the perceived error and one or more suggestions for its correction (see Figure 2-15).

2. You have these options for handling flagged spellings:

   - If you wish not to correct the perceived error, click **Ignore Once** for this one instance, or click **Ignore All** for all instances of the selected word.

   - Click **Change** for this one instance, or click **Change All** for all instances if you want to replace the perceived error with the highlighted suggestion. If one of the other suggestions is a better choice, click it before clicking **Change** or **Change All**.

   - Click **Add To Dictionary** if you want Word to add your spelling of the word to the dictionary to be used for future documents. If you want Word to automatically correct this misspelling with the selected correction every time you type the incorrect word, click **AutoCorrect**. (See Chapter 4 for more information on AutoCorrect.)

   - Click **Options** to display the Word Options Proofing dialog box (see Figure 2-14), where you can reset many of the spelling and grammar checking rules.

   - Click **Undo** to reverse the last action.

3. When Word has completed checking the spelling and grammar, you'll see a message to that effect. Click **OK**.

Save a Document for the First Time

The first time you save a document, you have to specify where you want to save it—that is, the disk drive and the folder or subfolder in which you want it saved. If this is your first time saving the file, the Save As dialog box will appear so that you can specify the location and enter a file name.

1. Click the **File** tab, and click **Save As**.

2. Click the icon on the left for the major area (for example, Favorites, Libraries, Computer) in which the file is to be saved.

3. If you want to store your new document in a folder that already exists in the major area, double-click that folder to open it.

Figure 2-15: The spelling checker is a gift to those of us who are "spelling challenged"!

4. If you want to store your new document in a new folder, click the **New Folder** button in the toolbar, type the name of the new folder, and click **OK**. The new folder will open. (You can create yet another new folder within that folder using the same steps.)

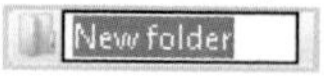

5. When you have the folder(s) open in which you want to store the document, enter the name of the document, as shown in Figure 2-16, and then click **Save**.

TIP

As good as Word's automatic saving is, I manually save my document frequently (like a couple of times an hour) on two different disk drives. I am truly paranoid about this after experiencing the frustration of working several hours on a document only to lose it.

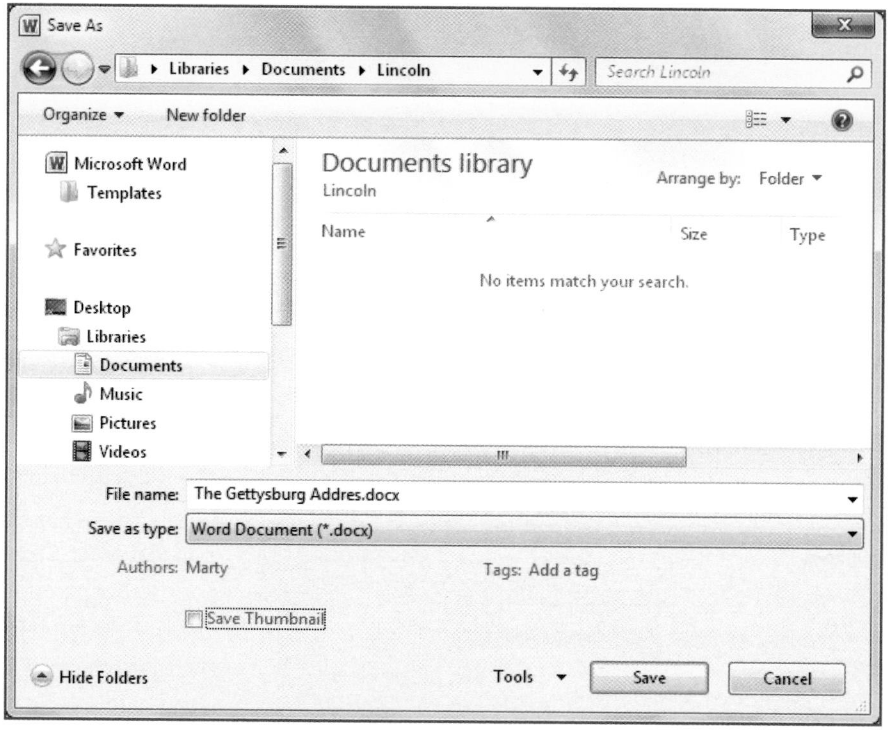

Figure 2-16: ***When saving a file, you don't have to enter a file extension. The ".docx" extension will be supplied by Word automatically.***

TIP

AutoRecover is a reserve parachute that you don't want to test unless you must. AutoRecover might give you the impression that you have lost your work. In fact, if you follow the instructions and choose to recover the AutoRecover document, you may not lose anything—at most, you might lose only the very last thing that you did.

Save a Document Automatically

It is important to save a document periodically as you work. Having Word save it automatically will reduce the chance of losing data in case of a power failure or other interruption.

QUICKSTEPS

SAVING A DOCUMENT

After you have initially saved a document and specified its location, you can quickly save it whenever you wish.

SAVE A DOCUMENT

To save a file:

- Click the **File** tab, and click **Save**.

  –Or–

- Click the **Save** icon on the Quick Access toolbar. 🖫

  –Or–

- Press **CTRL+S**.

SAVE A COPY OF YOUR DOCUMENT

When you save a document under a different name, you create a copy of it.

1. Click the **File** tab, and click **Save As**.

2. In the Save As dialog box, enter the new name in the File Name text box. Then open the **Save In** list box, and identify the path to the folder you want.

3. Click **Save**.

SAVE A DOCUMENT AS A TEMPLATE

To save a newly created document as a template from which to create new documents:

1. Click the **File** tab, and click **Save As**.

2. In the Save As dialog box, open the **Save As Type** drop-down list box, and click **Word Template (*.dotx)**.

3. Select the folder(s) in which to store the template and enter a name (without an extension) for it in the File Name text box.

4. Click **Save**.

1. Click the **File** tab, click **Options**, and click the **Save** option on the left.

2. Beneath Save Documents, make sure the **Save AutoRecover Information Every** check box is selected.

3. The save interval is initially set at 10 minutes. If you wish to change that, use the arrows in the Minutes box to select a time for how often Word is to save your document.

4. Click **OK** to close the dialog box.

Save documents

Save files in this format: Word Document (*.docx)   ▼

☑ Save AutoRecover information every 10 ⭥ minutes

   ☑ Keep the last Auto Recovered file if I close without saving

Chapter 3
Formatting a Document

Plain, unformatted text conveys information, but not nearly as effectively as well-formatted text, as you can see by the two examples in Figure 3-1. Word provides numerous ways to format your text. Most fall under the categories of text formatting, paragraph formatting, and page formatting, which are discussed in the following sections of this chapter. Additional formatting that can be applied at the document level is discussed in Chapter 4.

This chapter discusses the direct, or manual, application of formatting. Much of the character and paragraph formatting discussed in this chapter is commonly applied using styles that combine a number of different individual formatting steps, saving significant time over direct formatting. (Styles are discussed in Chapter 4.) Direct formatting is usually applied only to a small amount of text that needs formatting that is different from its style.

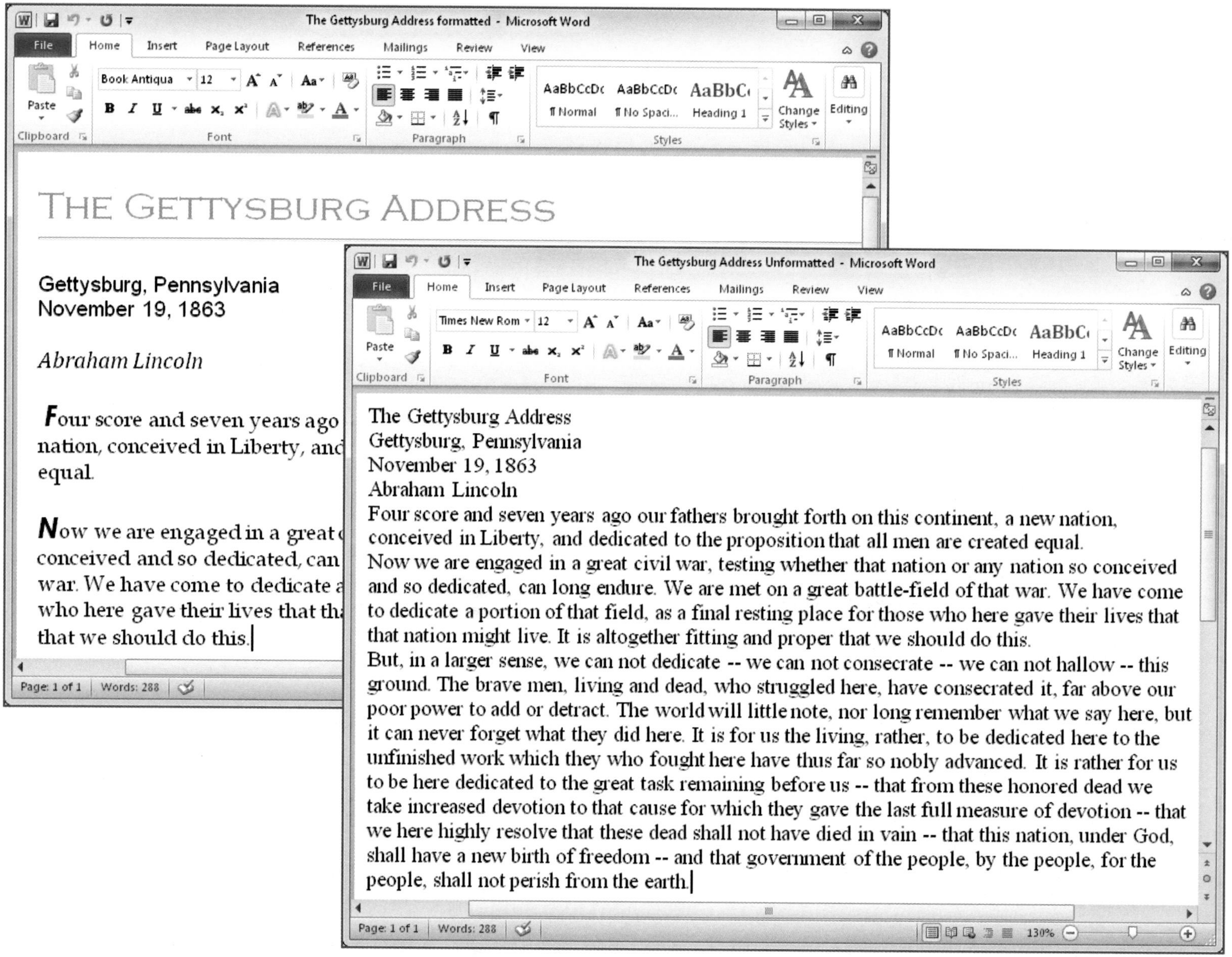

Figure 3-1: *Formatting makes text both more readable and more pleasing to the eye.*

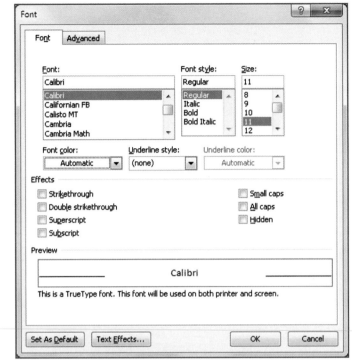

Figure 3-2: The Font dialog box provides the most complete set of character-formatting controls.

Format Text

Text formatting is the formatting that you can apply to individual characters, and includes the selection of fonts, font size, color, character spacing, and capitalization.

Apply Character Formatting

Character formatting can be applied using keyboard shortcuts, the Home tab on the ribbon, and a Formatting dialog box. Of these, clicking the **Home** tab and clicking the **Font Dialog Box Launcher** to open the Font dialog box (see Figure 3-2) provides a comprehensive selection of character formatting and spacing alternatives. In the sections that follow, the Font dialog box is used to accomplish the task being discussed. Keyboard shortcuts and the Font and Paragraph groups on the Home tab (see Figure 3-3) often provide a quicker way to accomplish the same task, and keyboard shortcuts (summarized in Table 3-1) allow you to keep your hands on the keyboard.

NOTE

Prior to applying formatting, you must select the text to be formatted. Chapter 2 contains an extensive section on selecting text.

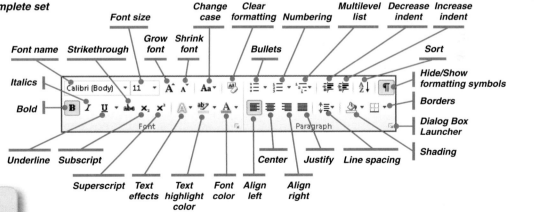

Figure 3-3: The Font and Paragraph groups on the Home tab provide fast formatting with the mouse.

APPLY FORMATTING	SHORTCUT KEYS
Align left	CTRL+L
Align right	CTRL+R
All caps	CTRL+SHIFT+A
Bold	CTRL+B
Bulleted list	CTRL+SHIFT+L
Center	CTRL+E
Change case	SHIFT+F3
Copy format	CTRL+SHIFT+C
Decrease font size	CTRL+SHIFT+<
Increase font size	CTRL+SHIFT+>
Decrease font size one point	CTRL+[
Increase font size one point	CTRL+]
Open Font dialog box	CTRL+D
Font name	CTRL+SHIFT+F
Hang paragraph	CTRL+T
Heading level 1	ALT+CTRL+1
Heading level 2	ALT+CTRL+2
Heading level 3	ALT+CTRL+3
Hidden character	CTRL+SHIFT+H
Indent paragraph	CTRL+M
Italic	CTRL+I
Justify paragraph	CTRL+J
Line space—single	CTRL+1
Line space—1.5 lines	CTRL+5
Line space—double	CTRL+2
Normal style	CTRL+SHIFT+N
Paste format	CTRL+SHIFT+V
Reset character formatting	CTRL+SPACEBAR
Reset paragraph formatting	CTRL+Q
Small caps	CTRL+SHIFT+K
Subscript	CTRL+=
Superscript	CTRL+SHIFT+=

Table 3-1: Formatting Shortcut Keys

USE THE MINI TOOLBAR

When you right-click text in Word 2010, you see both a context menu and a mini toolbar. This toolbar has several of the buttons available in the Home tab's Font and Paragraph groups. In the next sections, when we point out that you can use the Home tab Font group to accomplish a function, it is likely that you can do the same function with the mini toolbar. However, to reduce repetition, using the mini toolbar to carry out these tasks will not be included.

SELECT A FONT

A *font* is a set of characters that share a particular design, which is called a *typeface*. When you install Windows, and again when you install Office, a number of fonts are automatically installed on your computer. You can see the fonts available by clicking the down arrow next to the font name in the Home tab Font group and then scrolling through the list (your most recently used fonts are at the top, followed by all fonts listed alphabetically). You can also see the list of fonts in the Font dialog box, where you can select a font in the Font list and see what it looks like in the Preview area at the bottom of the dialog box.

By default, the Calibri font is used for body text in all new documents using the default Normal template. To change this font:

1. Select the text to be formatted (see Chapter 2).

2. Click the **Home** tab, and click the **Font** down arrow in the Font group. Scroll through the list until you see the font that you want, and then click it.

APPLY FORMATTING	SHORTCUT KEYS
Symbol font	CTRL+SHIFT+Q
Unhang paragraph	CTRL+SHIFT+T
Unindent paragraph	CTRL+SHIFT+M
Underline (continuous)	CTRL+U
Underline (double)	CTRL+SHIFT+D
Underline (word)	CTRL+SHIFT+W

Table 3-1: Formatting Shortcut Keys (Continued)

TIP

You can also open the Font dialog box by right-clicking the selected text you want to format and then clicking **Font** or by clicking the **Font Dialog Box Launcher** in the Font group.

NOTE

Several types of fonts are included in the default set that is installed with Windows and Office. Alphabetic fonts come in two varieties: serif fonts, such as Times New Roman or Century Schoolbook, where each letter is designed with distinctive ends, or *serifs*, on each of the character's lines, and *sans-serif* ("without serifs") fonts, such as Arial and Century Gothic, without the ends. Sans-serif fonts are generally used for headings and lists, while serif fonts are generally used for body text in printed documents, but often the reverse in Web pages. Finally, there are symbol fonts, such as Wingdings and Webdings, with many special characters, such as smiling faces ("smilies"), arrows, and pointing fingers.

APPLY BOLD OR ITALIC STYLE

Fonts come in four styles: regular (or "roman"), bold, italic, and bold-italic. The default is, of course, regular, yet fonts such as Arial Black and Eras Bold appear bold. To make fonts bold, italic, or bold-italic:

1. Select the text to be formatted (see Chapter 2).

2. Press **CTRL+B** to make it bold, and/or press **CTRL+I** to make it italic.

   –Or–

   Click the **Bold** icon in the Font group, and/or click the **Italic** icon.

CHANGE FONT SIZE

Font size is measured in *points*, which is the height of a character, not its width. For most fonts, the width varies with the character, the letter "i" taking up less room than "w." (The Courier New font is an exception, with all characters having the same width.) There are 72 points in an inch. The default font size is 11 points for body text, with standard headings varying from 11 to 14 points. The 8-point type is common for smaller print; anything below 6 point is typically unreadable. To change the font size of your text:

1. Select the text to be formatted (see Chapter 2).

2. On the Home tab, click the **Font Size** down arrow in the Font group, scroll through the list until you see the font size you want, and then click it.

   –Or–

   Press **CTRL+SHIFT+<** to decrease the font size, or press **CTRL+SHIFT+>** to increase the font size.

UNDERLINE TEXT

Several forms of underlining can be applied.

1. Select the text to be formatted (see Chapter 2).

2. Click the **Underline** down arrow in the Home tab Font group, and click the type of underline you want.

   –Or–

   Press **CTRL+U** to apply a continuous underline to the entire selection (including spaces).

   –Or–

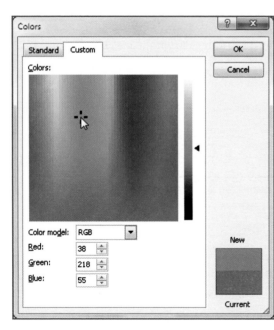

TIP

At the top of the Font Size list box, you can type in half-point sizes, such as <u>10.5</u>, as well as sizes that are not on the list, such as <u>15</u>.

TIP

The Underline Style drop-down list in the Font dialog box, as with the Underline button in the ribbon, contains underline choices beyond those the other methods provide—dotted, wavy, and so on.

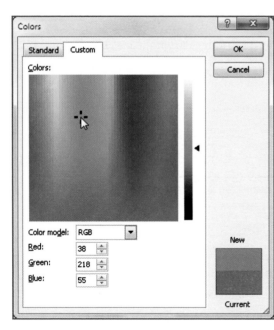

Figure 3-4: You can create any color you want in the Custom tab of the Colors dialog box.

Press **CTRL+SHIFT+W** to apply an underline to just each word in the selection.

–Or–

Press **CTRL+SHIFT+D** to apply a double underline to the entire selection.

USE FONT COLOR

To change the color of text:

1. Select the text to be formatted (see Chapter 2).

2. Click the **Home** tab, and click **Font Color** in the Font group to apply the currently selected color.

   –Or–

   Click the **Font Dialog Box Launcher** for the Font dialog box. Click the **Font Color** down arrow, click the color you want, and click **OK**.

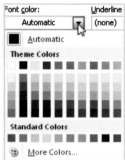

3. If, in selecting a color from either the Home tab Font group or the Font dialog box, you do not find the color you want within the 40-color palette, click **More Colors** to open the Colors dialog box. In the Standard tab, you can pick a color from a 145-color palette, or you can use the Custom tab to choose from an almost infinite range of colors by clicking in the color spectrum or by entering the RGB (red, green, and blue) values, as you can see in Figure 3-4, or the HSL (hue, saturation, and luminescent) values.

RESET TEXT

Figure 3-5 shows some of the formatting that has been or will be discussed. All of those can be reset to the plain text or the default formatting. To reset text to default settings:

1. Select the text to be formatted (see Chapter 2).

2. Click **Clear Formatting** in the Home tab, Font group.

   –Or–

   Press **CTRL+SPACEBAR**.

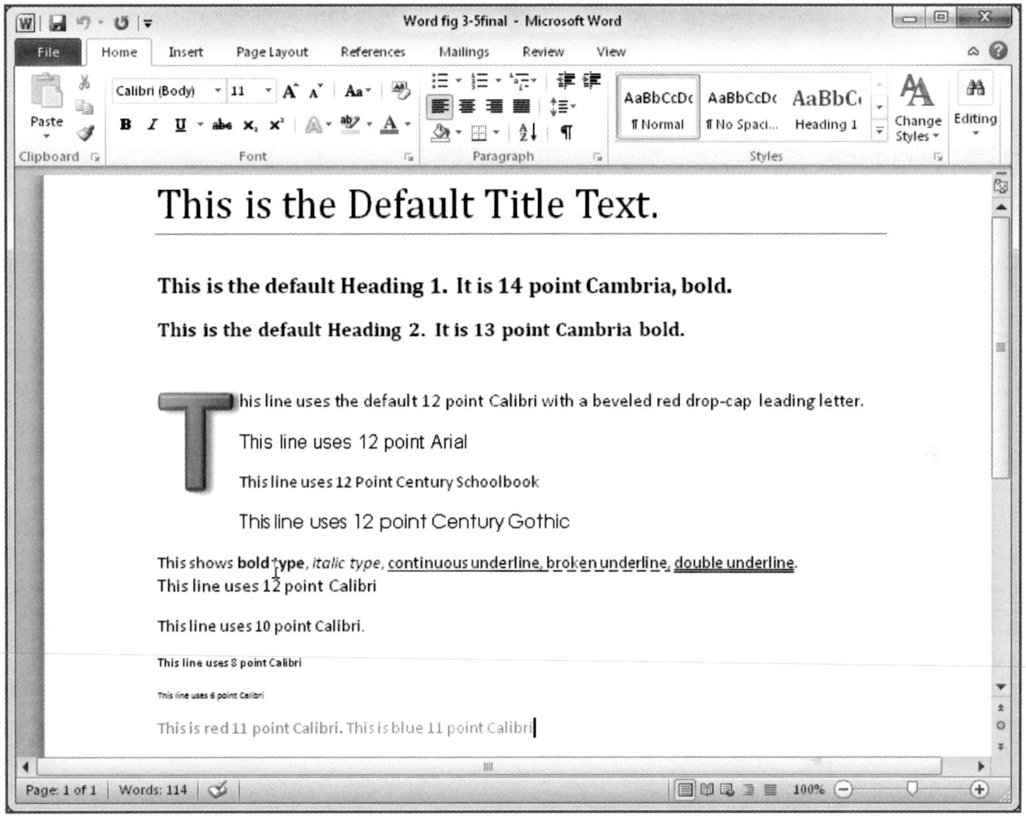

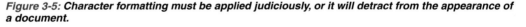

Figure 3-5: ***Character formatting must be applied judiciously, or it will detract from the appearance of a document.***

TIP

Word comes with a default set of formatting parameters for body text composed of Calibri, 11-point regular type, and black color. You can change this in the Font dialog box by clicking the **Font Dialog Box Launcher** in the Home tab. In the dialog box, select the font, style, size, and color you want. Click **Set As Default**, select either **This Document Only** or **All Documents**, and then click **OK** to make those settings the new default set.

Use Advanced Font Features

Word provides the ability to change two groups of advanced font features that deal with character spacing and OpenType features. Both of these are set in the Advanced tab of the Font dialog box, which is shown in Figure 3-6.

SET CHARACTER SPACING

Character spacing, in this case, is the amount of space between characters on a single line. Word gives you the chance to increase and decrease character spacing, as well as to scale the size of selected text, raise and lower vertically the position

NOTE

Character spacing, especially kerning, is predominantly used when you are creating something like a brochure, flyer, or newspaper ad in which you want to achieve a professional look.

QUICKSTEPS

USING TEXT EFFECTS

Word provides a number of text effects that can be applied directly from the Fonts group in the Home tab, such as superscript, subscript, and strikethrough, or from the Font dialog box's effects area (see Figure 3-2), such as double strikethrough, small caps, and hidden. In addition, Word 2010 has a new Text Effects button and menu in the Home tab Fonts group that allows you to apply a number of visual effects to selected characters, such as shadow, glow, and bevel.

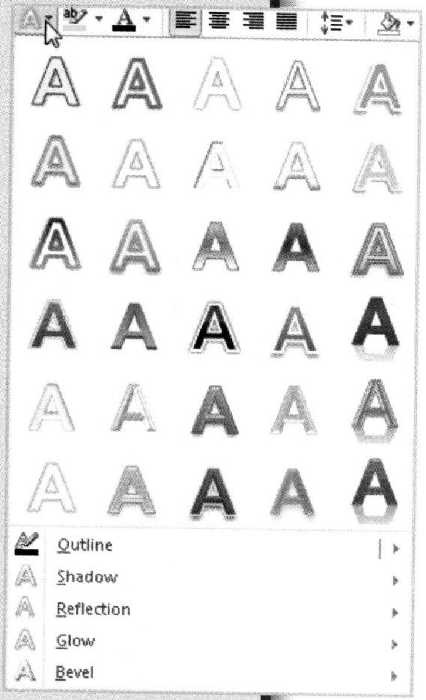

1. Select the text to which you want to apply the effect.
2. Click the **Home** tab, and click **Text Effects** in the Font group to open the text effects drop-down menu.
3. Slowly hover the mouse pointer over the various effects to see the results on the selected text.

Continued . . .

of text on the line, and determine when to apply kerning (how much space separates certain character pairs, such as "A" and "V," which can overlap). To apply character spacing:

1. Select the text to be formatted, click the **Home** tab, click the **Font Dialog Box Launcher** to open the Font dialog box, and click the **Advanced** tab. You have these character spacing options:
   - **Scale:** Select the percentage scale factor that you want to apply. (This is not recommended. It is better to change the font size so as not to distort the font).
   - **Spacing:** Select the change in spacing (expanded or condensed) that you want and the amount of that change in points (pt).
   - **Position:** Select the change in position (raised or lowered) that you want and the amount of that change in points.

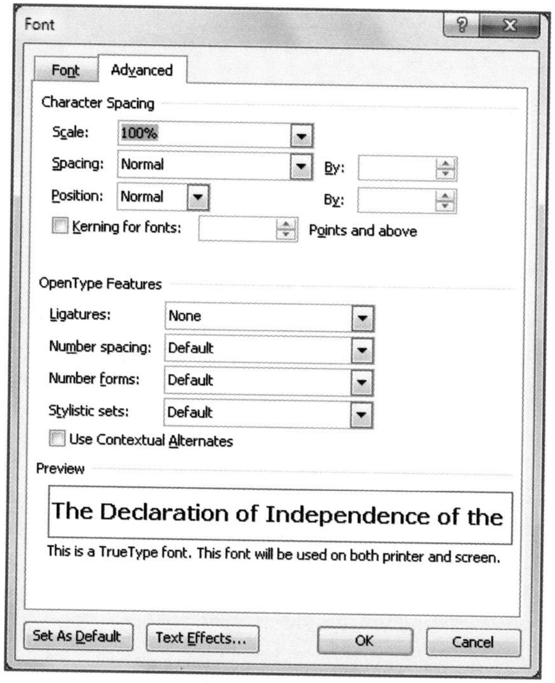

Figure 3-6: ***The spacing of text can have as much to do with its appearance as the choice of font.***

QUICKSTEPS

USING TEXT EFFECTS *(Continued)*

4. After looking at each of the 30 options, hover over each of the five sub-menus at the bottom. At the bottom of each of the final four sub-menus is an option that opens the Format Text Effects dialog box, shown in Figure 3-7.
5. Try various combinations of Text Fill, Text Outline, Outline Style, Shadow, Reflection, Glow And Soft Edges, and 3-D Format. The possibilities are close to infinite.
6. Select the effects you want to use, previewing them on your page. When you are satisfied, if you are using the Format Text Effects dialog box, click **Close**.

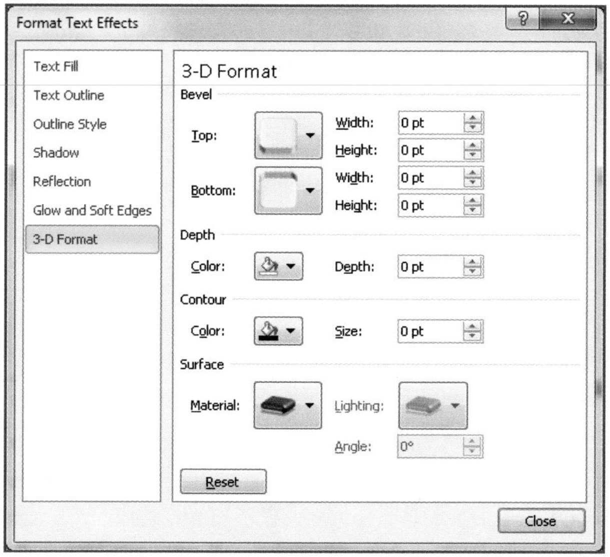

*Figure 3-7: **Using either the Text Effects drop-down menu or the Format Text Effects dialog box, you can make characters look any way you want.***

- **Kerning For Fonts:** Determine if you want to apply kerning rules and the point size at which you want to do that (it becomes more important in larger point sizes).

2. Check the results in the Preview area, an example of which is shown in Figure 3-7. When you are satisfied, click **OK**.

SET OPENTYPE FEATURES

OpenType is an open specification for defining computer fonts that is quite flexible, both in its ability to represent a great many of the world's alphabets, and in its ability to be easily scaled or sized. OpenType was started by Microsoft and added to by Adobe Systems and others to create a substantial enhancement to its predecessor, TrueType. OpenType is the predominant method used to create fonts on most computers today.

The Advanced tab of Word's Font dialog box contains a group of settings that provide stylistic alternatives for certain OpenType fonts, in addition to the control of the use of ligatures (stylistic pairs of letters like Æ), and the spacing and forms of numbers. These settings are applicable to fonts in which the font designer has added these options. One such font that is available with Windows Vista or Windows 7 and Office 2010 is Gabriola. Figure 3-8 shows the Gabriola font at 20 points with various OpenType features selected.

1. Select the text to be formatted, click the **Home** tab, click the **Font Dialog Box Launcher** to open the Font dialog box, and click the **Advanced** tab. The OpenType features available are (see the Note on the next page):
   - **Ligatures:** Select from among None, Standard, Standard And Contextual, Historical And Discretionary, or All. Turns on various levels of styling pairs of letters like Æ.
   - **Number Spacing:** Select Default, Tabular, or Proportional, depending on whether you are using the number in a sentence, where you might want proportional spacing, or in a tabular list where you want the numbers to line up. The proportional setting tends to take less horizontal space, but tabular is the default. Try this with the Calibri font.
   - **Number forms:** Select Default, Lining, where the tops and bottoms of the numbers line up, or Oldstyle, where the tops and bottoms of the numbers don't line up. Lining is the default, shown on the bottom in this example of Calibri numbers.

123,456,789
123,456,789

When in the Course of human events, it becomes necessary for one people to dissolve the political bands which have connected them with another, and to assume among the powers of the earth, the

(a)

When in the Course of human events, it becomes necessary for one people to dissolve the political bands which have connected them with another, and to assume among the powers of the earth, the

(b)

When in the Course of human events, it becomes necessary for one people to dissolve the political bands which have connected them with another, and to assume among the powers of the earth, the

(c)

When in the Course of human events, it becomes necessary for one people to dissolve the political bands which have connected them with another, and to assume among the powers of the earth, the

(d)

Figure 3-8: OpenType fonts give the font designer many added features that can be used in a given font. Here the Gabriola font is shown: (a) in its default configuration, (b) with stylistic set 4, (c) with Use Contextual Alternatives (note the letter "t" at the beginning of several lines), and (d) with stylistic set 7.

NOTE

The meaning of "standard," "default," "contextual," and the various stylistic sets in OpenType features are at the discretion of the font designer. Generally, the stylistic sets go from "1" being the least embellished to "20" being the most embellished, although some fonts only use some of these sets, such as Gabriola, which uses seven. The only way for you to know which fonts use these features and how the various feature selections look is for you to try them out. Do so at larger point sizes.

- **Stylistic Sets:** Select from up to 20 alternative embellishments to a font that have been added by the font designer (see Figure 3-8).

- **Use Contextual Alternatives:** When selected, this applies added flourishes that the designer wants used in only certain contextual circumstances, such as the first character in a line, as you can see in third example in Figure 3-8.

2. After making a selection, click **OK** and look at the effect on your page. The Preview area does not do justice to these changes.

Change Capitalization

You can, of course, capitalize a character you are typing by holding down **SHIFT** while you type. You can also press **CAPS LOCK** to have every letter that you type be capitalized and then press **CAPS LOCK** again to turn off capitalization. You can also change the capitalization of existing text.

1. Select the text whose capitalization you want to change.

2. In the Home tab Font group, click **Change Case**. Select one of these options:

NOTE

You can use **SHIFT+F3** to toggle between uppercase, lowercase, and sentence case or capitalize each word on selected text. For instance, if you select a complete sentence with a period at the end and press **SHIFT+F3** three times, you will get all caps, all lowercase, and sentence caps (only the first letter of the sentence capitalized), respectively. If the selection does not include a sentence-ending period, then each word will have leading caps with the final press of **SHIFT+F3**.

NOTE

To remove a drop cap, select the character or word, click **Drop Cap** in the Insert tab Text group, and click **None** on the context menu.

W hen In The Co For One Peopl connected the powers of the earth, th of Nature and of Natur opinions of mankind re impel them to the sepa

W e hold these truths to l that they are endowed that among these are l to secure these rights,

- **Sentence case** capitalizes the first letter of the first word of every selected sentence.
- **lowercase** displays all selected words in lowercase.
- **UPPERCASE** displays all selected words in all caps. All the characters of every selected word will be capitalized.
- **Capitalize Each Word** puts a leading cap on each selected word.
- **tOGGLE cASE** changes all lowercase characters to uppercase and all uppercase characters to lowercase.

Create a Drop Cap

A *drop cap* is an enlarged capital letter at the beginning of a paragraph that extends down over two or more lines of text (see the red "t" in Figure 3-5 earlier in this chapter). To create a drop cap:

1. Select the character or word that you want to be formatted as a drop cap.
2. Click the **Insert** tab, and click **Drop Cap** in the Text group. A context menu will open. You have these choices:

   - **None**, the default keeps a standard letter.
   - Click **Dropped** to have the first letter dropped within the paragraph text.
   - Click **In Margin** to set the capital letter off in the margin.
   - Click **Drop Cap Options** to see further options. You can change the font, specify how many lines will be dropped (3 is the default), and specify how far from the text the dropped cap will be placed. Click **OK** to close the Drop Cap dialog box.

   A≡ Drop Cap ▾ | 📧 ▾
   | None
   A≡ Dropped
   A≡ In margin
   A≡ Drop Cap Options...

3. Make the choice you want to use.

The paragraph will be reformatted around the enlarged capital letter. On the left are the two examples of putting the dropped cap in the paragraph or in the margin.

Format a Paragraph

Paragraph formatting, which you can apply to any paragraph, is used to manage alignment, indentation, line spacing, bulleted or numbered lists, and borders. In Word, a paragraph consists of a paragraph mark (created by pressing **ENTER**)

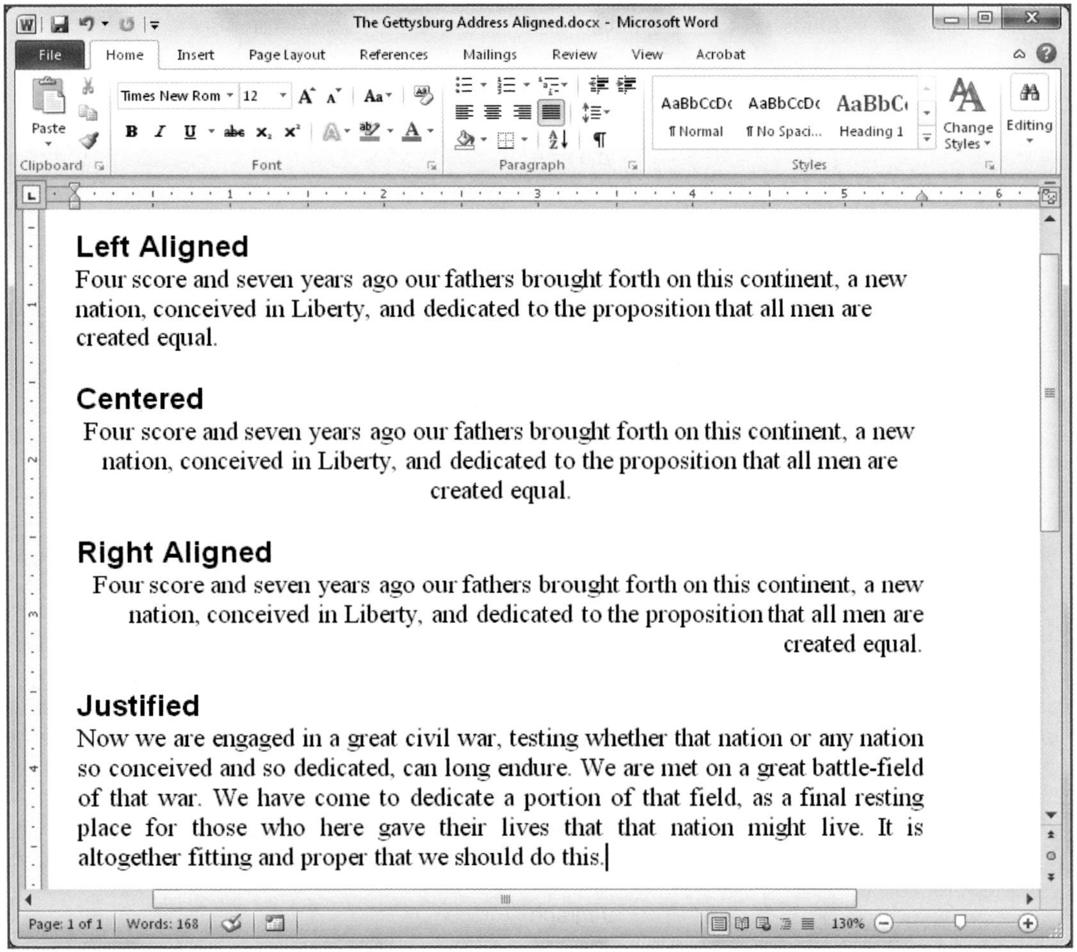
The Gettysburg Address Aligned.docx - Microsoft Word
File
Home
Insert
Page Layout
References
Mailings
Review
View
Acrobat
Paste
Clipboard
Times New Rom
12
Font
Paragraph
AaBbCcDc
¶ Normal
AaBbCcDc
¶ No Spaci...
AaBbCc
Heading 1
Change Styles
Styles
Editing
Left Aligned
Four score and seven years ago our fathers brought forth on this continent, a new nation, conceived in Liberty, and dedicated to the proposition that all men are created equal.
Centered
Four score and seven years ago our fathers brought forth on this continent, a new nation, conceived in Liberty, and dedicated to the proposition that all men are created equal.
Right Aligned
Four score and seven years ago our fathers brought forth on this continent, a new nation, conceived in Liberty, and dedicated to the proposition that all men are created equal.
Justified
Now we are engaged in a great civil war, testing whether that nation or any nation so conceived and so dedicated, can long endure. We are met on a great battle-field of that war. We have come to dedicate a portion of that field, as a final resting place for those who here gave their lives that that nation might live. It is altogether fitting and proper that we should do this.
Page: 1 of 1
Words: 168
130%

Figure 3-9: Paragraph alignment provides both visual appeal and separation of text.

and any text or objects that appear between that paragraph mark and the previous paragraph mark. A paragraph can be empty, or it can contain anything from a single character to as many characters as you care to enter.

Set Paragraph Alignment

Four types of paragraph alignment are available in Word (see Figure 3-9): left aligned, centered, right aligned, and justified. Left aligned, right aligned, and centered are self-explanatory. Justified means that the text in a paragraph is spread out between the left and right margins. Word does this by adding space between words, except for the last line of a paragraph. To apply paragraph alignment:

1. Click in the paragraph you want to align. (You don't need to select the entire paragraph.)
2. For left alignment, press **CTRL+L**; for right alignment, press **CTRL+R**; for centered, press **CTRL+E**; and for justified, press **CTRL+J**.

   –Or–

   In the Home tab Paragraph group, click the **Align Left**, **Center**, **Align Right**, or **Justify** button, depending on what you want to do.

   –Or–

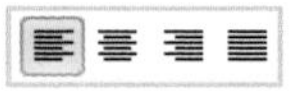

You can also open the Paragraph dialog box by right-clicking the paragraph you want to format and clicking **Paragraph**.

USING INDENTATION

There are four types of indentation:

- **Bulleted and numbered lists** are used to organize and group pieces of text so they can be viewed as elements within a given topic.

- **An indented paragraph**, either just on the left or on both the left and right, is used to separate and call attention to a piece of text.

- **An outline** is used to provide a hierarchical structure.

- **Indenting the first line** of a paragraph is used to indicate the start of a new paragraph.

- **Hanging indents** indent all of the lines in a paragraph except the first line, which hangs out to the left.

Indentation is a powerful formatting tool when used correctly. Like other formatting, it can also be overused and make text hard to read or to understand. Ask yourself two questions about indentation: Do I have a good reason for it? and Does it improve the readability and/or understanding of what is being said?

In the Home tab Paragraph group, click the **Paragraph Dialog Box Launcher** to open the Paragraph dialog box. On the Indents And Spacing tab, click the **Alignment** down arrow, click the type of alignment you want, and click **OK**.

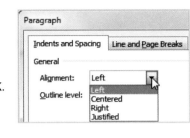

Indent a Paragraph

Indenting a paragraph in Word means to:

- Move the left or right edge (or both) of the paragraph inward towards the center

- Move the left side of the first line of a paragraph inward toward the center

- Move the left side of the first line of a paragraph leftward, away from the center, for a *hanging indent*

Figure 3-10 shows the various types of indenting styles available to you.

CHANGE THE LEFT INDENT

To move the left edge of an entire paragraph to the right:

1. Click in the paragraph to select it.

2. In the Home tab Paragraph group, click **Increase Indent** one or more times to indent the left edge a half-inch each time (the first click will move the left paragraph edge to the nearest halfinch or inch mark).

   –Or–

   Press **CTRL+M** one or more times to indent the left edge a half-inch each time.

   –Or–

   On the Page Layout tab Paragraph group, click the **Left Indent** spinner.

   –Or–

   Open the Paragraph dialog box. In the Home tab Paragraph group, click the **Paragraph Dialog Box Launcher**. On the Indents And Spacing tab, under Indentation, click the **Left** spinner's up arrow until you get the amount of indentation you want, and then click **OK**.

REMOVE A LEFT INDENT

To move the left edge of an entire paragraph back to the left:

1. Click in the paragraph to select it.

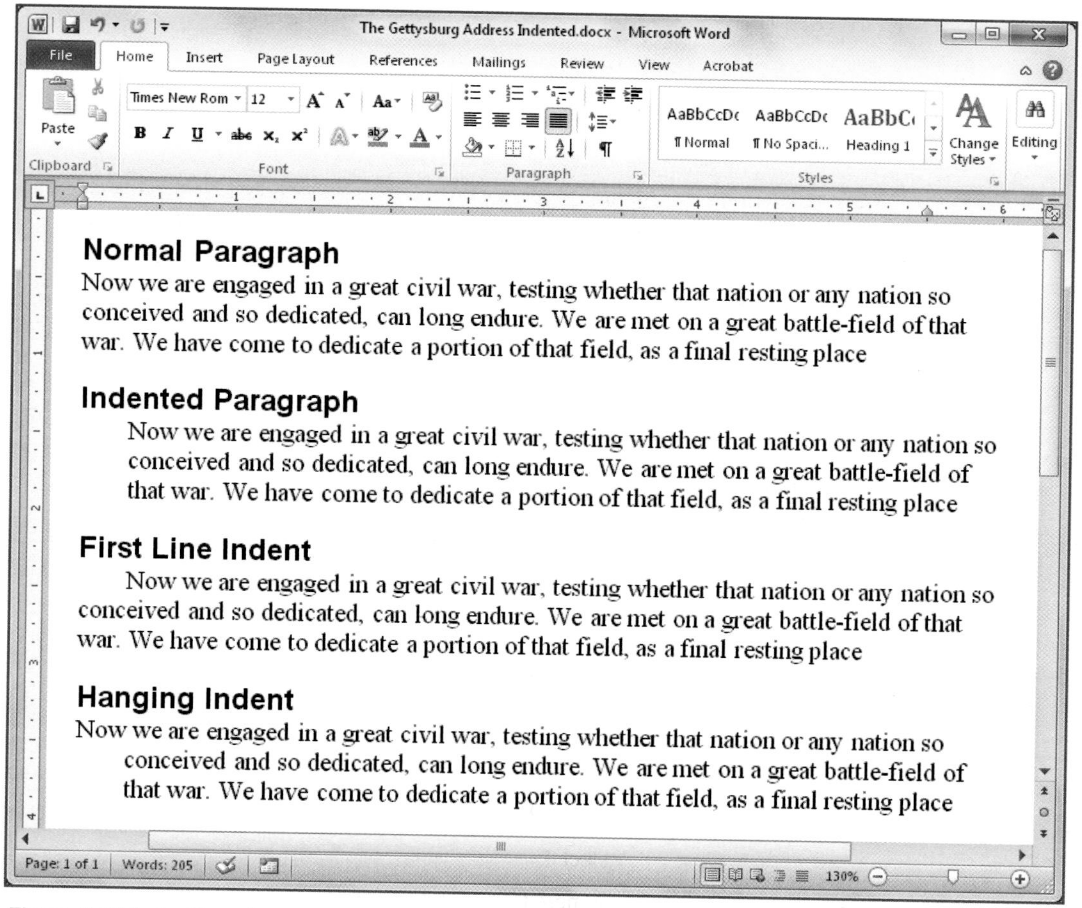

Figure 3-10: *Indenting allows you to separate a block of text visually.*

The document shown in the figure contains the following text:

Normal Paragraph

Now we are engaged in a great civil war, testing whether that nation or any nation so conceived and so dedicated, can long endure. We are met on a great battle-field of that war. We have come to dedicate a portion of that field, as a final resting place

Indented Paragraph

Now we are engaged in a great civil war, testing whether that nation or any nation so conceived and so dedicated, can long endure. We are met on a great battle-field of that war. We have come to dedicate a portion of that field, as a final resting place

First Line Indent

Now we are engaged in a great civil war, testing whether that nation or any nation so conceived and so dedicated, can long endure. We are met on a great battle-field of that war. We have come to dedicate a portion of that field, as a final resting place

Hanging Indent

Now we are engaged in a great civil war, testing whether that nation or any nation so conceived and so dedicated, can long endure. We are met on a great battle-field of that war. We have come to dedicate a portion of that field, as a final resting place

2. In the Home tab Paragraph group, click **Decrease Indent** one or more times to unindent the left edge a half-inch each time.

–Or–

Press **CTRL+SHIFT+M** one or more times to unindent the left edge a half-inch each time.

–Or–

In the Home tab Paragraph group, click the **Paragraph Dialog Box Launcher** to open the Paragraph dialog box. In the Indents And Spacing tab, under Indentation, click the Left spinner's down arrow until you get the amount of indentation you want, and then click **OK**.

CHANGE THE RIGHT INDENT

To move the right edge of an entire paragraph to the left:

1. Click in the paragraph to select it.

2. In the Page Layout tab, Paragraph group, click the **Right Indent** spinner.

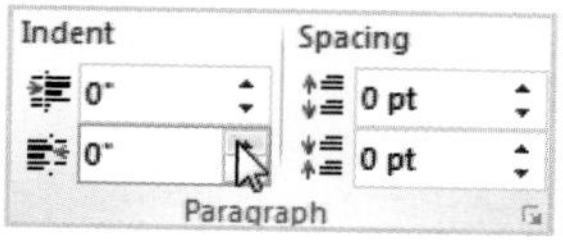

–Or–

Open the Paragraph dialog box. In the Home tab Paragraph group, click the **Paragraph Dialog Box Launcher**. In the Indents And Spacing tab, under Indentation, click the **Right** spinner's up arrow until you get the amount of indentation you want, and then click **OK**.

INDENT THE FIRST LINE

To move the first line of a paragraph to the right:

Click on the left edge of the first line of the paragraph and press **TAB**.

–Or–

Click in the paragraph. In the Home tab Paragraph group, click the **Paragraph Dialog Box Launcher**. In the Indents And Spacing tab, under Indentation, click the **Special** down arrow, and click **First Line**. If you want an indent different than the .5" default, click the **By** spinner to set the amount of indentation you want, and click **OK**.

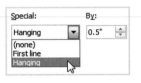

MAKE A HANGING INDENT

To indent all of a paragraph except the first line:

1. Click in the paragraph to select it.
2. Press **CTRL+T** one or more times to indent the left edge of all but the first line a half-inch each time.

   –Or–

   In the Home tab Paragraph group, click the **Paragraph Dialog Box Launcher**. In the Indents And Spacing tab, under Indentation, click the **Special** down arrow, and select **Hanging**. Enter the amount of the indent, and click **OK**.

REMOVE A HANGING INDENT

To unindent all but the first line of a paragraph:

1. Click in the paragraph to select it.
2. Press **CTRL+SHIFT+T** one or more times to unindent the left edge of all but the first line a half-inch each time.

   –Or–

   In the Home tab Paragraph group, click the **Paragraph Dialog Box Launcher**. In the Indents And Spacing tab, under Indentation, click the **Special** down arrow, and click **None**. Click **OK**.

TIP

You can reset *all* paragraph formatting, including indents, hanging indents, alignment, and paragraph spacing, to their default settings by pressing **CTRL+Q**.

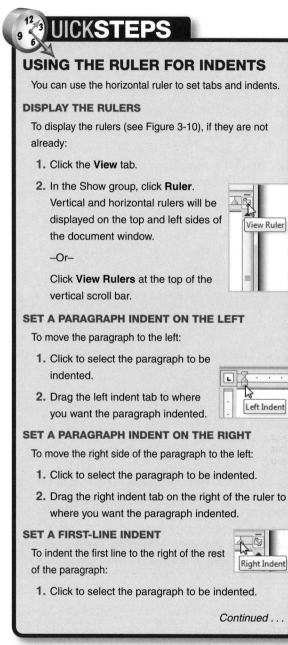

USING THE RULER FOR INDENTS

You can use the horizontal ruler to set tabs and indents.

DISPLAY THE RULERS

To display the rulers (see Figure 3-10), if they are not already:

1. Click the **View** tab.

2. In the Show group, click **Ruler**. Vertical and horizontal rulers will be displayed on the top and left sides of the document window.

   –Or–

   Click **View Rulers** at the top of the vertical scroll bar.

SET A PARAGRAPH INDENT ON THE LEFT

To move the paragraph to the left:

1. Click to select the paragraph to be indented.

2. Drag the left indent tab to where you want the paragraph indented.

SET A PARAGRAPH INDENT ON THE RIGHT

To move the right side of the paragraph to the left:

1. Click to select the paragraph to be indented.

2. Drag the right indent tab on the right of the ruler to where you want the paragraph indented.

SET A FIRST-LINE INDENT

To indent the first line to the right of the rest of the paragraph:

1. Click to select the paragraph to be indented.

Continued . . .

Determine Line and Paragraph Spacing

The vertical spacing of text is determined by the amount of space between lines, the amount of space added before and after a paragraph, and where you break lines and pages.

SET LINE SPACING

The amount of space between lines is most often set in terms of the line height, with *single-spacing* being one times the current line height, *double-spacing* being twice the current line height, and so on. You can also specify line spacing in points, as you do the size of type. Single-spacing is approximately 14 points for 12-point type. To set line spacing for an entire paragraph:

1. Click in the paragraph for which you want to set the line spacing.

2. In the Home tab Paragraph group, click the **Line Spacing** down arrow, and then click the line spacing, in terms of lines, that you want to use.

   –Or–

   Press **CTRL+1** for single line spacing, press **CTRL+5** for one-and-a-half line spacing, and press **CTRL+2** for double line spacing.

   –Or–

   In the Home tab Paragraph group, click the **Paragraph Dialog Box Launcher** to open the Paragraph dialog box. In the Indents And Spacing tab, under Spacing, click the **Line Spacing** down arrow. From the menu that appears, select the line spacing you want to use, as shown in Figure 3-11. Click **OK**.

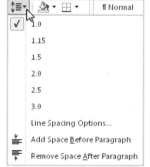

ADD SPACE BETWEEN PARAGRAPHS

In addition to specifying space between lines, you can add extra space before and after paragraphs. With typewriters, many people would add an extra blank line between paragraphs. That has carried over to computers, but it does not always look good. If you are using single spacing, leaving a blank line will leave an extra 14 points (with 12-point type) between paragraphs. Common

USING THE RULER FOR INDENTS

(Continued)

2. Drag the first line indent tab on the left of the ruler to where you want the paragraph indented.

First Line Indent

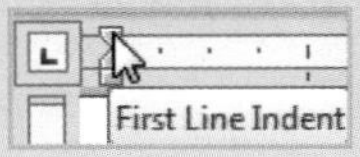

SET A HANGING INDENT

To indent all but the first line of a paragraph to the right of the first line:

1. Click to select the paragraph to be indented.

2. Drag the hanging indent tab on the left of the ruler to where you want the paragraph indented.

Hanging Indent

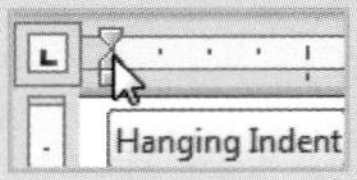

NOTE

In the Paragraph dialog box, you can specify the amount of space between lines in a format other than the number of lines. From the Line Spacing drop-down list, click **Exactly**, and then enter or select the number of points to use between lines. With 12-point type, single spacing is about 14 points, one-and-a-half line spacing (1.5) is about 21 points, and so on. With 11-point type, single spacing is about 12 points.

CAUTION

If you reduce the line spacing below the size of the type (below 12 points for 12 point type, for example), the lines will begin to overlap and become hard to read.

paragraph spacing is to leave 3 points before the paragraph and 6 points afterward, so if you have two of these paragraphs, one after the other, you would have a total of 9 points, in comparison to the 14 points from an extra blank line. To add extra space between paragraphs:

1. Click in the paragraph to which you want to add space.

2. In the Page Layout tab Paragraph group, click the **Spacing** spinners to set the spacing before and after the paragraph.

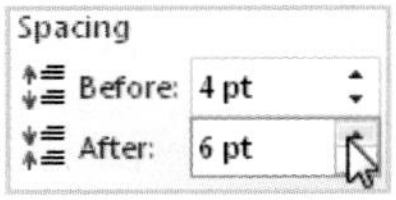

Spacing
Before: 4 pt
After: 6 pt

–Or–

In the Home tab Paragraph group, click the **Paragraph Dialog Box Launcher** to open the Paragraph dialog box. In the Indents And Spacing tab, under Spacing, click the **Before** spinner or enter a number in points ("pt") for the space you want to add before the paragraph. If desired, do the same thing for the space after the paragraph. When you are ready, click **OK**.

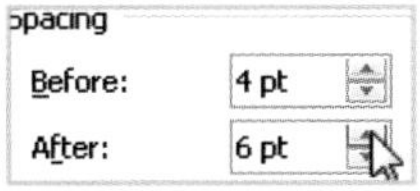

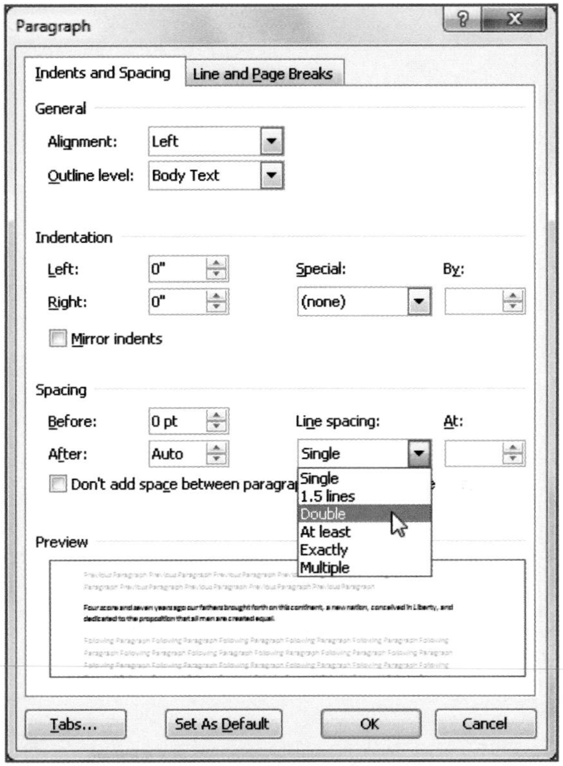

Spacing
Before: 4 pt
After: 6 pt

Figure 3-11: If a document is going to be edited on paper, it is a good idea to use double spacing to allow room for writing between the lines.

SET LINE AND PAGE BREAKS

The vertical spacing of a document is also affected by how lines and pages are broken and how much of a paragraph you force to stay together or be with text either before or after it.

You can break a line and start a new one, thereby creating a new line, a new paragraph, or a new page.

- **Create a new paragraph** by moving the insertion point to where you want to break the line and pressing **ENTER**.

- **Stay in the same paragraph** by moving the insertion point to where you want to break the line and pressing **SHIFT+ENTER**.

- **Break a page and start a new one** by pressing **CTRL+ENTER**.

    –Or–

    Click the **Insert** tab, and click **Page Break** in the Pages group.

    –Or–

    Click the **Page Layout** tab, and click **Breaks** in the Page Setup group. Click **Page** from the menu.

HANDLE SPLIT PAGES

When a paragraph is split over two pages, you have several ways to control how much of the paragraph is placed on which page.

1. Click in the paragraph you want to change.

2. Click the **Home** tab, click the **Paragraph Dialog Box Launcher**, and click the **Line And Page Breaks** tab.

3. Click the following options that are correct for your situation, and then click **OK**:

- **Widow/Orphan Control** adjusts the pagination to keep at least two lines on one or both pages. For example, if you have three lines, without selecting Widow/Orphan Control, one line is on the first page and two are on the second. When you select this option, all three lines will be placed on the second page. Widow/Orphan Control is selected by default.

- **Keep Lines Together** forces all lines of a paragraph to be on the same page. This option can be used for a paragraph title where you want all of it on one page.

- **Keep With Next** forces the entire paragraph to stay on the same page with the next paragraph. This option is used with paragraph headings that you want to keep with the first paragraph.

- **Page Break Before** forces a page break before the start of the paragraph. This option is used with major section headings or titles that you want to start on a new page.

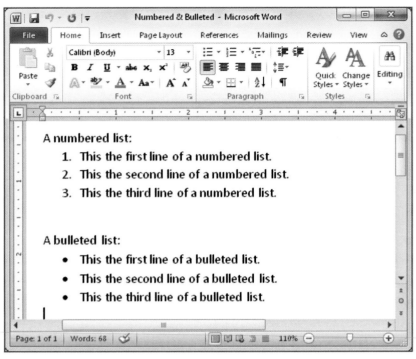

Figure 3-12: *Bullets and numbering help organize thoughts into lists.*

Use Numbered and Bulleted Lists

Word provides the means to automatically number or add bullets to paragraphs and then format the paragraphs as hanging indents so that the numbers or bullets stick out to the left (see Figure 3-12).

CREATE A NUMBERED LIST USING AUTOCORRECT

You can create a numbered list as you type, and Word will automatically format it according to your text. Word's numbered lists are particularly handy, because you can add or delete paragraphs in the middle of the list and have the list automatically renumber itself. To start a numbered list:

1. Press **ENTER** to start a new paragraph.

2. Type 1, press either the **SPACEBAR** *two* times or press **TAB** once, and then type the rest of what you want in the first item of the numbered list.

3. Press **ENTER**. The number "2" automatically appears, and both the first and the new lines are formatted as hanging indents. Also, the AutoCorrect lightning icon appears when you press **ENTER** on the first line.

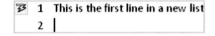

4. After typing the second item in your list, press **ENTER** once again. The number "3" automatically appears. Type the item and press **ENTER** to keep numbering the list.

5. When you are done, press **ENTER** twice. The numbering will stop and the hanging indent will be removed.

If you click the **AutoCorrect** icon, you may choose to undo the automatic numbering that has already been applied, stop the automatic creation of numbered lists, and control the use of AutoCorrect (see Chapter 4 for more information on AutoCorrect).

TIP

You can type 1 with or without a period, and 2 will be formatted in the same way. If you type the period and press **TAB** or two spaces, the AutoCorrect icon appears immediately and doesn't wait for you to press **ENTER**.

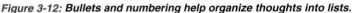

TIP

To select a number or bullet other than the default, click the **Numbering** or **Bullets** down arrow and click your choice from the context menu, as shown in Figure 3-13. See "Customize Bullets and Numbers" later in this chapter for additional ideas on how to vary bullets and numbering formats.

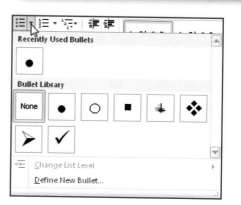

Figure 3-13: Clicking the Bullets down arrow displays a list of choices for formatting bullets. A similar menu is displayed when you click the Numbering down arrow.

NOTE

To apply bullets or numbering to a list that has already been typed, highlight the text, right-click it, and point to **Bullets** or **Numbering** on the context menu. Then click the format option you want. Or, on the Home tab Paragraph group, click **Numbering** to format the selected text as a numbered list, or click **Bullets** to format the text as a bulleted list.

CREATE A NUMBERED OR BULLETED LIST BEFORE YOU TYPE TEXT

You can also set up the formatting for a numbered or bulleted list before you start typing the text it will contain.

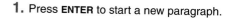

Bullets   Numbering

1. Press **ENTER** to start a new paragraph.

2. In the Home tab Paragraph group, click **Numbering** to begin a numbered list, or click **Bullets** to start a bulleted list.

3. Type the first item, and press **ENTER** to start the second numbered or bulleted item with the same style as the first. When you are done creating the list, press **ENTER** twice to stop the automatic list.

   –Or–

   Click **Numbering** or click **Bullets** in the Home tab Paragraph group to end the list.

CUSTOMIZE BULLETS AND NUMBERS

You saw in Figure 3-13 that Word offers seven different types of bullets. Word also offers eight different styles for numbering paragraphs, as you can see in Figure 3-14. For those to whom eight choices is not enough, there is a Define New option for both bullets and numbering that includes the ability to select from hundreds of pictures and to import others to use as bullets. To use custom bullets or numbering:

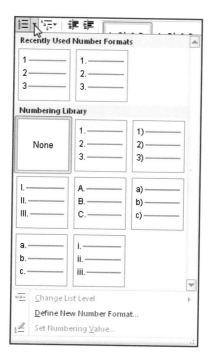

1. Click the **Home** tab, and click the **Bullets** or **Numbering** down arrow to open the Bullets or Numbering context menu.

2. Depending on whether you are using bullets or numbering, you have these choices:

   • For bullets, click **Define New Bullet**. The Define New Bullet dialog box appears (see Figure 3-15). Use one of the following:

     • Click **Font** and then select the font and other attributes in the dialog box for the

Figure 3-14: Numbered paragraphs can use numbers, letters, or even uppercase or lowercase roman numerals.

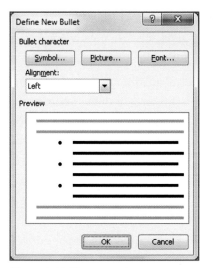

Figure 3-15: *You can select any character in any font to use as a bullet.*

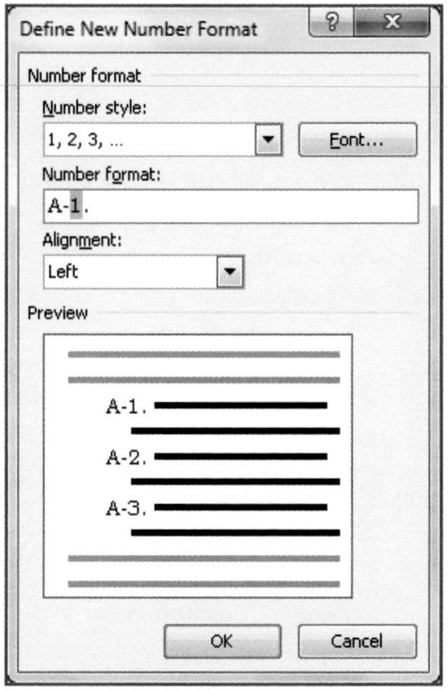

character that you want to use. Click **OK** to close the Font dialog box when you are ready.

- Click **Symbol** to select a symbol, and then click **OK**.

- Click **Picture** to choose from a number of picture bullets that are included in Office's clip art catalog (see Figure 3-16). To use your own picture, click **Import**, select the picture from the files on your computer, and click **Open**. With the picture you want selected, click **OK** to close the Picture dialog box. Then select the alignment for your new bullet, and click **OK** again. The new bullet will appear on your page.

- For numbering, click **Define New Number Format**. The Define New Number Format dialog box appears. Click the **Number Style** down arrow to choose the style (numbers, capital letters, lowercase letter, roman numerals, and so on). Click **Font** to choose the numbers formatted with a particular font, and click **OK** to close the Font dialog box. Press **TAB** to make any additions to the number in the Number Format text box. For example, delete the period for a number without the period or add a prefix such as "A-" to produce numbers A-1, A-2, and so on, as shown in Figure 3-17. Click the **Alignment** down arrow to choose between right alignment, left alignment, or centered. Click **OK** to apply the customized numbering.

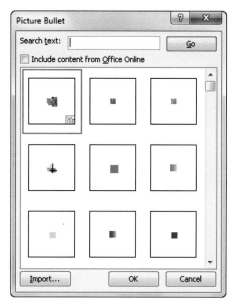

Figure 3-16: *Word provides a number of pictures that can be used as bullets.*

REMOVE NUMBERING AND BULLETING

To remove the numbering or bulleting (both the numbers or bullets and the hanging indent):

1. Select the paragraphs from which you want to remove the numbering or bulleting.

2. In the Home tab Paragraph group, click **Numbering** or **Bullets**, as appropriate.

Figure 3-17: *You can add a recurring prefix or suffix to automatically generated numbers.*

Add Borders and Shading

Borders and shading allow you to separate and call attention to text. You can place a border on any or all of the four sides of selected text, paragraphs, and pages; and you can add many varieties of shading to the space occupied by selected text, paragraphs, and pages—with or without a border around them (see Figure 3-18). You can create horizontal lines as you type, and you can add other borders from both the Formatting toolbar and the Borders And Shading dialog box.

CREATE HORIZONTAL LINES AS YOU TYPE

Horizontal lines can be added on their own paragraph as you type.

Hyphens
Underscores
Equal signs

1. Press **ENTER** to create a new paragraph.

2. Type --- (three hyphens) and press **ENTER**. A single, light horizontal line will be created between the left and right margins.

    –Or–

    Type === (three equal signs) and press **ENTER**. A double horizontal line will be created between the left and right margins.

    –Or–

    Type ____ (three underscores) and press **ENTER**. A single, heavy horizontal line will be created between the left and right margins.

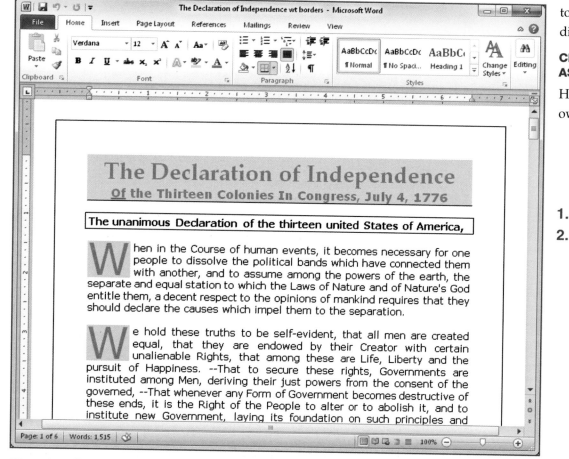

Figure 3-18: Borders and shading can be applied to text, blank paragraphs, phrases, characters, and words.

ADD BORDERS AND SHADING TO TEXT

Borders and shading can be added to any amount of text, from a single character to several pages.

1. Select the text for which you want to have a border or shading.

2. In the Home tab Paragraph group, click the **Borders** ⊞▾ down arrow, and then select the type of border you want to apply. If you have selected less than a full paragraph, you can only select a four-sided box (you actually can select less, but you will get a full box).

–Or–

In the Home tab Paragraph group, click the **Borders** down arrow, and click **Borders And Shading** on the context menu. The Borders And Shading dialog box will appear, as shown in Figure 3-19.

- To add text or paragraph borders, click the **Borders** tab, click the type of box (click **Custom** for fewer than four sides), the line style, color, and width you want. If you want fewer than four sides and are working with paragraphs, click the sides you want in the Preview area. Click **Options** to set the distance the border is away from the text.

- To add page borders, click the **Page Border** tab, click the type of box (click **Custom** for fewer than four sides), the line style, color, width you want, and art you want to use for the border, such as custom drawn lines or a row of miniature company logos. If you want fewer than four sides, click the sides you want in the Preview area. Click **Options** to set the distance the border is away from either the edge of the page or the text. (Figure 3-18 contains a page border.)

- To add shading, click the **Shading** tab, and click the color of shading, or *fill*, you want. If desired, select a pattern (this is independent of the fill), and choose whether to apply it to the entire page, paragraph, or just to the selected text.

- To add a graphic horizontal line, click **Horizontal Line**, click the line you want, and click **OK**.

When you are done with the Borders And Shading dialog box, click **OK** to close it.

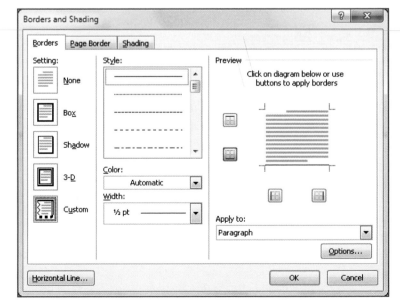

Figure 3-19: Borders can be created with many different types and widths of lines.

QUICKSTEPS

TURNING ON FORMATTING MARKS

To make any formatting and what is causing the spacing in a document easier to see, you can display some of the formatting marks. In the Home tab Paragraph group, click **Show/Hide Formatting Marks** ¶ to show all of the formatting marks—tabs, spaces, and paragraph marks, among other characters—as you can see in Figure 3-20.

→   This·has·a·tab,·spaces···,·and·paragraph·mark·¶

You can fine-tune exactly which formatting marks to display by clicking the **File** tab, clicking **Options**, and clicking the **Display** option. Under Always Show These Formatting Marks On The Screen, you can choose which marks to display. The default is to show no formatting marks.

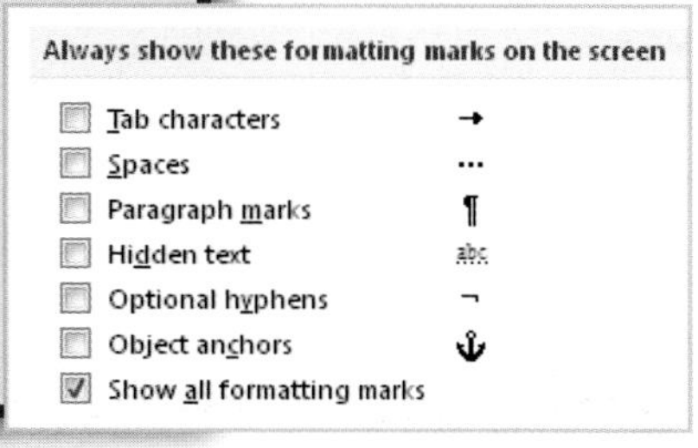

Always show these formatting marks on the screen

☐	Tab characters	→
☐	Spaces	···
☐	Paragraph marks	¶
☐	Hidden text	a̲b̲c̲
☐	Optional hyphens	¬
☐	Object anchors	⚓
☑	Show all formatting marks	

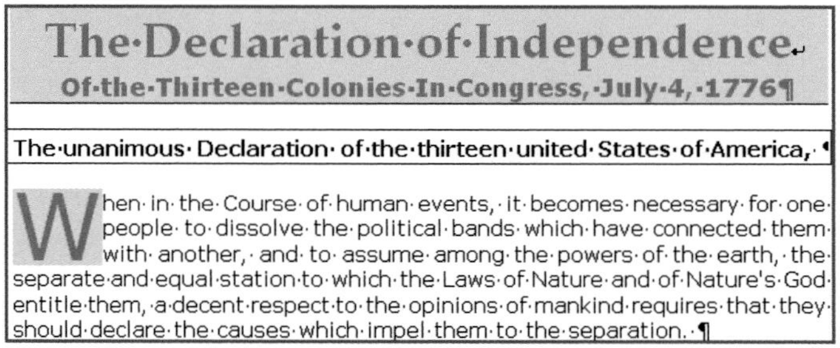

The·Declaration·of·Independence.
Of·the·Thirteen·Colonies·In·Congress,·July·4,·1776¶

The·unanimous·Declaration·of·the·thirteen·united·States·of·America,·

When·in·the·Course·of·human·events,·it·becomes·necessary·for·one·people·to·dissolve·the·political·bands·which·have·connected·them·with·another,·and·to·assume·among·the·powers·of·the·earth,·the·separate·and·equal·station·to·which·the·Laws·of·Nature·and·of·Nature's·God·entitle·them,·a·decent·respect·to·the·opinions·of·mankind·requires·that·they·should·declare·the·causes·which·impel·them·to·the·separation.·¶

Figure 3-20: Turning on formatting marks helps you see what is making your document look the way it does.

Format a Page

Page formatting has to do with the overall formatting of items, such as margins, orientation, size, and vertical alignment of a page. You can set options for page formatting either from the Page Layout tab or in a dialog box.

Set Margins

Margins are the space between the edge of the paper and the text. To set margins:

1. Open the document whose margins you want to set (see Chapter 2). If you want the margins to apply only to a selected part of a document, select that part now.

2. Click the **Page Layout** tab, and click **Margins** in the Page Setup group. A menu will open, as shown in Figure 3-21.

3. Click the option you want.

Use a Dialog Box to Format a Page

You can do a lot of page formatting using the Page Layout dialog box.

1. In the Page Layout tab, click the **Page Setup Dialog Box Launcher**. The Page Setup dialog box appears, as shown in Figure 3-22.

COPYING FORMATTING

Often, you'll want a word, phrase, or paragraph formatted like an existing word, phrase, or paragraph. Word allows you to copy just the formatting.

USE THE FORMAT PAINTER

1. Select the word, phrase, or paragraph whose formatting you want to copy. In the case of a paragraph, make sure you have included the paragraph mark (see the "Turning On Formatting Marks" QuickSteps).

2. In the Home tab Clipboard group, click the **Format Painter** button.

   • With the special pointer (brush and I-beam), select the word, phrase, or paragraph (including the paragraph mark) **⚐IThe Declaration** you want formatted.

COPY FORMATS WITH THE KEYBOARD

1. Select the word, phrase, or paragraph whose formatting you want to copy.

2. Press **CTRL+SHIFT+C** to copy the format.

3. Select the word, phrase, or paragraph (including the paragraph mark) you want formatted.

4. Press **CTRL+SHIFT+V** to paste the format.

COPY FORMATTING TO SEVERAL PLACES

To copy formatting to several separate pieces of text or paragraphs:

1. Drag across the text with the formatting you want to copy.

2. In the Home tab Clipboard group, double-click the **Format Painter** button.

3. Select each piece of text or paragraph that you want to format.

4. When you are done, click the **Format Painter** button again or press **ESC**.

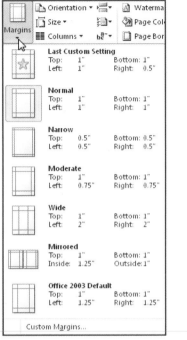

Figure 3-21: *You can select from a group of predefined margins, according to the needs of your document, or you can create a custom set of margins.*

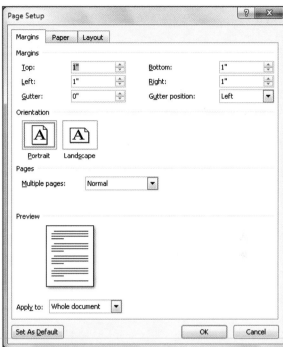

Figure 3-22: *Many page-formatting tasks can be done in the Page Setup dialog box.*

2. Click the **Margins** tab, if it isn't already visible. You have these options:

   • Under Margins, click the spinners or manually enter the desired distance in inches between the particular edge of the paper and the start or end of text.

   • Under Orientation, click either **Portrait** or **Landscape**, depending on which you want.

   • Under Pages, click the **Multiple Page** down arrow, and select an option: Click **Mirror Margins** when the inside gutter (the combined inside margin of two bound pages) is larger (if you will be printing and binding the document, for example). Click **2 Pages Per Sheet** when a normal sheet of paper is divided into two pages, and click **Book Fold** when you are putting together a section of a book ("a signature") with four, eight, or more pages in the signature.

TIP

If you are going to bind the document and want to add an extra amount of space on one edge for the binding, click the **Gutter** spinner to set the extra width you want, and click the **Gutter Position** down arrow to select the side that the gutter is on.

TIP

If you want to further differentiate between the left and right pages, you need to use sections (described in Chapter 4).

- If you want these changes to apply only to the selected part of a document, click **This Point Forward** under Preview Apply To.

3. When you are done setting margins, click **OK**.

Use Mirror Margins

Mirror margins allow you to have a larger "inside" margin, which would be the right margin on the left page and the left margin on the right page, or any other combination of margins that are mirrored between the left and right pages. To create mirror margins:

1. Open the document whose margins you want mirrored (see Chapter 2).

2. Click the **Page Layout** tab, and click **Margins** in the Page Setup group.

3. Click **Mirrored**. When you do that, the left and right margins change to inside and outside margins.

Determine Page Orientation

Page orientation specifies whether a page is taller than it is wide ("portrait") or wider than it is tall ("landscape"). For 8½-inch by 11-inch letter size paper, if the 11-inch side is vertical (the left and right edges), which is the standard way of reading a letter, then it is a portrait orientation. If the 11-inch side is horizontal (the top and bottom edges), then it is a landscape orientation. Portrait is the default orientation in Word. To change it:

1. Open the document whose orientation you want to set (see Chapter 2). If you want the orientation to apply only to a selected part of a document, select that part now, but you can only select whole pages to have a particular orientation.

2. In the Page Layout tab, click **Orientation** in the Page Setup group.

3. On the menu, click the option you want.

Specify Paper Size

Specifying the paper size gives you the starting perimeter of the area within which you can set margins and enter text or pictures.

TRACKING INCONSISTENT FORMATTING

When you turned on the formatting marks (see the "Turning On Formatting Marks" QuickSteps earlier in the chapter), you might have felt a bit disappointed that they didn't tell you more. You can direct Word to track inconsistencies in your formatting as you type.

1. Click the **File** tab, and click **Options**.

2. Click **Advanced** on the left pane.

3. Under Editing Options, click both **Keep Track Of Formatting** and **Mark Formatting Inconsistencies**.

☑ Keep track of formatting
☐ Mark formatting inconsistencies

1. In the Page Layout tab, click the **Size** down arrow in the Page Setup group. A menu will open, shown in Figure 3-23.

2. Click the size of paper you want.

Set Vertical Alignment

Just as you can right-align, center, left-align, and justify text between margins (see "Set Paragraph Alignment"), you can also specify vertical alignment so that text is aligned with the top, bottom, or center of the page or justified between the top and bottom.

1. In the Page Layout tab, click the **Page Setup Dialog Box Launcher**. The Page Setup dialog box appears.

2. In the Layout tab, under Page, click the **Vertical Alignment** down arrow, and click the vertical alignment that you want to use.

3. Click **OK** when you are done.

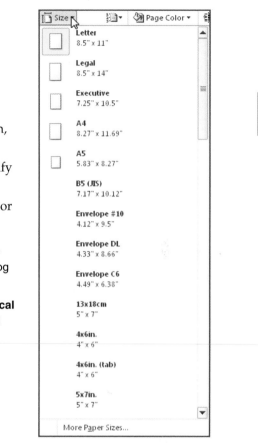

*Figure 3-23: **Choose the paper size from a selection of popular sizes in the Page Layout tab.***

Chapter 4

Customizing a Document

Microsoft Word 2010 provides a number of tools that combine text creation, layout, and formatting features that you can use to customize your documents. Two of the most common tools used at a broad level are styles and templates. Word also provides several other features, such as AutoFormat and AutoText, which help make document creation and formatting easier.

This chapter discusses creating documents through the use of styles and templates; formatting your documents using tabs, headers and footers, and outlines; and inserting front and end matter, such as tables of contents and indexes. The chapter also discusses Word's writing aids, such as AutoText, hyphenation, an equation builder, and the thesaurus.

Use Styles

Word 2010 provides a gallery of Quick Styles that provides you with sets of canned formatting choices, such as font, bold, and color that you can apply to headings, titles, text, and lists. You use Quick Styles by identifying what kind of formatting a selected segment of text needs, such as for a header or title. Then you select the style of formatting you want to apply to the document. You can easily apply Quick Styles, change them, and create new ones.

Identify Text with a Style

To identify a segment of text within your document with a consistent style, such as for a heading, you apply a Quick Style from the gallery.

1. Select the text to be formatted, for example, a title or heading.
2. Click the **Home** tab, and click the **Styles More** down arrow in the Styles group. The Quick Style gallery is displayed, as shown in Figure 4-1.
3. Point at the thumbnails to see the effects of each style on your text, and then click the thumbnail of the style you want to apply.

Apply Style Sets to a Document

Before you begin entering text, or after you have identified the components in your document, you can apply a consistent set of color, styles, and fonts to your document using the Change Styles function.

1. Open the document that you want to contain a style set. It can be either a blank document or one that has already had the components identified, such as title, headings, and lists.

2. Click the **Home** tab, click **Change Styles** in the Styles group, and click **Style Set**. A menu is displayed.

3. Click the style you want. The document will be changed. However, if you have components that are not identified with the Quick Styles, such as headings, they will not receive the formatting properly.

TIP

If you do not find the style you want in the Quick Style gallery for a segment of text, press **CTRL+SHIFT+S** to display the Apply Styles dialog box. Click the **Style Name** down arrow to find the style you want.

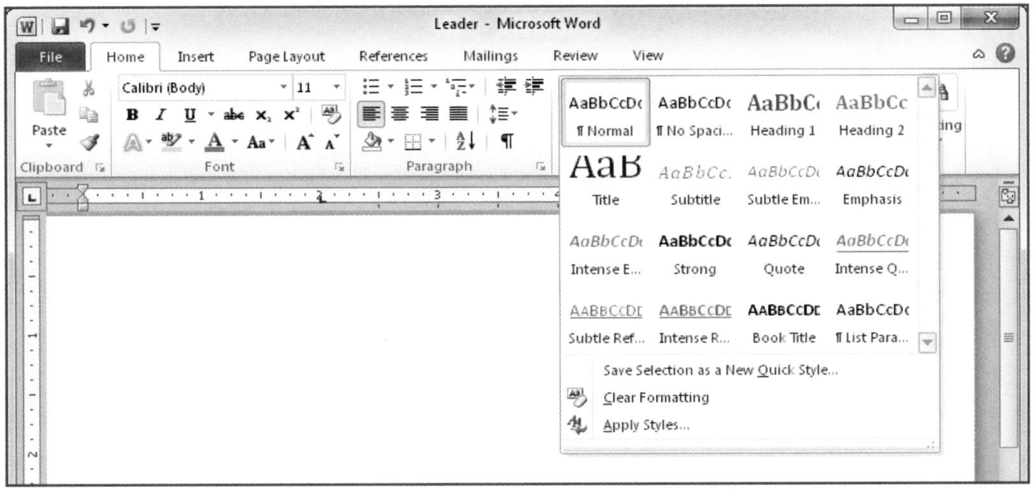

Figure 4-1: The Quick Style gallery shows you canned options for formatting headings, text, and paragraphs.

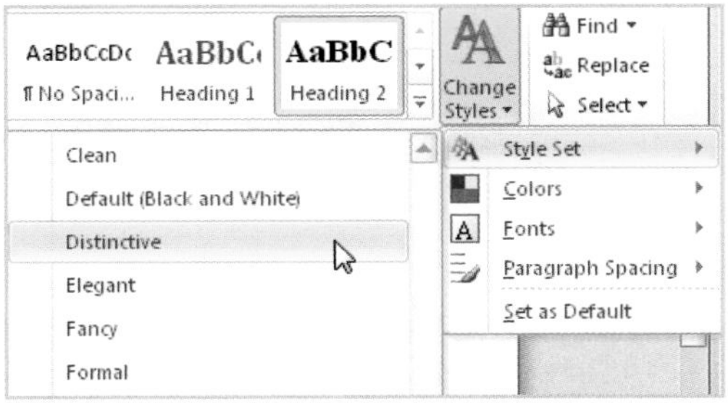

Save a New Quick Style

To create a new Quick Style option that will appear in the Quick Style gallery:

1. Format the text using the mini formatting toolbar or the commands in the Home tab Font group.

2. Select the text that represents the new style.

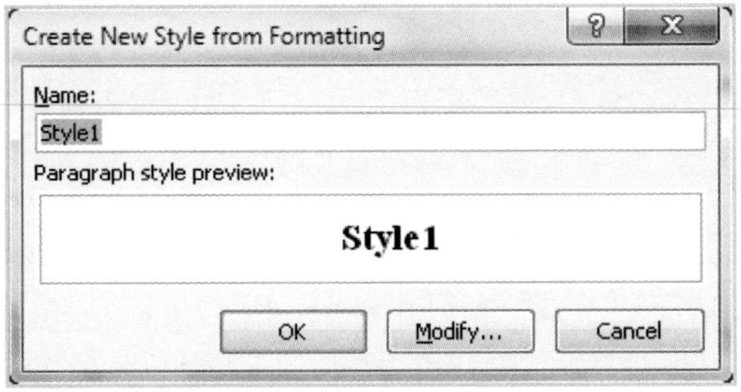

3. Right-click the selected text, click **Styles**, and click **Save Selection As A New Quick Style**. The Create New Style From Formatting dialog box appears.

4. Type the name you want for the style, and click **OK**. It will appear in the Quick Style gallery.

Modify a Style

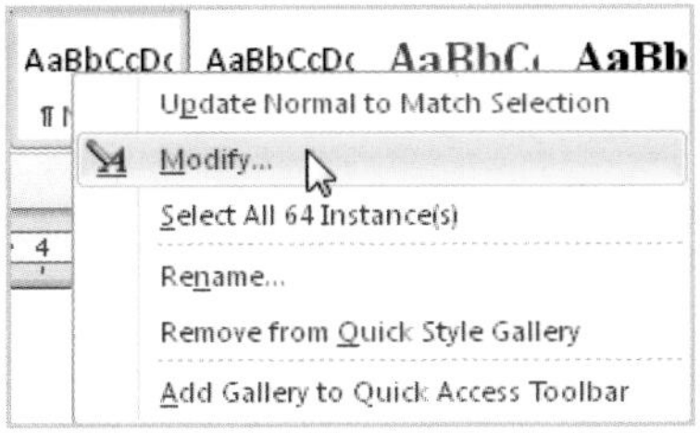

1. In the Home tab Styles group, click the **Styles More** down arrow. (If the window is narrow enough, the set of styles becomes a button, and you click the button in place of the down arrow.) The Quick Style gallery is displayed.

2. Right-click the style to be changed, and click **Modify**. The Modify Style dialog box appears, as shown in Figure 4-2.

   –Or–

   Click **Apply Styles** from the bottom of the gallery. The Apply Styles dialog box appears. Click the **Style Name** down arrow, and click the name of the style you wish to change. Click **Modify**, and the Modify Style dialog box appears.

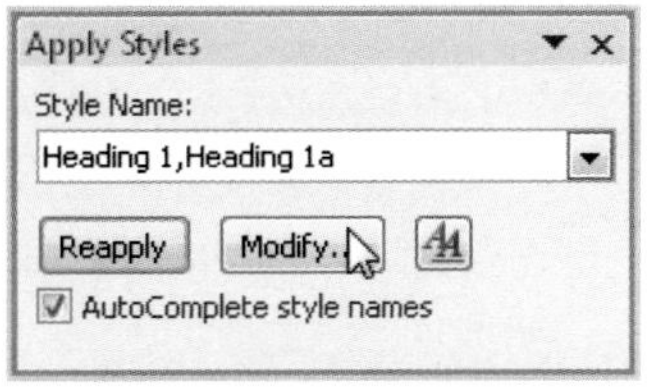

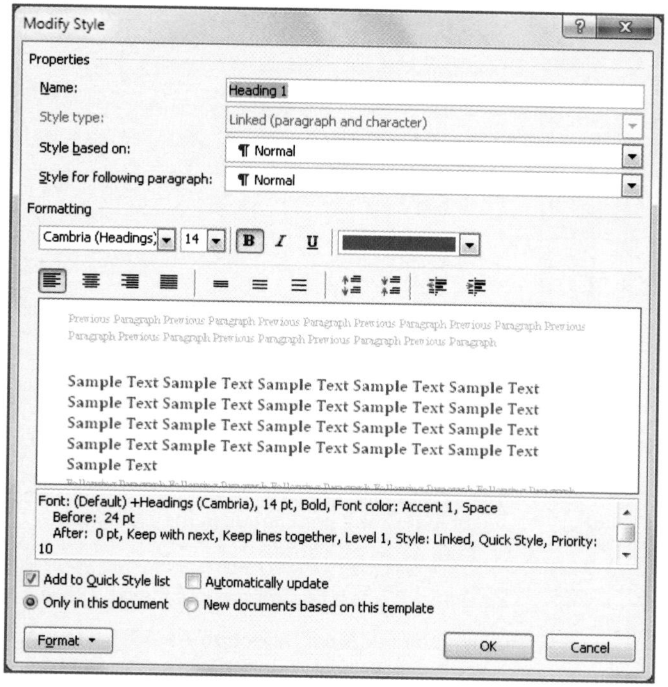

Figure 4-2: You can change a style by altering it in the Modify Style dialog box.

3. Change any formatting options you want.

4. To display more options, click **Format** in the lower-left area, and then click the attribute—for example, **Font** or **Numbering**—that you want to modify. Make that change and click **OK.**

5. Repeat step 4 for any additional attributes you want to change, clicking **OK** each time you are finished.

6. Type a new name for the style, if desired, unless you want to change existing formatted text.

7. Click **OK** to close the Modify Styles dialog box.

Automatically Update a Style

Sometimes, you may make changes to a style and want to have those changes automatically updated within a document.

1. Follow the steps in "Modify a Style" to display the Modify Style dialog box.

2. After making the changes you want, click the **Automatically Update** check box. Word will automatically redefine the style itself whenever you apply manual formatting in the document. ☑ Automatically update

Use Themes

One way that you can make a document look professional is by using themes. Themes combine coordinated colors, fonts (for body text and headings), and design effects (such as special effect uses for lines and fill effects) to produce a unique look. You can use the same themes with PowerPoint and Excel as well, thereby standardizing a look. All documents have themes; one is assigned to a new document by default.

ASSIGN A THEME TO YOUR DOCUMENT

To apply a theme to a document:

1. Click the **Page Layout** tab. Click **Themes** in the Themes group to display a gallery of themes, as seen in Figure 4-3.

2. Click the theme you want, and it will be applied to the current document.

TIP

To use a modified style in the New Styles gallery, click the **Add To Quick Style List** check box in the Modify Style dialog box. The modified style is added to the gallery of styles in the Styles group.  ☑ Add to Quick Style list

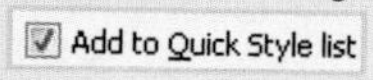

CAUTION

You should not click the Automatically Update check box when using the Normal style. Automatic Update can very easily change a style that you may not want to change.

DELETING A STYLE

You might choose to delete a style that you created for a one-time-use document and don't ever plan to use again. You can delete a style from the gallery or from the document being used.

DELETE/RESTORE A STYLE FROM THE GALLERY

To delete a style just from the gallery:

1. In the Home tab Styles group, click the **Styles More** down arrow to display the Quick Style gallery.

2. Right-click the style you want to delete, and click **Remove From Quick Style Gallery**.

   The style will be removed from the Quick Style gallery. However, this does not mean that the style is gone; it is still in the list of styles.

To restore the style to the gallery:

1. In the Home tab Styles group, click the **Styles Dialog Box Launcher**. The Styles task pane is displayed.

2. Right-click the style that you want to restore, and click **Add To Quick Style Gallery**.

DELETE A STYLE FROM A DOCUMENT

To completely delete a style from a document:

1. In the Home tab Styles group, click the **Styles Dialog Box Launcher**. The Styles task pane is displayed.

2. Right-click the style to be deleted, and click **Delete** *stylename*. A dialog box appears.

3. Click **Yes** to confirm that you want to delete the style.

Some styles cannot be deleted; the command to delete them will be unavailable, or grayed out, such as with the Normal or Heading style. If you delete a style from the document, any text formatted with that style will be reformatted with the Normal style.

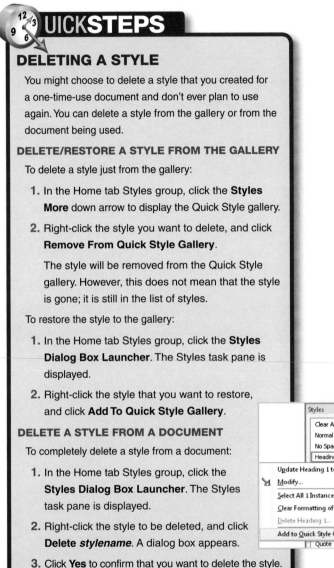

Figure 4-3: Use themes to standardize your documents with other Office products, such as PowerPoint and Excel.

Change a Theme

In addition to changing the overall theme of a document, you can customize a theme by altering the fonts, color, and design effects.

CHANGE THE COLOR OF A THEME

Each theme consists of a set of four colors for text and background, six colors for accents, and two colors for hyperlinks. You can change any single color element

NOTE

For a new theme to be applied, the text must already be formatted with common styles, such as titles, headings, normal text, and lists.

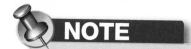

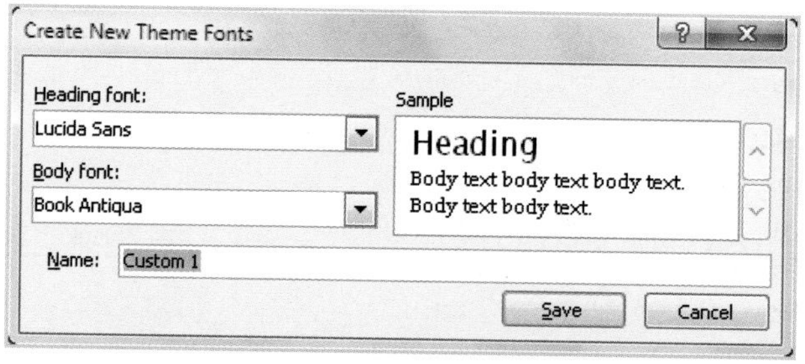

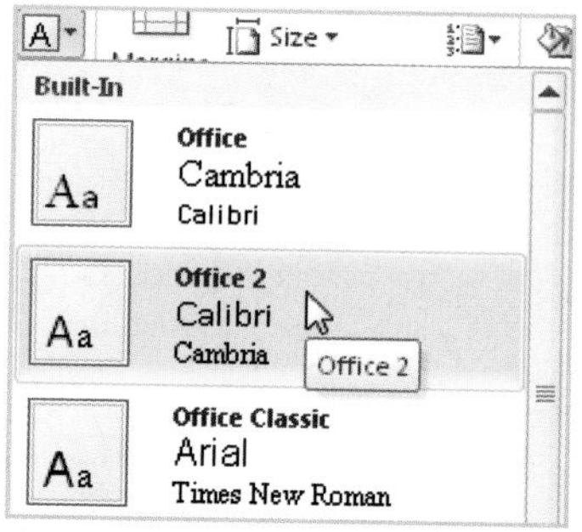

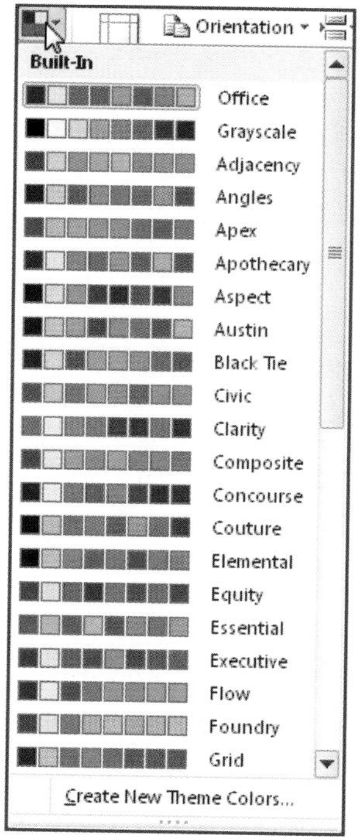

Figure 4-4: The menu of color combinations offers alternatives for your theme colors.

or all of them. When you change the colors, the font styles and design elements remain the same.

1. With your document open, click the **Page Layout** tab.
2. Click **Theme Colors**. The menu of color combinations will be displayed, as seen in Figure 4-4.
3. Point at the rows of color combinations to see which ones appeal to you.
4. When you find the one you want, click it.

CHANGE THEME FONTS

Each theme includes two fonts: The *body* font is used for general text entry, and a *heading* font is used for headings. The default fonts used in Word for a new document are Calibri for body text and Cambria for headings. After you have assigned a theme to a document, the fonts may be different, and they can be changed.

1. In the Page Layout tab Themes group, click **Theme** Fonts. The drop-down list displays various theme fonts. The current theme font combination is highlighted in its place in the list.
2. Point to each font combination to see how the fonts will appear in your document.
3. Click the font name combination you decide upon. When you click a font name combination, the fonts will replace both the body and heading fonts in your document on one or selected pages.

CREATE A NEW THEME FONT SET

You may also decide that you want a unique set of fonts for your document. You can create a custom font set that is available in the list of fonts for your current and future documents.

1. In the Page Layout tab Themes group, click **Theme Fonts**.
2. Click **Create New Theme Fonts** at the bottom of the drop-down list.
3. In the Create New Theme Fonts dialog box, click either or both the **Heading Font** and **Body Font** down arrows to select a new font combination. Click your choice(s) to view the new combination in the Sample area.

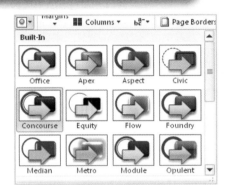

4. Type a new name for the font combination you've selected, and click **Save**. Custom fonts are available for selection at the top of the Theme Fonts drop-down list.

CHANGE THEMED GRAPHIC EFFECTS

Shapes, illustrations, pictures, and charts include graphic effects that are controlled by themes. Themed graphics are modulated in terms of their lines (borders), fills, and effects (such as shadowed, raised, and shaded). For example, some themes simply change an inserted rectangle's fill color, while other themes affect the color, the weight of the border, and whether it has a 3-D appearance. Theme effects do not affect text.

1. In the Page Layout tab Themes group, click **Theme Effects**. The drop-down list displays a gallery of effects combinations. The current effects combination is highlighted.

2. Point to each combination to see how the effects will appear in your document, assuming you have a graphic or chart inserted on the document page (see Chapters 7 and 8 for information on inserting tables, charts, graphics, and drawings).

3. Click the effects combination you want.

Create a Custom Theme

You can create a new theme, save it, and use it in your documents. You select a group of text, background, accent, and hyperlink colors, and then give them a collective name.

1. In the Page Layout tab Themes group, click **Theme Colors**.

2. At the bottom of the menu of colors, click the **Create New Theme Colors** link. The Create New Theme Colors dialog box appears, as shown in Figure 4-5.

3. To select a color for one of the color groups, click the text/background, accent, or hyperlink down arrow, and click the color you want to test. It will be displayed in the Sample area.

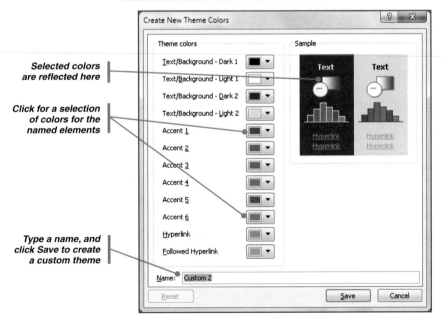

Selected colors are reflected here

Click for a selection of colors for the named elements

Type a name, and click Save to create a custom theme

Figure 4-5: The Create New Theme Colors dialog box allows you to create a new theme to use with multiple documents.

4. Go through each set of colors that you want to change.

5. When you have selected a group of colors that you like, type a name in the Name text box, and click **Save**.

Use Templates

A *template* is a collection of styles, associated formatting and design features, and colors used to determine the overall appearance of a document. A Word 2010 template file has an extension of .dotx. Templates are always attached to documents, as you saw in Chapter 2.

Create and Change Templates

Word 2010 comes with several templates that you can use to create letters, faxes, memos, and more. In addition, as you saw earlier, the Microsoft Office Web site has online templates that you can make use of. You can also create your own templates.

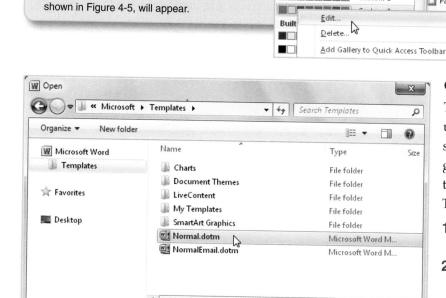

CHANGE THE DEFAULT NORMAL TEMPLATE

The *Normal* template is the default template used by Word unless you tell it otherwise. It, like all templates, includes default styles, AutoText, and other customizations that determine the general look of your document. You can customize the Normal template to include the styles you want to use on a regular basis. To change the default styles of the Normal template:

1. With a Word document open, click the **File** tab, click **Open**, and then click **Templates** under Microsoft Office Word.

2. If no templates are listed in the Open dialog box, click the **Files Of Type** down arrow (immediately above the Cancel button), and click **All Files (*.*)**. If you still do not see Normal.dotm (indicating a macro-enabled template) in the navigation or folder pane on the left, click **Computer**, click in the **Search** text box, type normal.dotm, and click **Go**.

3. Double-click **Normal.dotm** to open it. Ensure that you're working in the template by verifying that that "Normal.dotm" appears in the Word title bar.

4. Change the template by changing the styles using the steps described in "Modify a Style" earlier in this chapter.

5. When you are finished making the changes that you want, click the **File** tab, and click Save to resave Normal.dotm.

CREATE A TEMPLATE

1. With Word open, click the **File** tab, and click **New**. The new document window appears, as shown in Figure 4-6.

2. Under Available Templates, search through the Sample Templates to see if there are any that come close to what you want that you can modify, and if so select a template. Otherwise, click **Blank Document** if it is not already selected.

3. Click **Create**. A new document opens.

4. Add the recurring text, images, and formatting that you want to be in the template and, therefore, in each document that is created based upon the template.

5. Click the **File** tab, click **Save As**, enter the name of your template, click the **Save As Type** down arrow, click **Word Template (*.dotx)**, and click **Save**. The template should be saved in the default template folder.

6. Click the **File** tab, and click **Close**.

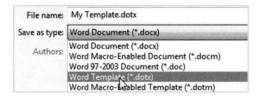

Figure 4-6: *Word comes with several templates you can use to create letters, faxes, and more.*

APPLY A TEMPLATE TO A NEW DOCUMENT

Having created your own template, you can use it to create a new document with the template's contents.

1. Click the **File** tab, and click **New** to open the new document window.

2. Under Available Templates, click **My Templates**, and double-click the template you want to use.

3. Add content and additional formatting to the document as desired, and then save it as a normal Word document (.docx).

Work with Documents

In addition to using styles and templates to format your documents, you can use section breaks, columns, tabs, headers and footers, tables of contents, and indexes to further refine your documents.

Create Section Breaks

A *section break* indicates the end of a section in a document. You can use section breaks to vary the layout of a document within a page or between pages. For example, you might choose to format the introduction of a magazine article in a single column and format the body of the article in two columns. You must separately format each section, but the section break allows them to be different. Section breaks allow you to change the number of columns, page headers and footers, page numbering, page borders, page margins, and other characteristics and formatting within a section. The section break retains the formatting above it, not after it.

INSERT A SECTION BREAK

1. Open the document and click where you want to insert a section break.

2. Click the **Page Layout** tab, and click **Breaks** in the Page Setup group. The Breaks menu appears.

3. To create a new section, in the Section Break Types area, select what comes after the break. You have the following options:

   - Click **Next Page** to begin a new section on the next page.
   - Click **Continuous** to begin a new section on the same page.
   - Click **Even Page** to start the new section on the next even-numbered page.
   - Click **Odd Page** to start the new section on the next odd-numbered page.

Breaks ▾ — Watermark ▾ — Indent

Page Breaks

Page
Mark the point at which one page ends and the next page begins.

Column
Indicate that the text following the column break will begin in the next column.

Text Wrapping
Separate text around objects on web pages, such as caption text from body text.

Section Breaks

Next Page
Insert a section break and start the new section on the next page.

Continuous
Insert a section break and start the new section on the same page.

Even Page
Insert a section break and start the new section on the next even-numbered page.

Odd Page
Insert a section break and start the new section on the next odd-numbered page.

¶...Section Break (Continuous)...

4. When you click the option you want, the section break is inserted. If the Show/Hide Formatting feature is turned on (in the Home tab Paragraph group), you'll be able to see the section breaks in the text.

DELETE A SECTION BREAK

When a section break is inserted on a page, you will see a note to that effect if the Show/Hide Formatting feature is turned on. You can delete the break by selecting that note.

1. Click the section break that you want to delete.

2. Press **DELETE**.

Create and Use Columns

You can format your documents in a single column or in two or more columns, like text found in newspapers or magazines. You must first create either a continuous break or a page break, not a column break, before you create the columns in order to prevent columns from forming in the previous section. To create columns in a document:

1. Place the insertion point at the place where you want the columns to begin. On the Page Layout tab, click **Breaks** in the Page Setup group, and click **Continuous**.

2. Click the **Page Layout** tab, and click **Columns** in the Page Setup group to display a menu.

3. Click the thumbnail option that corresponds to the number or type of columns you want.

–Or–

If you do not see what you want, click **More Columns** to display the Columns dialog box (see Figure 4-7). Then:

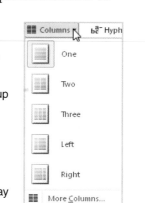

- Click an icon in the Presets area, or type a number in the Number Of Columns box to set the number of columns you want.

- Use the options in the Width And Spacing area to manually determine the dimensions of your columns and the amount of space between columns. If One Preset is selected, you will have to clear the **Equal Column Width** check box. (Clicking any other preset will make the check box available; clicking Left or Right will clear it.)

NOTE

When you delete a section break, you also delete the specific formatting for the text in the paragraphs immediately above that break. That text becomes part of the following section and assumes the relevant formatting of that section.

TIP

If you don't see section breaks displayed in your document, click the **Home** tab, and click the **Show/Hide** button in the Paragraph group. ¶

NOTE

You can change a section break by clicking the section break line in the document, clicking the **Page Layout** tab, and then clicking **Breaks** in the Page Setup group. Click the change you would like from the drop-down menu.

TIP

You can also set or change a section break from the Page Setup dialog box. In the Page Layout tab Page Setup group, click the **Page Setup Dialog Box Launcher**, and click the **Layout** tab. The section settings are at the top of the dialog box.

Page Setup

| Margins | Paper | Layout |

Section

Section start: | Continuous | ▾

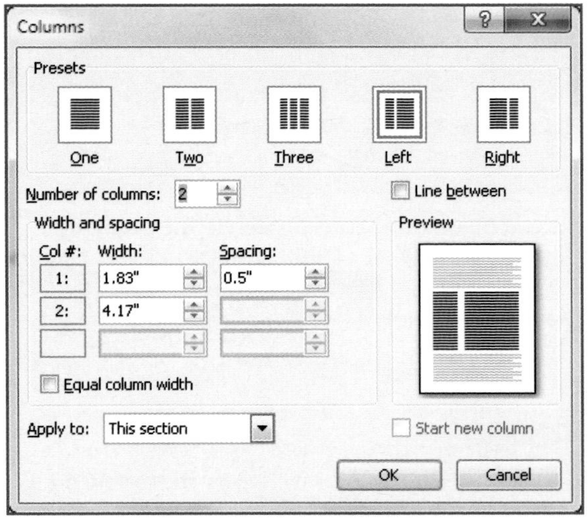

Figure 4-7: Use the Columns dialog box to create and format columns in your documents.

TIP

The Preview area in the Columns dialog box displays the effects as you change the various column settings.

TIP

To see tabs, the ruler needs to appear on the screen. If you do not see the ruler, click the **View** tab, and click **Ruler** in the Show group.

- Click the **Line Between** check box if you want Word to insert a vertical line between columns.
- Use the **Apply To** list box to select the part of the document to which you want your selections to apply: Whole Document, This Section, or This Point Forward. Click **This Point Forward**, and then click the **Start New Column** check box if you want to insert a column break at an insertion point.

4. Click **OK** when finished.

Use Tabs

A *tab* is a type of formatting usually used to align text and create simple tables. By default, Word has *tab stops* (the horizontal positioning of the insertion point when you press **TAB**) every half-inch. Tabs are better than space characters in such instances, because tabs are set to specific measurements, while spaces may not always align the way you intend due to the size and spacing of individual characters in a given font. Word supports five kinds of tabs:

- **Left tab** left-aligns text at the tab stop.
- **Center tab** centers text at the tab stop.
- **Right tab** right-aligns text at the tab stop.
- **Decimal tab** aligns the decimal point of tabbed numbers at the tab stop.
- **Bar tab** left-aligns text with a vertical line that is displayed at the tab stop.

  To align text with a tab, press the **TAB** key before the text you want aligned.

SET TABS USING THE RULER

To set tabs using the ruler at the top of a page:

1. Select the text, from one line to an entire document, in which you want to set one or more tab stops.
2. Click the **Left Tab** icon ⌊ from the tab area located to the left of the horizontal ruler until it changes to the type of tab you want: Left Tab, Center Tab ⊥, Right Tab ⌋, Decimal Tab ⊥, or Bar Tab ⏐.
3. Click the horizontal ruler where you want to set a tab stop.
4. Once you have the tabs set, you can:
   - Drag a tab off the ruler to get rid of it.
   - Drag a tab to another spot on the ruler to change its position.

First Line Indent

- Click the tab area until you get the First Line Indent ▽ , and then click the ruler where you want the first line of a paragraph to start.

  –Or–

  Drag the **First Line Indent** located on the top of the ruler to where you want the first line of a paragraph to start.

- Click the tab area until you get the Hanging Indent ⬒ , and then click the ruler where you want to start the second and following lines of a paragraph, creating a hanging indent.

  –Or–

  Drag the **Hanging Indent** on the bottom of the ruler to where you want the second and following lines of a paragraph to start, creating a hanging indent.

Hanging Indent

- Drag the **Left Indent** on the bottom of the ruler to where you want an entire paragraph indented.

Left Indent

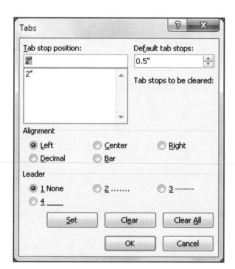

Figure 4-8: From the Tabs dialog box, you can format specific tab measurements and set tab leaders.

SET TABS USING MEASUREMENTS

To set tabs according to specific measurements:

1. In the Home tab, click the **Paragraph Dialog Box Launcher**, and click **Tabs** at the bottom-left area of the Paragraph dialog box that appears.

   –Or–

   Double-click a tab or an indent in the ruler.

   In either case, the Tabs dialog box will appear, as shown in Figure 4-8.

2. Enter the measurements you want in the Tab Stop Position text box.

3. Click the tab alignment option you want. Click **Set**.

4. Repeat steps 2 and 3 for as many tabs as you want to set. Click **OK** to close the dialog box.

SET TABS WITH LEADERS

You can also set tabs with *tab leaders*—characters that fill the space otherwise left by a tab—a dotted line, a dashed line, or a solid underscore.

1. Open the Tabs dialog box shown in Figure 4-8 using either method described in the previous section.

2. In the Tab Stop Position text box, type the position for a new tab, or select an existing tab stop to which you want to add a tab leader.

3. In the Alignment area, select the alignment for text typed at the tab stop.

4. In the Leader area, select the leader option you want, and then click **Set**.

5. Repeat steps 2–4 for additional tabs. When you are done, click **OK** to close the dialog box.

Add Headers and Footers

Headers and footers are parts of a document that contain information such as page numbers, revision dates, the document title, and so on. The header appears at the top of every page, and the footer appears at the bottom of every page. Figure 4-9 shows the buttons available on the Header And Footer Tools Design tab.

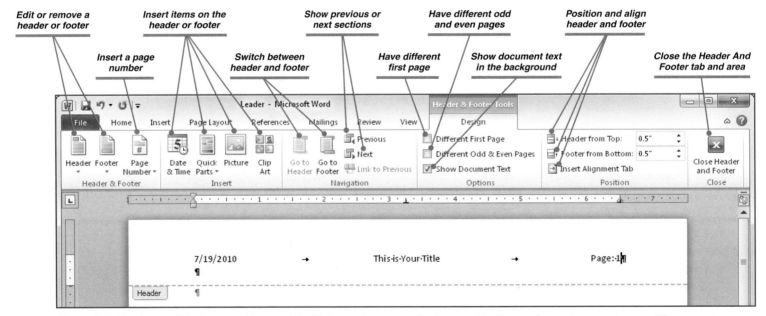

Figure 4-9: Headers and footers provide consistent information across the tops and bottoms of your document pages. These areas can also have unique tabs and other formatting.

CREATE A HEADER OR FOOTER

1. Open the document to which you want to add a header or footer (see Chapter 2).

2. Click the **Insert** tab, and click **Header** or **Footer** in the Header & Footer group. A list of predefined headers and footers will be shown. Either click one in the list or click **Edit Header** or **Edit Footer**. The header or footer area will be displayed along with the special contextual Header & Footer Tools Design tab.

   –Or–

   If you have some white space above your top line of text, double-click in the top area of the document where a header would be. If you do not have white space but you have content on at least two pages, double-click the split between pages, and then double-click the header or footer area. (If the page break and header area are hidden, you can't use the double-click method.)

3. Begin by using the elements like the page number and date on the Header & Footer Tools Design tab with the page number first, because if you type the text you want first and then add a page number, it will wipe out your text (a bad design). To use the tab's tools, do so in this order:

   a. When you first click Header or Footer, choose **Blank**, **Edit Header**, or **Edit Footer**; or double-click the blank area at the top or bottom of the page to provide a blank header or footer.

   b. Insert a page number by clicking **Page Number** in the Header & Footer group, clicking a location in the drop-down menu (given you are already in the header or footer, choose **Current Position**), scrolling down, and clicking a format.

   c. Insert a date and/or time by clicking **Date & Time** in the Insert group and then clicking one of the available formats to insert a date or time.

   d. To enter a left-aligned date, a centered title, and a right-aligned page number, as shown in Figure 4-9, either type the date or click **Date & Time** in the Insert group, press TAB, type the title, press TAB, if desired type Page, and leave a space. With the insertion point immediately after "Page" and the space in the tab, click **Page Number**, click **Current Position**, and click **Plain Number**. If desired, adjust the tab marks in the ruler.

   e. Type the text you want displayed in the header or footer, and align and format it.

   f. Switch between typing text in the header and typing it in the footer by clicking the **Go To Header** or **Go To Footer** button in the Navigation group, and type the text you want.

g. To go to the next or last section to enter a different header or footer, click **Previous Section** or **Next Section** in the Navigation group.

4. When finished, double-click in the document area or click the Close Header And Footer button.

EDIT A HEADER OR FOOTER

1. Open the document in which you want to edit a header or footer (see Chapter 2).

2. Click the **Insert** tab, and click **Header** or **Footer** in the Header & Footer group. A list of predefined headers and footers will be shown. Either click one in the list or click **Edit Header** or **Edit Footer**. The header or footer area will be displayed along with the special contextual Header & Footer Tools Design tab, as shown in Figure 4-9.

–Or–

If there is white space above or below the text on a page, double-click in this header or footer area. If there is no white space but you have content on at least two pages, double-click the line indicating the split between pages to display the header and footer areas. Then double-click the header or footer area to display the header and/or footer along with the Header And Footer Tools Design tab, as shown in Figure 4-9.

3. If necessary, click the **Previous Section** or **Next Section** button in the Navigation group to display the header or footer you want to edit.

4. Edit the header or footer. For example, you might revise text, change the font, apply bold formatting, or add a date or time.

5. When finished, double-click in the document area or click the **Close Header And Footer** button in the Close group.

DELETE A HEADER OR FOOTER

1. Open the document from which you want to delete a header or footer (see Chapter 2).

2. Double-click the header or footer area of the document. Or, first double-click the split between pages, and then double-click the header or footer area. The header or footer area will be displayed along with the Header And Footer Tools Design tab.

3. If necessary, click **Previous Section** or **Next Section** in the Navigation group to move to the header or footer you want to delete.

4. Select the text or graphics you want to delete, and press **DELETE**.

–Or–

Click **Header** or **Footer** in the Header & Footer group, and click **Remove Header** or **Remove Footer**.

Previous Section
Next Section

NOTE

When you edit a header or footer, Word automatically changes the same header or footer throughout the document, unless the document contains different headers or footers in different sections.

NOTE

When you delete a header or footer, Word automatically deletes the same header or footer throughout the entire document. To delete a header or footer for part of a document, you must first divide the document into sections, and then create a different header or footer for part of a document. (See "Create Section Breaks" earlier in this chapter for more information.)

Edit Header
Remove Header
Save Selection to Remove Header

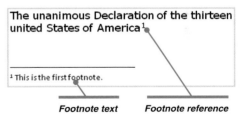

QUICKSTEPS

USING DIFFERENT LEFT AND RIGHT HEADERS

Different left and right pages use section breaks to allow different margins and tabs. Sometimes, you might want to create a document that has different left and right headers and/or footers. For example, you might have a brochure, pamphlet, or manuscript in which all odd-numbered pages have a title in the header and all even-numbered pages have the section name or other information.

To create different left and right headers and/or footers:

1. Open the document to which you want to add a different left and right header or footer (see Chapter 2).

2. Display the header and/or footer and its tab by either double-clicking in the header area or clicking the appropriate option in the Insert tab, as explained in previous sections.

3. In the Options group, click **Different First Page** to enter a separate title or no title for the first page. Create a different first page in the First Page Header area, create the normal header in the Header area of the second page, and so on.

–Or–

Continued . . .

In either case, the *content* of the header or footer will be removed, but the blank header or footer area will remain. These are removed in the Layout tab of the Page Setup dialog box (Page Layout tab, Page Setup Dialog Box Launcher).

Add Footnotes and Endnotes

Footnotes and *endnotes* are types of annotations in a document usually used to provide citation information or to provide additional information for readers. The difference between the two is where they appear in a document. Footnotes appear either after the last line of text on the page or at the bottom of the page on which the annotated text appears. Endnotes appear either at the end of the section in which the annotated text appears or at the end of the document.

INSERT A FOOTNOTE OR ENDNOTE

1. To display the Print Layout view, click the **View** tab, and then click **Print Layout** in the Document View group.

2. In the Print Layout view, position the insertion point immediately after the text you want to annotate.

3. Click the **References** tab, and then click **Insert Footnote** or **Insert Endnote** in the Footnotes group. For a footnote, the insertion point will be positioned at the bottom of the page; for an endnote, it will be positioned at the end of the document.

4. Type the text of the endnote or footnote.

5. To return to the text where the footnote reference was placed, right-click the footnote and click **Go To Footnote** or **Go To Endnote**. Before continuing to type, move the cursor to the right of the footnote/endnote reference symbol or number.

The unanimous Declaration of the thirteen united States of America[1]

––––––––––––––
[1] This is the first footnote.

Footnote text   *Footnote reference*

CHANGE FOOTNOTES OR ENDNOTES

If you want to change the numbers or formatting of footnotes or endnotes, or if you want to add a symbol to the reference, use the Footnotes dialog box.

1. On the References tab, click the **Footnotes Dialog Box Launcher** in the Footnotes group. The Footnote And Endnote dialog box appears (see Figure 4-10).

2. You have these options:

- In the Location box, click the **Footnotes** or **Endnotes** option, and click the down arrow to the right to choose where the footnote or endnote will be placed.

- Click the **Number Format** down arrow, and select the type of numbering you want from the drop-down list.

- To select a custom mark (a character that uniquely identifies a footnote or endnote), click the **Symbol** button. A dialog box appears. Scroll through the symbols, and double-click the one you want to select. It will be displayed in the Custom Mark text box. Click **Insert** to insert it in your text. You can also just type a character into the text box and then click **Insert** to place it in your text.

- Click the **Numbering** down arrow, and choose how the numbering is to start.

- Click the **Apply Changes To** down arrow to select the part of the document that will contain the changes.

3. Click Insert. Word makes the changes as noted.

4. Type the note text.

5. When finished, return the insertion point to the body of your document, and continue typing.

DELETE A FOOTNOTE OR ENDNOTE

In the document, select the number of the note you want to delete, and then press DELETE. Word automatically deletes the footnote or endnote and renumbers the notes.

CONVERT FOOTNOTES TO ENDNOTES OR ENDNOTES TO FOOTNOTES

1. Select the reference number or symbol in the body of a document for the footnote or endnote.

2. Click the **References** tab, and click the **Footnotes And Endnotes Dialog Box Launcher**. The Footnote And Endnote dialog box appears.

Figure 4-10: Footnotes and endnotes provide supplemental information to the body of your document. Use the dialog box to control location and formatting.

NOTE

When deleting an endnote or footnote, make sure to delete the number corresponding to the annotation and not the actual text in the note. If you delete the text but not the number, the placeholder for the annotation will remain.

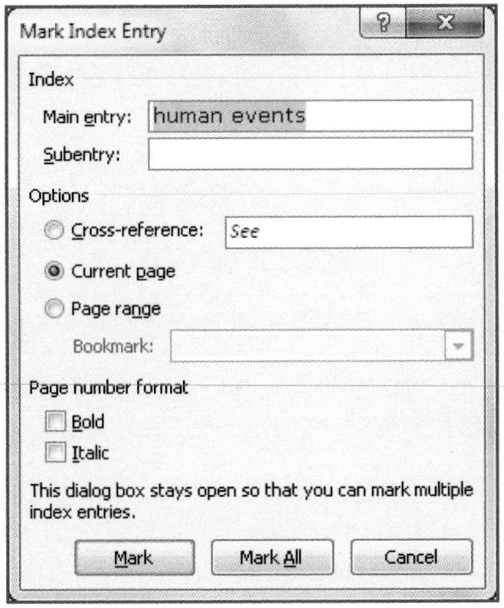

3. Click **Convert**. The Convert Notes dialog box appears.

4. Select the option you want, and then click **OK**.

5. Click **Close**.

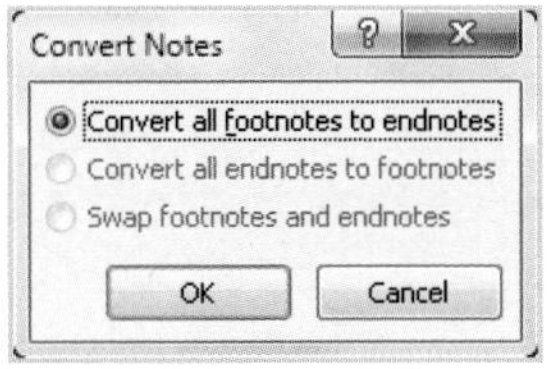

Create an Index

An *index* is an alphabetical list of words or phrases in a document and the corresponding page references. Indexes created using Word can include main entries and subentries as well as cross-references. When creating an index in Word, you first need to tag the index entries and then generate the index.

TAG INDEX ENTRIES

1. In the document in which you want to build an index, select the word or phrase that you want to use as an index entry. If you want an index entry to use text that you separately enter instead of using existing text in the document, place the insertion point in the document where you want your new index entry to reference.

2. Click the **References** tab, and click **Mark Entry** in the Index group (you can also press **ALT+SHIFT+X**). The Mark Index Entry dialog box appears (see Figure 4-11).

3. Type or edit the text in the Main Entry box. Customize the entry by creating a subentry or by creating a cross-reference to another entry, if desired.

4. Click the **Bold** or **Italic** check box in the Page Number Format area to determine how the page numbers will appear in the index.

5. Click **Mark**. To mark all occurrences of this text in the document, click **Mark All**.

6. Repeat steps 3–5 to mark additional index entries on the same page.

7. Click **Close** to close the dialog box when finished.

8. Repeat steps 1–7 for the remaining entries in the document.

GENERATE AN INDEX

1. Position the insertion point where you want to insert the finished index (this will normally be at the end of the document).

2. Click the **References** tab, and click **Insert Index** in the Index group. The Index dialog box appears (see Figure 4-12).

Figure 4-11: You need to tag index entries before you can generate an index.

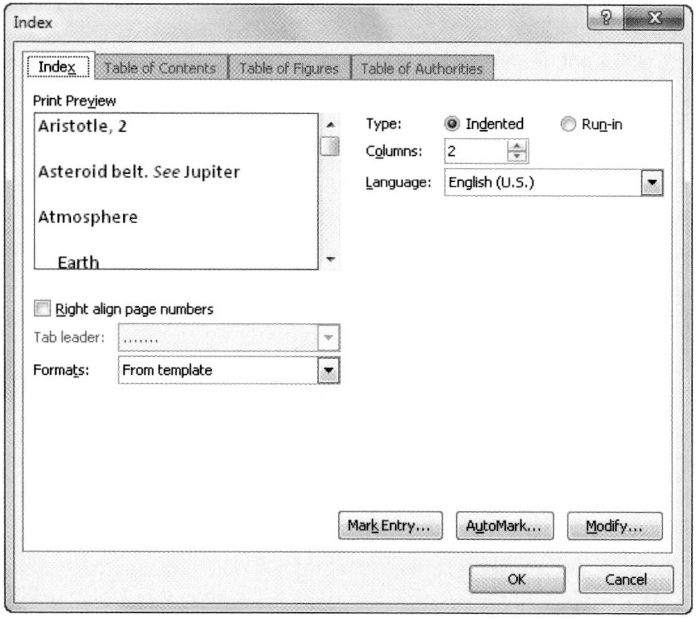

Figure 4-12: Use the options and settings in the Index dialog box to determine how your index will look.

3. In the Index tab of the Index dialog box, set the formatting for the index. You have these options:

- Click the **Type** option to indent subentries beneath and indented, or click **Run-In** to print subentries beside the upper-level category.

- Click the **Columns** spinner to set the number of columns in the index page.

- Click the **Language** down arrow to set the language for the index.

- Click **Right Align Page Numbers** to right-align the numbers.

- Click **Tab Leader** to print a leader between the entry and the page number.

- Click the **Formats** down arrow to use an available design template, such as Classic or Fancy.

4. Click **OK** when finished. Word generates the index, a small sample of which is shown next.

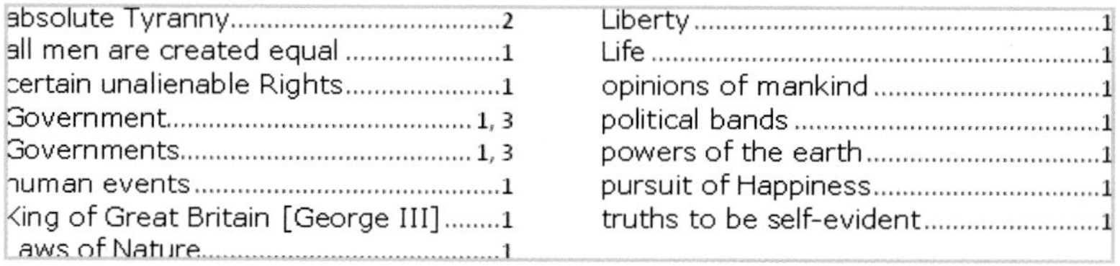

absolute Tyranny......................................2	Liberty...1
all men are created equal 1	Life 1
certain unalienable Rights.....................1	opinions of mankind 1
Government.......................................1, 3	political bands 1
Governments.....................................1, 3	powers of the earth................................1
human events 1	pursuit of Happiness...............................1
King of Great Britain [George III].........1	truths to be self-evident.........................1
Laws of Nature.......................................1	

Create a Table of Contents

A *table of contents* is a list of the headings in the order in which they appear in the document. If you have formatted paragraphs with heading styles, you can automatically generate a table of contents based on those headings. If you have not used the heading styles, then, as with indexes, you must first tag table of contents (or TOC) entries and then generate the table of contents. (See "Use Styles" earlier in this chapter.)

TAG ENTRIES FOR THE TABLE OF CONTENTS

Use the Quick Style gallery to identify a segment of text within your document so that it can contain a consistent style for headings and other text that you want contained in a table of contents.

1. Select the text to be formatted, for example, a title or heading.

2. Click the **Home** tab, and click the **Styles More** down arrow in the Styles group.

TIP

To make sure that your document is paginated correctly (and, therefore, that the index has the correct page numbers), you need to hide field codes and hidden text. If the XE (Index Entry) fields are visible, click the **Show/Hide** button.

You can also tag TOC entries by selecting the text that you want to include in your table of contents. Press **ALT+SHIFT+O**. The Mark Table Of Contents Entry dialog box appears. In the Level box, select the level and click **Mark**. If you have multiple tables of contents, you can identify to which TOC the current entry belongs by using the Table Identifier feature. To mark additional entries, select the text, click in the **Entry** box, and click **Mark**. When you have finished adding entries, close the dialog box.

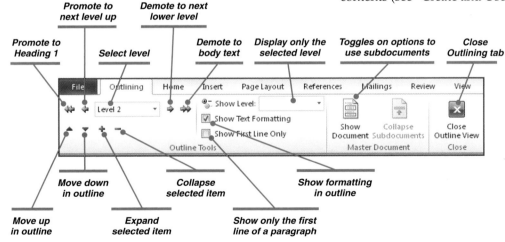

3. Point at each thumbnail to determine which style it represents, and then click the thumbnail of the style you want to apply.

PLACE OTHER TEXT IN A TABLE OF CONTENTS

To add text other than identified headings in a table of contents:

1. Highlight the text or phrase to be shown in the table of contents.

2. Click the **References** tab, and click **Add Text** in the Table Of Contents group. A menu is displayed.

3. Click the option you want. You have these choices:

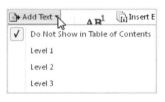

- **Do Not Show In Table Of Contents** removes the identification that something should be included in the TOC.

- **Level 1**, **Level 2**, or **Level 3** assigns selected text to a level similar to Heading 1, Heading 2, or Heading 3.

USE THE OUTLINING TAB FOR THE TABLE OF CONTENTS

The outlining tab contains an easy way to tag or identify entries for the table of contents (see "Create and Use Outlines" later in this chapter).

1. Click the **View** tab, and click **Outline** in the Document Views group. An Outlining tab will become available (see Figure 4-13). Within the Outlining tab, Figure 4-14 shows the Master Document group from which you can insert and manipulate subdocuments.

2. Click the right or left arrows to promote or demote the levels, respectively.

3. Click **Close Outline View** when you are finished and ready to generate the table of contents.

Figure 4-13: Use the Outlining tab to mark entries for a table of contents. The Outlining toolbar provides a number of ways to work with outlines.

It is a good idea to place a table of contents in its own section, where you can have separate formatting, margins, and page numbers. If you want to do this, create the section before creating the TOC. See "Create Section Breaks" earlier in this chapter.

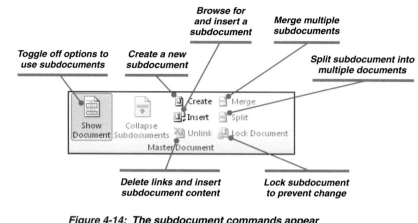

Figure 4-14: The subdocument commands appear when Show Documents on the Outlining tab is clicked. These commands allow subdocuments to be inserted and manipulated.

GENERATE A TABLE OF CONTENTS

1. Place the insertion point where you want to insert the table of contents (normally at the beginning of the document).

2. Click the References tab, and click Table Of Contents in the Table Of Contents group. A menu is displayed.

3. Click one of the two automatic built-in styles that will have a title and indented levels, or click **Insert Table Of Contents** to automatically generate a table of contents with formatting that you specify. In the latter case, the Table of Contents dialog box, shown in Figure 4-15, is displayed.

4. The Print Preview and Web Preview features show how the TOC will appear based on the options selected. You have these options:

- Clear the **Show Page Numbers** check box to suppress the display of page numbers.

- Clear the **Right Align Page Numbers** check box to allow page numbers to follow the text immediately.

- Clear the **Use Hyperlinks Instead Of Page Numbers** check box to use page numbers in place of hyperlinks.

- Click the **Tab Leader** down arrow, and click **(None)** or another option for a leader between the text in the TOC and the page number.

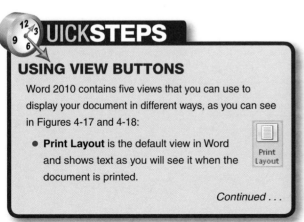

Figure 4-15: Use the options and settings in the Table Of Contents dialog box to determine how your table of contents will look.

QUICKSTEPS

USING VIEW BUTTONS

Word 2010 contains five views that you can use to display your document in different ways, as you can see in Figures 4-17 and 4-18:

• **Print Layout** is the default view in Word and shows text as you will see it when the document is printed.

Continued . . .

• Click the **Formats** down arrow to use one of the available designs.

• Click the **Show Levels** down arrow, and click the highest level of heading you want to display in the TOC.

5. Click OK when finished.

Create and Use Outlines

An *outline* is a framework upon which a document is based. It is a hierarchical list of the headings in a document. You might use an outline to help you organize your ideas and thoughts when writing a speech, a term paper, a book, or a research project. The Outline tab in Word makes it easy to build and refine your outlines, as shown in Figure 4-16.

1. Open a new blank document (see Chapter 1). Click the **View** tab, and click **Outline** in the Document Views group. Word switches to the Outlining tab, displayed earlier in Figures 4-13 and 4-14.

2. Type your first-level heading text, and press **ENTER**. Word formats the headings using the built-in heading style Heading 1. Type your second-level heading text, and continue throughout the document. You have these ways of setting the levels:

   • Assign a heading to a different level by selecting it from the Outline Level drop-down list box.

   –Or–

   Place the insertion point in the heading, and then click the **Promote** or **Demote** button on the Outlining toolbar until the heading is at the level you want.

   • To move a heading to a different location, place the insertion point in the heading, and then click the **Move Up** or **Move Down** button ▲ ▼ on the Outlining tab Outline Tools group until the heading is where you want it. (If a heading is collapsed, the subordinate text under the heading moves with it.)

3. You can display as much or as little of the outline as you want by collapsing or expanding it. To collapse the sublevels under a heading in the outline, double-click the plus sign opposite the heading. To expand the same heading, double-click the plus sign again.

   –Or–

QUICKSTEPS

USING VIEW BUTTONS *(Continued)*

- **Full Screen Reading** displays the document as a "book" with facing pages. You can "flip" through the pages rather than scroll through them. This view uses the full screen in order to display as much of the document as possible. On the top is a restricted toolbar with limited options for using the document.

- **Web Layout view** displays a document as it would look as a Web page.

- **Outline view** displays the document's framework as it has been laid out, with the various levels of headers identified.

- **Draft** suppresses headings and footer and other design elements in order to display the text in draft form so that you can have an unobstructed view of the contents.

To display any of these views, click the **View** tab, and click the view you want in the Document Views group (Figure 4-17); or click the relevant button on the View toolbar on the right of the status bar (Figure 4-18).

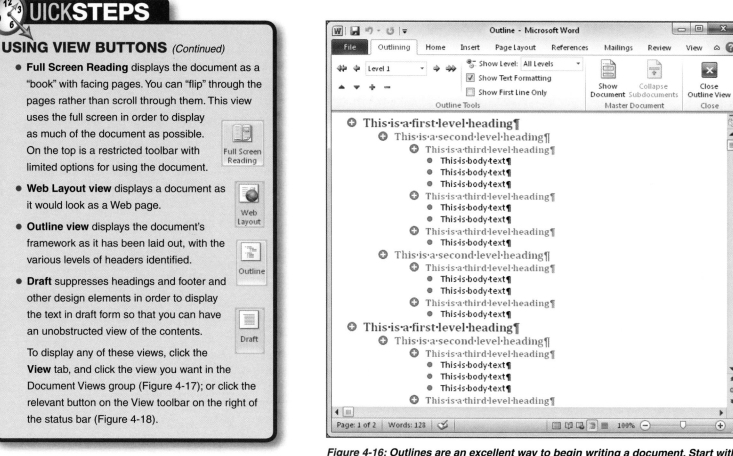

Figure 4-16: Outlines are an excellent way to begin writing a document. Start with the overall ideas and drill down to your core thoughts.

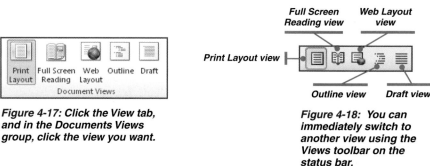

Figure 4-17: Click the View tab, and in the Documents Views group, click the view you want.

Figure 4-18: You can immediately switch to another view using the Views toolbar on the status bar.

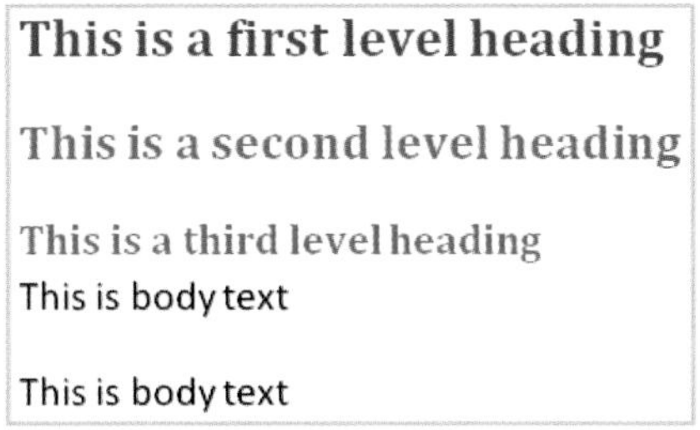

This is a first level heading

This is a second level heading

This is a third level heading
This is body text

This is body text

Select the heading and click the **Expand** or **Collapse** button ⊞ ⊟ on the Outlining tab Outline Tools group.

4. When you're satisfied with the organization, click **Close Outline View**, which automatically switches to Print Layout view (see the QuickSteps "Using View Buttons" for more information), which looks like the illustration at left.

Use Word Writing Aids

Word 2010 provides several aids that can assist you in not only creating your document, but also in making sure that it is as professional-looking as possible. These include AutoCorrect, AutoFormat, AutoText, AutoSummarize, an extensive equation-writing capability, character and word counts, highlighting, hyphenation, and a thesaurus.

Implement AutoCorrect

The AutoCorrect feature automatically corrects common typographical errors when you make them. While Word 2010 comes preconfigured with hundreds of AutoCorrect entries, you can also manually add entries.

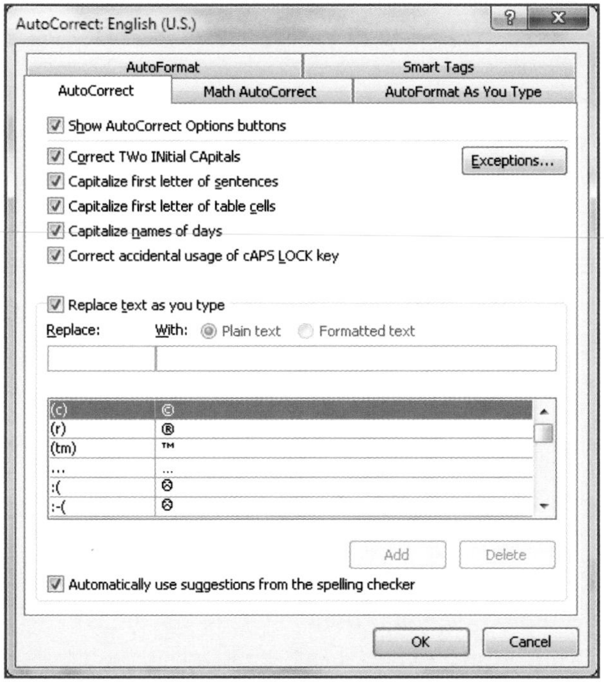

CONFIGURE AUTOCORRECT

1. Click the **File** tab, click **Options**, click **Proofing** in the left column, and click **AutoCorrect Options**. The AutoCorrect: *Language* dialog box appears.

2. Click the **AutoCorrect** tab (if it is not already displayed), and select from the following options, according to your preferences (see Figure 4-19):

- **Show AutoCorrect Options Buttons** displays a small blue button or bar beneath text that was automatically corrected. Click this button to see a menu, where you can undo the correction or set AutoCorrect options.

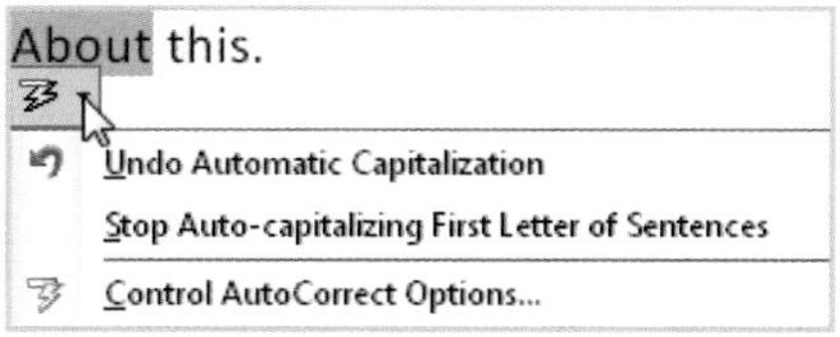

- **Correct TWo INitial CApitals** changes the second letter in a pair of capital letters to lowercase.

- **Capitalize The First Letter Of Sentences** capitalizes the first letter following the end of a sentence.

Figure 4-19: Use the AutoCorrect tab to determine what items Word will automatically correct for you as you type.

- **Capitalize The First Letter Of Table Cells** capitalizes the first letter of a word in a table cell.

- **Capitalize Names Of Days** capitalizes the names of the days of the week.

- **Correct Accidental Usage Of cAPS LOCK Key** corrects capitalization errors that occur when you type with the **CAPS LOCK** key depressed and turns off this key.

- **Replace Text As You Type** replaces typographical errors with the correct words as shown in the list beneath it.

- **Automatically Use Suggestions From The Spelling Checker** tells Word to replace spelling errors with words from the dictionary as you type.

3. Click OK when finished.

ADD AN AUTOCORRECT ENTRY

1. Click the **File** tab, click **Options**, click **Proofing** in the left column, and click **AutoCorrect Options**. The AutoCorrect: *Language* dialog box appears.

2. Click the **AutoCorrect** tab (if it is not already displayed).

3. Type the text that you want Word to automatically replace in the Replace box. Type the text that you want to replace it with in the With box.

4. Click **Add** and click **OK**.

DELETE AN AUTOCORRECT ENTRY

1. Click the **File** tab, click **Options**, click **Proofing** in the left column, and click **AutoCorrect Options**. The AutoCorrect: *Language* dialog box appears.

2. Click the **AutoCorrect** tab (if it is not already displayed).

3. Scroll through the list of AutoCorrect entries, and click the entry you want to delete.

4. Click **Delete** and click **OK**.

Use AutoFormat

AutoFormat automatically formats a document as you type it by applying the associated styles to text, depending on how it is used in the document. For example, Word will automatically format two dashes (--) into an em dash (—) or will automatically format Internet and e-mail addresses as hyperlinks.

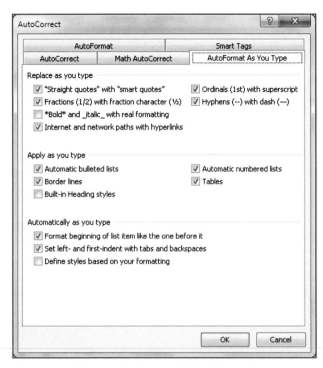

Figure 4-20: Use the AutoFormat As You Type tab to determine what items Word will automatically format for you as you type.

To choose the formatting you want Word to apply as you type:

1. Click the **File** tab, click **Options**, click **Proofing** in the left column, and click **AutoCorrect Options**. The AutoCorrect: *Language* dialog box appears. Click the **AutoFormat As You Type** tab.

2. Select from among the following options, depending on your preferences (see Figure 4-20):

   - **"Straight Quotes" With "Smart Quotes"** replaces plain quotation characters with curly quotation characters.

   - **Ordinals (1st) With Superscript** formats ordinal numbers (numbers designating items in an ordered sequence) with a superscript. For example, 1st becomes 1st.

   - **Fractions (1/2) With Fraction Character (½)** replaces fractions typed with numbers and slashes with fraction characters.

   - **Hyphens (--) With Dash (—)** replaces a single hyphen with an en dash (–) and two hyphens with an em dash (—).

   - ***Bold* And _Italic_ With Real Formatting** formats text enclosed within asterisks (*) as bold and text enclosed within underscores (_) as italic.

   - **Internet And Network Paths With Hyperlinks** formats e-mail addresses and URLs (Uniform Resource Locator—the address of a Web page on the Internet or an intranet) as clickable hyperlink fields.

   - **Automatic Bulleted Lists** applies bulleted list formatting to paragraphs beginning with *, o, or – followed by a space or tab character.

   - **Automatic Numbered Lists** applies numbered list formatting to paragraphs beginning with a number or letter followed by a space or a tab character.

   - **Border Lines** automatically applies paragraph border styles when you type three or more hyphens, underscores, or equal signs (=).

   - **Tables** creates a table when you type a series of hyphens with plus signs to indicate column edges.

   - **Built-In Heading Styles** applies heading styles to heading text.

   - **Format Beginning Of List Item Like The One Before It** repeats character formatting that you apply to the beginning of a list item. For example, if you format the first word of a list item in bold, the first word of all subsequent list items are formatted in bold.

   - **Set Left- And First-Indent With Tabs And Backspaces** sets left indentation on the tab ruler based on the tabs and backspaces you type.

- **Define Styles Based On Your Formatting** automatically creates or modifies styles based on manual formatting that you apply to your document.

3. Click **OK** when finished.

Use Building Blocks

Building blocks are blocks of text and formatting that you can use repeatedly, such as cover pages, a greeting, phrases, headings, or a closing. Word provides a number of these for you, but you can identify and save your own building blocks, and then use them in different documents.

CREATE A BUILDING BLOCK

1. Select the text or graphic, along with its formatting, that you want to store as a building block. (Include the paragraph mark in the selection if you want to store paragraph formatting.)

2. Click the **Insert** tab, click **Quick Parts** in the Text group, and then click Save Selection To Quick Parts Gallery.

3. The Create New Building Block dialog box appears. Accept the suggested name for the building block, or type a short abbreviation for a new one. For example, I changed this one to "mt" for Matthews Technology.

4. In most cases, you will accept the Quick Parts gallery, the General category, and the Building Blocks.dotx file name, since those provide for the easiest retrieval.

5. Click the **Options** down arrow, and, depending on what you are saving in your building block, click the option that is correct for you. If you want paragraph formatting, you must include the paragraph mark.

6. Click **OK**.

–Or–

1. After selecting the text or graphic that you want as a building block, press **ALT+F3**. The Create New Building Block dialog box appears.

2. Follow steps 3–6 in the preceding procedure.

INSERT ONE OF YOUR BUILDING BLOCKS

1. Place the insertion point in the document where you want to insert the building block.

2. Click the **Insert** tab, click **Quick Parts** in the Text group, and then double-click the entry you want, as shown in Figure 4-21.

–Or–

General

m

Marty

marty

Martin (Marty) Matthews

mt

Matthews Technology
http://matthewstechnology.com

QUICKSTEPS

AutoText	▶
Document Property	▶
Field...	
Building Blocks Organizer...	
Save Selection to Quick Part Gallery...	

Figure 4-21: Quick Parts provides direct access to your building block entries so that you can insert them in documents.

At the point in the document where you want to insert the building block, type its name or the short abbreviation you entered in place of the name, and press **F3**. For example, if I type <u>mt</u> and press **F3**, I get "Matthews Technology."

INSERT ONE OF WORD'S BUILDING BLOCKS

1. Place the insertion point in the document where you want to insert the building block.

2. Click the **Insert** tab, click **Quick Parts** in the Text group, and then click **Building Blocks Organizer**. The Building Blocks Organizer dialog box appears, as shown in Figure 4-22.

3. Scroll through the list of building blocks until you find the one that you want. Click the entry to see it previewed on the right. When you have selected one you want to use, click **Insert**.

Building Blocks Organizer

Building blocks:

Name	Gallery	Category	Template
Classic 2	Cover Pages	From Micros...	TC10163146...
Mod	Cover Pages	Built-In	Building Blo...
Sideline	Cover Pages	Built-In	Building Blo...
Contrast	Cover Pages	Built-In	Building Blo...
Conservative	Cover Pages	Built-In	Building Blo...
Alphabet	Cover Pages	Built-In	Building Blo...
Median	Cover Pages	Report	TC10179305...
Tiles	Cover Pages	Built-In	Building Blo...
Exposure	Cover Pages	Built-In	Building Blo...
Soft gradient	Cover Pages	From Micros...	TC10163147...
Transcend	Cover Pages	Built-In	Building Blo...
Cubicles	Cover Pages	Built-In	Building Blo...
Austin	Cover Pages	Built-in	TC10179306...
Origin	Cover Pages	Report	Origin.dotx
Equity	Cover Pages	Report	TC10179306...
Classic	Cover Pages	From Micros...	TC10163106...
Contrast	Cover Pages	Built-In	TC10179306...
Grid	Cover Pages	Built-in	TC10179306...
Puzzle	Cover Pages	Built-In	Building Blo...
Annual	Cover Pages	Built-In	Building Blo...
Motion	Cover Pages	Built-In	Building Blo...

Click a building block to see its preview

[Type the document title]

[Type the document subtitle]

Conservative
Top-aligned information block with accent line between title and subtitle; bottom-aligned abstract

Edit Properties...   Delete   Insert

Close

Figure 4-22: Word comes with a large number of building blocks that you can access.

NOTE

You cannot undo the deletion of a building block. The only way to restore it is to re-create it.

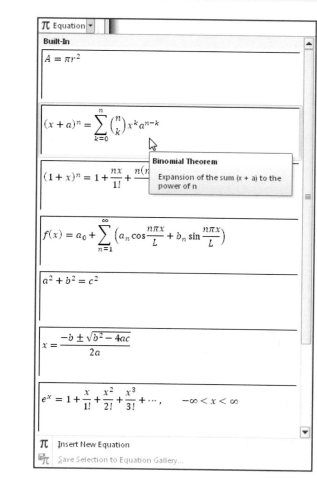

Figure 4-23: Word provides a number of ready-made equations for your use.

DELETE A BUILDING BLOCK

1. Click the **Insert** tab, click **Quick Parts** in the Text group, and then click **Building Blocks Organizer**. The Building Blocks Organizer dialog box appears.

2. Scroll through the list of building blocks until you find the one that you want. Click the entry to see it previewed on the right.

3. When you have selected the entry you want to delete, click **Delete**, click **Yes** to confirm the deletion, and click **Close**.

Enter an Equation

If you include mathematical equations in the documents you produce, Word has several helpful tools for producing them. These include ready-made equations, commonly used mathematical structures, a large standard symbol set, and many special mathematical symbols that can be generated with Math AutoCorrect. These tools allow you to create equations by modifying a ready-made equation, using an equation text box with common mathematical structures and symbols, and simply typing an equation as you would ordinary text.

MODIFY A READY-MADE EQUATION

1. Click at the location in the document where you want the equation.

2. Click the **Insert** tab, and click the **Equation** down arrow in the Symbols group. The list of built-in equations appears, as shown in Figure 4-23.

3. Click the equation you want to insert. An equation text box will appear, containing the equation, and the Equation Tools Design tab will display, as shown in Figure 4-24.

4. Click in the equation, and make any needed changes. Use the **RIGHT ARROW** and **LEFT ARROW** keys to move through the text.

5. When you have completed the equation, click outside the text box to close it and leave the equation looking like it is part of ordinary text.

An example of a complex theorem is the Binomial Theorem:

$$(x + a)^n = \sum_{k=0}^{n} \binom{n}{k} x^k a^{n-k}, \text{ which in an early form was}$$

discussed by Euclid in the 4th century BC and a number of other mathematicians. Its current form was described by Blaise Pascal in the 17th century.

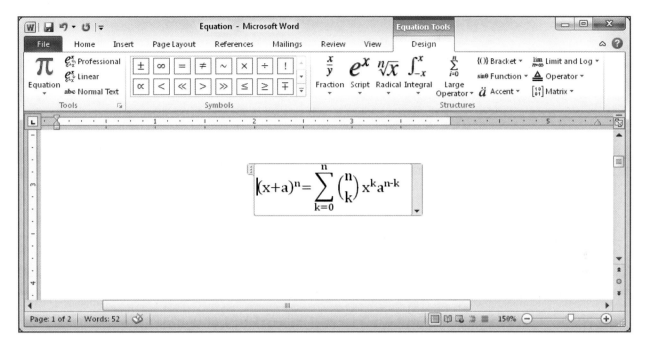

Figure 4-24: *The equation text box automatically formats equations, which can be built with the structures and symbols in the Equation Tools Design tab.*

NOTE

Treat an equation in its text box as you would ordinary text and the text box itself as an object in a line of text.

Type equation here.

NOTE

If you save a document with an equation in any format prior to Word 2007, the equation will be converted to a .tif image and you will not be able to edit it after you reopen it.

CREATE AN EQUATION IN A TEXT BOX

You can open an equation text box and use the Equation Tools Design tab to create a professional-looking equation.

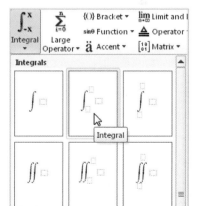

1. Click at the location in the document where you want to insert the equation.

2. Click the **Insert** tab, and click **Equation** (not the down arrow) in the Symbols group. An empty equation text box appears.

3. Either begin typing the equation or click one of the structures in the Structures group on the Equation Tools Design tab. If a drop-down menu appears, click the specific format you want.

NOTE

You can see the Math AutoCorrect text sequences by clicking the **File** tab, clicking **Proofing**, clicking **AutoCorrect Options**, and clicking the **Math AutoCorrect** tab. Scroll through the list to see the text sequences (see Figure 4-25). Click the option at the top of the dialog box to have Math AutoCorrect work outside of an equation text box. Click **OK** twice to close both dialog boxes.

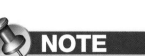

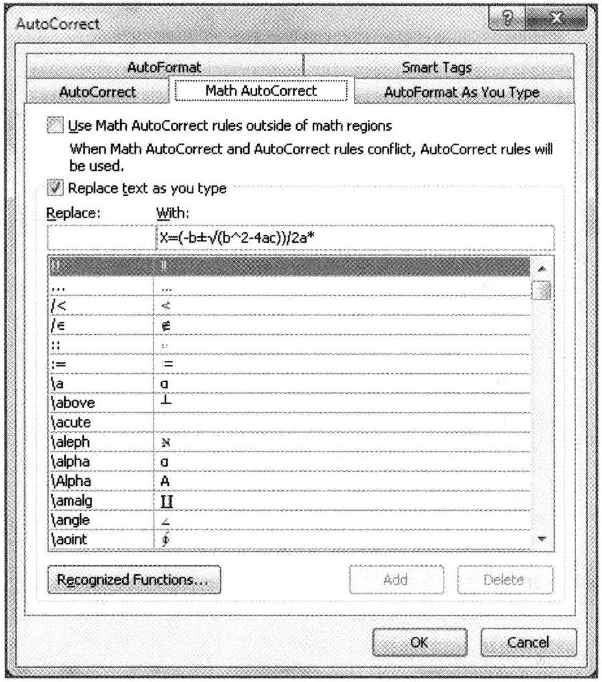

Figure 4-25: Math AutoCorrect allows you to insert math symbols by typing text sequences.

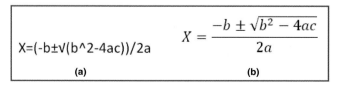

4. If you use one of the structures, click in the small text boxes, and type the characters or select the appropriate symbols from the Symbols group for the Equation Tools Design tab.
5. Finish the equation using additional structures, symbols, and normal characters, if needed.
6. When you have completed the equation, click outside the text box to close it and leave the equation looking like it is part of ordinary text.

CREATE AN EQUATION FROM SCRATCH

You can also type an equation in a line of text using standard keyboard keys plus special symbols and then convert it to a professional-looking equation.

1. Click at the location in the document where you want to insert the equation.
2. Begin typing using the keys on your keyboard, and, when needed, enter special characters by either:
   - Typing one of the Math AutoCorrect text sequences, like \sqrt to get a square root symbol.

   –Or–

   - On the Insert tab, click **Symbol** in the Symbols group, and click the symbol you want if you see it; or click **More Symbols**, scroll through the symbols list until you see the one you want, double-click it, and click **Close**.
3. Finish the equation using the techniques in step 2. When you have completed it (Figure 4-26a shows a quadratic equation created in this manner), select the entire equation, and, in the Insert tab Symbol group, click Equation. An equation text box forms around the new equation.
4. In the Equation Tools tab, click Professional [Professional] in the upper-right area of the Tools group. Click outside the text box to close it. The professionally formatted quadratic equation looks like Figure 4-26b.

X=(-b±√(b^2-4ac))/2a

(a)

$$X = \frac{-b \pm \sqrt{b^2 - 4ac}}{2a}$$

(b)

Figure 4-26: You can type an equation with normal text (a), and then convert it to a professional-looking equation (b).

TIP

To see how to format typed equations, select several of the ready-made equations, and click **Normal Text** `abc Normal Text` in the Equation Tools Design tab Tools group.

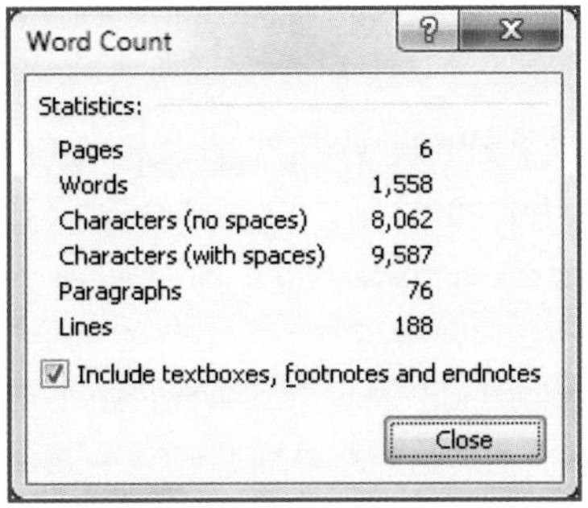

Word Count

Statistics:

Pages	6
Words	1,558
Characters (no spaces)	8,062
Characters (with spaces)	9,587
Paragraphs	76
Lines	188

☑ Include textboxes, footnotes and endnotes

Close

Figure 4-27: The Word Count feature is a quick and easy way to view the specifics of your document.

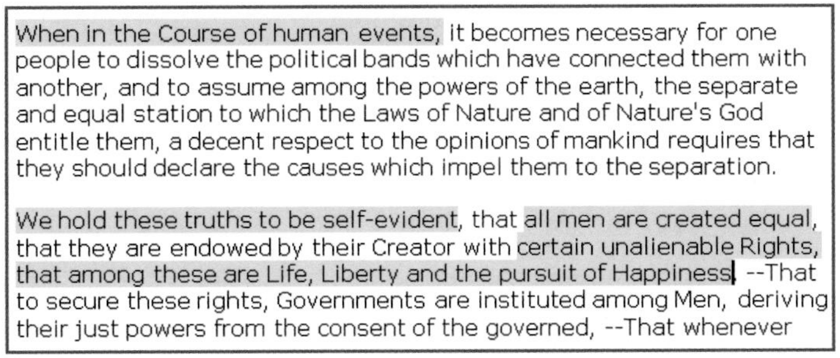

When in the Course of human events, it becomes necessary for one people to dissolve the political bands which have connected them with another, and to assume among the powers of the earth, the separate and equal station to which the Laws of Nature and of Nature's God entitle them, a decent respect to the opinions of mankind requires that they should declare the causes which impel them to the separation.

We hold these truths to be self-evident, that all men are created equal, that they are endowed by their Creator with certain unalienable Rights, that among these are Life, Liberty and the pursuit of Happiness| --That to secure these rights, Governments are instituted among Men, deriving their just powers from the consent of the governed, --That whenever

Figure 4-28: Highlighting is a great way to call attention to specific sections or phrases of your document.

TIP

You can also apply highlighting by selecting the text first and then clicking **Highlight** in the Home tab Font group.

Count Characters and Words

Word can tell you the number of characters and words in a document or in just a portion of the document you select.

On the Review tab, click **Word Count** `ABC 123 Word Count` in the Proofing group. The Word Count dialog box appears, displaying the following information about your document (see Figure 4-27):

- Number of pages
- Number of words
- Number of characters (not including spaces)
- Number of characters (including spaces)
- Number of paragraphs
- Number of lines

Use Highlighting

The Highlight feature is useful for marking important text in a document or text that you want to call a reader's attention to. Keep in mind, however, that highlighting parts of a document works best when the document is viewed online. When printed, the highlighting marks often appear gray and may even obscure the text you're trying to call attention to.

APPLY HIGHLIGHTING

1. In the Home tab Font group, click Highlight `aby ▾`.
2. Select the text or graphic that you want to highlight. The highlighting is applied to your selection (see Figure 4-28).
3. To turn off highlighting, click **Highlight** again or press **ESC**.

REMOVE HIGHLIGHTING

1. Select the text that you want to remove highlighting from, or press **CTRL+A** to select all of the text in the document.
2. In the Home tab Font group, click **Highlight**.

   –Or–

   In the Home tab Font group, click the **Highlight** drop-down arrow, and then click **No Color**.

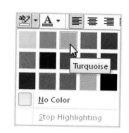

CHANGE HIGHLIGHTING COLOR

In the Home tab Font group, click the **Highlight** drop-down arrow, and then click the color that you want to use.

FIND HIGHLIGHTED TEXT IN A DOCUMENT

1. In the Home tab, click **Find** in the Editing group.

2. In the navigation pane that opens, click the magnifying glass, and click **Find** to open the Find dialog box.

3. If you don't see the Format button, click the **More** button.

4. Click the **Format** button, and then click **Highlight**.

5. Click **Find Next** and repeat this until you reach the highlight you are searching for or the end of the document.

6. Click **OK** when the message box is displayed indicating that Word has finished searching the document, and click Close in the Find And Replace dialog box.

Add Hyphenation

The Hyphenation feature automatically hyphenates words at the ends of lines based on standard hyphenation rules. You might use this feature if you want words to fit better on a line, or if you want to avoid uneven margins in right-aligned text or large gaps between words in justified text. (See Chapter 3 for information on text alignment.)

AUTOMATICALLY HYPHENATE A DOCUMENT

To automatically hyphenate a document:

1. In the Page Layout tab, click **Hyphenation** in the Page Setup group. A drop-down menu appears.

2. Click **Hyphenation Options** to open the Hyphenation dialog box. Select the option you want (see Figure 4-29):

   - **Automatically Hyphenate Document** either enables automatic hyphenation as you type or after the fact for selected text (this option is turned off in Word by default).

   - **Hyphenate Words in CAPS** hyphenates words typed in all uppercase letters.

   - **Hyphenation Zone** sets the distance from the right margin within which you want to hyphenate the document (the lower the value, the more words are hyphenated).

TIP

You can also hyphenate existing text by selecting the text, clicking **Hyphenation** in the Page Layout tab, and clicking **Automatic** in the Page Setup group.

Figure 4-29: You can determine how Word will automatically hyphenate words.

- **Limit Consecutive Hyphens** sets the maximum number of hyphens that can appear in consecutive lines.

3. Click **OK** when finished.

MANUALLY HYPHENATE TEXT

1. In the Page Layout tab, click **Hyphenation** in the Page Setup group. A drop-down menu appears.

2. Click **Manual**.

3. Word searches for possible words to hyphenate. When it finds one, the Manual Hyphenation dialog box appears.

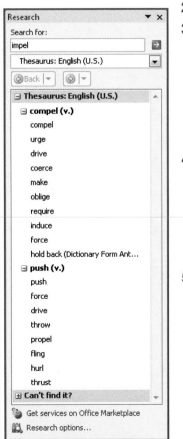

Manual Hyphenation: English (U.S.)

Hyphenate at: en-ti-tle

Yes | No | Cancel

4. Do one of the following:
   - Click **Yes** to hyphenate the word at the suggested blinking hyphen.
   - Click one of the other hyphen choices, if there are more than one, and then click **Yes**.
   - Click **No** to continue without hyphenating the word.

5. Word will continue searching for words to hyphenate and display the Manual Hyphenation dialog box until the entire document has been searched. A message box is displayed to that effect. Click **OK**.

EXPLORING THE THESAURUS

A *thesaurus* is a book or list of synonyms (words that have similar meanings), and Word contains a Thesaurus feature that will help you find just the right word to get your message across.

1. Select the word in your current document for which you want a synonym. You can also type a word later.

2. Press **SHIFT+F7**.

   –Or–

   In the Review tab, click **Thesaurus** in the Proofing group.

   In either case, the Research task pane is displayed (see Figure 4-30.)

3. If you did not select a word in step 1, type the word you want to find synonyms for in the Search For field.

4. Click the green arrow button to start searching.

5. A list of possible words is displayed. Point to the word you want to use. Click the arrow that appears, and click Insert.

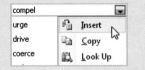

6. Close the Research pane when finished.

Research

Search for:
impel

Thesaurus: English (U.S.)

Back |

Thesaurus: English (U.S.)
- compel (v.)
  - compel
  - urge
  - drive
  - coerce
  - make
  - oblige
  - require
  - induce
  - force
  - hold back (Dictionary Form Ant...
- push (v.)
  - push
  - force
  - drive
  - throw
  - propel
  - fling
  - hurl
  - thrust
- Can't find it?

Get services on Office Marketplace

Research options...

Figure 4-30: The Thesaurus feature enables you to find exactly the right word.

Chapter 5
Printing and Using Mail Merge

The printing capabilities provided by Word 2010 go beyond just printing a document. You can preview your document before printing it and set specific parameters with regard to what is printed. Word also includes a convenient feature called Mail Merge that you can use to merge mailing lists into documents, including letters or envelopes.

This chapter covers these topics and more, including how to print envelopes and labels and how to set up a name and address list.

Print Documents

While printing documents may seem like a fairly basic function, there are several tasks associated with it that deserve attention, including setting up your printer, using Print Preview, and printing envelopes and labels.

Set Up Your Printer

Your printer will come with documentation that specifically tells you how to set it up, but there are two basic areas that you need to consider when setting up a printer: installing it on your computer and setting it as the default printer.

INSTALL A PRINTER

Follow the manufacturer's instructions to unpack, set up, and connect the printer to your computer or identify the network printer you want to use. If

you install a Plug and Play printer, it will automatically install itself and you can ignore the following instructions. Otherwise, to install a printer:

1. From Windows 7, click **Start** and then click **Devices And Printers**. The Devices And Printers window opens, as shown in Figure 5-1.

2. Click **Add A Printer** in the toolbar. The Add Printer Wizard starts.

3. Follow the instructions in the Add Printer Wizard, clicking **Next** as needed.

4. If you are using a local printer and you want to print a test page, make sure the printer is turned on and ready to print. When you are done, click **Finished**.

SET A DEFAULT PRINTER

1. From Windows 7, click **Start** and then click **Devices And Printers**, if it isn't already displayed.

2. Right-click the icon for the printer you want to use as the default printer, and then click **Set As Default Printer** from the context menu that appears. A check mark is displayed next to the icon you have selected.

3. Click **Close** in the Devices And Printers window.

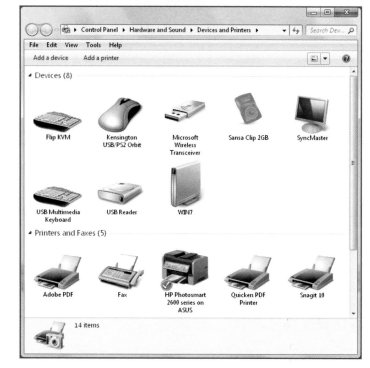

Figure 5-1: In addition to your printers the Devices And Printers window may display one or more virtual printers that produce files, not paper output, such as a PDF "printer."

Define How a Document Is Printed

The Properties dialog box for your printer is where you define how your document will be printed. From here, you can set such things as orientation, number of copies to print, effects, and so on. An example of a Properties dialog box for an HP Photosmart 2600 printer is shown in Figure 5-2. Keep in mind that the Properties dialog box for your printer will probably have some different options, and can even be different for the same printer, depending on whether the printer is connected directly to the computer or is accessed over the network. Consult the documentation that came with your printer for specific instructions.

Figure 5-2: Use the Properties dialog box for your printer to define how your documents will be printed.

To open the Properties dialog box for your printer:

1. In Word, click the **File** tab, and click **Print**.

2. In the Print window, beneath the Printer selection drop-down list, click **Printer Properties** (see Figure 5-3). The Document Properties dialog box for your printer appears. This particular printer model has five tabs in its dialog box.

3. The Printing Shortcut tab for the HP Photosmart 2600 has the following options, as shown in Figure 5-2. Other printers will have different tabs and different options, but within the Properties dialog box, they will generally cover the same functions. Make your selections accordingly.

   - **Print Quality** determines the quality of your print job. You can choose speed over quality or quality over speed.

   - **Paper Type** determines the type of paper you are printing on, for example, plain or photo glossy.

   - **Paper Size** determines the size of the paper you are printing on, for example, letter, legal, or postcard.

   - **Orientation** determines how the document is aligned on the page and the order in which the pages will be printed.

   - **Print On Both Sides** allows you to select from several options for two-sided printing.

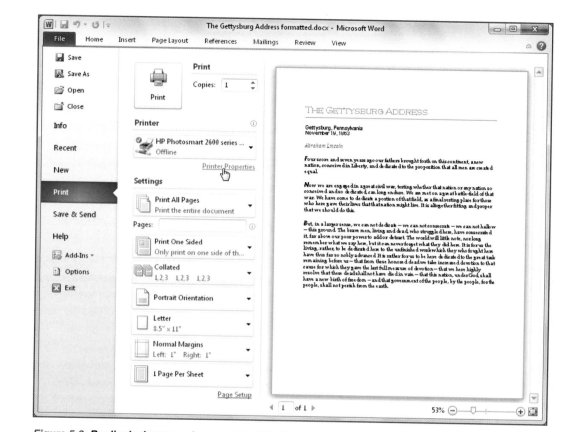

4. Other tabs will have a variety of options, depending on your printer. Some of the more common options are:

- **Copies** determines the number of copies to be printed.

- **Collate Copies** determines whether multiple copies of a document are printed one at a time. In other words, all the pages of one copy are printed, then the next copy is printed, and so on.

- **Source** determines which of several paper trays, if you have more than one, is used as the source of the paper.

- **Rotate** allows you to rotate the printing on the page by either a fixed or selectable number of degrees.

- **Pages Per Sheet** allows you to print two or more pages on a single sheet of paper, either directly (if the pages are sized accordingly) or by scaling.

5. When you have the settings the way you want them, click **OK** to close the dialog boxes.

Figure 5-3: **By displaying your document in Print Preview, you can see how it will look when printed.**

Preview What You'll Print

NOTE

Print Layout view, set in the View tab Documents Views group, provides almost the exact same view as Print Preview view, and the View tab provides many of the same options.

You can use the Print Preview feature to view your document on the screen before you print it. Print Preview displays the page(s) of your document as they will appear when printed. You can also see page breaks and margins using this feature.

To use Print Preview:

Click the File tab, and click Print. You'll see a preview of what will print in the right pane, as shown in Figure 5-3.

ZOOM IN AND OUT

Word 2010 Print Preview has a set of controls that allow you to increase or decrease the magnification of the print image, as shown in Figure 5-3. These are:

- **The zoom tools** in the lower-right corner of the Print Preview area provide five separate tools:

  - **The Zoom button** on the left, which shows you the current percentage of magnification. Clicking this button opens the Zoom dialog box.
  - **Zoom Out**, which is clicked to reduce the magnification and see more of the page.
  - **Zoom slider**, which you can drag in either direction to increase or decrease the magnification.
  - **Zoom In**, which is clicked to increase the magnification and see less of the page.
  - **Fit To Page**, which, when clicked, reduces the magnification so the entire page can be seen in the Print Preview area.

- **The Zoom dialog box**, which is opened by clicking the **Zoom** button (the percentage number on the left of the slider). Click one of the preset percentages, directly enter a percent, or use the spinner to set the level of magnification you want. You can also click **Many Pages** to view a number of page thumbnails on one page.

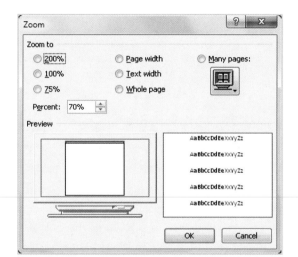

CHANGE MARGINS

The Print option of Word's File window, shown in Figure 5-3, provides the same margin menu and access to the Page Setup dialog box as available in the Page Layout tab Page Setup group (see Chapter 3 for more information).

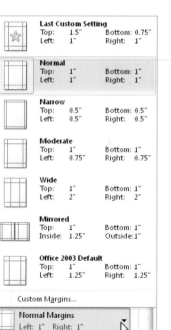

1. In the File window's Print option, click **Margins** (depending on what was previously selected, it will have a different title—the default is "Normal Margins"). A pop-up menu of margin options will open.

NOTE

The zoom tools in the lower-right corner of most Word windows is the same as the zoom tools in the Print Preview pane. In addition, on the View tab Zoom group, you'll find similar tools, one of which, Zoom, displays the Zoom dialog box.

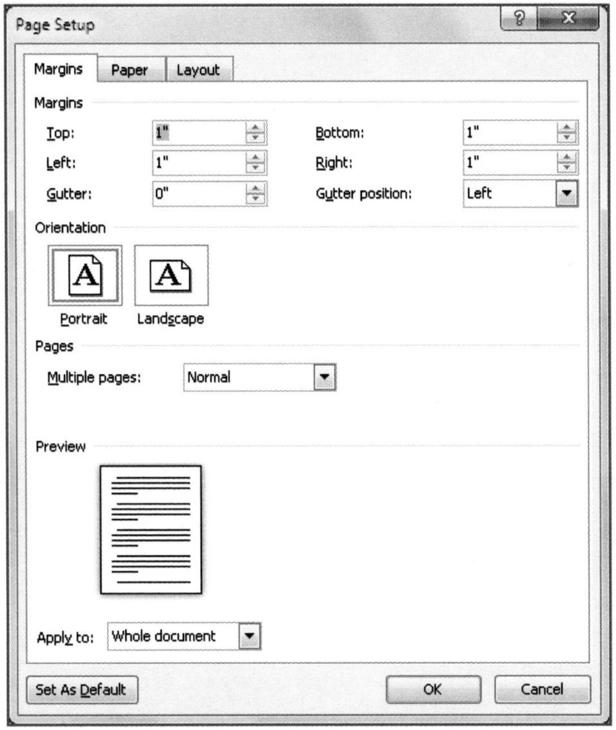

![Page Setup dialog box showing Margins tab with Top, Left, Gutter, Bottom, Right, Gutter position settings, Orientation (Portrait/Landscape), Pages Multiple pages Normal, Preview, Apply to Whole document, Set As Default, OK, Cancel buttons.]

Figure 5-4: *You can either select preset margins from the Margin drop-down menu or enter the custom margins you want in the Page Setup dialog box.*

2. Select the option that is correct for your document; or click **Custom Margins** at the bottom of the menu to open the Page Setup dialog box and directly enter or select the individual margins you want to use (see Figure 5-4).

–Or–

Click **Page Setup** at the bottom of the Print option window to open the Page Setup dialog box.

MOVE FROM PAGE TO PAGE

In the lower-left area of the Print Preview pane, click **Previous Page** or **Next Page** to move forward or backward one page at a time, or enter a page number in the text box.

◄ 2 of 6 ►

EXIT PRINT PREVIEW

Click **File** or another tab in the tab bar of the File window to return to a normal Word window.

VIEW YOUR DOCUMENT IN FULL-SCREEN MODE

A feature that was available in earlier versions of Word's Print Preview but that is not in Print Preview in Word 2010 is the ability to view a document in full-screen mode without the ribbon, status bar, or scroll bars present, as shown in Figure 5-5. This view, however, is available in Word 2010 from the View tab Document Views group. Click **Full Screen Reading** to see what is shown in Figure 5-5. Use the **Next** and **Previous** arrows in the margin at the bottom of the page to see other pages. When you are finished, click **Close** on the far right of the title bar to return to the regular Word window.

Print a Document

If you're in a hurry, or if you don't care about changing margins, then printing a document can be as easy as clicking a Print icon on the Quick Access toolbar. By default, that icon isn't on that toolbar, but you can add it. To set specific options before printing your document, you need to use the Print option of the File window.

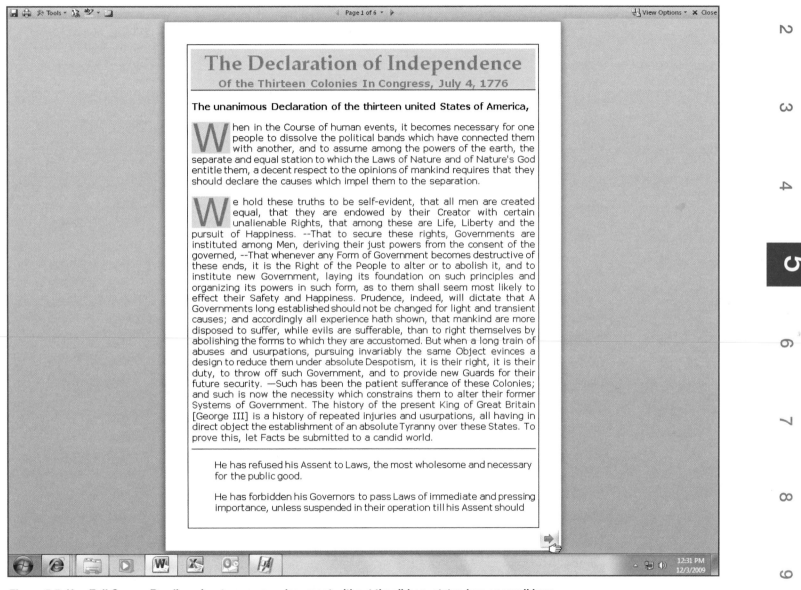

Figure 5-5: Use Full-Screen Reading view to see your document without the ribbon, status bar, or scroll bars.

Figure 5-6: *The Print Settings area provides many options for printing your document.*

ADD THE QUICK PRINT ICON

To add a single-click Print icon to the Quick Access toolbar: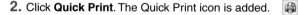

1. Click **Customize** on the right of the Quick Access toolbar.

2. Click **Quick Print**. The Quick Print icon is added. 🖨

   Clicking the Quick Print icon immediately prints the open document without further interruptions.

CUSTOMIZE A PRINT JOB

Customizing the print settings is done in the Print option of Word's File tab window.

1. Click the **File** tab, and click **Print.** The Print options appear with the Print Settings area in the left part of the window, as shown in Figure 5-6.

2. Type or use the spinner in the Copies box to select the number of copies you want to print.

3. Under Printer, the default printer is displayed automatically in the list box. If more than one printer is available to you and you want to consider alternatives, click the down arrow and select the printer you want to use from the Printer drop-down list.

4. By default, all the pages in the document are printed. If you want to further customize that, the options beneath Settings allow you to either:

   ● Retain the default, print all pages, or, beneath Print All Pages in the Pages text box, enter the specific pages to be printed in a list of pages separated by commas (1, 4, 7), or a range of pages separated by a hyphen (3-5), or a combination of the two (1-3, 6, 8-10, 12).

   –Or–

   ● Click the down arrow beside Print All Pages and select one of the following options:

     ● **Print All Pages** prints your entire document (the default).

     ● **Print Selection** prints only the content you have selected. Select text to print by dragging over it to highlight it.

     ● **Print Current Page** prints the currently selected page or the page in which the insertion point is active.

5. In addition, from the Print drop-down list you can choose to print several special areas:

   ● **Document Properties** prints the information about the document, such as the file name, the date the document was created, and when it was last saved.

NOTE

Word 2010 gives you the option of Quick Print, where you don't have worry about any other settings, and a very detailed set of options to produce professional looking documents.

- **List Of Markup** prints the revision marks that are present. These are the changes made to the document while Track Changes is enabled. (See Chapter 10 for more information on revision marks).

- **Styles** prints a list of the styles used in the document. (See Chapter 4 for more information on styles.)

- **AutoText Entries** prints a list of AutoText entries. (See Chapter 4 for more information on AutoText.)

- **Key Assignments** prints a list of shortcut keys defined by the user and available in Word. (See Chapter 6 for more information on shortcut keys.)

- **Print Markup** prints the selected pages showing the changes that have been made while using Track Changes.

- **Print Odd Pages Only** prints all the odd-numbered pages in the document or in the range you specify (see step 4).

- **Print Even Pages Only** prints all the even-numbered pages in the document or in the range you specify (see step 4).

6. Under Settings you have six additional settings that you can control by clicking the down arrow on each option:

- **Print One Sided** allows you to choose options for two-sided printing if your printer supports it.

- **Collated** allows you to choose between collated, where all the pages of a document are printed before a second document is printed, and uncollated.

- **Print Orientation** allows you to choose between portrait orientation (taller than it is wide) and landscape orientation (wider than it is tall).

- **Letter** allows you to choose the size of paper you will use in your printer.

- **Normal Margins** allows you to reset the document margins (see "Change Margins" earlier in this chapter, as well as Chapter 3).

- **1 Page Per Sheet** allows you to choose the number of pages to print on a sheet of paper.

- **Scale To Paper Size**, which is at the bottom of the pages per sheet pop-up menu, allows you to select a paper size and have your document scaled to that size. For example, you might select Executive (7.25 × 10.5 in) and have your document shrunk to that size paper.

7. When you have selected all the options you want and are ready to print your document, click **Print** at the top of the Print Settings area. Your document is printed.

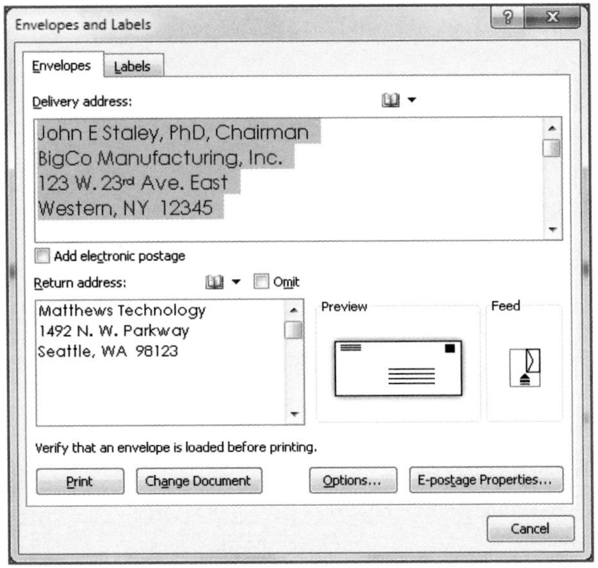

Figure 5-7: *Printed envelopes give your correspondence a professional look.*

NOTE

The Feed area in the lower-right area shows a default view that may be totally wrong for your printer. You need to use trial and error (which you can do on plain paper to save envelopes) to find the correct way to feed envelopes. When you find the correct pattern, click the feed image, select the correct image, and click **OK**.

TIP

For many HP ink-jet printers, the envelopes are fed with the flap up on the left of the envelope and positioned on the far right of the feed tray, like this:

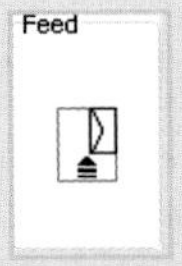

Print an Envelope

You can print a mailing address on an envelope to give your correspondence a more professional look. If you have a business letter with an address in the normal location, Word will pick up that address and suggest it for the envelope. If you don't have a letter, you can still create and print an envelope.

1. In the Mailings tab Create group, click **Envelopes**. The Envelopes And Labels dialog box appears with the Envelope tab selected, as shown in Figure 5-7.

2. In the Delivery Address box, if an address wasn't picked up from a letter, enter the mailing address.

3. In the Return Address box, accept the default return address, or enter or edit the return address. (If you are using preprinted envelopes, you can omit a return address by clicking the **Omit** check box.)

4. Click the **Add Electronic Postage** check box if you have separately installed electronic postage software and want to add it to your envelope.

5. To set options for the electronic postage programs that are installed on your computer, click **E-postage Properties**.

6. To select an envelope size, the type of paper feed, and other **options**, click Options, select the options you want, and then click **OK**.

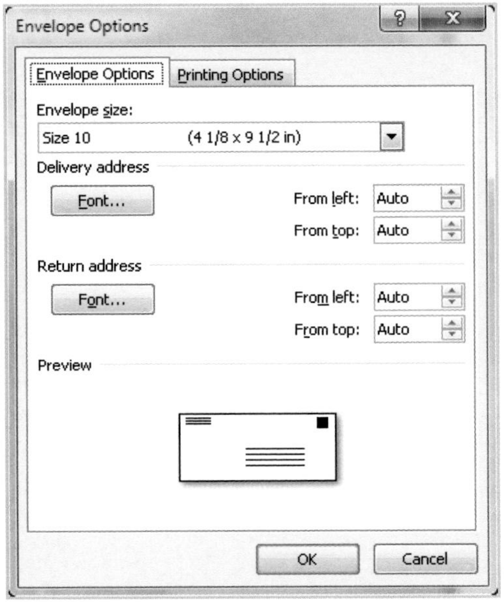

7. To print the envelope now, insert an envelope in the printer, as shown in the Feed area in the lower-right area (see the accompanying Note), and then click **Print**.

8. To attach the envelope to a document you are currently working on and print it later, click **Add To Document**. The envelope is added to the document in a separate section, as shown in Figure 5-8.

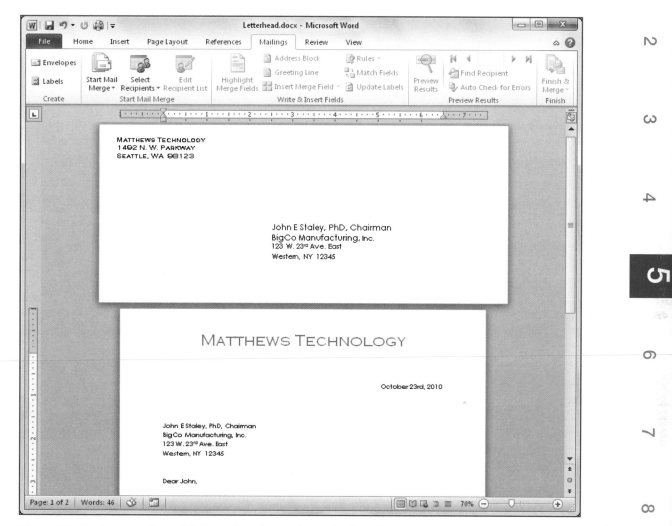

Figure 5-8: Word can create a printed envelope for you from a business letter.

Print Labels

You can print labels for a single letter or for a mass mailing, such as holiday cards, invitations, or for marketing purposes. See the section "Merge to Labels" later in this chapter for instructions on how to create labels for a mass mailing.

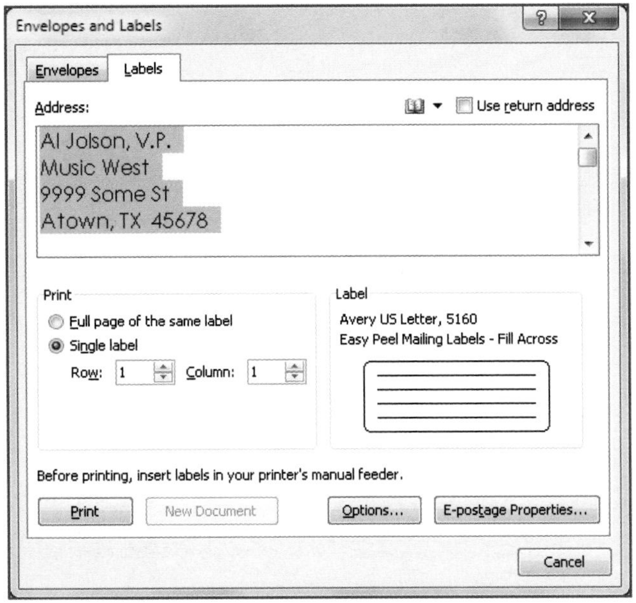

Figure 5-9: You can print a sheet of labels one at a time by specifying the row and column to be printed.

NOTE

In the Label Options dialog box, you can use the Find Updates On Office Online link to locate newly introduced labels as well as changes to existing labels.

NOTE

Later in this chapter, in the "Merge to Labels" section, we'll discuss printing many different labels on one or more sheets.

To print a single label:

1. In the Mailings tab Create group, click **Labels**. The Envelopes And Labels dialog box appears with the Labels tab displayed, as shown in Figure 5-9.

2. In the Address box, do one of the following:

   - If you have a business letter open in Word with an address in the normal location, that address will appear in the Address box and can be edited.

   - If you are creating a mailing label, enter or edit the address.

   - If you want to use a return address, click the **Use Return Address** check box, and then edit the address if necessary.

   - If you are creating another type of label, such as labels for file folders, type the text you want.

3. In the Print area, do one of the following:

   - Click the **Single Label** option to print a single label. Then type or select the row and column number on the label sheet for the label you want to print.

   - Click **Full Page Of The Same** Label to print the same information on a sheet of labels.

4. To select the label type, the type of paper feed, and other options, click **Options**, select the options you want, and then click **OK**. Pay attention to the Label Vendors choice since that determines the product numbers you'll see. If the type of label you want to use is not listed in the Product Number box, you might be able to use one of the listed labels, or you can click **New Label** to create your own custom label.

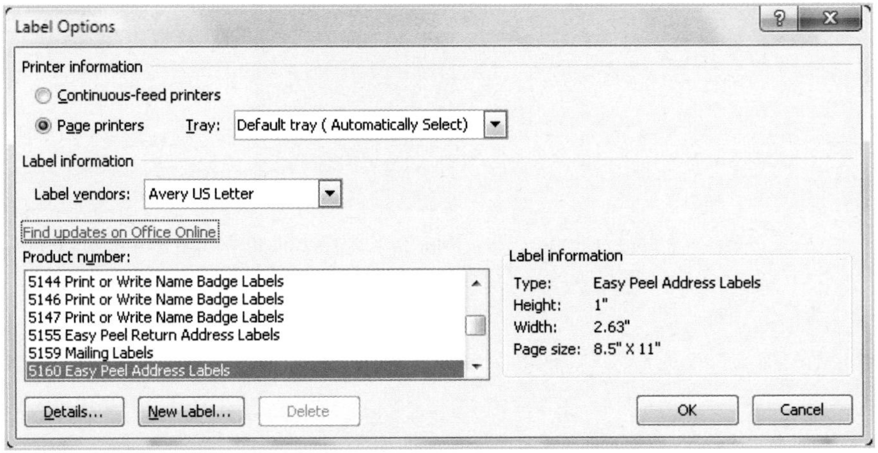

FAXING

You can send faxes directly from your computer. There are two ways to send faxes: via a faxing service and via a fax modem.

USE A FAX SERVICE

To send a fax using an online fax service (also called "eFax"):

1. Click the **File** tab, click **Save & Print**, and then, in the middle pane, ensure that **Send Using E-mail** is selected (select it if necessary), and click **Send As Internet Fax** in the right pane, as shown in Figure 5-10.

2. The first time you use fax services, you will be prompted to sign up with a provider. Click **OK** to open your Web browser, and then follow the sign-up instructions on the Web site. There is often a fee for this service.

3. When finished, close your Web browser, and then repeat step 1. An e-mail message will open with your document attached as an image file, or you can attach a file to the e-mail message.

4. Fill in the **Fax Recipient**, **Fax Number**, and **Subject** fields. Click **Send**.

USE A FAX MODEM

This procedure requires that your fax modem be set up as a printer on your system. To send a fax using a fax modem:

1. Click the **File** tab, and click **Print**. The Print view appears displaying the print settings.

Continued . . .

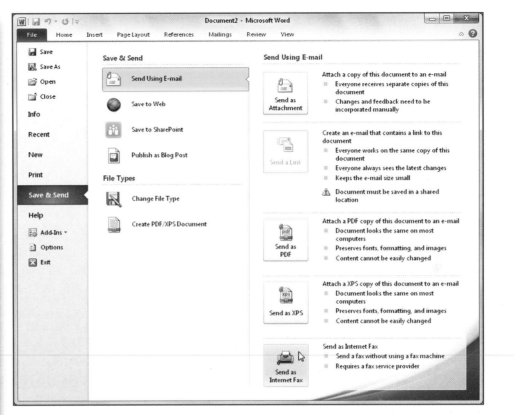

Figure 5-10: *Sending an Internet fax lets you fax a document using e-mail.*

5. To print one or more labels, insert a sheet of labels into the printer, and then click **Print**.

6. To save a sheet of labels for later editing or printing, click **New Document** and the labels will be displayed in the regular Word window. Save the labels document by clicking **File**, clicking **Save As**, and following the standard steps to save a file.

FAXING *(Continued)*

2. Click the **Printer** drop-down list to open it, click **Fax**, select what to print and other settings, and click **Print**. The first time you do this, the Fax Setup window will open. After that, you'll go directly to the New Fax message form and you can jump to step 4.

3. Click **Connect To A Fax Modem**, enter a name for the fax, and click **Next**. Select how you want to receive faxes, and click **Continue** when Windows asks for confirmation.

4. A New Fax message form will open, as shown in Figure 5-11. Your Word document will be attached as an image file. Type the fax number in the To text box, the subject, and any message.

5. Click **Send**. You should hear your modem dialing the number and sending the fax.

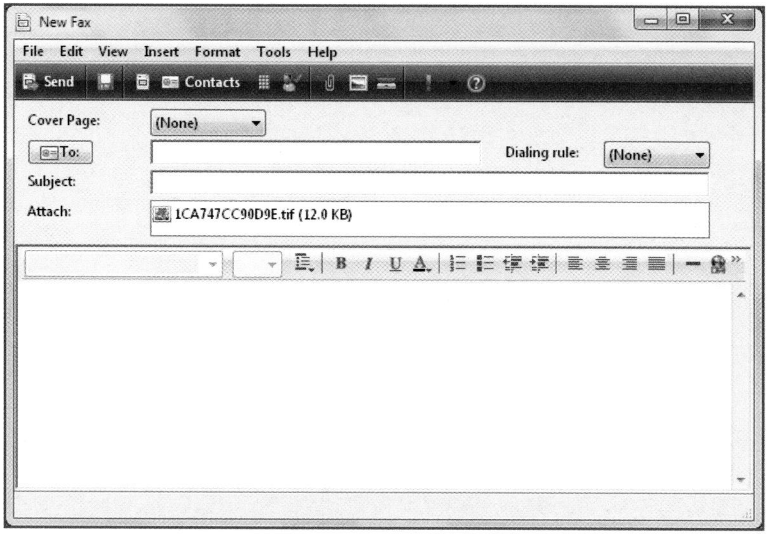

HP Photosmart 2600 series on ASUS
Ready

Adobe PDF
Ready

Fax
Ready

Quicken PDF Printer
Ready

Snagit 10
Ready

Add Printer...

Print to File

TIP

You cannot use the Mail Merge feature unless a document is open, although it can be a blank document.

NOTE

Word also allows you to take a list other than a mailing list—a parts list, for example, and merge it with a document to create a catalog or directory.

Figure 5-11: **With e-mail, faxing has become less popular, but it is still useful.**

Merge Lists with Letters and Envelopes

The *Mail Merge* feature allows you to combine a mailing list with a document to send the same thing to a number of people. You can merge a mailing list with letters, e-mail messages, envelopes, and labels. A mail merge combines two kinds of documents: the *main document*, which is the text of the document—for example, the body of a letter, and the *data source*, which is the information that changes with each copy of the document—for example, the individual names and addresses of the people who will be receiving the letter.

The main document has two parts: static text and merge fields. *Static text* is text that does not change—for example, the body of a letter. *Merge fields* are placeholders that indicate where information from the list or data source goes. For example, in a form letter, "Dear" would be static text, while <<First Name>>

You can e-mail documents that you create in Word as attachments to e-mail messages. To attach and send a document in an e-mail:

1. Click the **File** tab, click **Save & Send**, and then click **Send Using E-mail**. Displayed in the right pane are five choices about how you want to send the open Word document to your e-mail message:

   - As an attached Word (.docx) file that can be edited by the recipient

   - As a link to a file that has been stored on an Internet or intranet shared server

   - As an attached Adobe PDF file that is difficult to edit

   - As an attached Microsoft XPS file that is difficult to edit

   - As an Internet fax, as explained in the "Faxing" QuickSteps

2. Click your choice. A new e-mail message is opened with your document title automatically displayed in the Subject line and the document automatically attached to the e-mail.

3. Fill in the **To** and possibly **Cc** fields (if you are sending the document to multiple recipients), add anything you want to the body of the message, and click **Send**. Your e-mail message is sent with the document attached.

<<Last Name>> are merge fields. When the main document and the data source are combined, the result is "Dear John Doe," "Dear Jane Smith," and so on.

The following sections will show you how to create a data source, create a main document, and then merge them together using the six-step Mail Merge Wizard. You can also start out with an existing main document, an existing data source, or both and just use the parts of the wizard that you want to use.

Perform a Mail Merge

You can compose the static text in a document first and then insert the merge fields, or you can compose the static text and insert the merge fields as you go. You cannot insert merge fields into a main document until you have created the data source and associated it with your main document.

The mail merge process consists of the following six steps, which are described in the following sections:

- Select a document type
- Identify the starting document
- Select recipients
- Finalize the main document
- Preview the merge
- Complete the merge

SELECT THE TYPE AND IDENTIFY THE DOCUMENT

To begin the mail merge process:

1. In Word, open the document you want to use as your primary document, or open a new document (see Chapter 2).

2. Click the **Mailings** tab, click **Start Mail Merge** in the Start Mail Merge group, and click **Step By Step Mail Merge Wizard**. The Mail Merge task pane is displayed, as shown in Figure 5-12.

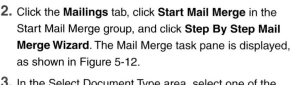

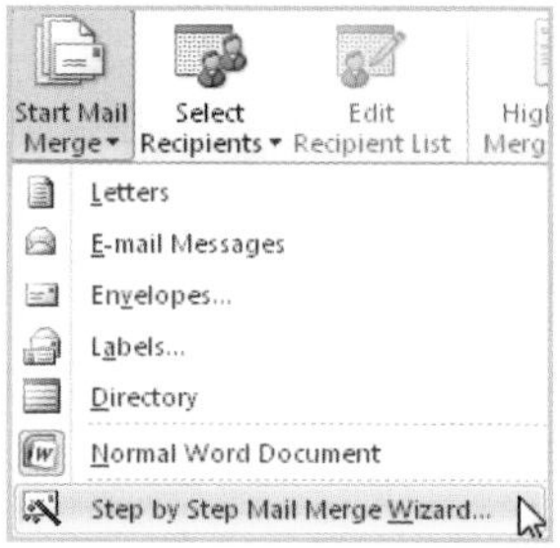

3. In the Select Document Type area, select one of the following options:

- **Letters** are form letters designed to be sent to multiple people.

- **E-mail Messages** are form letters designed to be sent to multiple people via e-mail.

- **Envelopes** are envelopes addressed to multiple people.

- **Labels** are labels addressed to multiple people.

- **Directory** is a collection of information regarding multiple items, such as a parts catalog or phone directory.

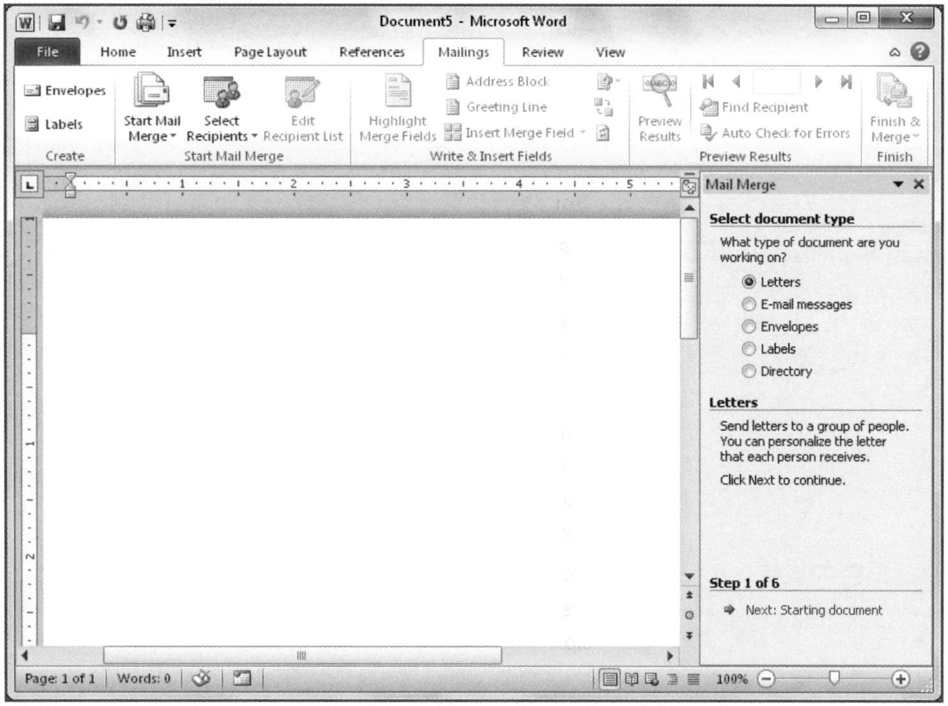

4. Click **Next: Starting Document** at the bottom of the task pane.

5. In the Select Starting Document area, select one of the following options:

- **Use The Current Document** uses the currently open document as the main document for the mail merge (it can initially be blank).

- **Start From A Template** uses a template you designate as the basis for the main document of the mail merge.

- **Start From Existing Document** uses an existing document you can retrieve from your computer or network and designate as the main document for the mail merge.

Figure 5-12: The Mail Merge task pane is where you begin the merge process.

TIP

Sort the merge recipients by clicking the field name at the top of the list that will provide the sort order. For example, if you want the list ordered alphabetically by last name, click **Last Name.**

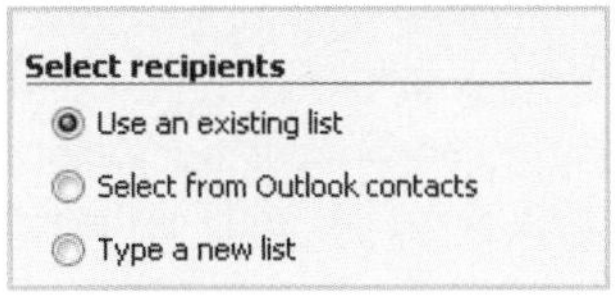

Select recipients
- ◉ Use an existing list
- ○ Select from Outlook contacts
- ○ Type a new list

SELECT RECIPIENTS

Your recipients are a name and address list, which is a data source. A data source has two parts: fields and records. A *field* is a category of information. For example, in a mailing list, First Name, Last Name, and Street Address are examples of fields. A *record* is a set of information across the fields for an individual. For example, in a mailing list, the record for John Doe would include information for all the relevant fields for this individual—his first and last name, street address, city, state, and ZIP code.

To set up a name and address list continuing from the previous section:

1. Click **Next: Select Recipients** at the bottom of the task pane. In the Select Recipients area, click **Type A New List**.
2. Click **Create** in the middle of the pane in the Type A New List area. The New Address List dialog box appears, as shown in Figure 5-13.
3. Enter the information for the first record in the fields you want to use. You may want to delete some of the columns or reorder them to facilitate entering data. Click **Customize Columns** to do that. Press **TAB** to move to the next field, or press **SHIFT+TAB** to move back to the previous field.
4. When you have completed all the fields you want for the first record, click **New Entry** and provide information for the second record.
5. Repeat steps 3 and 4 until you have added all the records you want to your list. When you are done, click **OK**.
6. A Save Address List dialog box appears. Type a file name for the list, select the folder on your computer where you want to save it, and click **Save**.
7. The Mail Merge Recipients dialog box appears, as shown in Figure 5-14. Clear the check boxes next to the recipients you do not want to include in the list. To make further changes to the name list, select the file name in the Data Source list box, and click **Edit**.
8. If you opened the Edit Data source dialog box, click **OK** to close it, and click **Yes** to update your recipient list. Click **OK** to close the Mail Merge Recipients dialog box.

New Address List

Type recipient information in the table. To add more entries, click New Entry.

Title ▼	First Name ▼	Last Name ▼	Company Name ▼	Address Line 1 ▼
▷				

New Entry   Find...
Delete Entry   Customize Columns...   OK   Cancel

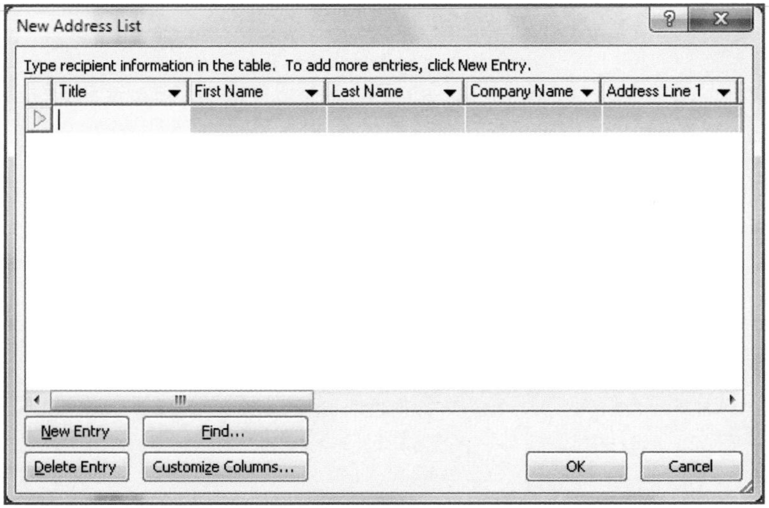

Figure 5-13: Use the New Address List dialog box to create your mailing list.

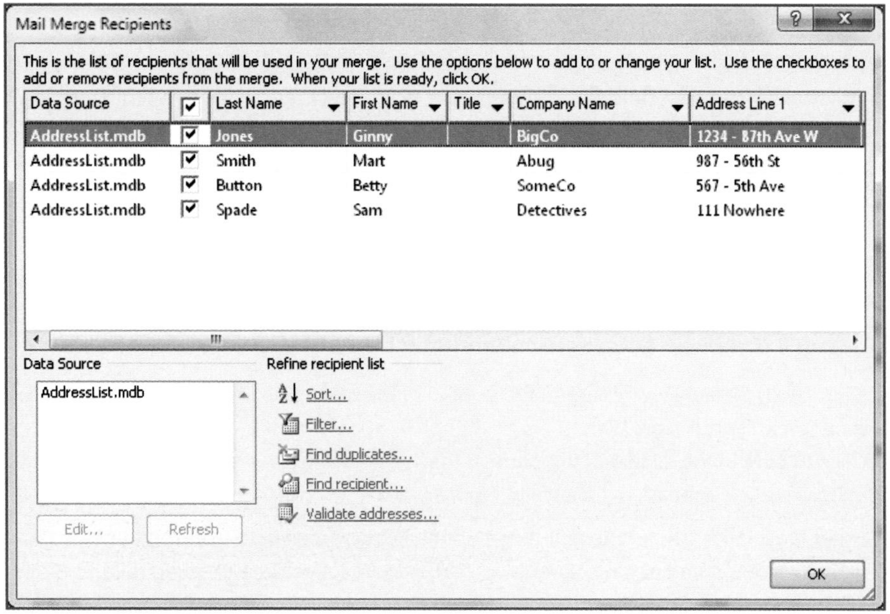

Figure 5-14: *Use the Mail Merge Recipients dialog box to manage your mailing list prior to completing the merge.*

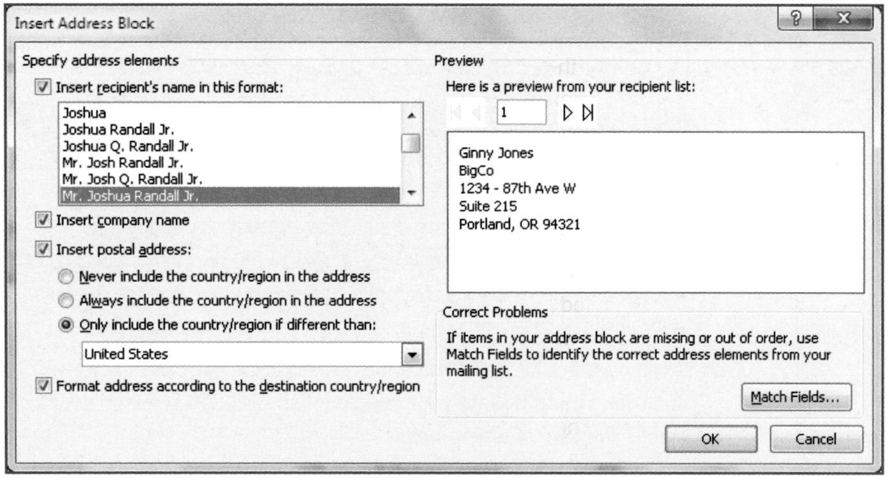

Figure 5-15: *You can customize the predefined field blocks to meet your mail merge needs.*

FINALIZE THE MAIN DOCUMENT

After creating the data source, you need to finalize the main document and insert the merge fields. This section will tell you how, after creating the main document, to insert merge fields in general. The example uses a letter; additional sections will show you how to use merge fields when creating envelopes and labels.

1. Continuing from the previous two sections, click **Next: Write Your Letter** at the bottom of the Mail Merge task pane. In the document pane, if it has not already been done, write the body of the letter—don't necessarily worry about the addressee and the greeting until you're satisfied with the text. (Although you can enter the fields and text together if you find it makes more sense to you.)

2. Place the cursor in the document where you want to insert a merge field, such as the addressee. Do one of the following:

   ● Select one of the three items in the top of the Mail Merge task pane if you want to insert a predefined block of merge fields, such as an address or a greeting. If you select anything other than More Items, a dialog box will appear and ask you to select options and formatting for that item (see Figure 5-15). When the block is the way you want it, click **OK**.

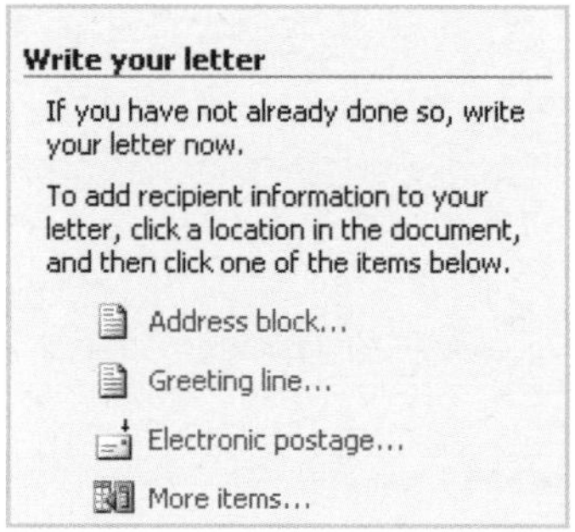

USING RULES

Rules (also called *Word Fields*) apply to merge fields or static text if certain conditions are met. One of the most common variable fields is the If/Then/Else rule. The IF rule performs one of two alternative actions, depending on a condition you specify. For example, the statement "If the weather is sunny, we'll go to the beach; if not, we'll go to the museum," specifies a condition that *must* be met (sunny weather) for a certain action to take place (going to the beach). If the condition is not met, an alternative action occurs (going to the museum).

This is an example of how using an IF rule in Word looks with the field codes turned on:

{IF { MERGEFIELD City } = "Seattle" "Please call our office." "Please call our distributor." }

This works as follows: If the current data record contains "Seattle" in the City field, then the first text ("Please call our office.") is printed in the merged document that results from that data record. If "Seattle" is not in the City field, then the second set of text ("Please call our distributor.") is printed. Using a rule is easy and doesn't require writing such a complex statement at all.

To insert a variable field into a merge document:

1. Position the insertion point where you want the rule.

2. In the Mailings tab, click **Rules** in the Write & Insert Fields group. A drop-down list appears.

Continued . . .

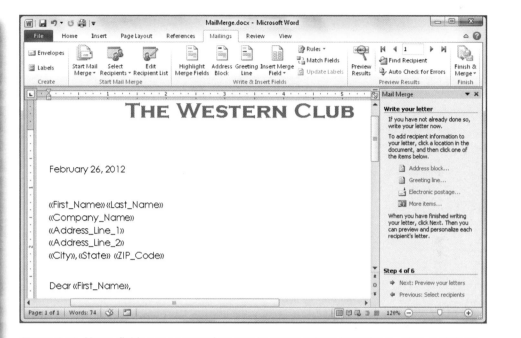

Figure 5-16: *Merge fields are a convenient way to create a form letter for multiple recipients.*

- Click **More Items** (the fourth item in the list) to insert an individual merge field. The Insert Merge Field dialog box appears. Verify that **Database Fields** is selected, and then select the field that you want to insert (for example, First Name or Last Name). Click **Insert** to insert the merge field into your document. Click **Close** when you are done inserting all the fields you need.

3. Add commas, spaces, and other punctuation marks to the address as needed. If you have some conditional fields that are printed only if some condition is met, like printing the country if it isn't the "United States," see the "Using Rules" QuickSteps." Figure 5-16 shows an example of a letter with merge fields inserted.

PREVIEW THE MERGE

Prior to actually completing the merge, the Mail Merge task pane presents you with an opportunity to review what the merged document will look like. This way, you can go back and make any last-minute changes to fine-tune your merge.

USING RULES *(Continued)*

3. Select the rule you want, for example, **If...Then... Else**.

> Ask...
> Fill-in...
> If...Then...Else...
> Merge Record #
> Merge Sequence #
> Next Record
> Next Record If...
> Set Bookmark...
> Skip Record If...

4. The Insert Word Field dialog box appears. Fill in the text boxes with your criteria, and click **OK** when finished.

Insert Word Field: IF

IF

Field name: City
Comparison: Equal to
Compare to: Seattle

Insert this text:
Please call our office.

Otherwise insert this text:
Please call our distributor.

[OK] [Cancel]

To preview a merge:

1. Continuing from the previous sections, click **Next: Preview Your Letters** at the bottom of the Mail Merge task pane.

Preview your letters

One of the merged letters is previewed here. To preview another letter, click one of the following:

[<<] Recipient: 4 [>>]

Find a recipient...

2. Use the right and left arrow buttons under Preview Your Letters in the Mail Merge task pane to scroll through the recipient list.

3. Click **Find A Recipient** to enter a recipient name and search for it in all fields or a particular field.

Find Entry

Find: Spade
Look in: ○ All fields
         ● This field: Last Name

[Find Next] [Cancel]

4. If you want to exclude a particular recipient from the merge, while that recipient is displayed, click **Exclude This Recipient**. (You can add the excluded recipient back by placing a check mark next to the name in the Mail Merge Recipient dialog box, which is displayed when you click **Edit Recipient List**.)

–Or–

Click **Edit Recipient List** to edit a particular recipient's information. If you click this link, the Mail Merge Recipients dialog box appears again (see Figure 5-13). Click the file name under the lower data source, click **Edit**, modify the information, click **OK**, and click **Yes** to update the recipient list. Click **OK** again to close the Mail Merge Recipients dialog box.

COMPLETE THE MERGE

The last step in performing a mail merge is to complete the merge; that is, to accept the preview of how the merge will look and direct Word to perform the merge.

To complete a merge:

1. Continuing from the previous sections, click **Next: Complete The Merge** at the bottom of the Mail Merge task pane.

2. If you wish, click **Edit Individual Letters** and select the letters to edit. The merged letters will appear as their own document in a new Word window, where you can make any changes you want and then print and save them as you normally would.

3. Click **Print** in the Merge area. The Merge To Printer dialog box appears.

4. Select one of the following options:

- **All** prints all records in the data source that have been included in the merge.
- **Current Record** prints only the record that is displayed in the document window.
- **From/To** prints a range of records you specify. Enter the starting and ending numbers in the text boxes.

5. Click **OK** when ready. The Print dialog box appears.

6. Select the print options you want, and click **OK**. Your merged document is printed.

7. When you are ready, save your merge document.

Merge to Envelopes

The process for merging to envelopes is similar to that for merging to letters; you must first define your envelope, type your return address if you don't have one defined, find your source of recipient addresses, insert the merge fields, preview your envelope results, finish the merge, and print the envelopes. This can be done with the Mail Merge Wizard, as described earlier with letters, or by using the options on the Mailings tab.

The following steps use the options on the Mailing tab.

1. In Word, open a new document. In the Mailings tab Start Mail Merge group, click **Start Mail Merge**, and click **Envelopes**. The Envelope Options dialog box appears, as shown in Figure 5-17.

2. Select the options you want from the Envelope Options and Printing Options tabs. Click **OK** when finished.

3. An envelope will appear with your default return address in the upper-left corner (if you have entered one, see "Print an Envelope" earlier in this chapter) and an indented paragraph mark where you will put the addressee. Type a return address, if needed, or make any changes you want to the return address and any other static text that you want. This will be printed on all envelopes.

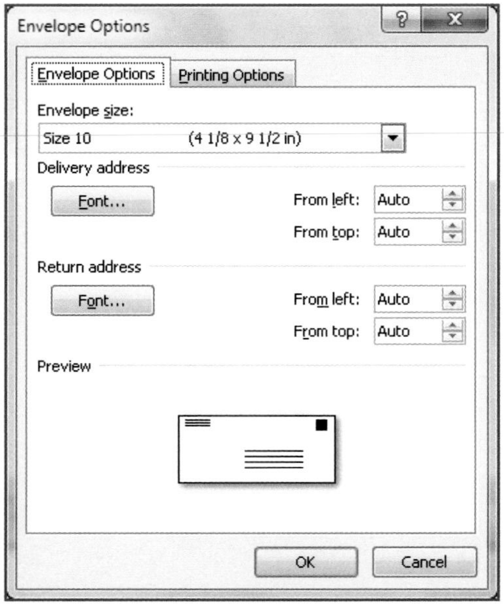

Figure 5-17: Word provides almost as many envelope sizes as it does paper sizes that you can use in printing.

4. In the Mailings tab Start Mail Merge group, click **Select Recipients**, choose the type of list you are using and follow the steps needed to identify or create the list; see the earlier section "Select Recipients."

5. When you have your recipient list ready, in the Mailing tab Write & Insert Fields group, click either **Address Block** or **Insert Merge Field**, depending on whether you want work with the address as a single predefined block or a set of discrete elements, and complete the steps needed to place the merge fields on the envelope. See "Finalize the Main Document" earlier in this chapter.

6. In the Mailings tab Preview Results group, click **Preview Results**. Your envelope should look similar to that shown in Figure 5-18. Use the **Previous Record** and **Next Record** buttons, or the record number text box to look through your merged envelopes.

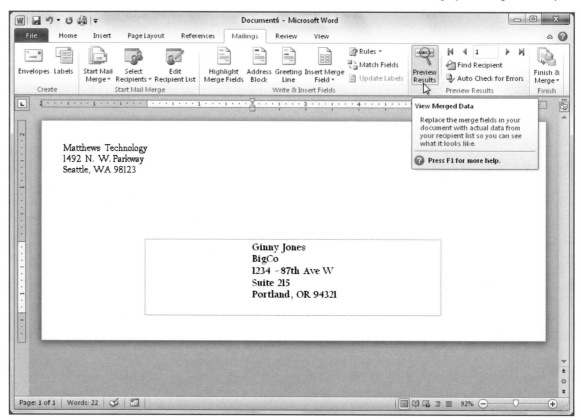

*Figure 5-18: **You can see how your merged envelope will look when completed prior to printing.***

7. When you are ready, in the Mailings tab Finish group, click **Finish & Merge**. If you want to make changes to some of the envelopes before they are printed, click **Edit Individual Documents**. The data will be merged to a new document that can then be modified. Otherwise, click **Print Documents**. Choose the records to be printed, and click **OK** to open the Print dialog box, where you can choose how the envelopes will be printed.

Label Options dialog box:

Label Options

Printer information
- ○ Continuous-feed printers
- ● Page printers   Tray: Default tray (Default) ▾

Label information
Label vendors: Avery US Letter ▾
Find updates on Office Online
Product number:
- 5147 Print or Write Name Badge Labels
- 5155 Easy Peel Return Address Labels
- 5159 Mailing Labels
- 5160 Easy Peel Address Labels
- 5161 Easy Peel Address Labels
- 5162 Easy Peel Address Labels

Label information
Type: Easy Peel Address Labels
Height: 1"
Width: 2.63"
Page size: 8.5" X 11"

Details...   New Label...   Delete   OK   Cancel

Merge to Labels

The process for merging to labels is similar to that for merging to letters and envelopes, and can be done with the Mail Merge Wizard, as described earlier with letters, or by using the options on the Mailings tab, as described with envelopes. The following steps use the options on the Mailing tab.

1. In Word, open a new document. In the Mailings tab Start Mail Merge group, click **Start Mail Merge**, and click **Labels**. The Label Options dialog box appears.

2. Select the options you want, and click **OK** when finished. A page formatted for labels will appear in Word.

3. In the Mailings tab Start Mail Merge group, click **Select Recipients**, choose the type of list you are using, and follow the steps needed to identify or create the list; see the earlier section "Select Recipients."

4. When you have your recipient list ready, click in the blank space for the first label. Then in the Mailing tab Write & Insert Fields group, click either **Address Block** or **Insert Merge Field**, depending on whether you want to work with the address as a single predefined block or a set of discrete elements, and complete the steps needed to place the merge fields on the envelope. See "Finalize the Main Document" earlier in this chapter.

5. In the Mailing tab Write & Insert Fields group, click **Update Labels** to copy the fields in the first label to all the labels, as shown in Figure 5-19.

6. In the Mailings tab Preview Results group, click **Preview Results**. Your labels should look something like this:

Ginny Jones	Mary Smith	Betty Button
BigCo	Abug	SomeCo
1234 - 87th Ave W, Suite 215	987 - 56th St,	567 - 5th Ave, Suite 3
Portland, OR 94321	Seattle, WA 98321	Seattle, WA 98765

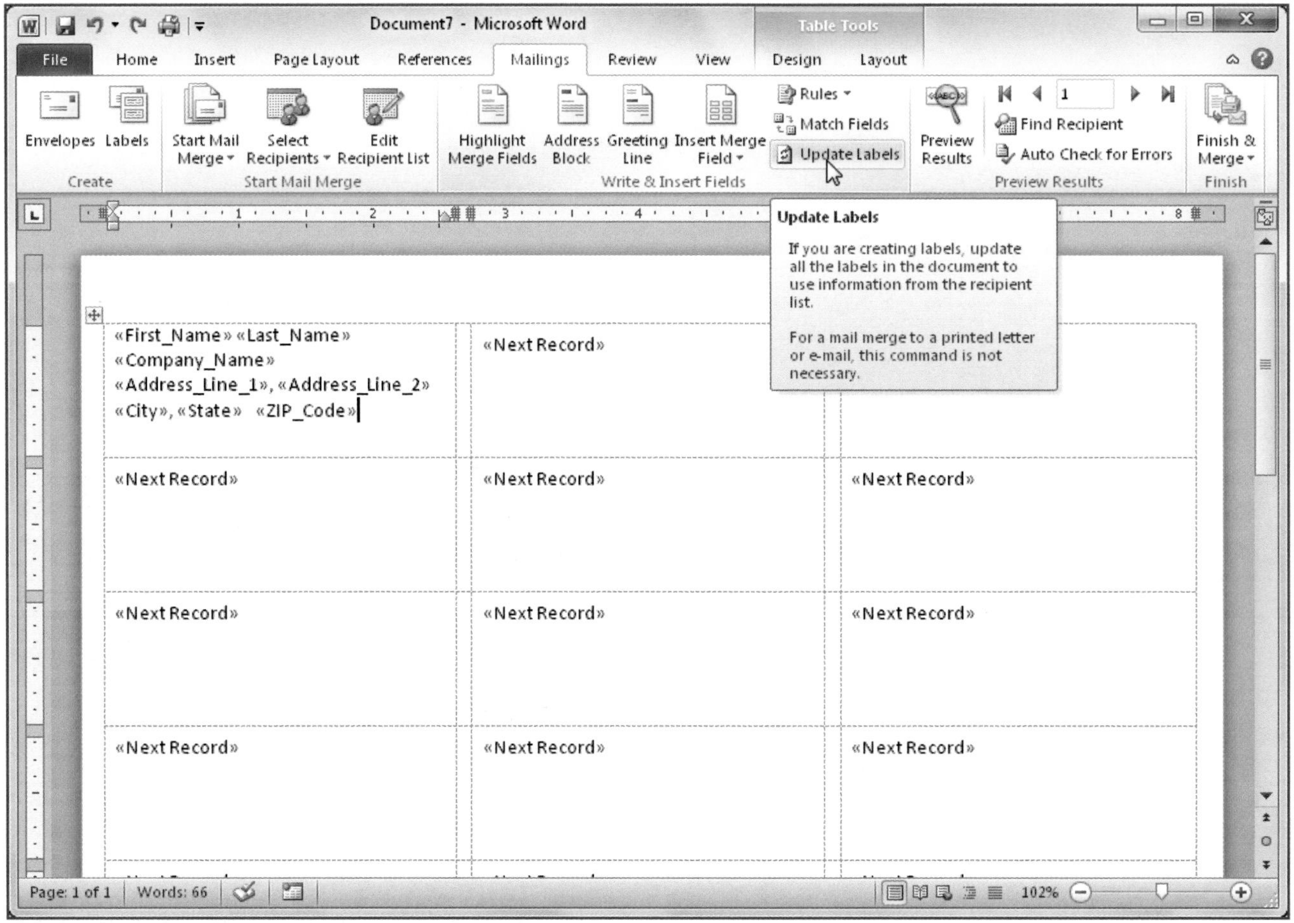

Figure 5-19: *You can replicate the fields in the first label to all the other labels.*

7. When you are ready, in the Mailings tab Finish group, click **Finish & Merge**. If you want to make changes to some of the envelopes before they are printed, click **Edit Individual Documents**. The data will be merged to a new document that can then be modified. Otherwise, click **Print Documents**. Choose the records to be printed, and click **OK** to open the Print dialog box, where you can choose how the envelopes will be printed.

Chapter 6

Using Tables

Documents can be composed of text only, but using visual elements to support information helps emphasize, organize, and clarify your written words. *Tables* provide a familiar column-and-row matrix that lets you easily define terms, list items, and lay out data in a convenient and organized manner. Word provides extensive features that support creating, using, and formatting tables to accomplish a variety of purposes. (See Chapters 7 and 8 for more information on the use of tables—Chapter 7 covers graphics, and Chapter 8 describes using charts.)

Create Tables

Tables allow you to divide a portion of a page into rows and columns that create *cells* at their intersections. Tables can be used to systematically arrange information in rows and columns, or they can be used to lay out text and graphics in a document.

QUICK**FACTS**

DISSECTING A TABLE

A table comes with an extensive vocabulary of terms that describe many of its elements, features, and how it's used, as shown in Figure 6-1.

Some of the ways that you can use tables are:

- Tabular data display, with or without cell borders
- Side-by-side columns of text
- Aligning labels and boxes for forms
- Separating and positioning text and graphics
- Placing borders around text or graphics
- Placing text on both sides of graphics or vice versa
- Adding color to backgrounds, text, and graphics

Create a Table

When you create a table, you can specify the number of rows and columns in it. In addition, depending on how you created the table, you can select how the columns' width is determined and choose a table style. In all cases, you can easily modify the table attributes after the original table displays in your document. With the document open in Word, place the insertion point at the appropriate location in the document where you want a table.

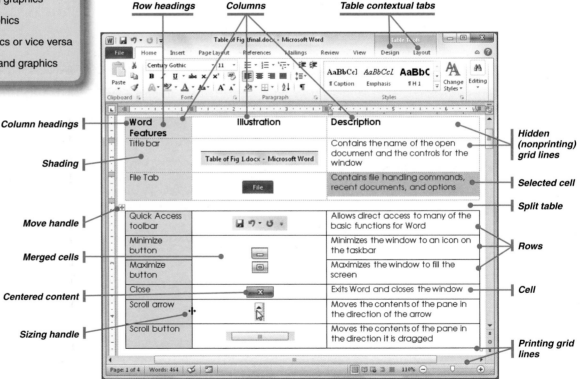

Figure 6-1: *Tables have a vocabulary all their own.*

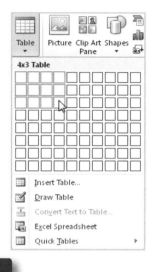

INSERT A TABLE QUICKLY

The Insert tab Tables group offers a variety of methods for creating a table using the default settings. The quickest method is to use the Insert tab.

1. In the Insert tab Tables group, click the **Table** down arrow. In the drop-down menu that opens, click the lower-right cell needed to give you the number of rows and columns you want.

2. Type the information you want in the table, pressing **TAB** as needed to move from cell to cell (see the "Entering Information" QuickSteps later in this chapter).

INSERT A TABLE FROM A DIALOG BOX

The Insert Table dialog box provides several options when initially setting up a table.

1. In the Insert tab Tables group, click the **Table** down arrow. In the drop-down menu that opens, click **Insert Table**. The Insert Table dialog box appears, as shown in Figure 6-2.

> Insert Table... ▷

  a. Under Table Size, click the respective spinners or enter a value to determine the number of rows and columns in the table.

  b. Under AutoFit Behavior, choose a fixed column width by clicking the spinner or entering a value (*Auto*, the default, sizes the columns equally so that they fill the available width of the table), have Word set each column's width to fit the contents in each column, or have Word size the columns to fit the window the table is in. (See "Change Column Width and Row Height" later in the chapter for more ways to adjust column width after a table is created.)

2. If you want the size settings you choose to apply to future tables you create, select the **Remember Dimensions For New Tables** check box.

3. Click **OK** to display the table in your document.

DRAW A TABLE

The most hands-on way to create a table is to draw it.

1. With the document open in Word, scroll to the location where you want to draw a table.

2. In the Insert tab Tables group, click the **Table** down arrow. In the drop-down menu that opens, click **Draw Table**. The mouse pointer turns into a pencil.

> Draw Table ▷   ⌀

TIP

If you want to insert a table that is larger than the 8 rows by 10 columns shown in the Table drop-down menu, you can easily add rows or columns to an initial table that you create from the menu. See "Change the Table Size" later in this chapter.

*Figure 6-2: **You can determine several table attributes when creating a table using the Insert Table dialog box.***

NOTE

It is not important to get the initial size and grid perfectly aligned. You can adjust them after the table has been drawn.

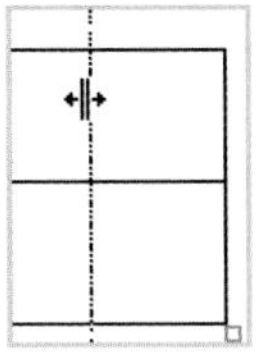

NOTE

If you make a mistake or change your mind, you can erase individual table segments with the Table Eraser. See the Note near "Remove Cells, Rows, and Columns," later in this chapter.

3. Place the pencil-shaped pointer where you want the upper-left corner of the table, and drag it diagonally across and down the page, creating a table outline that is the height and width of the outer border of the table you want.

4. Place the pencil-shaped pointer on the top border at the location of the right edge of the leftmost column you want, and drag down to the bottom border. Repeat that for the other columns you want.

5. Place the pencil-shaped pointer on the left border at the location of the bottom of the topmost row you want, and drag to the rightmost edge where you want the row to end. This may not be the last column in the table (the right outer border) if you don't want the border to span the table. Repeat that for the other rows you want.

6. When you are done drawing, press **ESC** to return the pencil-shaped pointer to the I-beam pointer.

7. If you want to adjust the location of any of the outer borders or the row or column borders, point at the border you want to adjust. The mouse pointer will turn into a double-headed resize arrow. Drag the selected line to the location you want it.

8. Enter the information you want in the table, pressing **TAB** as needed to move from cell to cell.

Use Table Tools

Once you have created a table, you have two sets of tools with which to work with it: the table contextual tabs in the ribbon and the context menus that open when you right-click in a table.

USE THE TABLE'S CONTEXTUAL TABS

When you create a table in Word 2010, the ribbon automatically displays two table-related tabs: Table Tools Design and Table Tools Layout. The Table Tools Design tab, shown in Figure 6-3, allows you to apply various styles to tables, as well as apply shading, customize the border, and draw and erase tables or their segments.

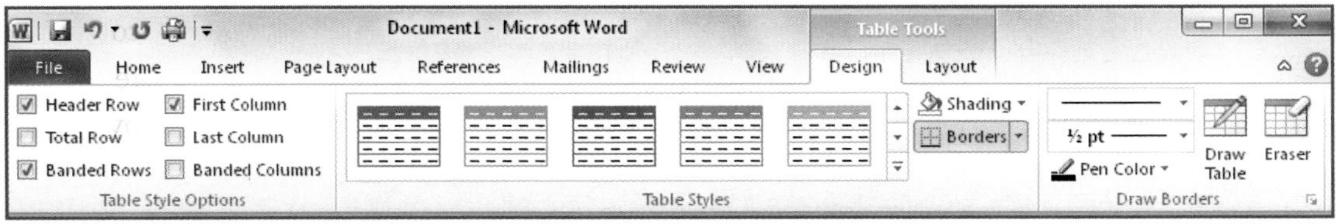

Figure 6-3: The Table Tools Design tab is used to change the style of a table.

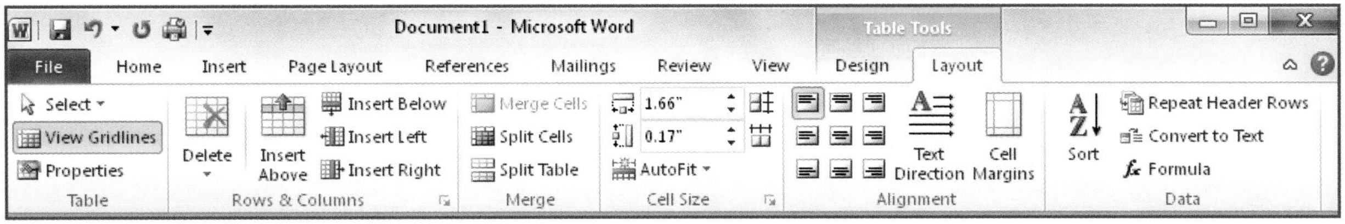

Figure 6-4: *The Table Tools Layout tab is used to modify tables.*

QUICKSTEPS

SELECTING TABLES, ROWS, COLUMNS, OR CELLS

Before you can perform many actions in a table, you must first select the element you are working with. With the table open in Word, perform any of the actions discussed in the following sections.

SELECT A TABLE

Click the **Move Handle** located in the upper-left area of the table.

–Or–

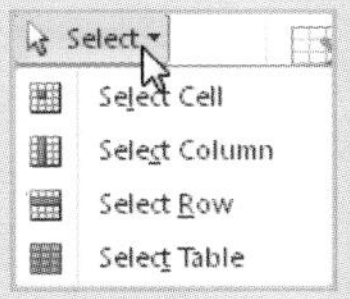

Click anywhere in the table, and in the Table Tools Layout tab Table group, click **Select** and click **Select Table**.

SELECT ROWS OR COLUMNS BY CLICKING

• Move the mouse pointer to the left border, if selecting rows, so that the pointer becomes an angled rightward-pointing arrow, and then click.

• Move the mouse pointer to the top border, if selecting columns, so that the pointer becomes a vertical black arrow, and then click.

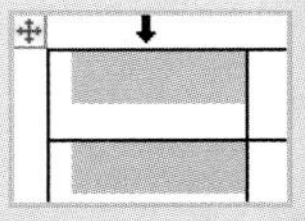

–Or–

Continued . . .

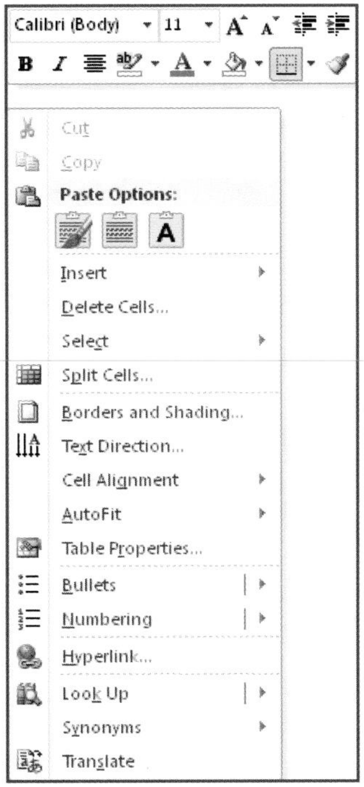

Figure 6-5: *The context menu allows you to format and modify tables.*

The Table Tools Layout tab, shown in Figure 6-4, allows you to modify tables in many different ways, including selecting, deleting, and inserting various table elements, as well as working with cells and their contents.

Both contextual tabs are discussed throughout this chapter.

USE THE TABLE'S CONTEXT MENU

When you right-click a table or its contents, you see a context menu that, depending on what you clicked, may look similar to Figure 6-5. This context menu allows you to do many of the formatting tasks in the Home tab, as well as many of the table modification tasks in the Layout tab.

Change the Table Size

Rows, columns, and cells can be added to a table using the Layout tab Rows & Columns group or the context menus. You can also change a table's size by removing elements, splitting a table, or resizing the overall dimensions.

QUICKSTEPS

SELECTING TABLES, ROWS, COLUMNS, OR CELLS *(Continued)*

1. Click anywhere in the row or column you want to select.

2. In the Table Tools Layout tab Table group, click **Select** and click **Select Column** or **Select Row**.

SELECT ROWS OR COLUMNS BY DRAGGING

Move the mouse to the first cell of the row or column, and drag it to the last cell. You can easily select multiple rows and/or columns this way.

SELECT A CELL BY CLICKING

1. Move the mouse pointer to the left border of the cell so that the pointer becomes an angled rightward-pointing black arrow.

2. Click the mouse to select the cell.

SELECT A CELL FROM THE MENU

1. Click your mouse pointer in the cell you want selected.

2. In the Layout tab Table group, click **Select** and click **Select Cell**.

SELECT CELLS BY DRAGGING

Place your mouse pointer in the upper-leftmost cell you want to select, and drag down and to the right across the remaining cells in the range you want selected, as shown in Figure 6-6. (If you are left-handed, you might find it easier to click in the upper-rightmost cell and then drag down and to the left.)

Click here ...   **... and drag...**   **...to here to select a range of cells**

Superior Office Supply	1st Qtr	2nd Qtr	3rd Qtr	4thQtr	Total
Paper Supplies	$23,567	$35,938	$38,210	$39,876	$137,591
Writing Instruments	5,482	5,836	5,923	6,082	$23,323
Cards and Books	14,986	15,021	15,934	16,732	$62,673
Forms	2,342	2,756	3,456	3,678	$12,232
Labels	3,522	4,621	5,361	5,476	$18,980
Equipment	45,328	47,934	51,830	55,638	$200,730
Furniture	37,278	38,429	38,328	39,103	$153,138
Total	$132,505	$150,535	$159,042	$166,585	$608,667

Figure 6-6: **The fastest way to select contiguous cells is to drag across them.**

ADD CELLS

Cells can be added to a table above and to the left of existing cells.

1. Select the cells adjacent to where you want to add the new cells. (To add a single cell, select only the cell below or to the right of where you want the new cell. If adding more than one cell, you can select the number of cells you want added, and an equal number will be added above or to the left of your selection.) See the "Selecting Tables, Rows, Columns, or Cells" QuickSteps.

2. In the Layout tab Rows & Columns group, click the **Dialog Box Launcher**.

   –Or–

   Right-click the existing cell, click **Insert**, and click **Insert Cells**.

   In either case, the Insert Cells dialog box appears.

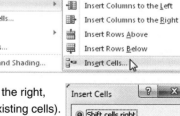

3. In the Insert Cells dialog box, click **Shift Cells Right** (existing cells are "pushed" to the right, inserting the new cell or cells to the left of the existing cells).

   –Or–

   Click **Shift Cells Down** (existing cells are "pushed" down, inserting the new cells above the existing cells).

4. Click **OK**.

INSERT ROWS OR COLUMNS

You can quickly add rows or columns from either the Layout tab Rows & Columns group or the context menu.

1. Select the rows or columns in the table next to where you want to add rows or columns (the number of rows or columns added will equal the number of rows or columns selected).

2. In the Layout tab Rows & Columns group, click **Insert Above** or **Insert Below** (for new rows) or **Insert Left** or **Insert Right** (for new columns).

   –Or–

   Right-click an existing row or column, click **Insert**, and click **Insert Columns To The Left**, **Insert Columns To The Right**, **Insert Rows Above**, or **Insert Rows Below**.

RESIZE BY DRAGGING

1. In the View tab Document Views group, click **Print Layout** (the sizing handle doesn't display in other views).

2. Place your mouse over the table whose size you want to change, and drag the sizing handle that appears in the lower-right corner of the table to increase or decrease the table size. The rows and columns increase or decrease proportionately within the constraints of the cell contents.

ADD ROWS AT THE BOTTOM OF A TABLE

As you are entering information into a table and you reach the bottom-rightmost cell, simply pressing **TAB** will add another row to the table.

REMOVE CELLS, ROWS, AND COLUMNS

1. Select the cells, rows, or columns you want to remove (see the QuickSteps "Selecting Tables, Rows, Columns, or Cells").

2. Right-click the selection.

3. Click **Delete Columns** to remove selected columns.

   –Or–

   Click **Delete Rows** to remove selected rows.

   –Or–

   Click **Delete Cells** to open the Delete Cells dialog box. Choose whether to fill the vacant area of the table by shifting cells to the left or up. Click **OK**.

NOTE

You can also remove parts of a table by erasing the elements you don't want. In the Table Tools Design tab Draw Borders group, click **Eraser**. Drag a rectangle using the eraser pointer over the elements you want removed. The borders of the elements to be removed within the red rectangular selection are bolded. Release the mouse button to remove the selected elements (when cells are removed within the interior of the table, the "hole" that remains is one large merged cell). Press **ESC** to return to the standard pointer, or click the **Eraser** button again.

TIP

To see the dimensions of each column's width or each row's height, hold down **ALT** as you drag a column or row border. The horizontal ruler displays the column widths, and the vertical ruler displays the row heights.

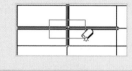

Figure 6-7: *You can set exact dimensions for each column's width or as a percentage of the table width.*

SPLIT A TABLE

You can divide a table along any of its rows to split it into segments. Word will divide longer tables when it creates automatic page breaks, although you might find it handy to be able to control exactly where the break occurs in the table.

1. Click a cell in the row below where you want the split to occur.
2. In the Table Tools Layout tab Merge Group, click **Split Table**. A blank paragraph is inserted between the two tables (see Figure 6-1).

Change Column Width and Row Height

By default, tables are created with equal column widths spanning the width of the table (margin-to-margin across the document) unless you manually draw them. You can change each column to a specific width you set or use AutoFit to adjust the width to fit the longest entry in the column. Row heights change vertically as needed to accommodate lines of text or larger font sizes (all cells in a row increase to match the highest cell in the row).

CHANGE COLUMN WIDTH AND ROW HEIGHT BY DRAGGING

1. Place the mouse pointer on the right border of the column whose width you want to change or on the bottom border of the row height you want to change. The mouse pointer changes to a resize pointer, showing the opposing directions in which you can drag.
2. Drag the border to increase or decrease the size.

CHANGE COLUMN WIDTH PRECISELY

1. Right-click the table that contains the columns whose width you want to change, and click **Table Properties** on the context menu.
2. In the Table Properties dialog box, click the **Column** tab, shown in Figure 6-7.
3. Click **Previous Column** or **Next Column** to select the initial column you want to set. (You may need to drag the dialog box to one side to see the table beneath it.)
4. Click the **Preferred Width** check box, and set a width in inches or as a percentage of the table width.
5. Repeat steps 3 and 4 to change the width of other columns.
6. Click **OK**.

CHANGE COLUMN WIDTH TO FIT CONTENTS

You can use AutoFit to dynamically adjust the column widths in a table to fit the longest single-line entry in that column.

Right-click the table whose columns you want to adjust to fit their content, click **AutoFit**, and click **AutoFit To Contents**. (To return to the default text-wrapping behavior, right-click the table, click **AutoFit**, and click **Fixed Column Width**. You will need to manually narrow any wide column widths to wrap text that has stretched the cell width.)

SPACE COLUMN WIDTHS OR ROW HEIGHTS EQUALLY

1. Select the columns or rows that you want to make the same size, and right-click that selection to open the context menu.

2. Click **Distribute Columns Evenly** to space selected column widths equally.

   –Or–

   Click **Distribute Rows Evenly** to space selected row heights equally.

Work with Tables

Tables can be set up for many purposes, and Word provides features to support many of them. You can use special shortcut key combinations to move through the cells in a table, you can sort lists, and you can work with formulas. You can also move, copy, and delete tables.

Sort Data

You can sort information in ascending or descending order according to the values in one or more columns. You can sort an entire table or selected cells (all data in the table or range is realigned so that the data in each row remains the same, even though the row might be placed in a different order than it was originally) or just a column (data in columns outside the sorted column does not change order).

ENTERING INFORMATION (Continued)

MOVE AROUND IN A TABLE

The most straightforward way to move between cells in a table as you are entering data is to press **TAB**. You can also simply click the cell where you want to add text or graphics. However, if you're adding a lot of data to a table, it's more efficient to keep your hands on the keyboard. See Table 6-1 for several keyboard shortcuts you can use.

MOVE CONTENT AROUND

You can cut and copy text and other content using the same techniques for basic text. Just select the content in the cells you want and, for example, press **CTRL+C** to copy the content. When pasting the content into other cells in the table, place the insertion point in the cell where you want the content to appear. Press **CTRL+V**. Any content in existing cells overlaid by the range of pasted cells will be overwritten with the new content.

TO MOVE TO...	PRESS...
Cells to the right and down at row end (with cell contents selected)	**TAB**
Cells to the left and up at row end (with cell contents selected)	**SHIFT+TAB**
First cell in a column	**ALT+PAGE UP**
Last cell in a column	**ALT+PAGE DOWN**
First cell in a row	**ALT+HOME**
Last cell in a row	**ALT+END**

Table 6-1: **Keyboard Shortcuts to Move Around in a Table**

SORT A TABLE OR SELECTED CELLS

1. Place your insertion point in the table you want to sort, or select a range of cells to sort.
2. In the Layout tab Data group, click **Sort**. The Sort dialog box appears, as shown in Figure 6-8.
3. Click the **Sort By** down arrow, and click the column of primary importance in determining the sort order in the drop-down list (if the columns have headings, select one of the titles; if there are no headings, select a column based on numbers that start with the leftmost column).
4. Click the **Type** down arrow, and click whether the column contains numbers, dates, or anything else (the Text option sorts anything). Click **Ascending** or **Descending**.

5. Click the first **Then By** down arrow, and click the column in the drop-down list that you want to base the sort on that is secondary in importance. Select the type of information in the column, and click **Ascending** or **Descending**.
6. Repeat, if necessary, for the second Then By section to sort by a third column of information.
7. Under My List Has, click whether the table or selection has a heading row.
8. Click **OK** when finished. An example of a table sorted by two columns is shown in Figure 6-9.

Figure 6-8: **You can reorganize information in a table by sorting by one or more columns in ascending or descending order.**

Primary sort arranges list by publisher **Secondary sort arranges list by date within publisher**

ISBN-13	Category	Title	Author	Pub Date	Price
9780072229387	Computers	HT DO EVERYTHING W/ACCESS 2003	ANDERSEN VIRGINIA	8/1/2003	26.99
9780072232288	Computers	MS OFFICE EXCEL 2003 QUICKSTEP	CRONAN JOHN	1/1/2004	19.99
9780072232295	Computers	MS OFFICE ACCESS 2003 QUICKSTE	CRONAN JOHN	2/1/2004	16.99
9780072263725	Computers	MICROSOFT OFFICE EXCEL 2007 QU	CRONAN JOHN	11/1/2006	19.99
9780072263718	Computers	MICROSOFT OFFICE ACCESS 2007 Q	CRONAN JOHN	1/1/2007	16.99
9780071601450	Computers	BUILD AN EBAY BUSINESS QUICKST	CRONAN JOHN	12/1/2008	19.99
9780071487672	Computers	QUICKBOOKS 2007 QUICKSTEPS	FOX CINDY	1/1/2007	19.99
9780071497879	Computers	CISSP ALLINONE EXAM GDE E04	HARRIS SHON	11/1/2007	79.99
9780072263879	Computers	HOW TO DO EVERYTHING W/IPOD	HART-DAVIS GUY	1/1/2008	24.99
9780071487641	Computers	A+ CERTIFICATION STUDY GDE	HOLCOMBE JANE	6/1/2007	49.99

Figure 6-9: **Sort by multiple columns to arrange entries that have the same secondary sort value.**

SORT A SINGLE COLUMN

You can sort a single column, independent of the rest of the table, but make sure
that is what you want, because there is no way to return the table to the way it
was originally.

1. Select the column you want to sort (see the QuickSteps "Selecting Tables, Rows,
   Columns, or Cells").
2. In the Layout tab Data group, click **Sort**.
3. In the Sort dialog box, click **Options**.   [Options...]
4. In the Sort Options dialog box, click the **Sort Column Only** check
   box. 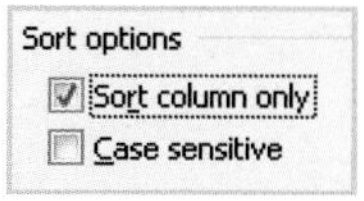
5. Click **OK** twice.

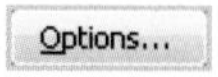

Sort options
- ☑ Sort column only
- ☐ Case sensitive

SORT BY MORE THAN ONE FIELD IN A COLUMN

If you combine two or more fields of information in a single column, such
as city, county, and state (for example, Everett, Snohomish, WA), instead of
splitting them out into separate columns, you can sort your list by choosing
which fields to sort by.

1. Place your insertion point in the table.
2. In the Layout tab Data group, click **Sort**.

QUICKSTEPS

MOVING AND COPYING TABLES, COLUMNS, AND ROWS

A table is easily moved or copied by dragging its move handle (the move handle is only displayed when viewing the document in Print Layout view). Columns and rows also can be dragged into new positions.

MOVE A TABLE

1. Point at the upper-leftmost cell in the table you want to move to display its move handle.

   Title

2. Drag the table to the position you want.

COPY A TABLE

Hold **CTRL** and drag the table's move handle to position where you want the copy of the table.

–Or–

In the Layout tab Table group, click **Select** and click **Select Table**. Press **CTRL+C** to copy the table to the Clipboard. Place your insertion point where you want the new table, and press **CTRL+V**.

MOVE COLUMNS AND ROWS

1. Select the columns or rows you want to move (see the QuickSteps "Selecting Tables, Rows, Columns, or Cells" earlier in the chapter).

2. Select the columns or rows that will be to the right (if a column) or below (if a row) of where you want the elements moved.

COPY COLUMNS AND ROWS

Use the previous procedure for moving columns and rows, except hold down **CTRL** while dragging to leave the selected elements in place while adding a copy of them to the new location.

Windows 7
Title

3. In the Sort dialog box, click **Options**. In the Sort Options dialog box, under Separate Fields At, click the character used to separate the fields in a single column, or click **Other** and type the separator character. Click **OK** to close the Sort Options dialog box.

Separate fields at
◉ Tabs
○ Commas
○ Other: -

4. In the Sort dialog box, click the **Sort By** down arrow, and click the primary column that contains multiple fields. Click the **Type** down arrow, click an information type, and click **Ascending** or **Descending**. Click the **Using** down arrow, and click the record group, such as paragraphs, or Field 1, Field 2, etc.

5. Use the **Then By** sections if you want to sort by additional columns or fields.

6. Click **OK** when finished.

Calculate Values Using Formulas

You can use formulas in tables to perform arithmetic calculations and provide a result, either by putting together your own formulas or using an AutoSum feature.

ASSEMBLE YOUR OWN FORMULAS

1. Place your mouse pointer in the cell where you want the result displayed.

2. In the Layout tab Data group, click **Formula** _fx_ Formula. The Formula dialog box appears, as shown in Figure 6-10.

3. In the Formula text box, keep the Word-suggested formula, apply a number format, and click **OK** to display the result.

   –Or–

   Delete everything except the equal (=) sign.

4. Click the **Paste Function** down arrow, and click the function you want to use.

Paste function:

ABS
AND
AVERAGE
COUNT
DEFINED
FALSE
IF
INT

Formula

Formula:
=SUM(ABOVE)

Number format:

Paste function: Paste bookmark:

OK   Cancel

*Figure 6-10: **The Formula dialog box provides tools to set up formulas for basic calculations.***

QUICKSTEPS

WORKING WITH FORMULAS

Word provides a basic spreadsheet capability with tables to perform calculations on numeric entries. Knowing a number of terms and concepts used when working with formulas will make using them in tables much easier. (Any number-crunching other than basic calculations using simple formulas should be relegated to Microsoft Excel, the Office product devoted to performing serious work with numbers. See *Microsoft Office Excel 2010 QuickSteps*, published by McGraw-Hill, for more information on working with formulas, functions, and worksheets.) Common terms and concepts are as follows:

- **Syntax** is the set of rules Word uses for you to communicate how to perform calculations with formulas. For instance, to identify to Word that a calculation is to be performed, you must precede the calculation with an equal sign.

- **Cell reference** is the scheme formulas use to provide a unique address for each cell, consisting of its column-and-row intersection. Columns are designated alphabetically, starting with the leftmost column as "A"; rows are sequentially numbered from top to bottom, with the topmost row as "1." For example, the third cell from the left in the second row would be identified as cell C2.

- **Cell reference operators** are the syntax used to identify multiple cells in a formula. For example, to add the values in cells A1, A2, B1, and B2, you use commas to list the cells the function is to sum: =SUM(A1,A2,B1,B2) or use a colon (:) operator to identify a range of contiguous cells: =SUM(A1:B2).

Continued ...

---

5. In the Formula text box, type the cell references or attribute the function applies to between the parentheses following the function.

6. Click the **Number Format** down arrow, and click the style you want applied to the result.

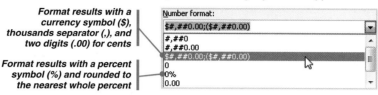

Format results with a currency symbol ($), thousands separator (,), and two digits (.00) for cents

Format results with a percent symbol (%) and rounded to the nearest whole percent

Number format:
$#,##0.00;($#,##0.00)
#,##0
#,##0.00
$#,##0.00;($#,##0.00)
0
0%
0.00

7. Click **OK** to display the result.

Convert Tables to Text and Text to Tables

If you have information in text format, Word can convert it to a table and similarly convert information in a table to ordinary text.

CONVERT TEXT TO A TABLE

Converting text to a table requires that the text be appropriately formatted with tabs, commas, or another character between columns and a separate character, like a paragraph mark, between rows.

1. Drag to select the text you want to convert to a table. In the Insert tab Tables group, click **Table** and click **Convert Text To Table**. The Convert Text To Table dialog box appears. Do not be concerned if the number of rows and columns do not yet match your expectations.

Convert Text to Table...

Convert Text to Table

Table size
Number of columns: 3
Number of rows: 4

AutoFit behavior
○ Fixed column width: Auto
○ AutoFit to contents
○ AutoFit to window

Separate text at
○ Paragraphs ○ Commas
● Tabs ○ Other: -

OK   Cancel

2. Under Separate Text At, click the character used to separate columns of text, or click **Other** and type the character. The number of columns and rows should now reflect how you formatted the text to be displayed in a table.

3. Under AutoFit Behavior, choose a fixed column width by clicking the spinner or entering a value (*Auto*, the default, sizes columns equally so that they fill the available width of the table), having Word set each column's width so that the contents fit in

QUICKSTEPS

WORKING WITH FORMULAS *(Continued)*

- **Functions** are prewritten formulas that you can use to perform specific tasks. For example, some functions perform arithmetic calculations, such as SUM and AVERAGE; some apply Boolean logic, such as AND, TRUE, and NOT; others are used for unique purposes, such as to COUNT the number of values in a list.

- **Attributes** communicate instructions to a function to perform an action. For example, if you click the bottom cell in a column and open the Formula dialog box, Word suggests a formula: =SUM(ABOVE). The ABOVE attribute eliminates the need for you to reference each cell in the column above the selected cell. Another frequently used attribute is LEFT, as in =COUNT(LEFT) to count the numeric entries in the cells to the left of the selected cell.

NOTE

If you see a formula inside brackets ⟨=SUM(ABOVE)⟩ where you want the number that results from the formula, select the formula with its brackets and press **SHIFT+F9**. The formula will be replaced by the number.

TIP

You must manually update formulas after changing an underlying cell value. To recalculate a formula, select the resulting value, and press **F9**.

each column, or having Word size the columns to fit the window the table is in. (AutoFit To Window is primarily used when sizing tables in Web pages. See Chapter 9 for more information on saving Word documents as Web pages.)

4. Click **OK** when finished. Figure 6-11 shows the original text data, as well as the resulting table that was created from it. (Under normal circumstances, the table replaces the text. Here, a copy was converted to show both states.)

Superior·Office·Supply	→	1st·Qtr	→	2nd·Qtr¶
Paper·Supplies	→	23,567	→	35,938¶
Writing·Instruments	→	5,482	→	5,836¶
Cards·and·Books	→	14,986	→	15,021¶

Superior·Office·Supply¤	1st·Qtr¤	2nd·Qtr¤
Paper·Supplies¤	23,567¤	35,938¤
Writing·Instruments¤	5,482¤	5,836¤
Cards·and·Books¤	14,986¤	15,021¤

Figure 6-11: **Text properly formatted with separators is easily converted to a table in Word.**

CONVERT A TABLE TO TEXT

Converting a table to text converts the contents of each cell to normal text separated by a character you choose, with each row becoming a separate paragraph.

1. Select the table that you want to convert to text (see the QuickSteps "Selecting Tables, Rows, Columns, or Cells").

2. In the Layout tab Data group, click **Convert To Text**. The Convert Table To Text dialog box appears.

3. Under Separate Text With, click the formatting character you want to use to separate text in columns, or click **Other** and type the character you want.

4. If you have a table within a table, click the **Convert Nested Tables** check box to convert the nested table(s) as well.

5. Click **OK** when finished.

Repeat Header Rows

Headers are the column identifiers placed in the first row of a table (see Figure 6-1) to distinguish different categories of information. In tables, you can repeat the heading rows at the top of each page so that they span multiple document pages. The reader then does not have to remember the column category or keep returning to the beginning of the table. (Repeated headers only apply to Word-generated page breaks, not those you create manually.)

1. In the View tab Document Views group, click **Print Layout**, if it isn't already selected, so that you can see the headers displayed.

2. Select the header rows (see the QuickSteps "Selecting Tables, Rows, Columns, or Cells").

3. In the Layout tab Data group, click **Repeat Header Rows**.

Remove a Table

Removing a table removes the rows and columns of the table along with any text or data.

1. Place the insertion point in the table you want to remove.

2. In the Layout tab Rows & Columns group, click **Delete** and click **Delete Table**.

   –Or–

   In the Design tab Draw Borders group, click **Eraser**. Drag a rectangle using the eraser pointer over the table border, and then release the mouse button. Press **ESC** to return to the standard pointer.

   –Or–

   Click the move handle in the upper-left corner, just outside the table, to select the table, and press **CTRL+X**; or in the Home tab Clipboard group, click **Cut**. The table is removed but is available to be pasted elsewhere. (See Chapter 2 for information on using the Office Clipboard to paste material in Word documents.)

Change a Table's Appearance

A table chock full of data is informative, but not necessarily appealing. Word offers special features to help with this, including text wrapping and orientation options. You can also change the look of the table's structure by merging and splitting cells; adjusting margins surrounding cells; aligning the table on the document page; and applying color, shading, and emphasis to backgrounds and borders.

Merge and Split Cells

Cells can be *merged* by combining two or more cells into one cell. Merged cells can be used to create a banner that spans the width of a table, as a placeholder for larger inserted graphics, and for other special effects. You can also accomplish the opposite effect by subdividing a cell into multiple columns and/or rows by splitting the cell.

MERGE CELLS

1. Select the cells you want to combine into one cell (see the QuickSteps "Selecting Tables, Rows, Columns, or Cells").

| Document·paneo | □ | Displays·the contents of·the·document being·created·or·editedo |
| | □ | □ |

2. Right-click the selection and click **Merge Cells**.

   –Or–

   In the Layout tab Merge group, click **Merge Cells**.

   | Merge Cells |
   | Split Cells |
   | Split Table |
   | Merge |

Any content spans the merged cell.

| Document·paneo | Displays·the contents of·the document being·created·or·editedo |

FORMATTING CONTENT *(Continued)*

3. Click **Options** to open the Cell Options dialog box. Under Options, clear the **Wrap Text** check box. (Fit Text changes the font size to fit the cell size.)

4. Click **OK** twice to close the Cell Options and Table Properties dialog boxes.

Options
- ☐ Wrap text
- ☐ Fit text

ORIENT TEXT DIRECTION IN A CELL

For a special effect, you can change the typical horizontal text orientation to one of two vertical arrangements, as shown in Figure 6-12.

1. Select the cells whose text orientation you want to change.

2. Right-click the selected cells, and click **Text Direction** on the context menu. In the Text Direction – Table Cell dialog box, click an orientation and click **OK**.

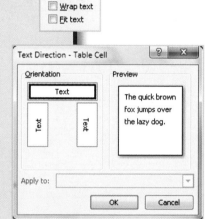

–Or–

In the Layout tab Alignment group, click **Text Direction** to cycle through the one horizontal and two vertical orientation options.

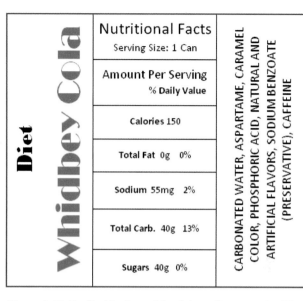

Figure 6-12: *Vertical text provides interesting opportunities for laying out logos and other information.*

SPLIT CELLS

1. Select the cell or cells you want to split into more columns or rows.

2. For a single cell, right-click it and click **Split Cells**.

–Or–

With one or more cells, in the Layout tab Merge group, click **Split Cells**.

In both cases, the Split Cells dialog box will appear.

Split Cells
Number of columns: 2
Number of rows: 1
☑ Merge cells before split
OK Cancel

3. Click the **Number Of Columns** spinner or enter a value to divide the selected cell vertically.

–And/or–

Click the **Number Of Rows** spinner or enter a value to divide the selected cells horizontally. (Other cells in the rows of the cells being split increase their height to accommodate the increase.)

Check out the alignment, lists, and indent options on the Home (and formatting mini toolbar), Page Layout, and Table Tools Layout tabs after you click a cell whose text direction has changed. The option faces become oriented vertically as well!

CHANGING A TABLE'S ALIGNMENT

ALIGN A TABLE QUICKLY

1. Point just above the leftmost column, and drag to the right to select all the columns, *except for the final mark at the end of each row, just outside the rightmost column.*

2. In the Home tab Paragraph group, click **Align Left**, **Center**, or **Align Right**. (See Chapter 3 for an explanation of the alignment buttons. Justify alignment doesn't work in tables.)

ALIGN AND INDENT A TABLE

1. Right-click the table you want to align, click **Table Properties** on the context menu, and click the **Table** tab, as shown in Figure 6-13.

2. Click the **Left** alignment icon. Click the **Indent From Left** spinner or enter a value to shift the left edge of the table relative to the page margin (use negative values to shift the left edge to the left of the margin).

3. Click **OK**.

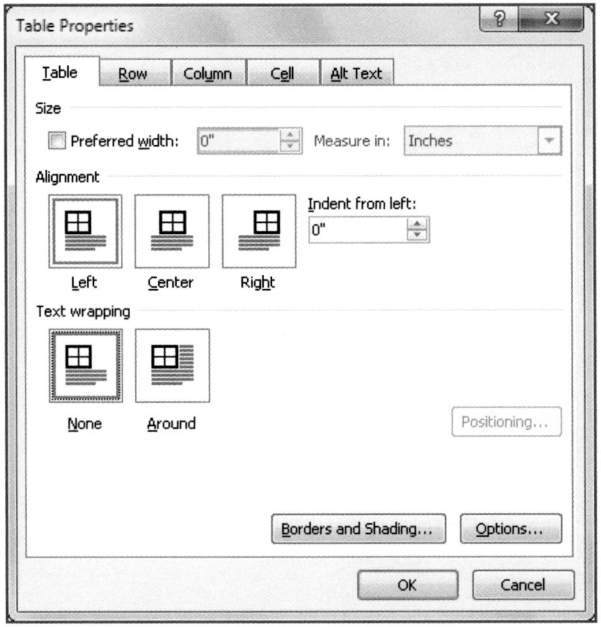

*Figure 6-13: **Use the Table tab of a table's properties dialog box to align and indent a table, as well as to size and determine text-wrapping options.***

4. To split each selected cell into the number of rows or columns entered, clear the **Merge Cells Before Split** check box.

–Or–

To split the merged block of selected cells into the number of rows or columns entered, select the **Merge Cells Before Split** check box.

5. Click **OK**.

Wrap Text Around a Table

By default, tables are inserted *inline* with other text and objects in the document so that the other content is either above or below the table's position. You can choose to have adjacent text wrap on either side of the table, as well as adjust how the table is positioned relative to the text.

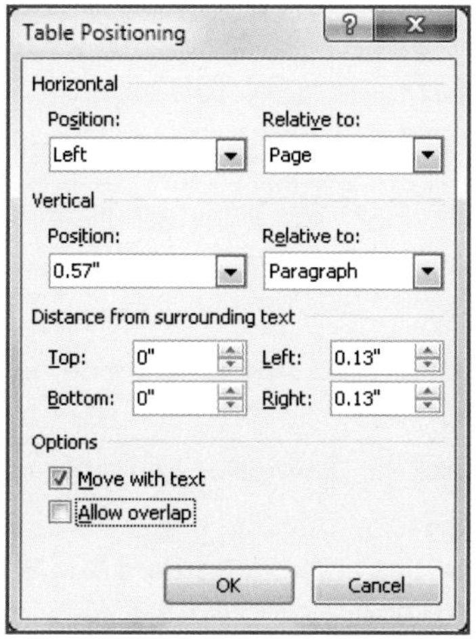

Figure 6-14: *You can lock a table's position relative to a document's elements and set options for how text displays near the table.*

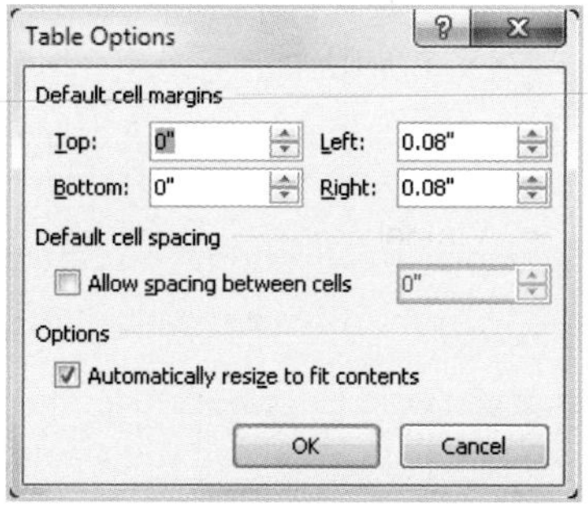

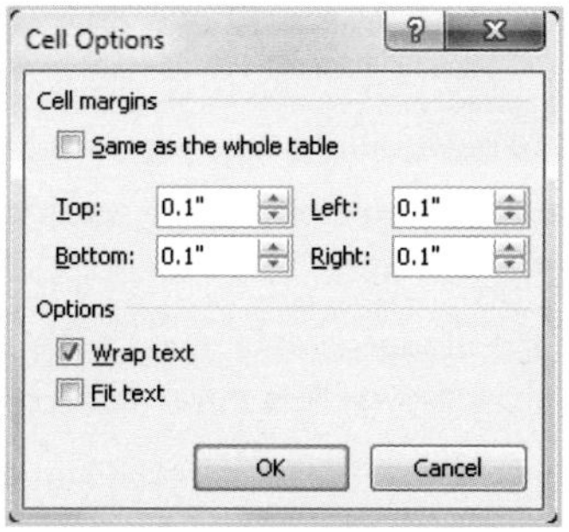

1. Right-click the table you want to align, click **Table Properties** on the context menu, and click the **Table** tab (see Figure 6-13).

2. Under Text Wrapping, click the **Around** icon to wrap text around the sides of the table (the table's width must be less than the margin width for text to appear on the sides).

3. Click **Positioning** to open the Table Positioning dialog box, shown in Figure 6-14.

   ● Under Horizontal and Vertical, set values to position the table relative to other elements on the page.

   ● Under Distance From Surrounding Text, determine how much of a gap you want to exist between the table and surrounding text.

   ● Select the **Move With Text** check box if you want the table to move with text flow; clear it to keep the table in a fixed position, regardless of whether content is added or removed on the page.

   ● Select **Allow Overlap** to let text flow over on top of the table.

4. Click **OK** twice.

Change Cell Margins

You can change the distance between content and the cell borders, both for an entire table and for selected cells.

SET MARGINS FOR ALL CELLS IN A TABLE

1. Right-click the table whose default cell margins you want to change, and click **Table Properties** on the context menu.

2. On the Table tab, click **Options**. In the Table Options dialog box, under Default Cell Margins, change the **Top**, **Bottom**, **Left**, and **Right** values as needed by clicking their respective spinners or entering numbers.

3. Click **OK** twice.

SET MARGINS FOR SELECTED CELLS

1. Select the cells whose default cell margins you want to change, right-click them, and click **Table Properties** on the context menu.

2. Click the **Cell** tab, and click **Options**.

3. In the Cell Margins dialog box, clear the **Same As The Whole Table** check box, and change the **Top**, **Bottom**, **Left**, and **Right** values as needed by clicking their respective spinners or entering numbers.

4. Click **OK** twice.

Apply Shading and Border Effects

Tables and individual cells can be emphasized using Word's broad set of tools to apply shading and border outlines.

1. Select the table or cells to which you want to apply a shading or border effect.

2. Open the Borders And Shading dialog box, shown in Figure 6-15, by one of the following means:

   ● Right-click the selected element, and click **Borders And Shading** on the context menu.

   ● In the Design tab Draw Borders group, click the **Dialog Box Launcher** in the lower-right corner.

   ● In the Layout tab Table group, click **Properties** and click **Borders And Shading** in the Table tab of the Table Properties dialog box.

> Borders and Shading...

(See Chapter 3 for information on how to apply borders and shading to text.)

Format a Table Automatically

Tables are easily changed after they are created, but when in a hurry, it is often helpful to give Word the first crack at applying a consistent look to a table. You can always modify the formatting or start over with a different appearance. In addition, you can create a format style from scratch and save it, or modify an existing format style and save it.

1. Select the table that you want to have Word format automatically. (You can also automatically format a table as you create it using the Insert Table dialog box. See "Insert a Table from a Dialog Box" earlier in the chapter.)

2. In the Design tab Table Styles group, a gallery of table styles is displayed, as shown in Figure 6-16.

APPLY A TABLE STYLE

1. In the Design tab Table Styles group, scroll through the gallery of table styles, and point the mouse at each one to see a preview of your table with that style. Figure 6-17 shows three examples of the options.

2. When you find the one that you want, click that style.

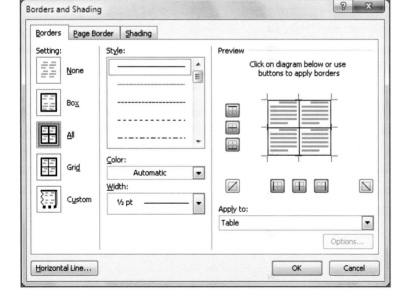

Figure 6-15: *You can choose borders for each side of cells and the table, as well as provide background fills and patterns.*

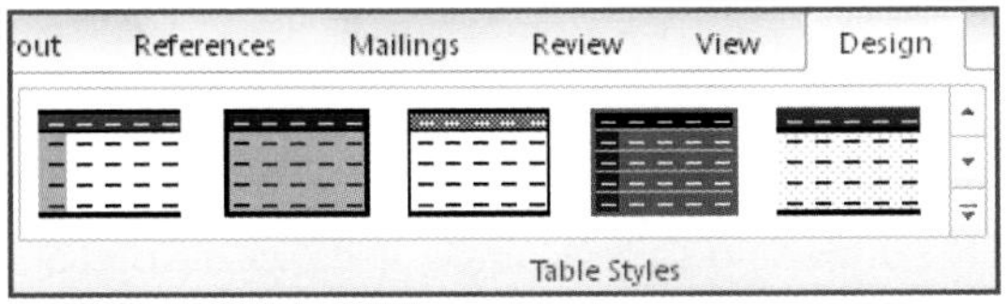

out	References	Mailings	Review	View	Design

Table Styles

Figure 6-16: *You can apply a preformatted table style, modify an existing style, or create your own and save any changes for future use.*

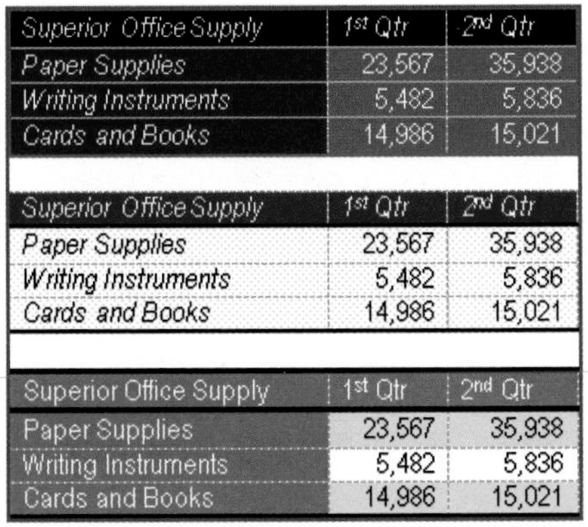

Superior Office Supply	1st Qtr	2nd Qtr
Paper Supplies	23,567	35,938
Writing Instruments	5,482	5,836
Cards and Books	14,986	15,021

Superior Office Supply	1st Qtr	2nd Qtr
Paper Supplies	23,567	35,938
Writing Instruments	5,482	5,836
Cards and Books	14,986	15,021

Superior Office Supply	1st Qtr	2nd Qtr
Paper Supplies	23,567	35,938
Writing Instruments	5,482	5,836
Cards and Books	14,986	15,021

Figure 6-17: *Word provides a number of attractive table styles you can apply.*

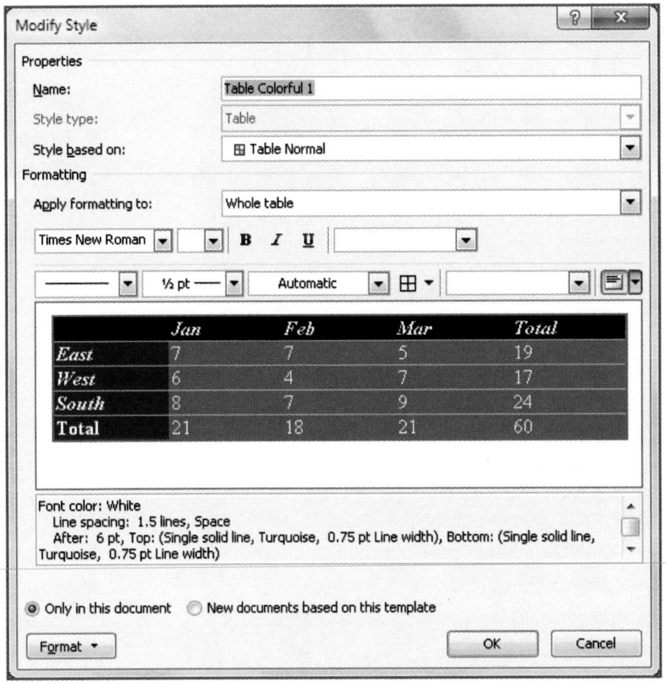

Modify Style

Properties

Name: Table Colorful 1

Style type: Table

Style based on: ⊞ Table Normal

Formatting

Apply formatting to: Whole table

Times New Roman **B** *I* <u>U</u>

½ pt — Automatic ⊞ ▾

	Jan	Feb	Mar	Total
East	7	7	5	19
West	6	4	7	17
South	8	7	9	24
Total	21	18	21	60

Font color: White
Line spacing: 1.5 lines, Space
After: 6 pt, Top: (Single solid line, Turquoise, 0.75 pt Line width), Bottom: (Single solid line, Turquoise, 0.75 pt Line width)

◉ Only in this document   ○ New documents based on this template

Format ▾   OK   Cancel

Figure 6-18: *There is no shortage of formatting options available to you when changing or creating a table style.*

CHANGE OR CREATE A TABLE STYLE

The Modify Style and Create New Style dialog boxes provide a number of options and tools that you can use to change or create a table style. (The Modify Style dialog box is shown in Figure 6-18.)

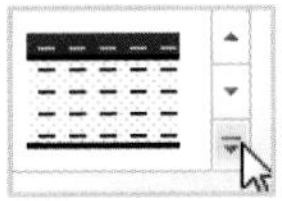

1. In the Design tab Table Styles group, click **More** beneath the scroll arrows on the right of the style gallery.

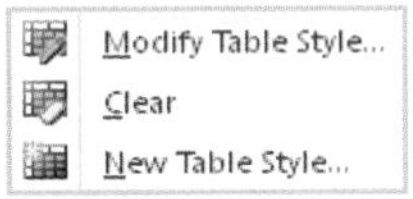

2. Click **Modify Table Style** to change an existing style.

   –Or–

   Click **New Table Style** to create a new one.

🗐 Modify Table Style...
🗐 Clear
🖼 New Table Style...

CAUTION

When modifying an existing table style, provide a new name for the style in the Name text box; otherwise, the original style will be overwritten with any changes you make and you won't be able to return to "square one" if need be.

TIP

You can choose a table style to be the default style for tables in the current document or for all of those that use the Normal template. Right-click the style you want from the table style gallery in the Design tab. Click **Set As Default**, click the applicable option in the Default Table Style dialog box, and click **OK**.

Microsoft Office Word   [?] [X]

Do you want to set the default table style to Table Colorful 1 for:
   ⦿ This document only?
   ○ All documents based on the Normal.dotm template?

                          [OK]   [Cancel]

3. In either dialog box:

- Under Properties, enter a name for the style, click the **Style Based On** down arrow, and click a style to start with (the style appears in the Preview area).

- Under Formatting, click the **Apply Formatting To** down arrow, and click the part of the table to which you want the style to be applied. Use the formatting tools in the center of the dialog box. Or, you can click **Format** at the bottom of the dialog box to open a drop-down list of options that open additional dialog boxes with even more formatting choices.

Format
Table Properties...
Borders and Shading...
Banding...
Font...
Paragraph...
Tabs...
Text Effects...

- Click **Only In This Document** if you want the formatting to apply only to your current document. Click **New Documents Based On This Template** if you want the style available to other documents.

4. Click **OK** to close all open dialog boxes when done.

DELETE A STYLE

1. In the Design tab Table Styles group, scroll through the table styles gallery, and right-click the style you want to delete.

2. Click **Delete Table Style**, and click **Yes** to confirm the action. The style is removed from the gallery.

Chapter 7
Working with Illustrations

Illustration is a term used to describe several forms of visual enhancements that can be added to a document. Illustrations include pictures, clip art, drawings, shapes, SmartArt, charts, and screenshots. In this chapter you will learn how to insert, format, and manage illustration files, such as digital photos and clip art images. You will see how to create your own drawings directly on a document and how to combine them with built-in shapes. In addition, you will see how to embed charts and screenshots alongside your text and how to produce organizational charts and other business-oriented diagrams.

LINKING PICTURE FILES

Pictures are *embedded* by default when inserted in a document. Embedding means that the picture files become part of the Word file and their file size is added to the size of the saved Word document. In a document with several high-resolution pictures, the document's size can quickly rise to several megabytes (the greater the number of pixels in a picture, the higher the resolution and the larger the file size). To dramatically reduce the size of a document that contains pictures, you can *link* to the picture files instead. In this case, the addresses of picture files are retained in the document file, not the pictures themselves. (Alternatively, you can reduce the resolution and compress embedded pictures, although the reduction in file size won't be as large as with linked files. See the section "Reduce a Picture's File Size," later in the chapter.) Another characteristic of linked picture files is that any changes made and saved in the source file will be updated in the Word document. Linking does have the downside of requiring the picture files to remain in the same folder location they were in when the link was created. In addition, documents with linked files are not suitable for sharing outside your local network.

1. To link a picture file when you are inserting a picture into a document, click the **Insert** tab, and click **Picture** in the Illustrations group to open the Insert Picture dialog box.

2. Click the **Insert** down arrow in the lower-right corner, and click **Link To File**.

Insert ▾	Cancel
Insert	
Link to File	
Insert and Link	
Show previous versions	

Work with Pictures

Pictures, which include both digital photos and *clip art* (small drawings or commercial photos), are separate files that can be manipulated in a number of ways once you have them within Word. You can organize your picture collections, resize images, and move them into the exact positions that you want.

Add Pictures

You can browse for picture files, use the Clip Art task pane to assist you, drag them from other locations, or import them directly from a scanner or digital camera.

BROWSE FOR PICTURES

1. Place your insertion point in the Word paragraph or table where you want to insert the picture.

2. In the Insert tab, click **Picture** in the Illustrations group. The Insert Picture dialog box appears, as shown in Figure 7-1.

3. Browse to the picture you want, and select it. (If you do not see your pictures, click the **Views** down arrow on the dialog box toolbar, and click **Large Icons** or a larger size.)

4. Click **Insert**. The picture is displayed in the document.

NOTE

Pictures are files that are produced by a device, such as a digital camera or scanner, or that are created in a painting or drawing program, such as Microsoft Paint or Adobe Illustrator. In either case, the files are saved in a graphic format, such as JPEG or GIF (popular formats used on the Internet) or TIF (used in higher-end printing applications). Table 7-1 lists the graphic file formats supported by Word.

NOTE

Often, when you insert a picture or illustration, it is not the size that you want it to be. You can easily make a picture the size you want by dragging the corners of the picture to resize it.

Figure 7-1: *The Insert Picture dialog box displays thumbnails of picture files accepted by Word.*

FILE TYPE	EXTENSION
Computer Graphics Metafile	CGM
Encapsulated PostScript	EPS
Graphics Interchange Format	GIF, GFA
Joint Photographic Expert Graphics	JPG, JPEG, JFIF, JPE
Macintosh PICT/Compressed	PCT, PICT/PCZ
Portable Network Graphics	PNG
Tagged Image File Format	TIF, TIFF
Windows Bitmap	BMP, BMZ, RLE, DIB
Windows Enhanced Metafile/Compressed	EMF/EMZ
Windows Metafile/Compressed	WMF/WMZ
WordPerfect Graphics	WPG

Table 7-1: *Picture File Formats Accepted by Word*

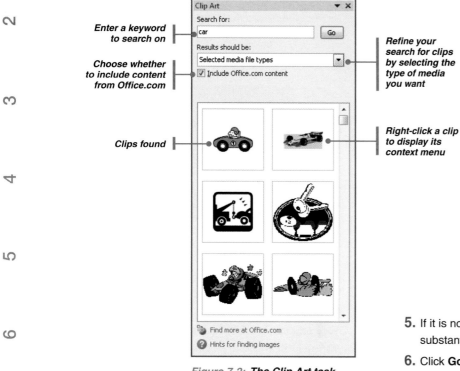

Enter a keyword to search on

Choose whether to include content from Office.com

Clips found

Refine your search for clips by selecting the type of media you want

Right-click a clip to display its context menu

Figure 7-2: The Clip Art task pane helps you find clips on your computer and on Office Online.

ADD CLIP ART

1. Place your insertion point in the paragraph or table where you want to insert the picture.

2. In the Insert tab Illustrations group, click **Clip Art**. The Clip Art task pane opens.

3. In the Search For text box, type a keyword.

4. Click the **Results Should Be** down arrow, and clear all file types other than Illustrations.

5. If it is not already set, click **Include Office.com Content** if you want to include substantial additional content other than what is on your computer.

6. Click **Go**. In a few moments, thumbnails of the search results will appear, as shown in Figure 7-2.

7. Click the thumbnail to insert it in your document and resize it as needed (see the Note on resizing on the previous page). When you are ready, click **Close** in the Clip Art task pane.

ADD PICTURES DIRECTLY

In addition to adding pictures to Word from files on your computer or from clip art, you can bring pictures directly into Word from a camera plugged into your computer.

1. Place your insertion point in the paragraph or table where you want to insert the picture.

2. Make sure that the digital camera is connected to your computer and is turned on.

3. In the Insert tab Illustrations group, click **Picture**. The Insert Picture dialog box appears.

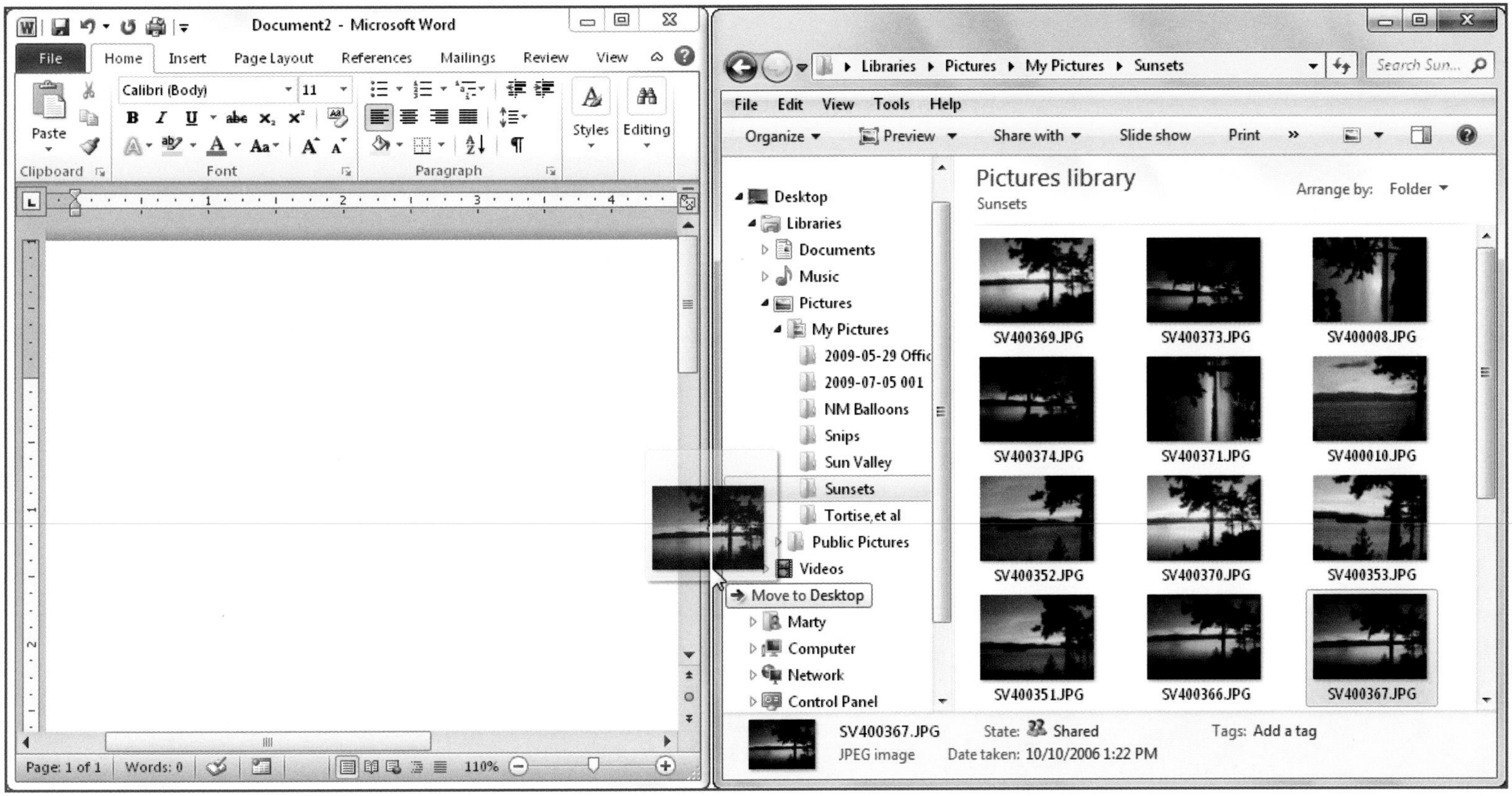

Figure 7-3: *You can directly drag any art you have on your computer to an open Word document.*

7

TIP

If you have plugged in and turned on your camera, and everything looks like it should be working but you can't find it, click **Start** and click **Control Panel**. In Control Panel Category view, click **Hardware And Sound**, and click **Devices And Printers**. If your camera is not listed, click **Add A Device**. Select your camera, click **Next**, enter a name for the device, and click **Finish**.

4. Drag the **Folders** pane to the top of its area, and select the device that represents your camera. This may be called a "removable disk," as shown in Figure 7-4.

5. Double-click the picture you want to use. The picture will appear in Word.

6. On the Picture tools Format tab, you can adjust custom settings, such as adjusting brightness and contrast or choosing to display the image with various borders and effects, as you can see in Figure 7-5. (If the Format tab is not visible, click the picture to select it.)

Material you copy from the Internet, books, magazines, and other sources is normally protected by copyright; therefore, before you put it on your Web site or use it for any commercial purpose, be sure to check the licensing agreement or contact the copyright owner.

NOTE

You can organize your clips in the Clip Art task pane into collections on your hard disk by selecting the clip, clicking its down arrow, and clicking **Copy To Collection**. In the Copy To Collection dialog box that appears you can create new folders and organize them into folder trees.

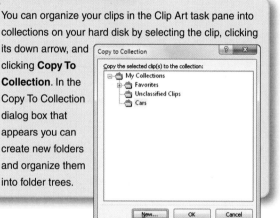

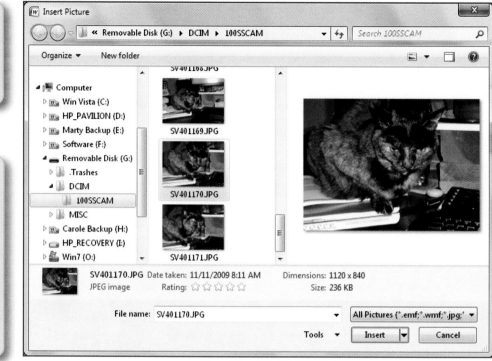

Figure 7-4: **Plugging your camera into your computer makes it an extension of the computer and allows you to get pictures directly from it.**

QUICKFACTS

USING THE PICTURE TOOLS FORMAT TAB

Pictures are manipulated primarily by using the Picture Tools Format tab, shown in Figure 7-6. The Format tab automatically appears when an illustration is selected in a document. The tab has five groups that allow you to adjust the characteristics of an image, determine its style, remove its background, arrange an image on a page or in relation other images or text, and size an image. In addition, the two Dialog Box Launchers in the Picture Styles and Size groups provide a number of other settings.

Remove Unwanted Areas

You can remove areas from a picture that you do not want by using the Crop tool on the Picture toolbar.

1. Open and select the picture you want to crop. See "Add Pictures" earlier in this chapter.

2. On the Picture Tools Format tab, click **Crop** in the Size group. The picture redisplays with eight sizing handles on the corners and sides, and the mouse pointer becomes a four-headed arrow, as shown in Figure 7-7.

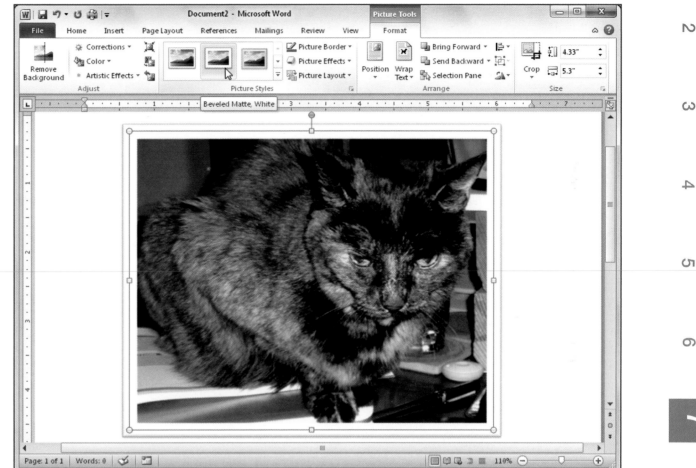

Figure 7-5: After bringing a picture into Word, you can set several image properties.

3. Place the cropping tool over one of the eight sizing handles (it will morph into an angle or T icon), and drag the tool so that the area of the picture is cut away or cropped by what you have dragged over.

4. Release the mouse button. The area of the picture is shown as it will be cropped. Press **ESC** or click outside of the image to complete the cropping and turn off the Crop tool. While the cropping handles are still shown, you can drag them to a different location and consider that cropping. If you change your mind after you complete the cropping, click **Undo** in the Quick Access toolbar or press **CTRL+Z** to reverse the cropping.

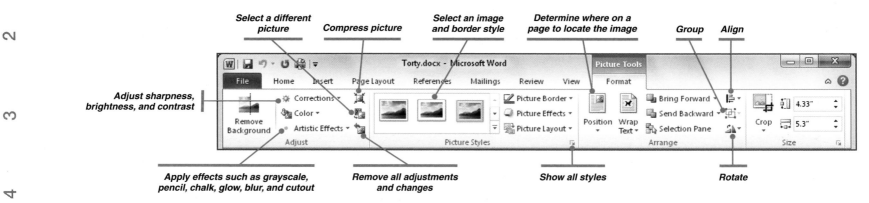

Select a different picture
Compress picture
Select an image and border style
Determine where on a page to locate the image
Group
Align
Adjust sharpness, brightness, and contrast
Apply effects such as grayscale, pencil, chalk, glow, blur, and cutout
Remove all adjustments and changes
Show all styles
Rotate

Figure 7-6: *The Picture Tools Format tab is your one-stop venue for accessing picture-related options.*

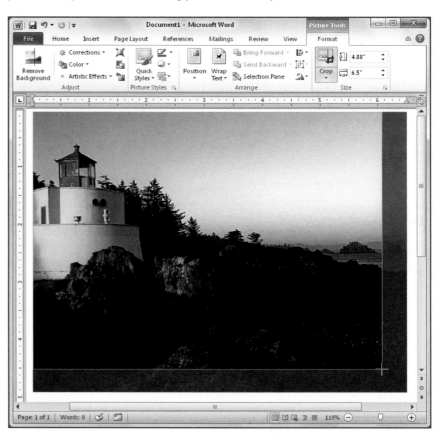

QUICKSTEPS

POSITIONING "IN-LINE" PICTURES

When you insert a picture, by default, the image is positioned in a paragraph similar to a character you enter from the keyboard; that is, the bottom of the image is aligned with the bottom of the text line at the insertion point. The paragraph will expand vertically the height of the picture and "push" any other text or objects down the page. The picture is "in-line with text" and maintains its *relative* position to surrounding content as text and other objects are added to or removed from the page. (You can change this orientation, however. See "Wrap Text Around a Picture.")

ALIGN PICTURES

When a picture is in-line with text, it will respond to paragraph formatting. Use one of the following

Continued . . .

Figure 7-7: *Cropping removes the area of a picture outside where the cropping handle has been dragged.*

POSITIONING "IN-LINE" PICTURES

(Continued)

paragraph-formatting tools to align pictures with text (see Chapter 3 for details on how to format paragraphs):

- The paragraph alignment tools in the Home tab Paragraph group

- The Paragraph dialog box, which is opened from either the paragraph's context menu or the Home tab Paragraph group's Dialog Box Launcher

- Tabs and indents, which are set in the horizontal ruler or the Tabs dialog box (opened from the Paragraph dialog box or by double-clicking a tab on the ruler)

MOVE PICTURES

1. Click the picture you want to move to select it.

2. Drag the picture to a new paragraph or table cell.

TIP

You can add a caption to inserted pictures to give a uniform appearance to your picture identifiers. Right-click a picture and click **Insert Caption**. In the Caption dialog box, choose a label (create your own labels by clicking **New Label**), where you want the caption, and a numbering format. You can also have Word use AutoCaption to automatically add a caption based on the type of picture or object inserted.

Reduce a Picture's File Size

Pictures embedded in a document add to the document's file size. Just a few high-resolution pictures or several lower-resolution pictures can quickly increase a document's file size beyond the threshold established by many e-mail servers and network administrators. To mitigate file size "bloat," you have a few options available to you. (An alternative method of reducing the impact of inserted pictures is to link the pictures to the document. See the QuickFacts "Linking Picture Files" earlier in this chapter for more information.)

1. Open the document that contains the picture whose file size you want to reduce, and select the picture.

2. In the Picture Tools Format tab Adjust group, click **Compress Pictures**.

3. Click **Apply Only To This Picture** if that is what you want (versus applying it to all the pictures in the document).

4. Choose whether to delete cropped areas of pictures, which removes any cropped areas not only from view, but totally from the document.

5. Choose whether the target output should be printing the document, viewing it on the screen, sending it via e-mail, or the current document resolution. For each option but the last, the resolution of the resulting image is shown in pixels per inch (ppi). The greater the ppi, the higher the resolution.

6. Click **OK** to close the Compress Pictures dialog box.

Wrap Text Around a Picture

Wrapping text around a picture requires positioning a picture independently of the text on a page, which is called "absolute positioning," and offers three features that the default paragraph-positioning feature does not. You can:

- Place a picture in a document so that it keeps its position, even if other content shifts on the page

- Drag a picture to any location on a page, regardless of paragraph considerations

- Place the picture according to distances or positions relative to document areas

TIP

Pictures that are in-line with text are, in a sense, treated like a big character and have paragraph-formatting characteristics. Pictures can also be positioned independently of text and display either on top of the text or behind it.

TIP

The Align option in the Arrange group of the Drawing Tools Format tab has a number of options that help with the relative placement of several objects. These allow you to align a common edge of several objects or to evenly distribute them.

To position a picture absolutely:

1. Click the picture to select it. In the Picture Tools Format tab, click **Position** in the Arrange group.

2. Click any wrapping style, except In Line With Text. You can now drag the picture to anywhere in the document.

Create Drawings

Drawings may be composed of prebuilt shapes, text you add effects to, and renderings you put together using one or more drawing tools. You can manipulate drawings by altering their position, size, color, shape, and other characteristics using the Drawing Tools Format tab, shown in

Figure 7-8. You can choose premade illustrations or *shapes*; add styles, color, and effects; and position and size illustrations using the tools available in the Drawing Tools Format tab.

Drawings are created within a drawing canvas, which is a rectangular area where you can move and size multiple drawings as one object. To start a new drawing:

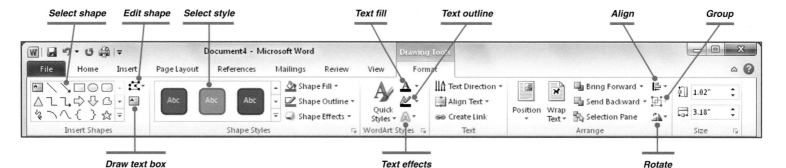

Figure 7-8: *The Drawing Tools Format tab provides tools to create and insert drawings and to apply effects.*

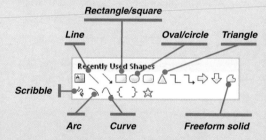
Open a new drawing canvas. In the Insert tab Illustrations group, click **Shapes** and then, at the bottom of the drop-down menu, click **New Drawing Canvas**.

–Or–

Start with one of the many prebuilt shapes on the Shapes drop-down menu, and a drawing canvas will be created for you.

Add Shapes

Shapes are prebuilt drawings that you can select, or you can create your own by modifying existing shapes or drawing your own freeform shapes. The prebuilt shapes and tools for creating your own are added either from the Insert tab Illustrations group or, with a drawing canvas open and selected, from the Drawing tools Format tab Insert Shapes group.

1. In the Insert tab Illustrations group, click **Shapes** to open the Shapes drop-down menu.

2. Choose a shape by:

   Clicking a shape from one of the several categories

   –Or–

   Clicking one of the lines or basic shapes to begin your own shape

3. Drag the mouse crosshair pointer in the approximate location and size you want. In the case of freeform tools, see the QuickSteps "Working with Curves."

WORKING WITH CURVES *(Continued)*

- Click **Scribble** and drag the pencil icon to create the exact shape you want. Release the mouse button to complete the drawing.

- Click **Freeform** and use a combination of curve and scribble techniques. Click the crosshair pointer to establish curvature points, and/or drag the pencil pointer to create other designs. Double-click to set the end point and complete the drawing.

ADJUST A CURVE

1. Right-click a handle or line of the curve, and click **Edit Points**. Black squares (*vertices*) appear at the curvature points.

2. Drag a vertex to reconfigure its shape.

3. Pull out the two curve handles, the white squares, and rotate them to change the degree and angle of the curve.

4. Change any other vertex, and click outside the curve when finished.

CLOSE A CURVE

Manually closing a curve is not always easy, so Word gives you an automated way to do it.

1. After completing a shape, right-click the curve and click **Edit Points**.

2. Right-click the curve again, and click **Close Path**.

OPEN A CURVE

Right-click a closed curve, click **Edit Points**, right-click again, and click **Open Path**.

Add Special Effects to Text

Special text effects, as shown in Figure 7-9, can be added easily to text using WordArt to simulate a graphic artist's professional touch.

APPLY A WORDART EFFECT

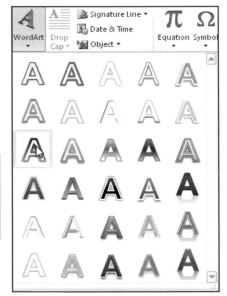

1. In the Insert tab Text group, click **WordArt** to display the WordArt gallery of text styles, shown in Figure 7-9.

2. Click a style that's close to what you want (you can "tweak" it later). The text "YOUR TEXT HERE" appears in a box with drawing handles.

3. Type the text you want styled, select that type, and use the:

   - Home tab's Font and Paragraph groups to format the text

   - Drawing Tools Format tab's WordArt Styles and Text groups to adjust the text fill and outline colors and/or the text effects, as explained next

   The text is displayed with the effect you have selected.

Figure 7-9: The WordArt Gallery provides 30 special effects that can be applied to text.

USE DRAWING TOOLS WITH WORDART

The Drawing Tools Format tab, shown earlier in Figure 7-8, displays when you select text that has a WordArt effect applied to it. Use its options to apply different styles, effects, and alignment.

TIP

If a curve doesn't have an edit point where you need one, right-click the curve, click **Edit Points,** and then place the pointer over the curve where it changes to a dot with four lines through it, then right-click and click **Add Point**.

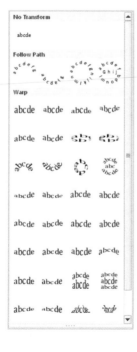

- In the WordArt Styles group, click a **Quick Styles** thumbnail (or if the window is maximized, click **More** styles) to display the same WordArt gallery you originally saw from the Insert tab WordArt option. Point at a different WordArt style to preview the effects on your text. Click the style to make it permanent.

- Click **Text Fill** to open the standard color chart and point at a color or a gradient to preview it on your text (see "Use Color Effects" later in this chapter). Click the selection to make it permanent.

- Click **Text Outline** to open the standard color chart, and point at a color, line weight, or line type to preview it on your text. Click a selection to make it permanent.

- Click **Text Effects** to open a drop-down menu of effects, each of which opens a sub-menu with a number of options for the particular effect, and at the bottom, an option to open the Format Text Effects dialog box. Click a selection to make it permanent.

- Click **Text Effects** and then click **Transform** to open a drop-down menu of text transformations that wrap and curve text. Click the selection to make it permanent.

- Click the **WordArt Styles Dialog Box Launcher** to open the Format Text Effects dialog box. This provides a comprehensive set of controls to manually set text fill, text outline, and text effects, as shown in Figure 7-10.

- In the Drawing Tools Format tab, click **Align Text** and click one of the several vertical alignment formats.

Create a Diagram

You can quickly create and modify several different types of diagrams, some of which are easily interchangeable. One type,

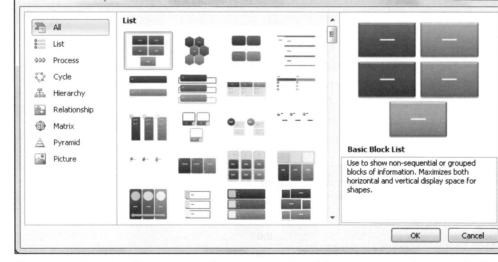

Figure 7-10: *Word provides both quick and detailed ways to control text fill, outline, and effects.*

an organization or hierarchy chart, provides special tools and features that streamline the structuring of this popular form of charting.

1. In the Insert tab Illustrations group, click **SmartArt**. The Choose A SmartArt Graphic dialog box appears, as shown in Figure 7-11.

2. Click **Hierarchy** in the left column, and then double-click the organization chart, which is on the top left. The start of an organization chart and the SmartArt Tools Design tab will be displayed, as shown in the example chart in Figure 7-12. You can then personalize your chart by doing one or more of the following:

● Click the highest level, or *manager*, position in your chart, and in the SmartArt Tools Design tab, click **Layout** in the Create Graphic group to open a menu of hierarchical options. Click the structure that best matches your organization.

● Click a current box on the chart. In the Create Graphic group, click **Add Shape** and select the type of new position you want to add to the current structure. For a higher level, click **Add Shape Above**; for a subordinate level, click **Add Shape Below**; for a co-worker level, click either **Add Shape Before** or **Add Shape After**; and for an assistant, click **Add Assistant**.

● To place text in a shape after adding a new shape or selecting one, simply start typing. You can also click **Text Pane** ("Type Your Text Here") in the Create Graphic group to open it, if it isn't already, and type text there. Type the name, title, and/or other identifiers for the position. The font size will change to fit the text box. Press **SHIFT+ENTER** after each line for a subordinate line (like a position after a name) that is spaced close to the previous line, or press **ENTER** for a second line equally spaced in the box. Format text in the shapes as you would standard text, using the Home tab and its associated options.

● Click **Right To Left** in the Create Graphic group to flip the entire chart so the names and shapes on the right are switched with the ones on the left.

● Click **Promote** or **Demote** in the Create Graphic group to move a shape and its text up or down in the organization chart.

Figure 7-11: *SmartArt allows you to easily create a number of diagram types, such as organizational charts.*

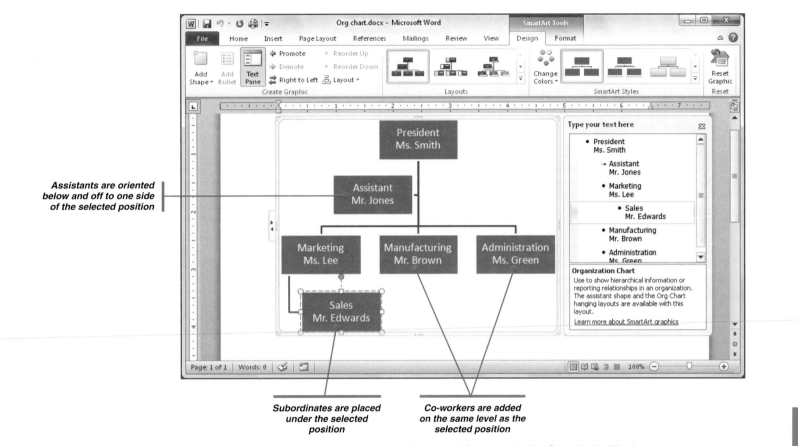

Assistants are oriented below and off to one side of the selected position

Subordinates are placed under the selected position

Co-workers are added on the same level as the selected position

Figure 7-12: Organization charts are easily laid out and formatted using SmartArt in Word.

NOTE

Diagrams are really just combinations of shapes that fit a specific need. As such, you can, for example, delete an element of a diagram by selecting it and pressing **DELETE**. Or you can delete the entire diagram by selecting its border and pressing **DELETE**. See "Modify Illustrations" to learn how to format the overall diagram, as well as how to change various components of shapes.

- Point at any of the alternative layouts, colors, or SmartArt styles to see how your chart would look with that change. Click the layout, color, or style to make the change permanent.

- If you make a "permanent" change, as just described, you can return to the previous layout, color, or style by pressing **CTRL+Z** or by clicking **Reset Graphic** in the Reset group.

- To select a group of shapes and their text so that they can be acted upon all at once, hold down **CTRL** while clicking each shape (including the connecting lines).

- Click the **SmartArt Tools Format** tab to display several options for changing the shape and its text, as shown in Figure 7-13.

Figure 7-13: *Quickly redesign the overall appearance of your organization chart.*

QUICKSTEPS

ADDING OBJECTS FROM OTHER PROGRAMS

You might want to include the product of another program in a document as an illustration. The major difference between adding the illustration as an *object* (these are technically *OLE objects*, named for "object linking and embedding," which is the technology involved) and copying and pasting it is that an object maintains a link to the program that created it. This means that in addition to changing formatting and other illustration options, you can change the *content* using the menus, task panes, and other tools of the originating program while still in Word.

1. In the Insert tab Text group, click **Object**. If a context menu opens, click **Object** again. The Object dialog box appears.

2. Choose whether to create a new object or use an existing one.

   - Click the **Create New** tab, select an object type, and click **OK**.

   –Or–

   - Click the **Create From File** tab, click **Browse**, locate an existing object, and click **OK**.

Continued . . .

Use Color Effects

Color can be added to interior fills, borders, and text in various shades, gradients, textures, and patterns. Click a drawing to select it, and in the Drawing Tools Format tab, click **Shape Fill** 🖌 Shape Fill ▾ or **Shape Outline** ✐ Shape Outline ▾ in the Shape Styles group. A menu of coloring options opens. Depending on what attribute you want to format, you will see all or part of the following options.

SELECT A COLOR QUICKLY

Click one of 10 standard colors or one of the 60 theme colors in the color matrix on the drop-down menu.

–Or–

Click **More (*Fill* Or *Outline*) Colors** to have access to more than 140 standard colors and many more custom colors.

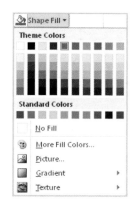

SET GRADIENTS

1. Click **Gradient** on the Shape Fill drop-down menu to open the sub-menu of basic gradient options.

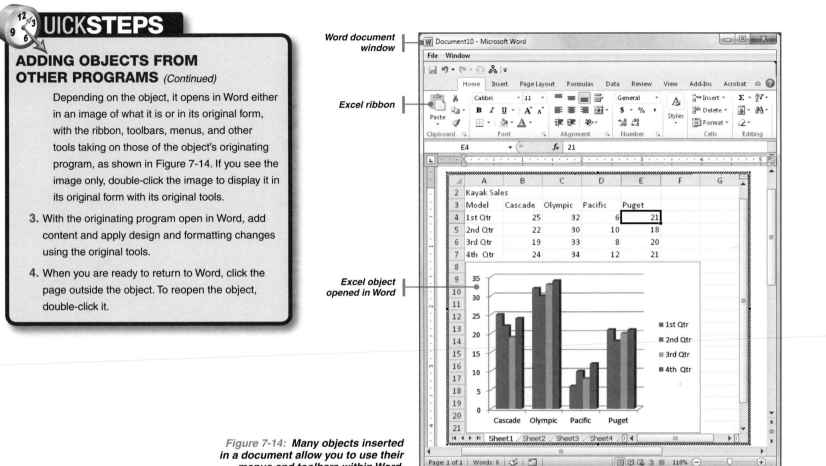

ADDING OBJECTS FROM OTHER PROGRAMS *(Continued)*

Depending on the object, it opens in Word either in an image of what it is or in its original form, with the ribbon, toolbars, menus, and other tools taking on those of the object's originating program, as shown in Figure 7-14. If you see the image only, double-click the image to display it in its original form with its original tools.

3. With the originating program open in Word, add content and apply design and formatting changes using the original tools.

4. When you are ready to return to Word, click the page outside the object. To reopen the object, double-click it.

Word document window

Excel ribbon

Excel object opened in Word

Figure 7-14: **Many objects inserted in a document allow you to use their menus and toolbars within Word.**

TIP

If you create an object from an existing file using the Create From File tab, you can create a *link* between the object in Word and the original file by clicking **Link To File** in the Object dialog box as you are bringing the object onto the document.

2. Click **More Gradients** to open the Format Shape dialog box. In the Fill option, select **Gradient Fill** under Fill, as shown in Figure 7-15.

3. Click **Preset Colors** and select one of the gradient color schemes from the drop-down list box.

–Or–

Click a gradient stop in the gradient bar, and click **Color** to open the color palette, and then click a color. Repeat this for each of the gradient stops you want. To add a stop, double-click the gradient bar or click the **Add Gradient Stop** button on the right. To delete a stop, drag it off the gradient bar or click the **Remove Gradient Stop** button.

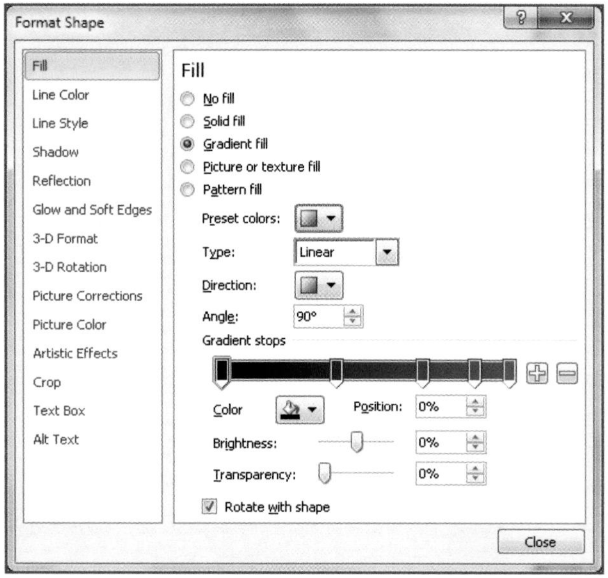

Figure 7-15: *You can blend colors to create gradient fills.*

4. Select a type of fill and its direction and angle, if applicable.

5. For each of the gradient stops, you can use the **Position** spinner to precisely set the location of the stop on the gradient bar.

6. Also for each gradient stop, you can use the relevant slider or the spinner to set the degree of brightness and transparency.

7. When you are done, click **OK**.

USE A PICTURE TO FILL YOUR DRAWING

With a shape in Word that you want to fill with a picture:

1. Select the shape. In the Drawing Tools Format tab, click **Shape Fill** and click **Picture** on the Shape Fill drop-down menu. The Select Picture dialog box appears.

2. Browse for the picture you want, select it, and click **Insert**. The picture will be inserted into the background of the drawing shape.

COLOR TEXT IN A TEXT BOX

1. Select the text to be colored by double-clicking or dragging. If you have trouble selecting the text you want, set your insertion point at the beginning or end of the selection, and press and hold **CTRL+SHIFT** while using the arrow keys to select the remaining characters.

2. On the mini toolbar (displayed when you select the text and place your pointer over the toolbar's vague outline), click the **Font Color** down arrow , and click the color you want from the color matrix. Your selected text is colored, and the Font Color button displays the selected color so that you can apply that same color to additional objects by just clicking the button.

REMOVE EFFECTS

- **To remove a fill**, select the drawing. In the Drawing Tools Format tab, click the **Shape Fill** down arrow in the Shape Styles group, and click **No Fill**.

- **To remove the outline border** around a drawing, select the drawing. In the Drawing Tools Format tab, click the **Shape Outline** down arrow in the Shape Styles group, and click **No Outline**.

- **To remove text coloring**, select the text, in the mini toolbar click the **Font Color** down arrow, and click **Automatic**. The text will turn black.

NOTE

You can make enhancements to lines much like adding effects to shapes. Using the Format Shape dialog box (Drawing Tools Format tab, Shape Styles Dialog Box Launcher), you can apply arrows to lines, change the thickness of a line, add shadows and 3-D effects to lines and drawings, and introduce other enhancements. The tools work similarly—select the line or drawing by clicking it, and then click the tool whose effect you want.

CAUTION

Do not remove the border or line around a drawing unless you have first added a fill. Without the line and a fill, the drawing is invisible, except for the handles that display when it's selected.

Take Screenshots

Screenshots (also called screen captures and screen grabs) allow you to copy a portion of what you see on your screen, be it an icon, window, or the entire screen. In Word, you can select any open windows to capture (except for Word itself, unless you have another Word window open), or you can drag a selection rectangle across whatever area of the screen you want. The capture is placed in your document and can be modified using the Picture Tools formatting features.

1. Minimize the Word window and arrange your desktop with the program(s), window(s), and objects you want to capture.

2. Restore the Word window, place the insertion point where you want the screenshot, and in the Insert tab Illustrations group, click **Screenshot**.

3. From the Available Screen Shots area, select one of your open windows.

–Or–

Click **Screen Clipping**. Use the large black cross to drag across the area you want, and release the mouse button when finished. This way you can capture several windows or the whole screen, as shown in Figure 7-16.

4. In both cases, the image you selected is displayed on your worksheet surrounded by selection handles.

*Figure 7-16: **Screenshots are a powerful tool, allowing you to use your screen to provide visual additions to your document.***

NOTE

Right-click an illustration and click **Format Shape** to open a dialog box that makes available the options that pertain to that type of illustration. For example, if you right-click a line you drew, the Line Style option is displayed, as shown in Figure 7-17. In the same dialog box for the line, the Picture Corrections options are not available.

CAUTION

Enlarging an image beyond the ability of the pixels to span it can distort the image.

TIP

Display the Word rulers to help you draw, align, and arrange drawings more precisely. Click **View Ruler** at the top of the vertical scroll bar on the right of the Word window to display the horizontal ruler and, if it is turned on, the vertical ruler. Alternatively, in the View tab Show group, click **Ruler**. If the vertical ruler is not visible in Print Layout view, click the **File** tab, click **Options**, and click **Advanced** in the left column. Under Display, click **Show Vertical Ruler In Print Layout View**. Click **OK**.

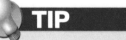

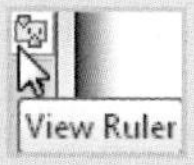

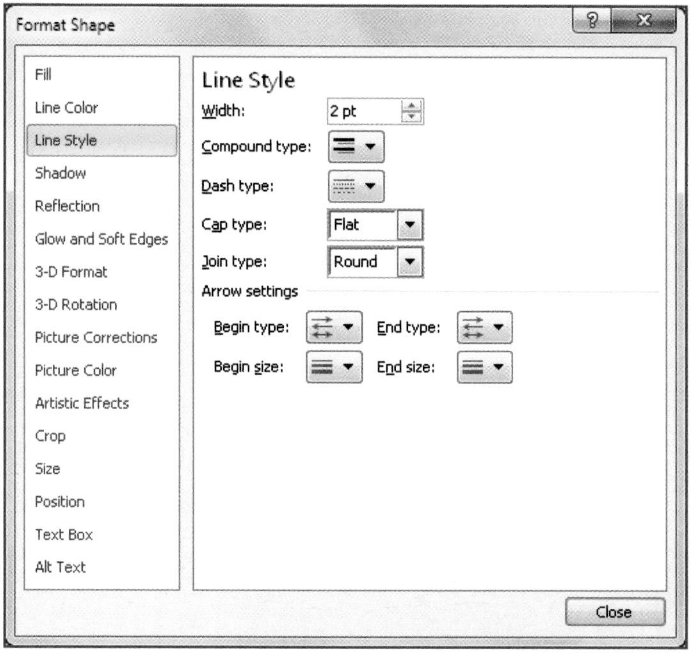

Figure 7-17: ***Each type of illustration has a set of options within the Format dialog box that apply to its unique characteristics.***

Modify Illustrations

Pictures, drawings, and shapes share a common Format dialog box, although not all of the features and options are available for every type of illustration you can add to a Word document. This section describes formatting and other modifications you can apply to illustrations.

Resize and Rotate Illustrations Precisely

You can change the size of illustrations by setting exact dimensions and rotating them. (You can also drag handles to change them interactively. See "Use Handles

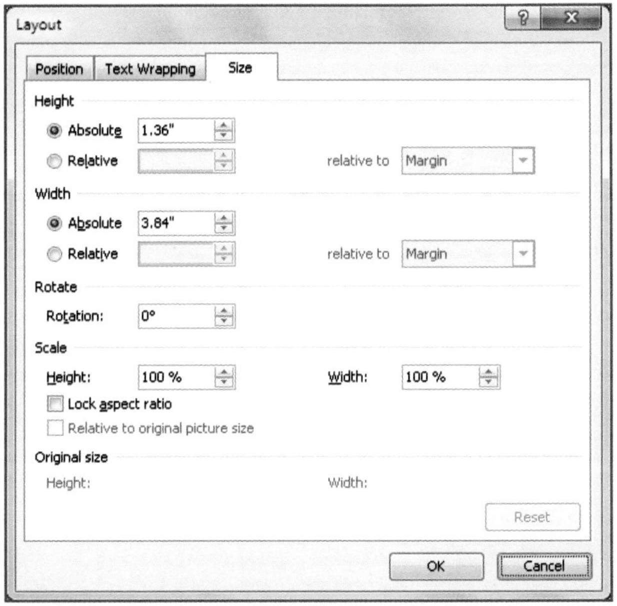

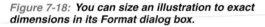

Figure 7-18: **You can size an illustration to exact dimensions in its Format dialog box.**

and Borders to Position Illustrations" later in this chapter for ways to resize and rotate illustrations with a mouse.)

1. Click the illustration you want to resize to select it. In the Picture (or other type of illustration) Tools Format tab, click the **Size Dialog Box Launcher** in the Size group. (For some illustrations, such as an organization chart, the Size Dialog Box Launcher will not exist.)

2. Click the Size tab, shown in Figure 7-18, and if it isn't already selected, click the **Lock Aspect Ratio** check box to size the illustration proportionally when entering either width or height values.

   ● Under Rotate, enter a positive (rotate clockwise) or negative (rotate counterclockwise) number of degrees of rotation if you want to rotate the image.

   ● Under either Height or Width, enter the height or the width dimension, or use the spinners to increase or decrease one of the dimensions from its original size.

   –Or–

   Under Scale, enter a percentage for either the height or the width to increase or decrease it, or use the spinners to increase or decrease the percentage of the original picture size.

3. Click **OK**. The picture will resize and/or rotate according to your values.

Position Illustrations

Illustrations (including pictures that use absolute positioning) can be positioned anywhere in the document by dragging or setting values. In either case, the illustration retains its relative position within the document as text and other objects are added or removed. You can override this behavior by anchoring the illustration to a fixed location. You can also change how text and other objects "wrap" around the illustration. Figure 7-19 shows several of these features.

CHANGE HOW CONTENT DISPLAYS AROUND AN ILLUSTRATION

By default, most illustrations come into a document in-line with the text, like just another character. In this mode, you can't control how the text flows, or *wraps*, around the illustration or where the illustration will be on the page if you

---

TIP

After you change a picture from its default style of being in-line with the text to a style that supports absolute positioning, it is difficult to return to the default style. It's easiest to just delete the picture and reinsert it.

NOTE

The default wrapping option (In Line With Text) is the only style that provides paragraph-like formatting to position pictures. If you change to any of the other wrapping styles, you can position the picture absolutely, that is, by dragging it into position or by selecting positions relative to document areas, such as margins or paragraphs.

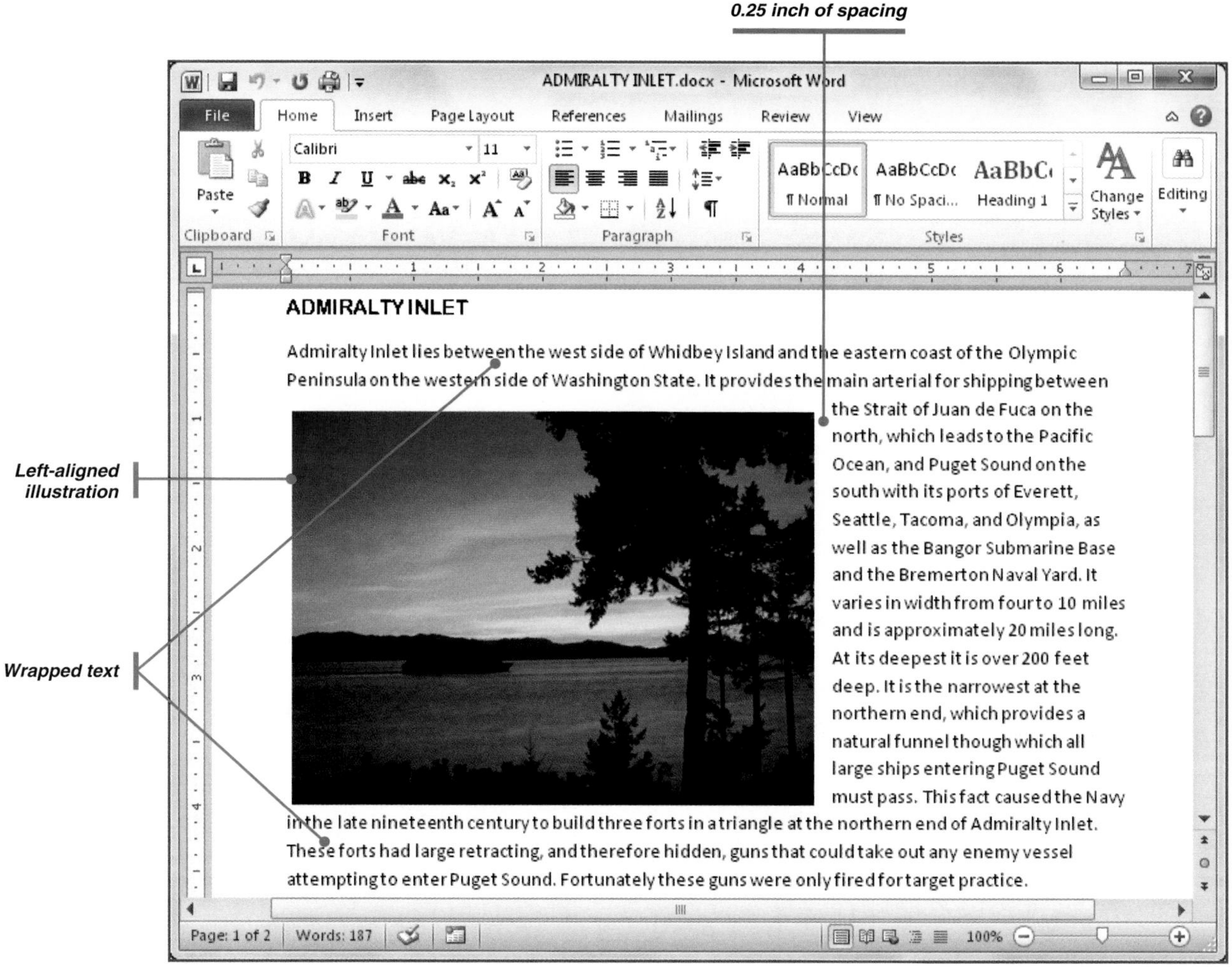
0.25 inch of spacing
Left-aligned illustration
Wrapped text
ADMIRALTY INLET.docx - Microsoft Word
File
Home
Insert
Page Layout
References
Mailings
Review
View
Paste
Clipboard
Font
Paragraph
Styles
Change Styles
Editing
ADMIRALTY INLET
Admiralty Inlet lies between the west side of Whidbey Island and the eastern coast of the Olympic Peninsula on the western side of Washington State. It provides the main arterial for shipping between the Strait of Juan de Fuca on the north, which leads to the Pacific Ocean, and Puget Sound on the south with its ports of Everett, Seattle, Tacoma, and Olympia, as well as the Bangor Submarine Base and the Bremerton Naval Yard. It varies in width from four to 10 miles and is approximately 20 miles long. At its deepest it is over 200 feet deep. It is the narrowest at the northern end, which provides a natural funnel though which all large ships entering Puget Sound must pass. This fact caused the Navy in the late nineteenth century to build three forts in a triangle at the northern end of Admiralty Inlet. These forts had large retracting, and therefore hidden, guns that could take out any enemy vessel attempting to enter Puget Sound. Fortunately these guns were only fired for target practice.
Page: 1 of 2
Words: 187
100%

Figure 7-19: ***You can easily arrange text and illustrations in several configurations using dialog box options.***

change the text. You can change this behavior, however, to gain control of how the illustration and the text relate to each other.

1. Click the illustration that you want to wrap text around to select it. Right-click the illustration and click **More Layout Options**. The Layout dialog box is displayed.

UNDERSTANDING ILLUSTRATION POSITIONING

When you position an illustration (picture, clip art, drawing, or shape) on the page, the position can be *inline*, or *relative*, to the text and other objects on the page, where the illustration moves as the text moves, like a character in a word. The alternative is *absolute* positioning, where the illustration stays anchored in one place, regardless of what the text does. If the illustration uses absolute positioning, you can then specify how text will wrap around the illustration, which can be on either or both sides or along the top and bottom of the illustration. Also, for special effects, the text can be all either on top of the illustration or underneath it.

If you find that the movement of the illustration is not as you intended, or if you want to change the way the illustration behaves as you add text, use the Layout dialog box. Right-click the illustration and click **More Layout Options**. On the Position tab, you'll see horizontal and vertical absolute position options, as shown in Figure 7-20. On the right, you'll see what the illustration is positioned relative to: the margin, page, paragraph, or column. See "Position an Illustration Relative to Areas in a Document," later in this chapter.

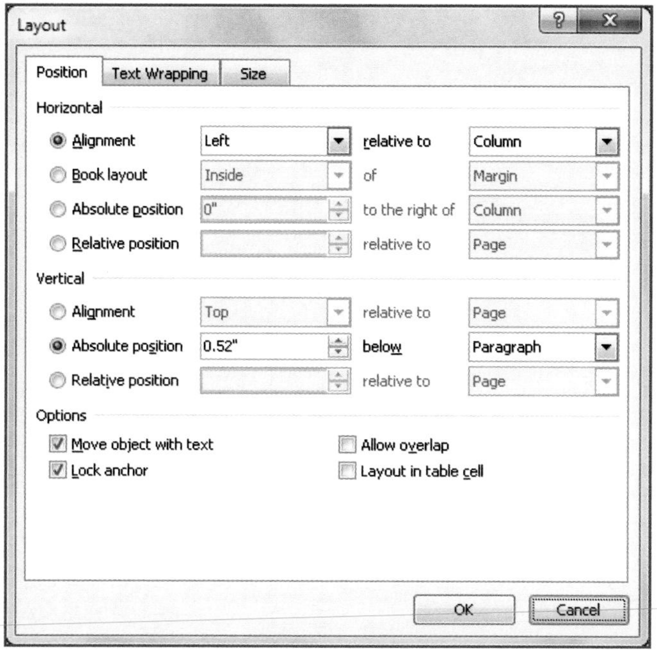

Figure 7-20: **Using absolute positioning, you can choose where to place an illustration relative to other objects in the document.**

2. Click the **Text Wrapping** tab, shown in Figure 7-21, and under Wrapping Style, click one of the styles to wrap as the icons indicate (if you select In Line With Text, the illustration will lose its absolute-positioning ability and can only be positioned using paragraph-like options, plus tabs, text, and spaces on the left).

3. Click where you want text to wrap, and under Distance From Text, click the relevant spinners to enter the distances you want between the text and the illustration.

4. Click **OK** to accept the wrapping style and other settings and to close the dialog box.

POSITION AN ILLUSTRATION RELATIVE TO AREAS IN A DOCUMENT

Besides dragging an illustration into position, you can select or enter values that determine where the illustration is placed in relation to document areas.

1. Right-click the illustration that you want to position to select it.

Figure dialog

Layout

Position | Text Wrapping | Size

Wrapping style

In line with text   Square   Tight   Through   Top and bottom

Behind text   In front of text

Wrap text

○ Both sides   ⦿ Left only   ○ Right only   ○ Largest only

Distance from text

Top   0"   Left   0.25"
Bottom 0"   Right   0.13"

OK   Cancel

*Figure 7-21: **Word allows you to determine with some precision how text and illustrations interact.***

TIP

When an illustration uses absolute positioning, an anchor icon may be displayed. If the anchor is locked, a padlock icon may also be displayed. If you don't see the anchor icon and the illustration is using absolute positioning, click the **File** tab, click **Options**, and click **Display** in the left column. Under Always Show These Formatting Marks, click the **Object Anchors** check box or click **Show All Formatting Marks**. Click **OK** to display anchor icons in the document.

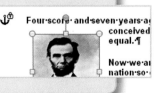

2. Click **More Layout Options**, and click the **Position** tab. Select or enter the horizontal- and vertical-positioning entries by selecting them from the drop-down menus, entering the values, or using the spinners to increase or decrease distances, as shown earlier in Figure 7-20.

3. To anchor an illustration in place, regardless of whether other content is added or removed—for example, an illustration you want in the upper-left corner of a specific page—click the **Lock Anchor** check box, and clear all other options.

4. Click **OK** to close the Layout dialog box.

Use Handles and Borders to Position Illustrations

Illustrations are easily manipulated using their sizing handles and borders.

SELECT AND ROTATE AN ILLUSTRATION

You select an illustration by clicking it. Handles appear around the illustration and allow you to perform interactive changes. Even text boxes and their text behave similarly.

- Click in a text box. A dotted border with handles appears around the perimeter of the text box. Drag the green rotation handle at the top, and the text box and its text will rotate.

- Place the mouse pointer in the text in a text box; it will become an I-beam pointer. Click it to place an insertion point, or drag across the text to select it. The mini toolbar will dimly appear. Move the mouse pointer over the toolbar for it to fully appear, and then make a selection to change the formatting.

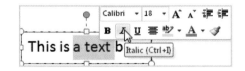

WORKING WITH ILLUSTRATIONS

While illustrations can be positioned absolutely by simply dragging them or choosing placement relative to other objects in a document, Word also provides a number of other techniques that help you adjust where an illustration is in relation to other illustrations.

MOVE ILLUSTRATIONS INCREMENTALLY

Select the illustration or group of illustrations (see "Combine Illustrations by Grouping"), hold **CTRL**, and press one of the arrow keys in the direction you want to move the illustration by very small increments (approximately .01 inch).

REPOSITION THE ORDER OF STACKED ILLUSTRATIONS

You can stack illustrations by simply dragging one on top of another. Figure 7-22 shows an example of a three-illustration stack. To reposition the order of the stack, right-click the illustration you want to change, click **Bring To Front** or **Send To Back** on the context menu, and then click one of the following:

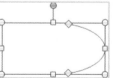

- **Bring To Front** moves the illustration to the top of the stack.

- **Send To Back** moves the illustration to the bottom of the stack.

- **Bring Forward** moves the illustration up one level (same as Bring To Front if there are only two illustrations in the stack).

Continued . . .

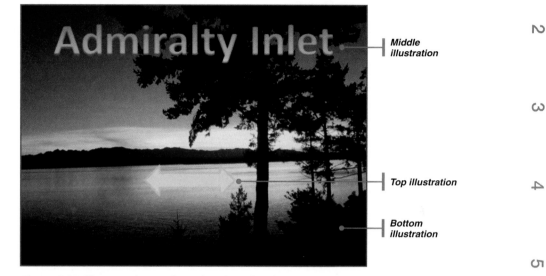

Figure 7-22: **You can change the order of stacked illustrations to achieve the look you want.**

Middle illustration

Top illustration

Bottom illustration

RESIZE AN ILLUSTRATION

Drag one of the square or round sizing handles surrounding the illustration—or at either end of it, in the case of a line—in the direction you want to enlarge or reduce the illustration. Hold **SHIFT** when dragging a corner sizing handle to change the height and length proportionately (if you have Lock Aspect Ratio selected in the Size tab of Format Pictures, the picture will remain proportionally sized without pressing **SHIFT**).

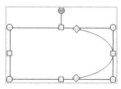

ROTATE AN ILLUSTRATION

Drag the green dot in the direction you want to rotate the illustration. Hold **SHIFT** when dragging to rotate in 15-degree increments (see the earlier illustration with a text box).

QUICKSTEPS

WORKING WITH ILLUSTRATIONS

(Continued)

- **Send Backward** moves the illustration down one level (same as Send To Back if there are only two illustrations in the stack).
- **Bring In Front Of Text** moves the illustration on top of overlapping text.
- **Send Behind Text** moves the illustration behind overlapping text.

ALIGN ILLUSTRATIONS

To align two or more illustrations relative to one another, select the illustrations by holding down **SHIFT**. In the Picture (or Drawing) Tools Format tab Arrange group, click **Align** and click one of the alignment choices.

EVENLY SPACE ILLUSTRATIONS

Select the illustrations by holding down **SHIFT**. In the Picture (or Drawing) Tools Format tab Arrange group, click **Align** and then click **Distribute Horizontally** or **Distribute Vertically**, depending on their orientation.

Align ▾
Align Left
Align Center
Align Right
Align Top
Align Middle
Align Bottom
Distribute Horizontally
Distribute Vertically
Align to Page
Align to Margin
✓ Align Selected Objects
View Gridlines
Grid Settings...

NOTE

If you don't see Order on the context menu when you right-click one of the illustrations in a stack, click outside all the illustrations, and then click one of the other illustrations.

CHANGE AN ILLUSTRATION'S PERSPECTIVE

If the illustration supports interactive adjustment, a yellow diamond adjustment handle is displayed. Drag the yellow diamond toward or away from the illustration to get the look you want.

Combine Illustrations by Grouping

You can combine illustrations for any number of reasons, but you typically work with multiple illustrations to build a more complex rendering. To prevent losing the positioning, sizing, and other characteristics of the individual components, you can group them so that they are treated as one object.

GROUP ILLUSTRATIONS

1. Select the illustrations to be grouped by clicking the first illustration and then holding down **SHIFT** while selecting other drawings and pictures.

2. In the Picture (or Drawing) Tools Format tab Arrange group, click **Group** and then click **Group** again; or right-click one of the selected illustrations, click **Grouping**, and click **Group**. A single set of selection handles surrounds the perimeter of the illustrations. Coloring, positioning, sizing, and other actions now affect the illustrations as a group instead of individually.

UNGROUP ILLUSTRATIONS

To separate a group into individual illustrations, select the group. In the Picture (or Drawing) Tools Format tab Arrange group, click **Group** and click **Ungroup**; or right-click the group, click **Group**, and click **Ungroup**.

Chapter 8
Using Special Features

Word comes with a number of special features that facilitate communications. Forms, which you can quickly generate in Word, provide the means to gather information. Language is no barrier, as Word can translate words and even entire documents. When working with data in Word, you can use Excel's charting capability to create a chart and embed it in Word to provide a more visual representation of data than that provided by a table.

Work with Forms

If you want to collect a consistent set of information from a number of people, an easy way is to use a form that asks for just the information you want. You can, of course, use Word's normal features, especially tables (see Chapter 6) to create a fairly good form. However, Word has some specialized tools that you can use to create professional-looking forms and allow someone using Word

2007 and later versions to interactively fill out the form. Using these same tools, Microsoft has both built in and included on Microsoft Office Online a number of form templates for various purposes. You can use these templates as is, you can modify them, and you can create your own forms from scratch.

Use Microsoft Form Templates

You can use the Microsoft Office Online form templates directly from Word, or you can download and store them on your computer, where they are available from My Templates.

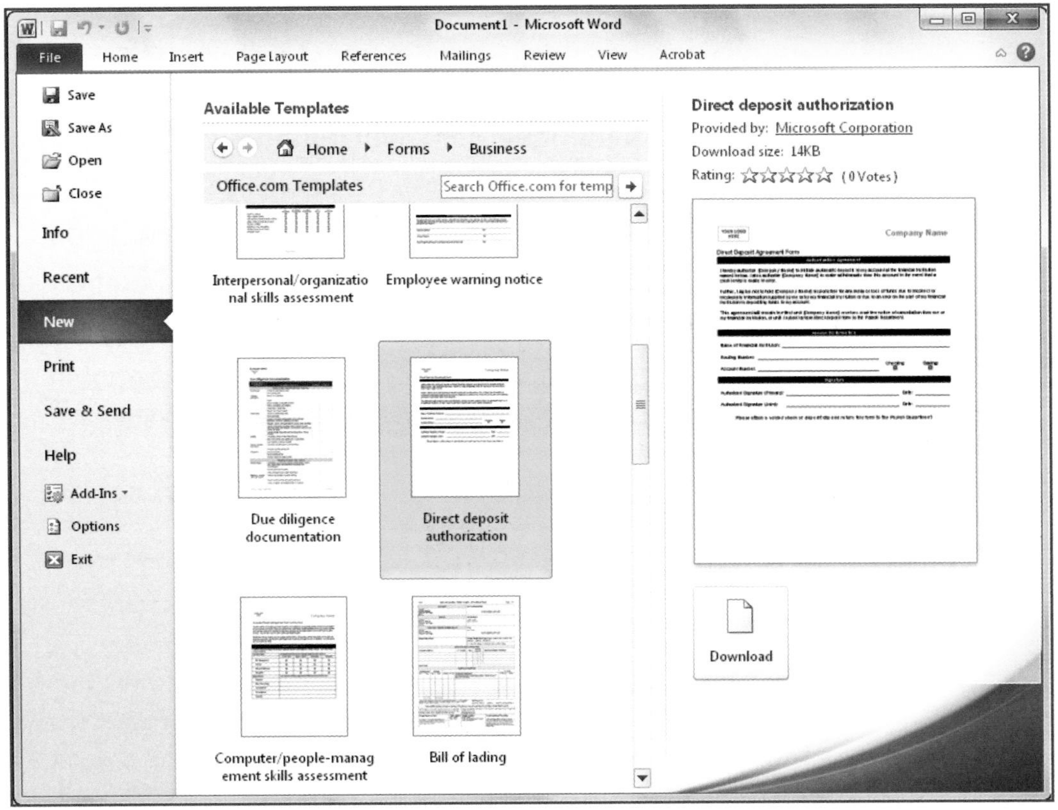

*Figure 8-1: **Microsoft Office Online provides a number of form templates for your use.***

OPEN FORM TEMPLATES IN WORD

If you want to just use the Microsoft-provided templates, you can do so directly from Word.

1. Click **File**, click **New**, and click **Forms** under Office.com Templates in the lower part of the middle pane. Microsoft Office Online is searched, and a list of forms is presented.

2. Click the category of form that you want. For example, click **Business**.

3. Scroll down, reviewing the forms that are available to you, and click the form that you want to use. For example, click **Direct Deposit Authorization**, as shown in Figure 8-1.

4. Click **Download**. The form is opened in Word.

5. Click **File** and click **Save As**.

   If you want to use the form only once, leave the default type **Word Document**.

   –Or–

If you want to use the form a number of times or modify it, change the default type to **Word Template**.

6. In either case, select a folder in which to store the form, enter a file name, and click **Save**. See the "Using a Form" QuickSteps in this chapter.

DOWNLOAD TEMPLATES TO YOUR COMPUTER

While you can save the templates obtained in the previous section as template files (instead of document files), another way is to download Microsoft Office Online templates using your browser and save them as template files.

1. Open your browser and in the address line, type office.microsoft.com/templates, and press **ENTER**.

2. Scroll down the page. Under Browse Templates, click **Forms**, scroll down, and click the category that is correct for you. For example, click **Employment**.

3. Scroll down and click the form that you want to use. For example, click **Absence Request Form (For Employees)**. Scroll down to see a large image of the form. If this is what you want to use, click **Download**.

   A message box will open telling you the status of the download. When this completes, the form will open in Word, as you can see in Figure 8-2.

4. You can save this file as either a template or a document, depending on your needs. Click the **File** tab and click **Save As**. The Save As dialog box will appear. If you want to save this file as a template, click the **Save As** Type down arrow, choose **Word Template (*.dotx)**, and select your Template folder. If you want to save it as a document with a .docx (or .doc) extension in a different folder, you must specify this. The default Template folder is C:\Users\username\AppData\Roaming\Microsoft\Templates.

5. When the Save As dialog box is as you want it, click **Save**. (Files saved as templates in the Templates folder can be accessed above the Favorites list on the upper-left area of the Save As dialog box.)

Modify a Template

The fields that you can fill out or select on a Microsoft form template are created or modified using the content controls on the Developer tab in Word.

1. If you don't see the Developer tab, click **File**, click **Options**, and click **Customize Ribbon** in the left pane. At the top of the right column, select **Main Tabs**, about halfway down the right column click the **Developer** check box to select it, and click **OK**.

Absence request form (for employees)
Provided by: Kalope Blue
Version: Word 2007
Downloads: 16700
Rating: ★★★★☆ (21 votes)

CAUTION

Microsoft Office Online form templates are created for several different programs. Make sure that the one you choose has been created for Word.

Main Tabs
- ☑ Home
- ☑ Insert
- ☑ Page Layout
- ☑ References
- ☑ Mailings
- ☑ Review
- ☑ View
- ☑ Developer
- ☑ Add-Ins
- ☑ Blog Post
- ☑ Insert (Blog Post)
- ☑ Outlining
- ☑ Background Removal

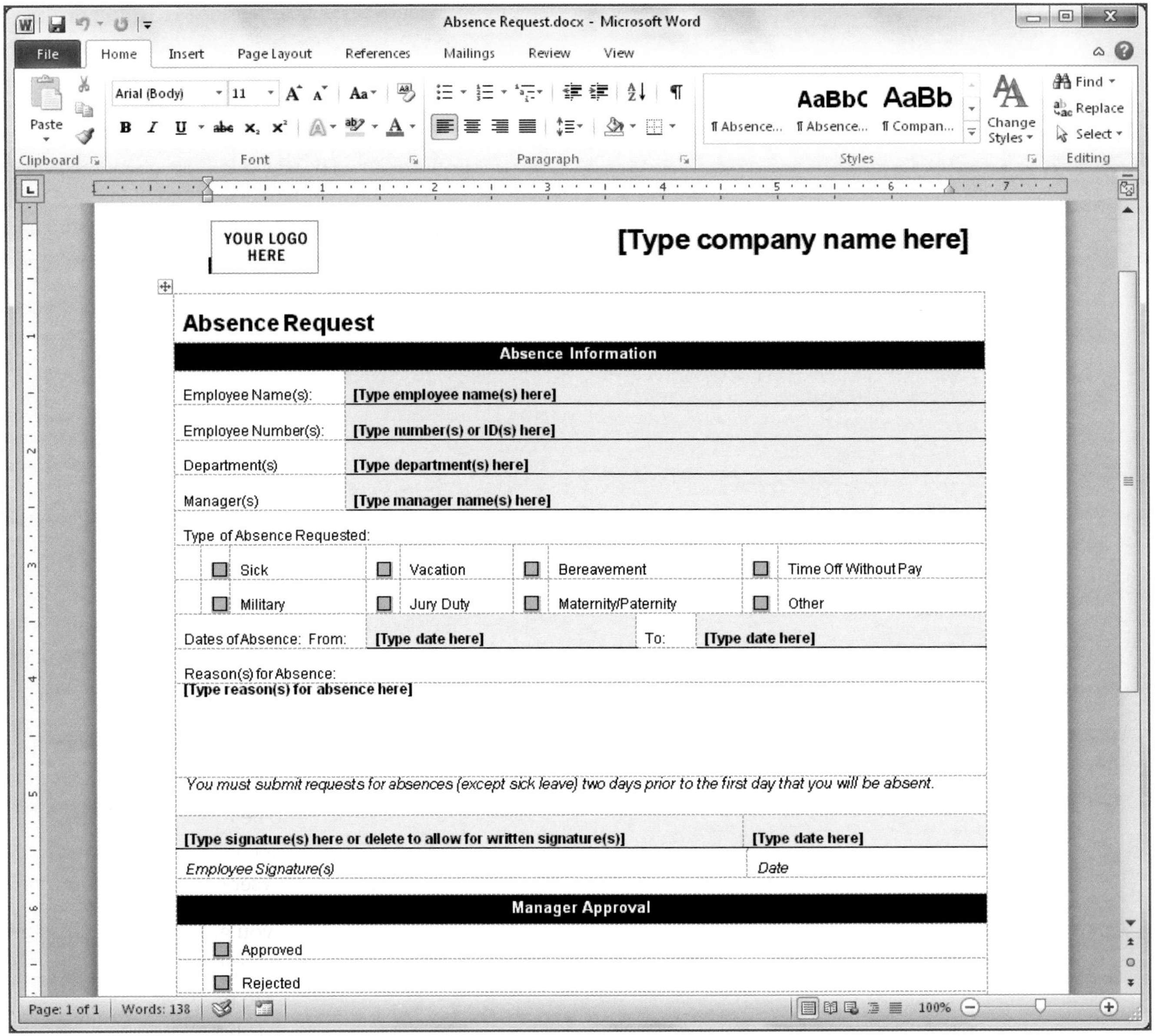

Figure 8-2: **The Microsoft Office Online form templates are ready to be filled out in Word—just click in a field.**

Check Box Form Field Options

Check box size
- ● Auto
- ○ Exactly: 10 pt

Default value
- ● Not checked
- ○ Checked

Run macro on
Entry:
Exit:

Field settings
Bookmark: Check3
- ☑ Check box enabled
- ☐ Calculate on exit

Add Help Text...   OK   Cancel

NOTE

If you choose to save a document or form in either .docx or .dotx format, you will see a message here saying "You are about to save your document to one of the new file formats..." Click **OK** to continue; or click **Cancel**, select the **Maintain Compatibility With Previous Versions Of Word** check box, and click **Save**.

Absence Request

Absence Information				
Employee Name(s):	[Type employee name(s) here]			
Employee Number(s):	[Type number(s) or ID(s) here]			
Department(s)	[Type department(s) here]			
Manager(s)	[Type manager name(s) here]			

Type of Absence Requested:

☐ Sick	☐ Vacation	☐ Bereavement	☐ Time Off Without Pay	
☐ Military	☐ Jury Duty	☐ Maternity/Paternity	☐ Other	

Dates of Absence: From: [Type date here] To: [Type date here]

*Figure 8-3: **Most Microsoft Office Word form templates are built using tables and can be easily modified.***

2. Open a Microsoft form template, and save it as a template, as explained in "Use Microsoft Form Templates" earlier in this chapter.

3. In the Developer tab Controls group, click **Design Mode** and take a minute to explore the form. Most forms are based on a table format. You can see this more easily if you right-click a section of the form, click **Borders And Shading**, click **All**, and click **OK**. You can see the results of doing this in Figure 8-3—using the form in Figure 8-2. (If the border lines do not show up, make sure the color of the lines is black.)

4. Click in the fields, and see how you can easily change the existing text or label simply by selecting it and typing new text. Depending on the type of field, field properties are available that you can work with. For example, if you double-click a check box, you'll see the following dialog box.

5. You can delete fields by selecting the table row and deleting it. You can also split and merge table cells to create fewer or more cells to hold fields. (See Chapter 6 for information on how to work with tables.)

6. You can add various kinds of fields, as described in the next section "Create a Form."

7. When you have the form template the way you want it, click **File**, click **Save As**, click the **Save As Type** down arrow, click either **Word Template (*.dotx)** to create a template for use with Word 2007 and 2010 or **Word 97-2003 Template (*.dot)** to create a template that can be used with previous versions of Word.

8. Select **Templates** under Microsoft Office Word on the top-left area of the Save As dialog box, adjust the file name as desired, and click **Save**.

Create a Form

Your first step in creating a form is to decide how the form is to be used. Is it going to be printed and filled out by hand; is it going to be filled out using Word and, if so, what is the oldest version of Word that will be used; or will it be filled out in a browser over either an intranet or the Internet?

Second, are you going to use an existing layout in one of Microsoft's templates or design your own layout, perhaps using a table to provide the overall structure? You then need to add fields (Microsoft calls them "controls") to the form, but you determine which set of controls to use.

LAY OUT A FORM

Laying out a form is one way of visualizing how the information you want to collect will appear. That is why it is so helpful to at least look at, if not start with, a form that is already completed. If you don't use an existing form, start by listing all of the fields you want on the screen. Then assign a type of control to each field.

- **Labels** are typed like any other text.
- **Text fields** allow the entry of text onto the form.
- **Check boxes** allow the selection of several options in a group.
- **Option buttons** allow the selection of one option in a group.
- **Spinners** allow the selection of a number in a series.
- **Combo boxes** (or drop-down lists) allow the selection of one item in a list, the first item of which is displayed.
- **List boxes** allow the selection of one item in a list where all items are displayed.
- **Command buttons** perform an action when clicked, such as saving or resetting the form.
- **Picture** (or image) allows the attachment of a picture or image when the form is filled out.

Next, sketch out the form so that you have a rough idea what will go where, and then create a table that has the general layout of the form (see Chapter 6 for information on creating tables). You can split and merge fields to make the final form layout.

SELECT CONTROLS

In the Developer tab Controls group, you have a choice of three different sets of form field controls: those that can be used only in Word 2010 forms, those that can be used in Word 2003 and later forms, and those that can be used in forms created in Word 97 and later. These are grouped into:

- Controls that must be saved in a .dotx file and accessed and used in Word 2007 and 2010. These are available in the upper-left area of the Developer tab Controls group.
- ActiveX controls that can be saved either in a .dot or .dotx file and accessed and used in Word 2003 or Word 2010. These are available in the lower part of the Legacy Tools flyout menu. (Legacy Tools is at the bottom-right corner in the Developer tab Controls group.)

Form fields for use in Word 2007/10

Form fields for use in early versions of Word

Form fields for use in Word 2003

- Legacy form controls that can be saved either in a .dot or .dotx file and accessed and used in Word 97 through Word 2010. These are available in the upper part of the Legacy Tools flyout menu.

Choosing the type of controls to use depends a lot on how the form will be used. If you are going to print the form and have it manually filled out, then any of the controls will work. If the form will be filled out using Word, then you need to decide which versions of Word the form will support. Similarly, if the form will be filled out using a browser, you will need to decide which browsers you will support. The latest controls for use with Word 2007 and 2010 only work with the latest browsers. The ActiveX controls for use with Word 2003 work with more browsers, but far from all of them.

The simple answer, of course, is to use the oldest set of controls. The problem is that these controls are the most limited and, therefore, restrict what you can do on the form. You need to determine which solution best meets your needs.

> **NOTE**
>
> ActiveX controls require knowledge of Visual Basic for Applications (VBA) to fully use their capabilities. Use of VBA is beyond the scope of this book.

INSERT FIELDS

The actual inserting of a field is anticlimactic.

1. Click in the table cell where you want a label for a field, and type the label.
2. Click in the table cell next to the label. In the Developer tab Controls group, click the control you want to use in that particular field.
3. Repeat steps 1 and 2 for each field in the form (see Figure 8-4).

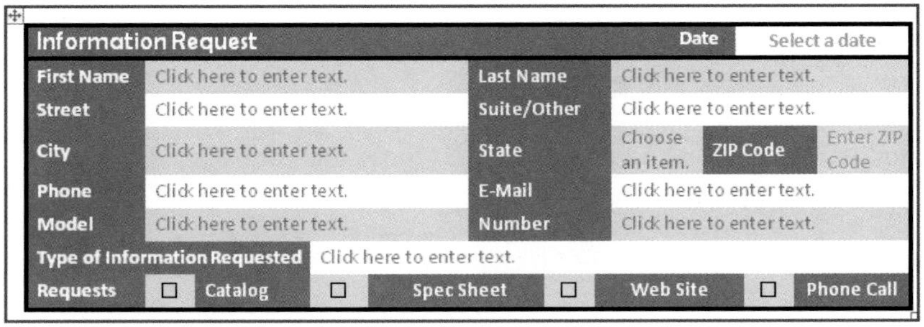

Information Request				Date	Select a date
First Name	Click here to enter text.	Last Name	Click here to enter text.		
Street	Click here to enter text.	Suite/Other	Click here to enter text.		
City	Click here to enter text.	State	Choose an item.	ZIP Code	Enter ZIP Code
Phone	Click here to enter text.	E-Mail	Click here to enter text.		
Model	Click here to enter text.	Number	Click here to enter text.		
Type of Information Requested	Click here to enter text.				
Requests	☐ Catalog	☐ Spec Sheet	☐ Web Site	☐ Phone Call	

Figure 8-4: ***A simple form in design mode created using Word 2007/2010 controls***

SET FIELD PROPERTIES AND SAVE A TEMPLATE

Once you have added the controls that you want in each field, you need to set the properties for those controls. The following steps are based on using the upper level of the Legacy Tools flyout menu. You'll find that the choices you have for the Properties dialog boxes differ, depending on which controls you use.

1. Click the control you want to work with, and click **Properties** in the Developer tab Controls group. The properties dialog box for the control will appear.

QUICKSTEPS

USING A FORM

Once you have created a form and saved it as a template, it can be used on any computer with a version of Word that is appropriate for the type of fields used on the form.

1. In Word, click **File** and click **New**. In the middle column, click **My Templates** and double-click your template. The form will open as a document.
2. Click in the first field, and enter the information requested. Press **TAB** to move to the next field.
3. Repeat step 2 until all fields are filled in. Figure 8-5 shows the form in Figure 8-4 after it is filled out.
4. Click **File** and click **Save As**. Opposite Save As Type, select either **Word Document** for a Word 2010 file or **Word 97-2003 Document** for earlier versions, select a folder in which to save the filled-out form, enter a file name, and click **Save**.

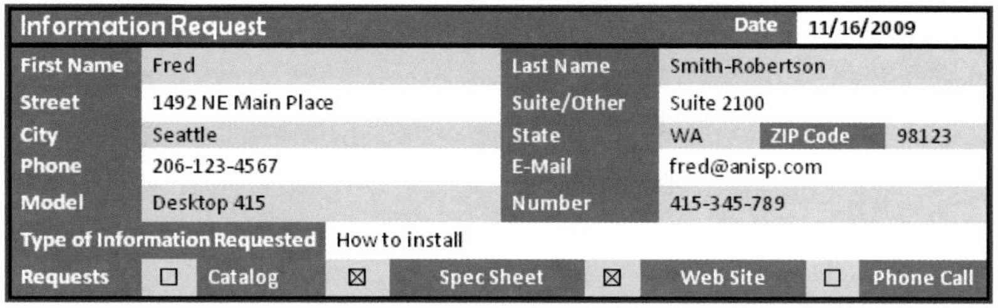

Information Request				Date	11/16/2009
First Name	Fred	Last Name	Smith-Robertson		
Street	1492 NE Main Place	Suite/Other	Suite 2100		
City	Seattle	State	WA	ZIP Code	98123
Phone	206-123-4567	E-Mail	fred@anisp.com		
Model	Desktop 415	Number	415-345-789		
Type of Information Requested	How to install				
Requests	☐ Catalog	☒ Spec Sheet	☒ Web Site	☐ Phone Call	

Figure 8-5: ***When you design a form, consider how easy it will be to gather information from it.***

NOTE

If you choose a language that does not display its translated words correctly, you might have to install additional language-support software. Go to the Microsoft Office Web site (office.microsoft.com), and search for "proofing tools." You can download a number of different options.

2. Select or enter the information needed for that control. For example, the following illustration shows the properties dialog box for a drop-down list box that will allow the selection of a state.

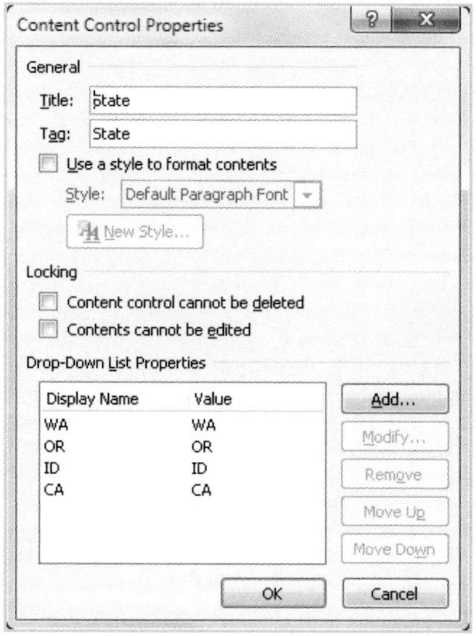

3. When the form is the way you want it, click **File** and click **Save As**. In the Save As dialog box, opposite Save As Type, select **Word Template (*.dotx)** if your template will be used with Word 2007 or 2010; otherwise, select **Word 97-2003 Template (*.dot)** for earlier versions of Word.
4. Select **Templates** under Microsoft Office Word on the top-left area of the Save As dialog box, adjust the file name as desired, and click **Save**.

Translate Text

Word's Translate feature allows you to choose the original and translated languages and whether you want to translate the whole document, selected text, or a word or phrase. This process uses either a bilingual dictionary, for smaller amounts of text, or a computer translation service offered by Microsoft.

Translate a Word or Phrase

To translate a word or phrase, the Mini Translator is your best option.

1. Open the document in Word with which you want translation help.

2. In the Review tab Language group, click **Translate** to open the drop-down menu, and click **Mini Translator**.

3. The first time you click Translate, the Translation Language Options dialog box appears. Click the **Translate To** drop-down list, click the language and country to which you want to translate, and click **OK**.

4. Point at the word or select the phrase you want translated. The Mini Translator's Bilingual Dictionary will faintly appear. Move your mouse into it to see your word or phrase and its translation to the language you selected.

Bilingual Dictionary

father
['fɑːðər] *noun* père *masculin*, *Father Martin* RELIGION le père Martin

5. To translate another word or phrase, point at or select it, and the Mini Translator will display the translation.

Translate Selected Text

To translate larger sections of text:

1. Open the document in Word, and select the section(s) of text you want translated.

2. In the Review tab Language group, click **Translate** and then click **Translate Selected Text**.

–Or–

Right-click your selected text, and click **Translate**.

In either case, the Research task pane appears on the right side of the Word window with the Translation option selected.

3. Under Translation, click the **From** and **To** down arrows, and click the language the text is in (From) and the language you want it translated into (To). The results are displayed in the Translation section of the Research task pane, as shown in Figure 8-6.

4. To translate another word or phrase, select the text and repeat steps 2 and 3.

Translate Document [English (U.S.) to French (France)]
Show a machine translation in a Web browser.

Translate Selected Text
Show a translation from local and online services in the Research Pane.

Mini Translator
Point to a word or select a phrase to view a quick translation.

Choose Translation Language...

NOTE

After the first time you click Translate, Word will assume that you want to continue to translate from and to the same languages you originally selected. If that is not true, click **Choose Translation Language**, select the From and To languages, and click **OK**.

NOTE

The Mini Translator's bilingual dictionary translation is fine for words or short translations, but the literal translation may lose the "sense" of the words. For a more "true" translation, use the online machine translation services that are offered. See "Translate Selected Text" and "Translate an Entire Document" for more information.

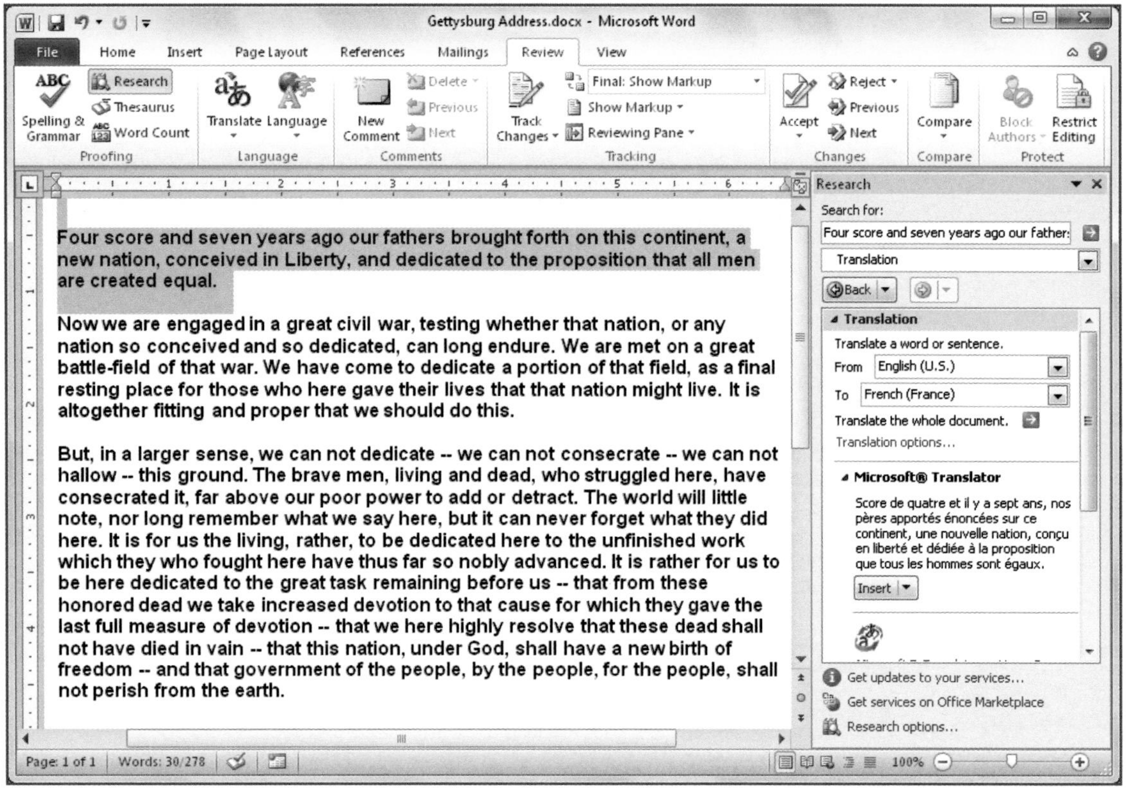

Translate an Entire Document

To translate a complete document, you can send the document unencrypted over the Internet to a Microsoft computer translator.

1. Open the document in Word to be translated. In the Review tab Language group, click **Translate** and then click **Translate Document**.

2. The first time you click Translate, the Translation Language Options dialog box appears. Click the **Translate To** drop-down list, click the language and country to which you want to translate, and click **OK**.

After the first time, when you click Translate, Word will assume that you want to continue to translate to the same language. If that is not true, click **Choose Translation Language**, select the From and To languages, and click **OK**.

3. Click **Send** to send the document unencrypted over the Internet.

Figure 8-6: Word provides the ability to translate a number of languages using both bilingual dictionaries and machine translation.

4. Your browser opens to the Windows Live Translator with the document translated using machine translation, similar to that shown in Figure 8-7. To see how a particular section will be translated, move your mouse to that section; it and the translation will be highlighted. You can also copy and paste the translation into your Word document.

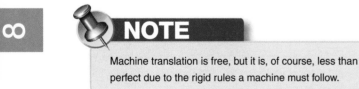

NOTE

Machine translation is free, but it is, of course, less than perfect due to the rigid rules a machine must follow.

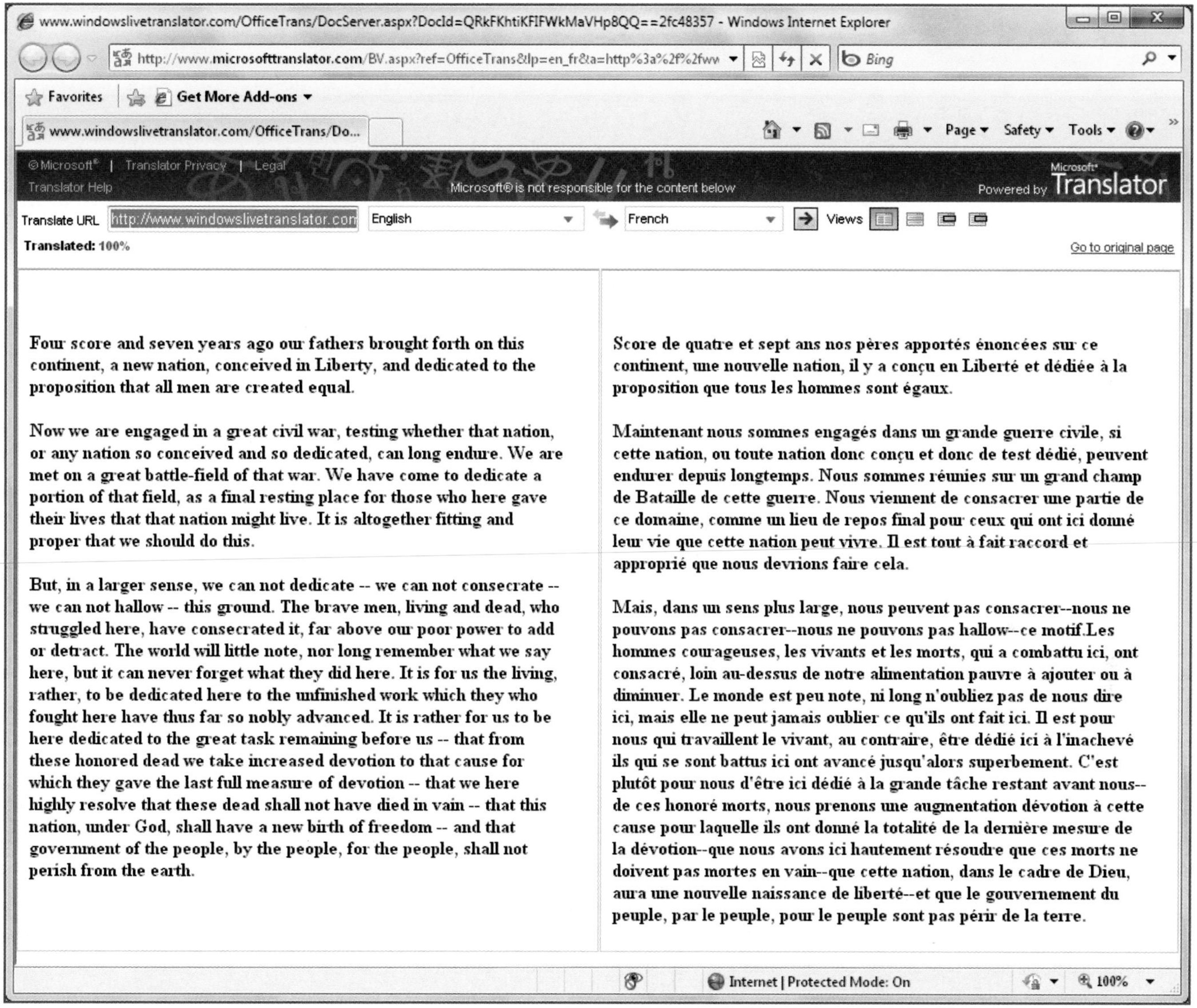

www.windowslivetranslator.com/OfficeTrans/DocServer.aspx?DocId=QRkFKhtiKFIFWkMaVHp8QQ==2fc48357 - Windows Internet Explorer
http://www.microsofttranslator.com/BV.aspx?ref=OfficeTrans&lp=en_fr&a=http%3a%2f%2fww
Bing
Favorites
Get More Add-ons
www.windowslivetranslator.com/OfficeTrans/Do...
Page
Safety
Tools
©Microsoft® | Translator Privacy | Legal
Translator Help
Microsoft® is not responsible for the content below
Powered by Microsoft® Translator
Translate URL
http://www.windowslivetranslator.com
English
French
Views
Translated: 100%
Go to original page
Four score and seven years ago our fathers brought forth on this continent, a new nation, conceived in Liberty, and dedicated to the proposition that all men are created equal.
Now we are engaged in a great civil war, testing whether that nation, or any nation so conceived and so dedicated, can long endure. We are met on a great battle-field of that war. We have come to dedicate a portion of that field, as a final resting place for those who here gave their lives that that nation might live. It is altogether fitting and proper that we should do this.
But, in a larger sense, we can not dedicate -- we can not consecrate -- we can not hallow -- this ground. The brave men, living and dead, who struggled here, have consecrated it, far above our poor power to add or detract. The world will little note, nor long remember what we say here, but it can never forget what they did here. It is for us the living, rather, to be dedicated here to the unfinished work which they who fought here have thus far so nobly advanced. It is rather for us to be here dedicated to the great task remaining before us -- that from these honored dead we take increased devotion to that cause for which they gave the last full measure of devotion -- that we here highly resolve that these dead shall not have died in vain -- that this nation, under God, shall have a new birth of freedom -- and that government of the people, by the people, for the people, shall not perish from the earth.
Score de quatre et sept ans nos pères apportés énoncées sur ce continent, une nouvelle nation, il y a conçu en Liberté et dédiée à la proposition que tous les hommes sont égaux.
Maintenant nous sommes engagés dans un grande guerre civile, si cette nation, ou toute nation donc conçu et donc de test dédié, peuvent endurer depuis longtemps. Nous sommes réunies sur un grand champ de Bataille de cette guerre. Nous viennent de consacrer une partie de ce domaine, comme un lieu de repos final pour ceux qui ont ici donné leur vie que cette nation peut vivre. Il est tout à fait raccord et approprié que nous devrions faire cela.
Mais, dans un sens plus large, nous peuvent pas consacrer--nous ne pouvons pas consacrer--nous ne pouvons pas hallow--ce motif.Les hommes courageuses, les vivants et les morts, qui a combattu ici, ont consacré, loin au-dessus de notre alimentation pauvre à ajouter ou à diminuer. Le monde est peu note, ni long n'oubliez pas de nous dire ici, mais elle ne peut jamais oublier ce qu'ils ont fait ici. Il est pour nous qui travaillent le vivant, au contraire, être dédié ici à l'inachevé ils qui se sont battus ici ont avancé jusqu'alors superbement. C'est plutôt pour nous d'être ici dédié à la grande tâche restant avant nous--de ces honoré morts, nous prenons une augmentation dévotion à cette cause pour laquelle ils ont donné la totalité de la dernière mesure de la dévotion--que nous avons ici hautement résoudre que ces morts ne doivent pas mortes en vain--que cette nation, dans le cadre de Dieu, aura une nouvelle naissance de liberté--et que le gouvernement du peuple, par le peuple, pour le peuple sont pas périr de la terre.
Internet | Protected Mode: On
100%

Figure 8-7: ***Your document is quickly translated by Microsoft's computer translation service.***

NOTE

The terms *chart* and *graph* can be used interchangeably; they mean the same thing here.

Work with Charts

Word 2010 uses Excel 2010's extensive chart-building capability to embed a chart in a Word document. You have the full functionality of the chart program available to you, as shown in Figure 8-8. After the chart is created, you can change how your data is displayed—for example, you can switch from column

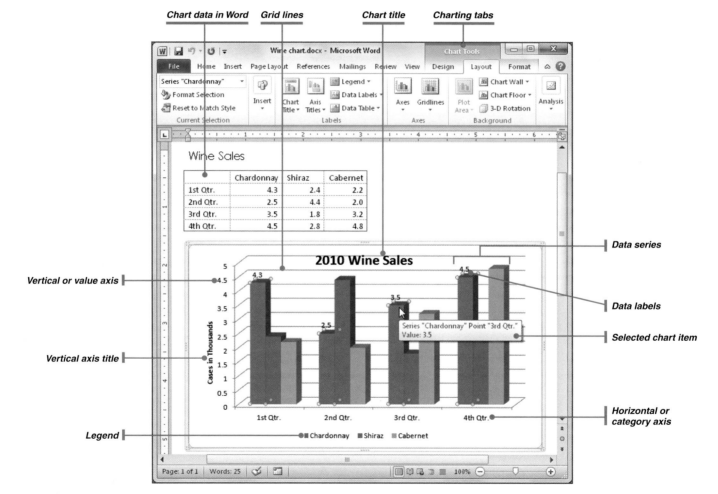

Figure 8-8: Word 2010 uses Excel 2010's chart tools to display your data in a Word document.

representation to a line chart. In addition, you can add or remove chart items, such as titles, axes, legends, and gridlines, as well as format text and several of the chart items with color and other attributes.

Create a Chart

Charts are created from Word by initially opening the charting capability in Excel and using a sample table there to embed and display a chart of that data in Word. This chart can be easily formatted and reconfigured to meet your needs. You can then replace the sample data with the real data you want displayed, either by typing the data or by cutting and pasting it.

1. In Word, open the document and click the insertion point where you want the chart displayed.

2. In the Insert tab Illustrations group, click Chart ⬛ Chart . The Insert Chart dialog box appears.

3. In the Insert Chart dialog box, first click the type of chart you want in the left column, and then double-click the variation of that type on the right.

Excel opens and displays a table of sample data, while in Word, a chart of the type you specified displays the sample data graphically. Figure 8-9 shows the two windows side-by-side (you must manually arrange the windows side by side).

4. You can replace the data in the Excel window by typing over it or by copying data from another table, perhaps in Word, to the Excel table. To directly replace the data in the Excel window, type your data over the sample data. To copy another table's data with one that exists in Word, select the Word table, copy it, click the upper-left cell in the Excel table, and paste the Word table there:

	Chardonnay	Shiraz	Cabernet
1st Qtr.	4.3	2.4	2.2
2nd Qtr.	2.5	4.4	2.0
3rd Qtr.	3.5	1.8	3.2
4th Qtr.	4.5	2.8	4.8

	A	B	C	D
1	Column1	Chardonna	Shiraz	Cabernet
2	1st Qtr.	4.3	2.4	2.2
3	2nd Qtr.	2.5	4.4	2
4	3rd Qtr.	3.5	1.8	3.2
5	4th Qtr.	4.5	2.8	4.8

Word data transferred to Excel

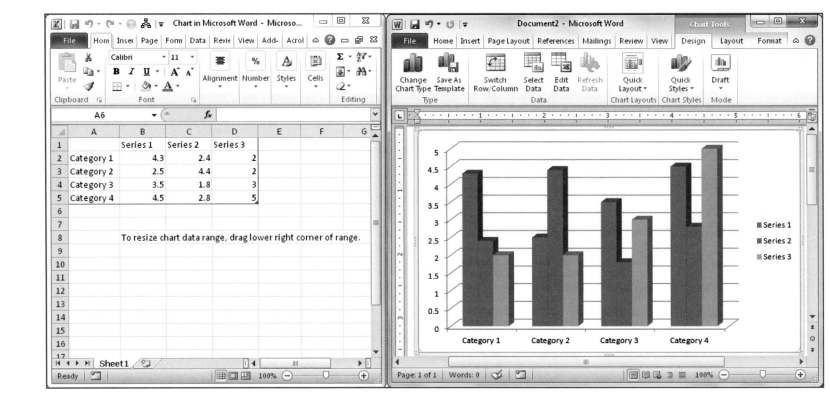

Figure 8-9: To create a chart, Word opens Excel, and the two programs can be displayed side-by-side.

Determine the Chart Type

In Excel, there are 11 standard chart types available to display your data. Each chart type has two or more variations you can choose. In addition, you can create a custom chart type based on changes you've made to a chart. Table 8-1 describes the different chart types.

CHANGE THE CHART TYPE

1. Click in the chart to select it.

2. Click the **Chart Tools Design** tab, and in the Type group, click **Change Chart Type**.

3. In the Change Chart Type dialog box, double-click a different chart type.

4. Repeat steps 2 and 3 as many times as needed to find the correct chart type for your data.

CHART TYPE	FUNCTION
Column, Bar, Line	Compares trends in multiple data series in various configurations, such as vertical and horizontal, and in several shapes, such as bar, cylinder, cone, and pyramid
Pie and Doughnut	Displays one data series (pie) or compares multiple data series (doughnut), either as part of a whole or 100 percent
XY (Scatter)	Displays pairs of data to establish concentrations
Area	Shows the magnitude of change over time; useful when summing multiple values to see the contribution of each
Radar	Connects changes in a data series from a starting or center point with lines, markers, or a colored fill
Surface	Compares trends in multiple data series in a continuous curve; similar to line chart with a 3-D visual effect
Bubble	Displays sets of three values; similar to an XY chart, with the third value being the size of the bubble
Stock	Displays three sets of values, such as a high, low, and closing stock price

Table 8-1: Chart Types

CREATE A CHART TEMPLATE

After you have applied formatting and added or removed chart items, your chart may not resemble any of the standard chart types provided by Excel. To save your work as a template so that you can build a similar chart at another time:

Save As Template

1. Create and customize the chart in Word, as described earlier in this chapter.

2. Select the chart (the sizing border and the Chart Tools tabs should appear), and in the Chart Tools Design tab Type group, click **Save As Template**.

3. In the Save Chart Template dialog box that appears, the default folder where you want the template stored will be selected. The default and recommended location (because it will automatically be found there) is C:\Users*username*\AppData\Roaming\Microsoft\ Templates\Charts.

4. Enter a chart name, and click **Save**.

USE A CHART TEMPLATE

You can use a chart template, either when creating a new chart or by making an existing chart look like the template.

1. Create and save a chart as a template, as described in the previous section.

2. In a new document, either:

QUICKSTEPS

SELECTING CHART ITEMS

You can select items on a chart using the Chart Tools Layout tab, the Chart Tools Format tab, the keyboard, or by clicking the item with the mouse. When selected, items will display small, round handles (for some items, these are sizing handles; for others, they just show that they have been selected).

SELECT CHART ITEMS FROM THE LAYOUT TAB

1. Click the chart you are working on.

2. In the Chart Tools Layout tab, click the major item in the Labels, Axes, and Background groups that you want to select (such as Chart Title or Data Labels). A context menu is displayed. Click the specific variation you want.

SELECT CHART ITEMS FROM THE CURRENT SELECTION GROUP

1. Click the chart you are working on.

2. In either the Chart Tools Layout or Format tab Current Selection group in the upper-left area of the ribbon, click the down arrow, and then click the chart item you want.

Continued . . .

Click in the document at the location where you want the chart. In the Insert tab Illustrations group, click **Chart**.

–Or–

Select the chart in the document that you want to change, and in the Chart Tools Design tab Type group, click **Change Chart Type**.

In either case, the chart type selection dialog box will appear (labeled either "Change Chart Type" or "Insert Chart").

3. Click **Templates** at the top of the left column, and then double-click the template you want to use on the right.

DELETE A CHART TEMPLATE

You can delete a chart template from your folder of templates.

1. In any document open in Word, in the Insert tab Illustrations group, click **Chart**.

2. Click **Manage Templates** at the bottom of the left column, find and right-click the template you want to remove, and click **Delete** on the context menu.

Work with Chart Items

You can add or modify items on a chart to help clarify and emphasize the data it represents.

1. In an open Word document, click to select the chart you want to work on.

2. In the Chart Tools Layout tab or directly on the chart, select the chart item you want to work on, as described in the "Selecting Chart Items" QuickSteps.

ADD A CHART TITLE

1. With the chart selected, in the Chart Tools Layout tab, click **Chart Title** in the Labels group.

2. Click either **Centered Overlay Title** or **Above Chart**. The words "Chart Title" appear in a selected text box at the top of the chart.

Chart Title

3. Type your own title.

QUICKSTEPS

SELECTING CHART ITEMS *(Continued)*

SELECT CHART ITEMS USING THE KEYBOARD

Click the chart. Use the arrow keys on your keyboard to cycle through the chart items. A set of selection handles will appear around the selected item.

SELECT CHART ITEMS BY CLICKING

Point your mouse at the item you want selected, and click. Again, a set of selection handles will appear around the selected item.

When you are selecting one element of a series, you click once to select the whole series, and a second time to get one single element in the series.

TIP

The chart item displayed at the top of the Current Selection group in the Chart Tools Format or Layout tab changes as you select an element on the chart. For example, when you select a column in a column chart, the option will be "Series *name*"; when you select an axis, the option will be "*named* Axis"; when you select a legend, the option will be "Legend." You can also use this technique to select an element that you may not easily be able to click or select any other way. You click the element in this drop-down list, and then click **Format Selection** to display a dialog box where it can be formatted.

ADD AN AXIS TITLE

1. With the chart selected, in the Chart Tools Layout tab, click **Axis Title** in the Labels group.

2. Click either **Primary Horizontal Axis Title** or **Primary Vertical Axis Title**. Then click the variant of the axis title you want to use. The words "Axis Title" appear in a selected text box either to the left of the vertical axis or below the horizontal axis.

3. Type your own title.

MOVE THE LEGEND

1. With the chart selected, in the Chart Tools Layout tab, click **Legend** in the Labels group.

2. Click where and how you want to display the legend. The legend will be moved accordingly.

SHOW DATA LABELS

Data labels are the actual numbers that generate the elements on a chart. For example, if you have a bar on a bar chart that represents 4.5 units sold, the data label, which you can optionally add to the chart, would be "4.5."

1. With the chart selected, click one of your data series (a column, bar, or line), and in the Chart Tools Layout tab, click **Data Labels** in the Labels group.

UNDERSTANDING DATA SERIES AND AXES

There are a few guidelines for setting up data for charting, as well as some assumptions that are used.

- Text, which is used solely to create labels, should only be in the topmost row and/or the leftmost column. Text encountered in the table outside these two areas is charted as zero.

- Each cell must contain a *value* (or data point). Values in the same row or column are considered to be related and are called a *data series*. The first data series starts with the first cell in the upper-left corner of the selected data that is not text or formatted as a date. Subsequent data series are determined by continuing across the rows or down the columns.

- If it is determined that there is a greater number of rows or columns selected, the lesser number is assumed to be the data series, and the greater number is assumed to be categories that are plotted on the horizontal or category (X) axis. In Figure 8-8, there are three columns and four rows of data. As a result, the rows become categories and the columns become data series. When the number of rows and columns are equal, this same pattern is the default.

- The vertical or value (Y) axis displays a scale for the values in the data series.

- To swap the categories and data series, in the Chart Tools Design tab Data group, click **Edit Data**, and then click **Switch Row/Column**.

2. Click **Show**. The numbers appear next to the selected element.

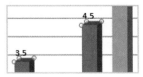

Format Chart Items

Each chart item has a number of attributes that can be formatted, such as the color, the fill, the line style, and the alignment. These attributes are set in the Format dialog box for that item, as shown in Figure 8-10. Table 8-2 shows the formatting options that are available in the Format dialog box for each item.

Figure 8-10: **A typical Format dialog box, tailored to a chart item.**

FORMATTING OPTIONS	DESCRIPTION	APPLIES TO
Number	Provides the same number formats as the Format Cells Number tab, such as currency, accounting, date, and time	Axis, data labels
Fill	Provides options for solid color fill, gradient colors and options, picture, or texture fill, as well as pattern fill and degrees of transparency	Axis, chart area, data labels/series, data tables, legend, plot area, titles, walls/floors
Line or Border Color	Offers solid or gradient lines and options, as well as color choices and degrees of transparency	Axis, chart area, data labels/series, data tables, error bars, grid lines, legend, plot area, titles, trend lines, walls/floors
Line or Border Style	Provides options for width, dashed, and compound (multiple) lines, as well as styles for line ends and line joins	Axis, chart area, data labels/series, data tables, error bars, grid lines, legend, plot area, titles, trend lines, walls/floors
Shadow	Provides preset shadow styles and controls for color, transparency, size, blur, angle, and distance	Axis, chart area, data labels/series, data tables, legend, plot area, titles, trend lines, walls/floors
Glow and Soft Edges	Provides presets for glow and soft edges and controls for color, transparency, and size	Axis, chart area, data labels/series, data tables, legend, plot area, titles, trend lines, walls/floors
3-D Format	Adds a 3-D effect to shapes; provides top, bottom, material, and lighting presets and controls for depth and contour color and size or degree	Axis, chart area, data labels/series, data tables, legend, plot area, titles, walls/floors
3-D Rotation	Provides angular rotation and perspective adjustments, as well as positioning and scaling controls	Walls/floors
Alignment	Vertically aligns, rotates, and stacks text	Axis, data labels, titles, legends
Alt Text	Provides a text title and description of the chart and the information it contains. This can be read to a person with a visual disability.	Chart area

Table 8-2: *Formatting Options Available to Chart Items*

NOTE

The options on the Format *elements* dialog box will vary, depending on the type of chart. For instance, a pie chart will have different options than a bar chart. In addition, the attributes within an option will be different. For example, the fill attributes for a pie chart are different from those for a bar chart.

To open the Format dialog box for a chart item:

- Select the item (see the "Selecting Chart Items" QuickSteps), and click **Format Selection** in the Current Selection group, either in the Chart Tools Format tab or the Chart Tools Layout tab.

  –Or–

- In the Chart Tools Layout tab, click a chart item in the Labels, Axes, or Background group. If needed, click a variation of that item, and then click **More (item name)**.

  –Or–

- Right-click the item on the chart, and click **Format (item name)**.

WORKING WITH THE DATA TABLE

In addition to the chart data in Excel, and possibly the original data in Word, you can display a *data table* as part of a chart with the same data. Data tables are for display only and simply reflect the data in Excel. The values in a data table cannot be changed on the chart without changing them in Excel. Figure 8-11 shows a chart with a data table that includes a legend.

DISPLAY THE DATA TABLE

Click the chart in Word to select it. Then in the Chart Tools Layout tab Labels group, click **Data Table**. From the context menu, click **Show Data Table** or **Show Data Table With Legend Keys**. The chart and data are displayed in Word.

FORMAT A DATA TABLE

A data table can be formatted in the same way as any other chart element.

- Right-click the data table and click **Format Data Table**.

  –Or–

- With the data table selected (see the "Selecting Chart Items" QuickSteps), click **Format Selection** in the Chart Tools Layout or Format tab Current Selection group.

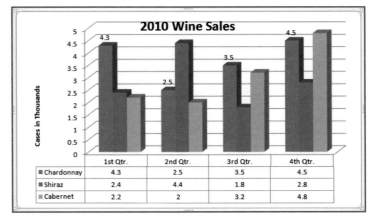

Figure 8-11: **Data tables add precision to the information presented in a chart.**

Format Text

You may have noticed that there is no capability to format text in the various chart item dialog boxes. To format text:

- Select a chart item (see the "Selecting Chart Items" QuickSteps), and in the Home tab Font group, use the formatting options or click the **Dialog Box Launcher** to open the Font dialog box.

  –Or–

- Right-click a chart item, and either use the mini font toolbar that appears, or click **Font** to open the Font dialog box.

Chapter 9
Creating Web Pages

You can use Word 2003 to create and save documents as Web pages. These features enable you to put Word documents on a Web site or an intranet site (a Web site that is internal to an organization) in a format in which they can be viewed using a Web browser, such as Internet Explorer. Word also allows you to work with existing Web pages and provides a number of settings to control them.

Create and Save a Web Page in Word

Word provides the means to produce a moderate quantity of Web pages, including the ability to save documents as Web pages, view a document as a Web page, and set a number of options unique to Web pages.

Create a Web Page

Creating a Web page in Word consists of creating a document page as you would for any other document, viewing it as a Web page, and then saving it as a Web page. Such a page can then be viewed with a browser, such as Microsoft Internet Explorer.

1. If Word is not already open, start it. Click **File** and click **New**.
2. In the New Document dialog box, double-click **Blank Document**.
3. In the View tab Document Views group, click **Web Layout**.

4. Create content on the page using standard Word techniques, as described in the earlier chapters of this book. For example:
   - To enter text, type it as usual.
   - To apply a style, select a style from the Quick Styles gallery in the Home tab Styles group.
   - To apply direct formatting (for example, bold or italic), select the text to which you want to apply it, and then click the appropriate button in the Home tab Font group.
   - To create tables and add pictures and other graphic elements, use Word's extensive table creation and graphics tools.
5. Save the document, as described in the next section.

Save Word Documents as Web Pages

To save an existing Word document as a Web page:

1. Start Word, if it is not already running, or switch to it.
2. Click **File**, click **Open**, select the existing document you want to save as a Web page, and then click **Open**. The document opens.

CHOOSING SUITABLE WEB FILE FORMATS

Word offers three HTML formats to choose from; before you save a file in HTML, you should understand how the formats differ from each other and which format is suitable for which purposes. Word offers the Single File Web Page format; the Web Page format; and the Web Page, Filtered format.

WEB PAGE FORMAT

The Web Page format creates an HTML file that contains the text contents of the document, together with a separate folder that contains the graphics for the document. This makes the Web page's HTML file itself smaller, but the page as a whole is a little clumsy to distribute because you need to distribute the graphics folder as well. The folder is created automatically and assigned the Web page's name followed by *files*. For example, a Web page named Products.htm has a folder named Products_files.

Files in the Web Page format use the .htm and .html file extensions. These files also use Office-specific tags to preserve in an HTML format all of the information the file contains.

SINGLE FILE WEB PAGE FORMAT

The Single File Web Page format creates a Web archive file that contains all the information required for the Web page: all the text contents and all the graphics. Use the Single File Web Page format to create files that you can easily distribute.

Files in the Single File Web Page format use the .mht and .mhtml file extensions. These files use Office-specific tags that preserve in an HTML format all of the information the file contains.

Continued . . .

3. Click **File** and click **Save As**. The Save As dialog box appears.

4. Select the folder in which you want to save the Web page.

5. Click the **Save As Type** down arrow, and click the file format you want to use. (Your choices are Single File Web Page; Web Page; or Web Page, Filtered. See the "Choosing Suitable Web File Formats" QuickFacts for a discussion of the available formats.)

6. In the File Name text box, type the file name. If you want to use the .html extension instead of the .htm extension (for a file in either the Web Page format or the Web Page, Filtered format) or the .mhtml extension instead of the .mht extension (for a file in the Single File Web Page Format), type the extension as well.

7. To enter or change the page title (see Figure 9-1—the page title is what appears in the title bar of the browser), click **Change Title**, type the new title in the Set Page Title dialog box, and then click **OK**.

Figure 9-1: Word's Save As dialog box for saving Web pages includes the Page Title area and the Change Title button.

CHOOSING SUITABLE WEB FILE FORMATS *(Continued)*

WEB PAGE, FILTERED FORMAT

The Web Page, Filtered format creates an HTML file that contains the text contents of the document, together with a separate, automatically named folder that contains the graphics for the document. However, this format removes Office-specific tags from the document. Removing these features reduces the size of the file, but the file uses items such as document properties and Visual Basic for Applications (VBA) code, so this format is not useful for round-tripping complex documents (bringing them back into Word and editing them).

Files in the Web Page, Filtered format use the .htm and .html file extensions.

NOTE

Word also offers one other Web-related file format, .xml, which uses the eXtensible Markup Language (XML) to organize and work with data. XML is beyond the scope of this book.

NOTE

You must set the Web options separately for each Office application. The settings you make in Word don't affect the settings in Excel, PowerPoint, or other applications.

8. Click **Save**. Word saves the document as a Web page.

9. If you've finished working with the document, click **File** and then click **Close**. If you've finished working with Word, click **Close** in the upper-right corner.

Work with Web Pages in Word

Word provides a number of tools and settings that allow you to work with Web pages and implement the features you want on a Web site.

Configure Web Options in Word

Before you start using Word to create Web pages, you must configure the Web options in Word. These options control how Word creates Web pages. Once you've specified the options you want, you probably won't need to change them. If you do need to change them for a particular file, you can do so when you're saving the file as a Web page.

DISPLAY THE WEB OPTIONS DIALOG BOX

To configure Web options, first display the Web Options dialog box.

1. If Word is not already running, start it now.

2. Click **File** and then click **Options**. The Word Options dialog box appears.

3. Click **Advanced** in the left column, scroll down to the bottom of the page, and then click **Web Options**. The Web Options dialog box appears, as shown in Figure 9-2.

4. Choose options, as discussed in the following subsections, click **OK** to close the Web Options dialog box, and then click **OK** to close the Word Options dialog box.

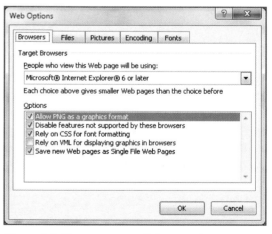

Figure 9-2: *You can create Web pages for specific browser versions.*

UNDERSTANDING HTML AND HOW WORD USES IT

Many Web pages, including those created with Word, use HTML to specify how the page will look and behave in a Web browser.

UNDERSTAND HTML

HTML (HyperText Markup Language) is responsible for many of the wonders of the Web. It enables you to specify the contents of a Web page and control how it looks and behaves in a Web browser. All modern computer operating systems have browsers, so pages created using HTML can be displayed on almost any computer. An HTML file consists of plain text and pictures with *tags*, or formatting codes, that specify how the text or pictures will look on the page.

For more information on HTML, see *HTML, XHTML, and CSS QuickSteps*, by Guy Hart-Davis, published by McGraw-Hill/Professional.

UNDERSTAND HOW WORD USES HTML

Word uses HTML to create Web content, automatically applying all necessary tags when you save a file in one of the Web formats. It uses standard HTML tags for creating standard HTML elements (such as headings, paragraphs, and tables) that will be displayed by a Web browser. It uses custom, Word-specific tags for saving Word-specific data in a Web-compatible format.

This combination of standard and custom tags enables Word to save an entire document. Saving all the information like this allows what is called *round-tripping*, saving a file with all its contents and formatting so that the application that created the file can reopen it with exactly the same information and formatting as when it saved the file.

Continued . . .

CHOOSE OPTIONS ON THE BROWSERS TAB

Figure 9-2 shows the Browsers tab of the Web Options dialog box for Word. Table 9-1 explains the options and shows for which browsers they're turned on (with the check box selected) or off (with the check box cleared).

OPTION	EXPLANATION	IE 5 OR LATER	IE 6, 7, 8, OR LATER	FIREFOX 3 OR LATER
Allow PNG As A Graphics Format	Enables Web pages to contain graphics in the PNG format. All current browsers can display PNG graphics.	Off	On	On
Disable Features Not Supported By These Browsers	Turns off HTML features the browsers don't support.	On	On	On
Rely On CSS For Font Formatting	Uses Cascading Style Sheets (CSS) for font formatting.	On	On	On
Rely On VML For Displaying Graphics In Browsers	Uses Vector Markup Language (VML) for displaying graphics.	On	On	On
Save New Web Pages As Single File Web Pages	Uses the Single File Web Page format for saving new files.	On	On	On

*Table 9-1: **Options on the Browsers Tab of the Web Options Dialog Box***

The best way to select the options is to click the **People Who View This Web Page Will Be Using** drop-down list and select the earliest browser version that you want to support. The choice you make in this list automatically selects the appropriate check boxes in the Options group box. You can then select or clear check boxes manually to fine-tune the choices you've made.

- Choosing **Microsoft Internet Explorer 6.0**, which came with Windows XP, provides a reasonable baseline for most Web sites and provides the largest feature set.

9

UNDERSTANDING HTML AND HOW WORD USES IT *(Continued)*

Round-tripping enables you to create HTML documents (.html files) instead of Word documents (.doc files). However, you should remember that the Word-specific data is saved along with the HTML data. Any visitor to your Web site can view the entire source code for a Web page, including any Word-specific data, by using a View Source command in a browser. See "Remove Personal Information from the File Properties" later in this chapter.

Word enables you to remove the Word-specific tags from a Web page you save (see "Remove Word-Specific Tags from a Document" later in this chapter). You may also choose to use Word to create specific HTML elements that you then paste into another HTML editor, such as Windows Notepad, where you can integrate them with the code you directly enter. (See the QuickSteps "Using Word to Create HTML Elements" later in this chapter.)

TIP

In late fall 2009, Internet Explorer had approximately 41 percent of the browser market (Internet Explorer 8 had 13 percent, Internet Explorer 7 had 15 percent, and Internet Explorer 6 had 13 percent). Mozilla Firefox had approximately 46 percent. Google Chrome had 8 percent, and other browsers had 5 percent altogether. These figures show that choosing Microsoft Internet Explorer 6.0 Or Later on the Browsers tab of the Web Options dialog box and then checking how your Web pages look and work with Mozilla Firefox will ensure that your pages are viewable by the vast majority of people online.

- If you want maximum browser compatibility, choose **Microsoft Internet Explorer 5.0**, which came with Windows 2000/ME; however, the percentage of users that will be picked up is less than 1 percent.

- To support Mozilla Firefox and Google Chrome, which you should, choose **Microsoft Internet Explorer 6.0 Or Later**.

CHOOSE OPTIONS ON THE FILES TAB

On the Files tab of the Web Options dialog box, choose options for controlling how Word handles file names and file locations for the Web pages you create, and specify whether to use Office as the default editor for Web pages created by Word. Figure 9-3 shows the Files tab of the Web Options dialog box.

The following options are included in the Files tab:

Figure 9-3: The Files tab of the Web Options dialog box determines where Web files are stored and how the files are edited.

- Select **Organize Supporting Files In A Folder** if you want the application to save graphics and other separate elements in a folder that has the same name as the Web page plus "_files"—for example, the Web page named "products.html" receives a folder named "products_files." The application automatically creates a file named "filelist.xml" that contains a list of the files required for the Web page.

- Clear the **Use Long File Names Whenever Possible** check box to prevent the application from creating long file names that include spaces, which may not be compatible with the Web server you're using. It's best to keep file names short and to use underscores instead of spaces when you need to separate parts of the file name.

- Click the **Update Links On Save** check box if you want the application to automatically check each link and update any information that has changed each time you save the file. In most cases, this automatic updating is helpful.

NOTE

Web documents in Word keep all their text and embedded elements (such as graphics) in the same file. Linked items, such as graphics or automation objects from other applications, are kept in separate files.

NOTE

Keeping the supporting files together in a folder is usually helpful, because you can move the Web page and its supporting files easily to another folder. If you clear the Organize Supporting Files In A Folder check box, Word saves the graphics and other separate elements in the same folder as the Web page. This behavior tends to make your folders harder to manage, as you cannot see at a glance which supporting files belong to which Web page. However, if you do not have permission to create new folders in the folder in which you are saving your Web pages (for example on an intranet site), you may need to clear the Organize Supporting Files In A Folder check box so that Word does not attempt to create new folders for your Web pages.

Web Options

| Browsers | Files | Pictures | Encoding | Fonts |

Encoding

Reload the current document as:

Western European (Windows)

Save this document as:

Western European (Windows)

☐ Always save Web pages in the default encoding

- Click the **Check If Office Is The Default Editor For Web Pages Created In Office** check box if you want Internet Explorer to check if Word is your default HTML editor for Web pages created by Word when you click the Edit button in Internet Explorer. Clear this check box if you want to use another application to edit the Web pages you've created with Word.

- Click the **Check If Word Is The Default Editor For All Other Web Pages** check box if you want Internet Explorer to open Word for the editing of all non-Office–created Web pages. Clear this check box if you want to use another application for this function.

CHOOSE OPTIONS ON THE PICTURES TAB

On the Pictures tab of the Web Options dialog box, choose options for the pictures you include in your Web pages.

Web Options

| Browsers | Files | Pictures | Encoding | Fonts |

Target monitor

Screen size: 1024 x 768

Pixels per inch: 96

- In the Screen Size drop-down list, select the minimum resolution that you expect most visitors to your Web site to be using. For most Web sites, the best choice is 1024 × 768, a resolution that almost all monitors manufactured since 2004 support. If you're creating an intranet site whose visitors will all use monitors with a higher resolution than 1024 × 768, you can choose a higher resolution.

- In the Pixels Per Inch drop-down list, select the number of pixels per inch (ppi) to use for pictures in your Web pages. The default setting is 96 ppi, which works well for most pages. You can also choose 72 ppi or 120 ppi.

CHOOSE OPTIONS ON THE ENCODING TAB

The Encoding tab of the Web Options dialog box lets you specify which character-encoding scheme to use for the characters in your Web pages. Word in North America and Western Europe uses the Western European (Windows) encoding by default. This works well for most purposes, but you may prefer to choose Western European (ISO) for compliance with the ISO-8859-1 standard for a more European flavor or Unicode (UTF-8) for compliance with the Unicode

Unicode is a scheme for representing characters on computers. For example, a capital A is represented by 0041 in Unicode, and a capital B is represented by 0042. *UTF-8* is the abbreviation for Universal Character Set Transformation Format 8-Bit. *ISO* is the acronym for the International Organization for Standardization.

QUICKFACTS

UNDERSTANDING HYPERLINKS

Hyperlinks provide the means to switch, or "jump," from one Web page to another or from one location on a Web page to another location on the same page. Hyperlinks can also be used to open files such as pictures and programs. The billions of hyperlinks on all the Web pages on the Internet are what give the Web its name. On a Web page, a hyperlink can be a word or words, a graphic, or a picture, which, when clicked, tells the browser to open a new page at another site whose address is stored in the hyperlink. A hyperlink's address is called a *URL*, or Uniform Resource Locator. A URL is used by a browser to locate and open a Web page or file. An example of a URL is http://en.wikipedia.org/wiki/Warren_Buffett#Acquisitions.

- The "http://" identifies the site as using Hypertext Transfer Protocol (HTTP), a set of standards for communication and identification.

- Next, there is often "www," which identifies the site as being on the Internet or World Wide Web; although, frequently, as in this case, the space used by "www" in a URL contains other information used to identify a major segmentation of the Web site. In this case, the "en" identifies the English language area.

Continued . . .

standard and many languages outside North America and Western Europe. You must have saved your document before this option is available.

Select the encoding you want in the **Save This Document As** drop-down list. Then, if you always want to use this encoding, click the **Always Save Web Pages In The Default Encoding** check box. Selecting this check box disables the Save This Document As drop-down list.

CHOOSE OPTIONS ON THE FONTS TAB

The Fonts tab of the Web Options dialog box (see Figure 9-4) offers the following options:

- Use the **Character Set** list box to specify the character set you want for your pages. Use the **English/Western European/Other Latin Script** item, unless you need to create pages in another character set, such as Hebrew or Arabic.

- Use the **Proportional Font** drop-down list and its **Size** drop-down list to specify the proportional font and font size for your pages.

Figure 9-4: Word gives you the capability of choosing a number of different character sets to use on Web pages.

- Use the **Fixed-Width Font** drop-down list and its **Size** drop-down list to specify the monospaced font and font size.

After you finish choosing settings in the Web Options dialog box, click **OK** to close the dialog box, and then click **OK** to close the Options dialog box.

Insert a Hyperlink

There are several different types of hyperlinks. All of them are inserted on a page in Word by first displaying the Insert Hyperlink dialog box, as described here.

UNDERSTANDING HYPERLINKS

(Continued)

- "wikipedia.org" is a *domain name* that is the principle identifier of a Web site.

- "/wiki/" is a folder name identifying a sub-area within a site.

- "Warren_Buffett" is a Web page in the wiki folder in the Web site. (Warren Buffett is one of the most successful of American investors.)

- "#Acquisitions" is a particular location on the Web page, and is called a *bookmark*.

You then need to follow the steps in the subsequent sections for the particular type of hyperlink you want to create.

1. Start Word and open the file in which you want to insert the hyperlink, as described in "Create a Web Page."

2. Select the text or graphic where you want the hyperlink to appear.

3. In the Insert tab Links group, click **Hyperlink**. The Insert Hyperlink dialog box appears (see Figure 9-5).

> 🔗 Hyperlink
> 📑 Bookmark
> 🔖 Cross-reference
> Links

4. Complete the hyperlink by following the steps in one of the following sections, depending on whether you want to create a hyperlink to an existing file or Web page, to a place in the current document, to a new document, or to an e-mail address.

CREATE A HYPERLINK TO AN EXISTING FILE OR WEB PAGE

To create a hyperlink to an existing file or Web page:

1. In the Link To column on the left, click the **Existing File Or Web Page** button, if it is not already selected.

2. Navigate to the file or Web page in one of these ways:

Use the **Look In** drop-down list (and, if necessary, the **Up One Folder** button) to browse to the folder.

–Or–

Click the **Browse The Web** button to open a window in a Web browser on your computer, browse to the page or pages to which you want to link, and then switch back to the Insert Hyperlink dialog box. If you have used Internet Explorer, Word will automatically enter the URL in the Address text box (see Figure 9-6). If you use a different browser, you need to copy and paste the URL into the Address text box. If a browser is opened by selecting Insert Hyperlink and you want to use a different one, close the open browser and open the one you want to use.

–Or–

Click the **Current Folder** button to display the current folder. Click the **Browsed Pages** button to display a list of Web pages you've browsed recently. Click the **Recent Files** button to display a list of local files you've worked with recently.

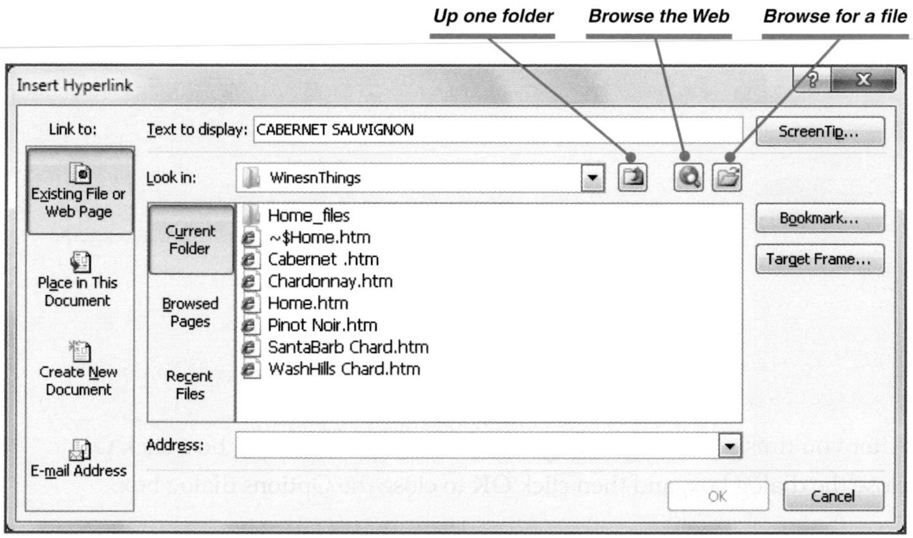

Up one folder   Browse the Web   Browse for a file

*Figure 9-5: **The Insert Hyperlink dialog box enables you to create hyperlinks to Web pages, places within the same file, files, or e-mail addresses.***

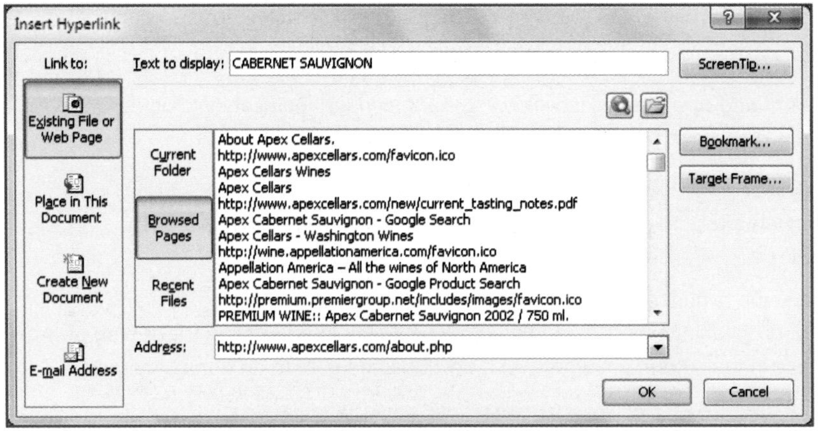

Figure 9-6: *Clicking the Browsed Pages button will give you a list of the Web pages and files that you have viewed with the browser so that you can select one of them for a hyperlink.*

NOTE

Bookmarks cannot have spaces, hyphens, or any other special characters in them, except an underscore (_).

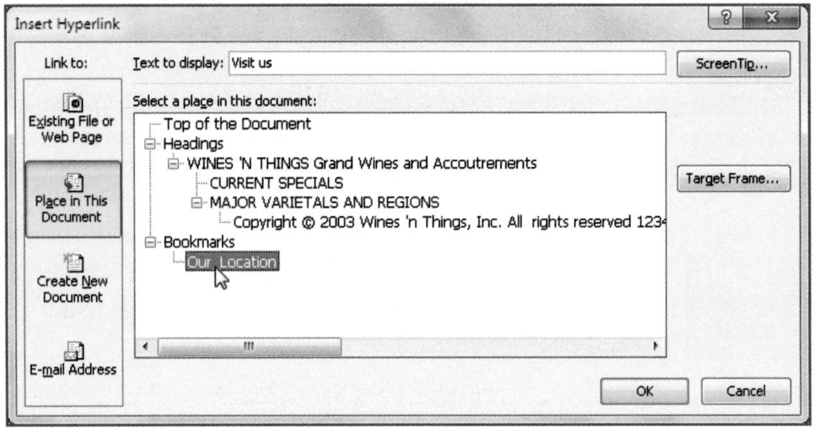

Figure 9-7: *Word enables you to link to a particular place in either the current or a destination document—for example, to a heading or bookmark in a Word document.*

–Or–

Select the address from the Address drop-down list.

3. If needed, change the default text in the Text To Display text box to the text you want displayed for the hyperlink. (This is the text that the user clicks to access the linked page.) If you have selected text instead of a graphic, for example, on your Web page, it will appear here and may not need to be changed.

4. To add a ScreenTip to the hyperlink, click **ScreenTip**, type the text in the Set Hyperlink ScreenTip dialog box, and then click **OK**.

5. To make the hyperlink connect to a particular location in the page rather than simply to the beginning of the page, click **Bookmark** and choose the location in the Select Place In Document dialog box (see "Create a Hyperlink to a Place in the Current Document").

6. Click **OK**. Word inserts the hyperlink.

CREATE A HYPERLINK TO A PLACE IN THE CURRENT DOCUMENT

To create a hyperlink to a place in the current document:

1. In the Link To column, click the **Place In This Document** button. Under Select A Place In This Document, click a heading or a bookmark that is displayed (see Figure 9-7).

2. If needed, change the default text in the Text To Display text box to the text you want displayed for the hyperlink. (This is the text that the user clicks to access the linked page.) If you have selected text instead of a graphic, that is what will be displayed. You may not want to change it in that case.

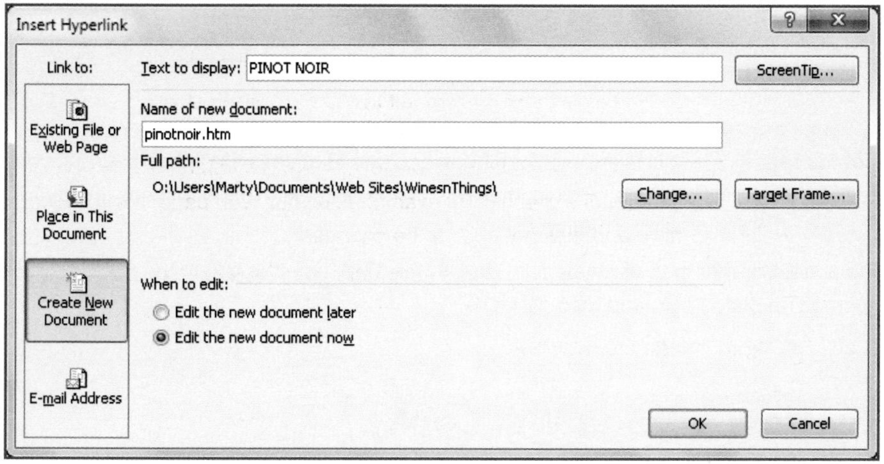

Figure 9-8: *When you need to link to a new document, Word lets you create the new document immediately to ensure that it is saved with the correct name and location.*

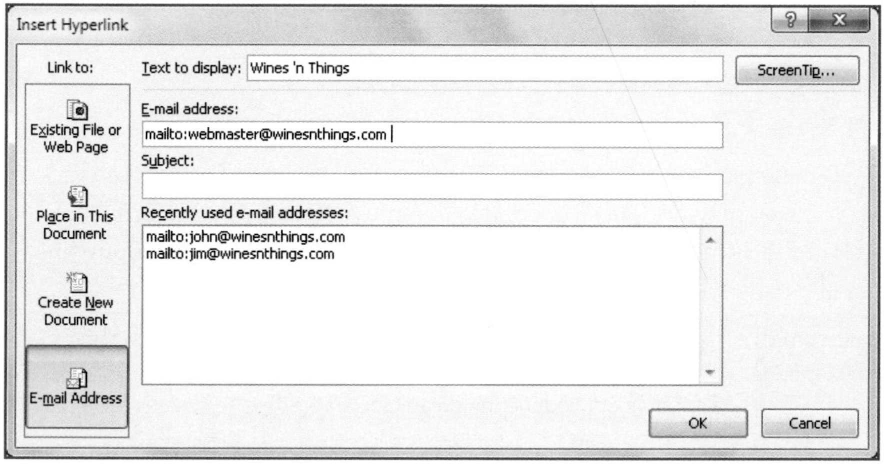

Figure 9-9: *The Insert Hyperlink dialog box lets you quickly create a mailto hyperlink to an e-mail address.*

3. To add a ScreenTip to the hyperlink, click **ScreenTip**, type the text in the Set Hyperlink ScreenTip dialog box, and then click **OK**.

4. Click **OK**. Word inserts the hyperlink.

CREATE A HYPERLINK TO A NEW DOCUMENT

To create a hyperlink to a new document:

1. In the Insert Hyperlink dialog box, in the Link To Column on the left, click the **Create New Document** button (see Figure 9-8).

2. Type the file name and extension in the Name Of New Document text box. Check the path in the Full Path area. If necessary, click **Change**; use the Create New Document dialog box to specify the folder, file name, and extension; and then click **OK**.

3. If needed, change the default text in the Text To Display text box to the text you want displayed for the hyperlink. (This is the text that the user clicks to access the linked page.) If you have selected text for the hyperlink instead of a graphic, it will be displayed in this field and you may not want it changed.

4. To add a ScreenTip to the hyperlink, click **ScreenTip**, type the text in the Set Hyperlink ScreenTip dialog box, and then click **OK**.

5. By default, Word selects the **Edit The New Document Now** option. If you prefer not to open the new document for editing immediately, click the **Edit The New Document Later** option.

6. Click **OK**. Word inserts the hyperlink.

CREATE A HYPERLINK TO AN E-MAIL ADDRESS

To create a mailto hyperlink that starts a message to an e-mail address:

1. In the Link To column, click the **E-mail Address** button (see Figure 9-9).

TIP

E-mail addresses you have recently used in other hyperlinks will be in the list of Recently Used E-Mail Addresses at the bottom of the Edit Hyperlink dialog box. If you want to use one of them in another hyperlink, click it instead of typing it again in the E-Mail Address text box.

NOTE

The "mailto:" entry in front of the e-mail address tells a browser to open the default e-mail program, open a new message, and place the address in the "To" line.

NOTE

Word automatically creates a hyperlink when you type a URL, e-mail address, or a network path in a document and then press **SPACEBAR**, **TAB**, **ENTER**, or a punctuation key. If you find this behavior awkward, you can turn it off: Click **File**, click **Options**, click **Proofing** in the left column, click **AutoCorrect Options**, click the **AutoFormat As You Type** tab, clear the **Internet And Network Paths With Hyperlinks** check box, and then click **OK** twice.

2. Type the e-mail address in the E-mail Address text box (or select it from the Recently Used E-mail Addresses list box), and type the subject for the message in the Subject text box.

3. Change the default text in the Text To Display text box to the text you want displayed for the hyperlink. (This is the text that the user clicks to access the linked page.) If you selected text, instead of a graphic, then this will be displayed in the text box. In this case, you may not want it changed.

4. To add a ScreenTip to the hyperlink, click **ScreenTip**, type the text in the Set Hyperlink ScreenTip dialog box, and then click **OK**.

5. Click **OK**. Word inserts the hyperlink.

Verify How a Page Will Look

After you have saved a Word document as a Web page, you'll probably want to check how it looks in your browser.

1. In Windows, click **Start**, click **Computer**, navigate to the folder where the Web page file is stored, and double-click the Web document. It will open in your default browser. Figure 9-10 shows an example file in Word on the left and then the file being previewed in Internet Explorer.

2. After viewing the Web page, click **Close** to close the Internet Explorer window.

Remove Personal Information from the File Properties

When creating a Web page that you will place on a Web site (as opposed to a site on a local network), it's a good idea to remove the personal information that Word includes by default in documents, which might include your name, company name, date, and comments. To remove this information:

1. Start Word, if it is not already running, and open the document that will become a Web page.

2. Click **File** and then click **Options**. The Options dialog box appears.

3. Click **Trust Center** in the left column, and then click **Trust Center Settings** to open the Trust Center dialog box.

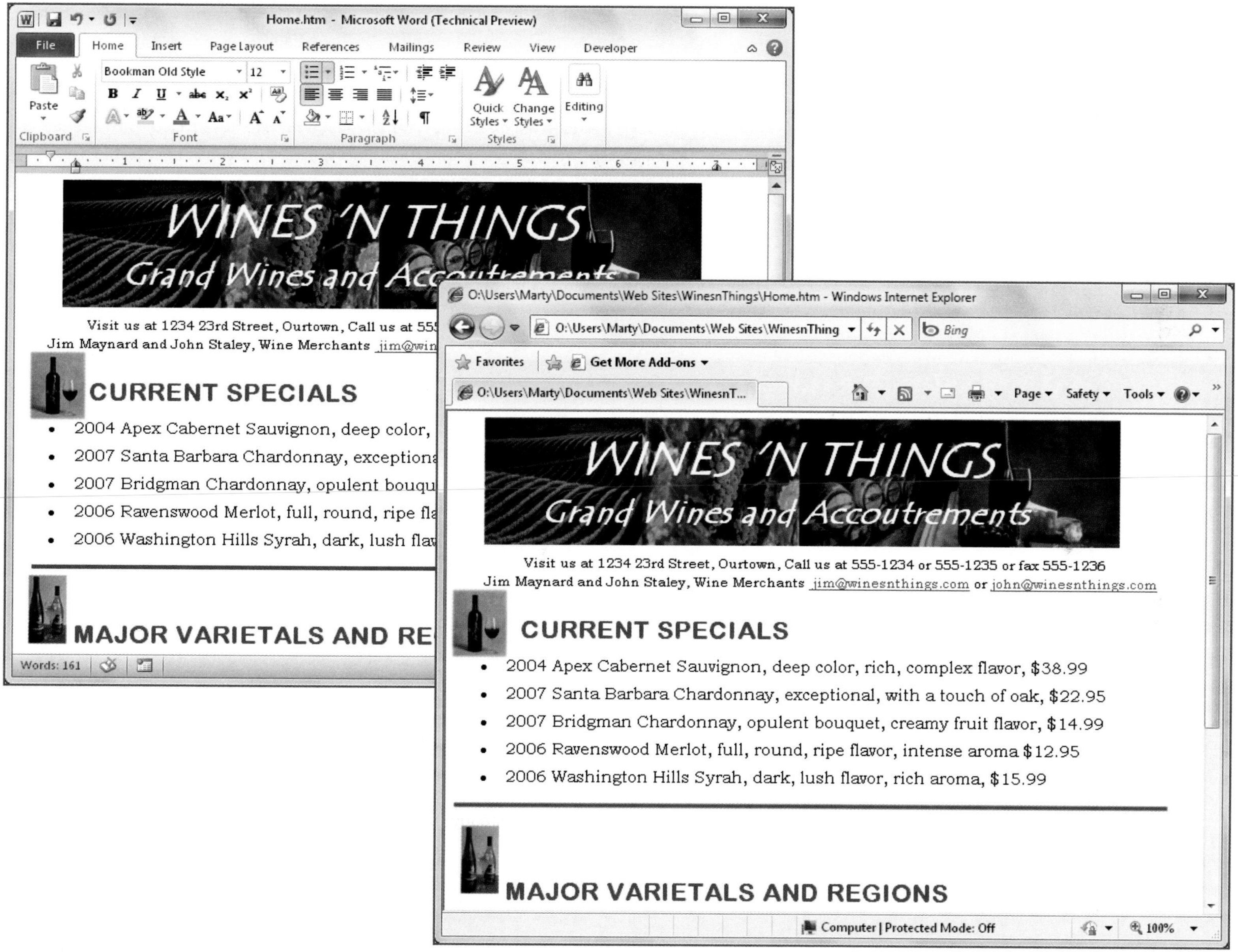

Figure 9-10: Previewing a Web page enables you to identify problems with your Web pages while you are still working on them in Word. Here, the original document in Word is shown on the left.

Figure 9-11: *Inspect and remove any personal information in the Web pages you save.*

4. Click **Privacy Options** in the left column, and click **Document Inspector**. Select the type of data you want to check for (the default is all of the options), and click Inspect. The Document Inspector dialog box appears and may show information you want to remove, as shown in Figure 9-11.

5. Click **Remove All** for all the information you want removed. Click **Close** and then click **OK** twice. Save the document, as described in an earlier section of this chapter.

Remove Word-Specific Tags from a Document

As discussed earlier in this chapter, Word uses custom HTML tags to store the Word-specific data required to save the entire Word document in an HTML format. Saving this data is good if you want to be able to again edit the document in Word with all its features present, but you don't need this extra data when you're using Word on a one-time basis to create pages for your Web site.

To remove the Word-specific tags from a document:

1. When you are ready to save the document one final time after you are sure it is the way you want it, click **File**, click **Save As**, click the **Save As Type** down arrow, and click the **Web Page**, **Filtered** format.

2. Click **Save**. A Microsoft Office Word dialog box appears, telling you that Office-specific tags will be removed. Click **Yes**. (If you click No, the save will not occur. You will be able to change the Save As Type setting.)

UICKSTEPS

USING WORD TO CREATE HTML ELEMENTS

If you choose not to use Word as your main HTML editor, you may still want to use it to create some HTML elements so that you can include them in your Web pages.

1. Start Word, if it is not already running.

2. Open an existing document, or create a new document that contains the desired content.

3. Save the Word document in one of the HTML formats.

4. View the resulting page in your browser.

5. View the source code of the Web page. For example, in Internet Explorer, click the **View** menu, and then click **Source** (in Internet Explorer 7 or 8, you must first turn on the menus by pressing **ALT**).

6. Select the code for the element you want to copy, and then issue a copy command (for example, press **CTRL+C**).

7. Switch to your HTML editor, position the insertion point, and then issue a paste command (for example, press **CTRL+V**).

8. Close Word and your browser if you have finished working with them.

3. Depending on the browser settings you have chosen in the Web Options dialog box, you may also see warnings about features that will be removed from the Word document. Click **Continue** if you want to proceed anyway; click **Cancel** if you want to choose another format.

If you wish to go beyond the basic Web page building you can do in Word, two books can be of help. The first, mentioned earlier, is *HTML, XHTML, and CSS QuickSteps*, by Guy Hart-Davis, which provides a good foundation in Web site creation; the second, *Dynamic Web Programming: A Beginner's Guide*, by Marty Matthews, provides the tools to create an interactive Web site, including using an online database to provide information to the Web site and collect information from it. Both books are published by McGraw-Hill/Professional. You can learn more on the author's Web site, http://matthewstechnology.com.

How to...

- *Track Changes*
- *Review Changes*
- *Creating Reviewing Shortcuts*
- *Add Comments*
- *Highlight Objects*
- *Setting Document Properties*
- *Save Several Copies of a Document*
- *Compare Documents*

Chapter 10

Using Word with Other People

In the first nine chapters of this book, we've talked about the many ways you can use Word on your own. In this chapter we'll talk about how you can use Word with other people. Word has a number of features that allow multiple people to work on the same document and see what each other has done. These include marking changes, both additions and deletions, that multiple people make to a document; adding comments to a document; highlighting words, lines, and paragraphs of a document; having multiple versions of a document; and comparing documents.

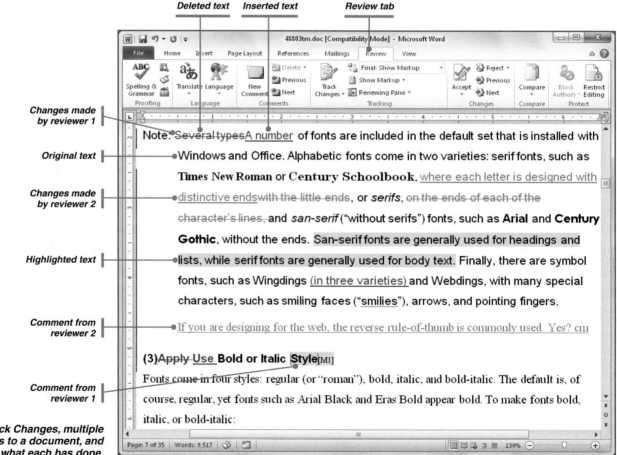

For major collaboration of multiple people and even teams, Microsoft has a product called SharePoint 2010 under which all the Office 2010 products run. See *SharePoint 2010 QuickSteps*, published by McGraw-Hill/Professional, for more information.

Mark Changes

When two or more people work on a document, it is helpful to see what the other people did without having to read every word and accurately remembering what it was before it was changed. You can do this in Word by using the Track Changes feature. *Track Changes* identifies the changes (additions or deletions) made to a document by everyone who works on it. Each person is automatically assigned a color, and their changes are noted in that color. For example, Figure 10-1 shows

Deleted text   **Inserted text**   **Review tab**

Changes made by reviewer 1

Original text

Changes made by reviewer 2

Highlighted text

Comment from reviewer 2

Comment from reviewer 1

Figure 10-1: By using Track Changes, multiple people can make changes to a document, and you can see what each has done.

Carole, 11/4/2009 1:36:00 AM inserted: where each letter is designed with distinctive ends

a section of a document in the editing process. After all the changes are made, they can be accepted or rejected, either one at a time or all together.

Track Changes

To use Track Changes, you must turn it on. Prior to this, anything anyone types looks like ordinary text, and there is no way of telling the difference between the new text and what was on the page before the change was made. Once Track Changes is turned on, however, anything anyone types or does to the document will be shown in the color automatically assigned to that person; furthermore, the changes are fully reversible, if desired. To turn on Track Changes:

1. Start Word and open the document in which you want to track changes.

2. In the Review tab Tracking group, click the upper part of the **Track Changes** button.

   –Or–

   Press **CTRL+SHIFT+E**.

USE THE REVIEW TAB

The Review tab provides a number of features that you can use as you and others edit a document, as shown in Figure 10-2.

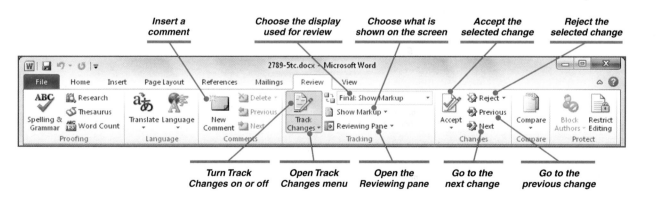

Figure 10-2: The Review tab can be used to go through an edited document and accept or reject changes.

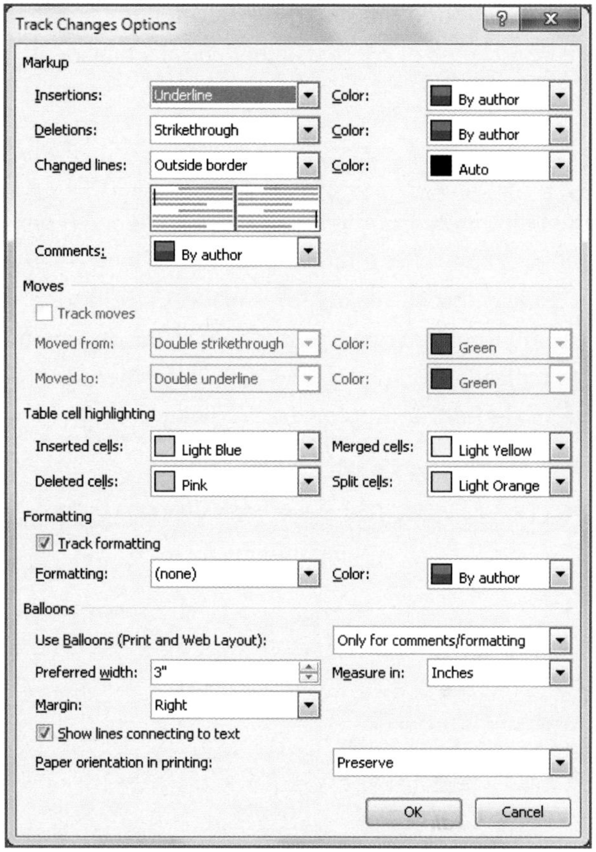

Figure 10-3: While you can select colors for each type of change, the best practice is to let Word automatically select the color for each reviewer (By Author).

SET OPTIONS FOR TRACK CHANGES

Word gives you a number of options for how changes are displayed with Track Changes. These are set in the Track Changes Options dialog box, shown in Figure 10-3. To open this dialog box and set the options:

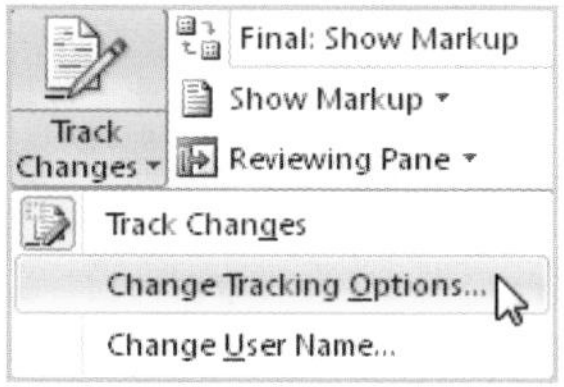

1. In the Review tab Tracking group, click the **Track Changes** down arrow, and click **Change Tracking Options**.

2. Open the drop-down lists next to **Insertions**, **Deletions**, **Changed Lines**, and **Comments** to review and change the options for displaying each of these items. Also, you can change the colors used for each of these.

3. Review and consider how moving text, changing tables, and revising formatting are handled, and make any changes you want. (Balloons are discussed in the following section.)

4. When you are done, click **OK**.

PUT CHANGES IN BALLOONS

Word gives you two ways of viewing changes, both on the screen and when you print out the document. One is an in-line method, where the changes are made within the original text, as shown in Figure 10-1. The other is to put changes in balloons to the right of the text, as shown in Figure 10-4. What is in the balloon and what is in the text depends on your choice in the Review tab's Display For Review drop-down list. The default option, shown in Figure 10-4, is Final Showing Markup, which shows the text with the final wording and the balloons with primarily deletions. The options available in the Display For Review drop-down list are described in Table 10-1.

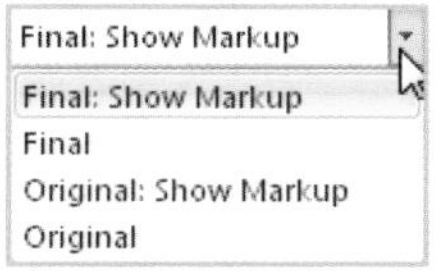

DISPLAY OPTION	WHAT IS IN THE TEXT	WHAT IS IN THE BALLOON
Final Showing Markup	Final text with insertions	Deletions and format changes
Final	Final text without markings	Nothing
Original Showing Markup	Original text with deletions	Insertions and format changes
Original	Original text without markings	Nothing

Table 10-1: Display For Review Options

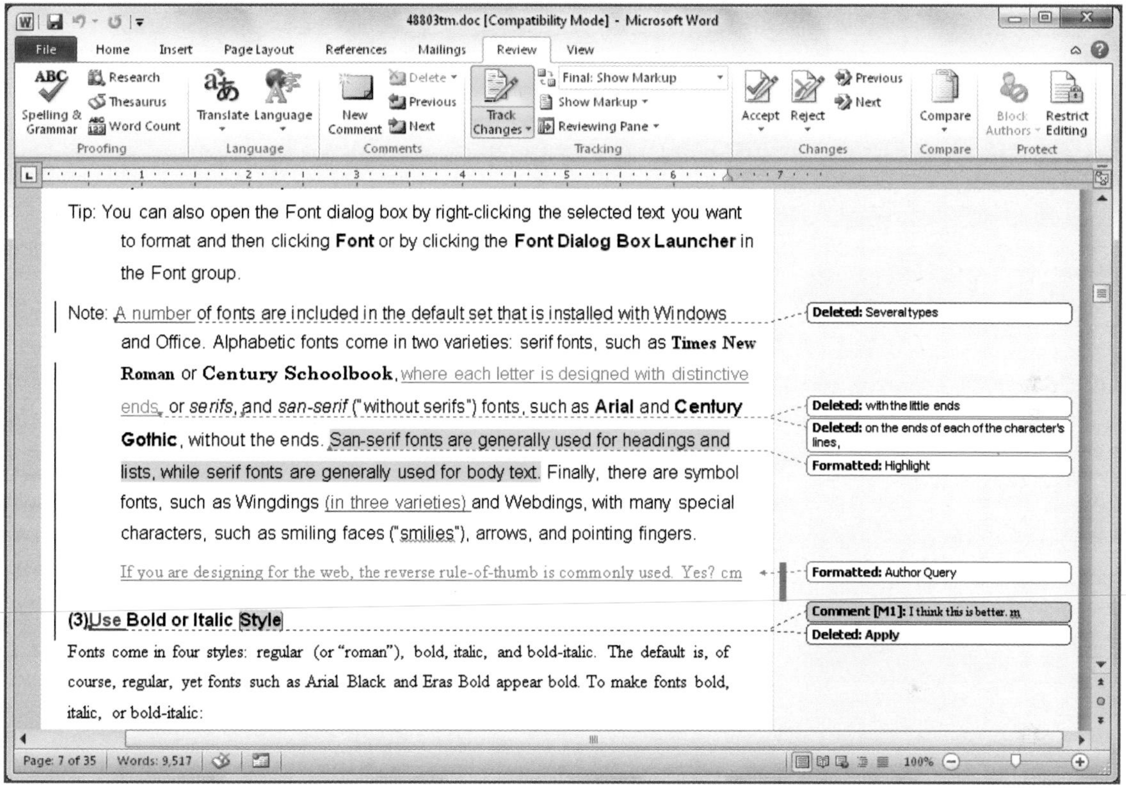

Figure 10-4: Using balloons for changes can provide for easier reading of the final text and can show changes in formatting, but it can be harder to see what has been changed.

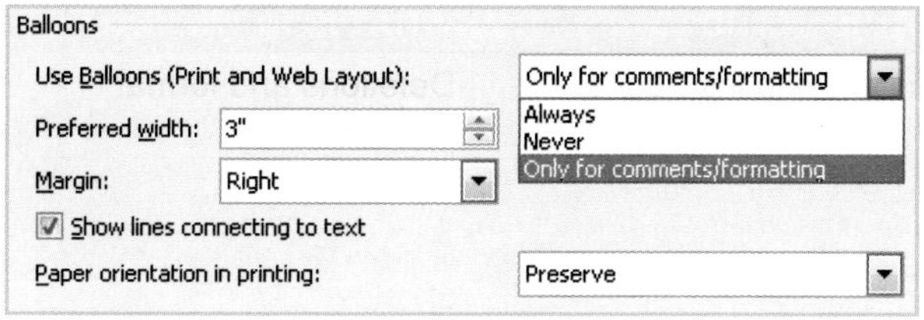

You can quickly turn the balloon changes on or off.

1. In the Review tab Tracking group, click the **Track Changes** down arrow, and click **Change Tracking Options**.

2. Under Balloons, opposite Use Balloons (Print And Web Layout), click **Never** to turn off balloons, click **Always** to turn on balloons, or click **Only For Comments/Formatting** (the default) to use balloons in that way.

3. If you choose to turn balloons on, you can:

   • Set how wide you want the balloons to be, along with the unit of measure to use.

   • Determine which margin the balloons should be on.

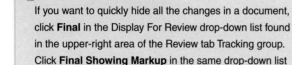
- Determine whether there are connecting lines between the balloons and the text.
- Determine whether to print a document with balloon changes in its normal portrait orientation or force it to be printed in landscape orientation to better keep the original text size.

4. When you are done setting balloon-related settings, click **OK**.

Review Changes

Changes are made to a document by simply adding, deleting, and reformatting the text. If Track Changes is turned on, the changes appear either in the text or in balloons in the margins. Once all changes have been made to a document, you will want to go through the document, look at the changes, and decide to accept or reject each one.

1. With the document you want to review and the Review tab open in Word (see "Use the Review Tab" earlier in this chapter), click **Track Changes** in the Tracking group, if it is turned on, to turn it off.

2. Press **CTRL+HOME** to position the insertion point at the beginning of the document, and click **Next** on the Review tab to select the first change.

3. Click **Accept** on the Review tab Changes group if you want to make the change permanent.

   –Or–

   Click **Reject** on the Review tab Changes group if you want to remove the change and leave the text as it was originally.

4. Repeat step 3 for each of the changes in the document. Each time you click **Accept** or **Reject**, you automatically move to the next change. (See the QuickSteps "Creating Reviewing Shortcuts" for creating keyboard shortcuts for these reviewing tasks.)

5. When you are finished, click **Save** on the Quick Access toolbar to save the reviewed document.

QUICKSTEPS

CREATING REVIEWING SHORTCUTS

If you are going through a large document, looking at each change and accepting or rejecting it, clicking the mouse repeatedly on Accept or Reject can become tedious. A partial solution for this is to make keyboard shortcuts.

To assign shortcut keys to each of the three functions—Next, Accept Change, and Reject Change:

1. Click **File**, click **Options**, click **Customize Ribbon** in the left column, and opposite Keyboard Shortcuts at the bottom of the dialog box, click **Customize** again. The Customize Keyboard dialog box appears.

2. Click **Review Tab** in the Categories list, click **AcceptChangesOrAdvance** in the Commands list, click in the **Press New Shortcut Key** text box, and press the key(s) you want to use. For example, press **ALT+A** for Accept Change (see Figure 10-5). Click **Assign**.

3. Repeat step 2, first for Next by clicking **NextChangeOrComment** in the Command list and assigning, for example, **ALT+N**; and then for Reject by clicking **RejectChangesOrAdvance** and assigning, for example, **ALT+R**, and clicking **Assign** for each.

4. When you are done, click **Close** and then click **OK**.

5. Open a document for which you want to review changes.

6. Press **ALT+N** to go to the first change. Then press either **ALT+A** to accept the change or **ALT+R** to reject the change and automatically move on to the next change. Repeat this for the remainder of the changes.

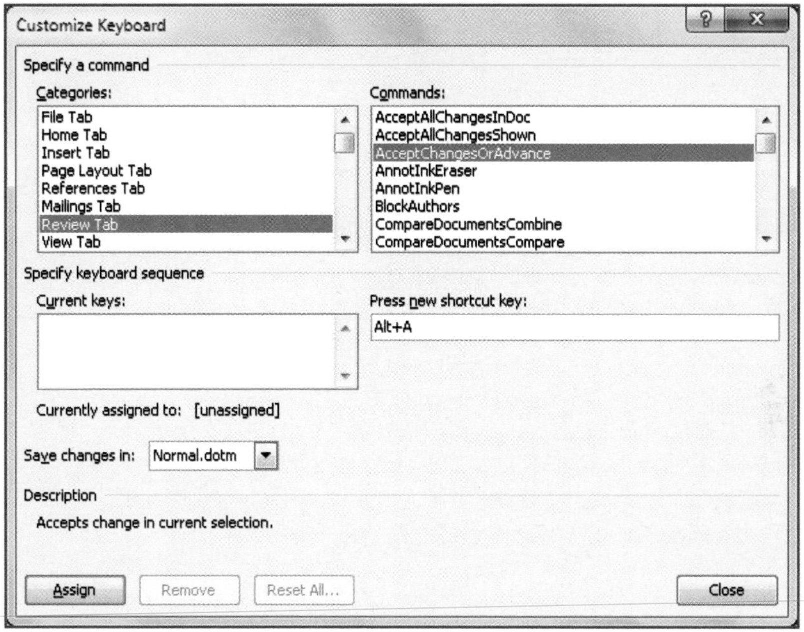

Figure 10-5: *For some people, keyboard shortcuts are faster than clicking the mouse, especially if you use two hands.*

USE THE REVIEWING PANE

Word provides another way to look at changes using the Reviewing pane, shown in Figure 10-6. This pane opens at left or at the bottom of the Word window and lists each individual change, with its type, the author, and the date and time the change was made (the latter is included only if the column is wide enough).

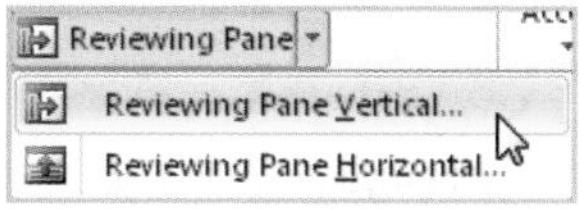

1. With the document you want to review and the Review tab open in Word, click **Reviewing Pane** in the Tracking group to open it.

2. Scroll through and click the changes in the Reviewing pane to see them in the document, and/or use the **Next** and **Previous** buttons on the Review tab (or your shortcut keys) to display each change in the Reviewing pane, as well as to highlight them in the document pane.

3. When you are finished making changes, click **Save** on the toolbar.

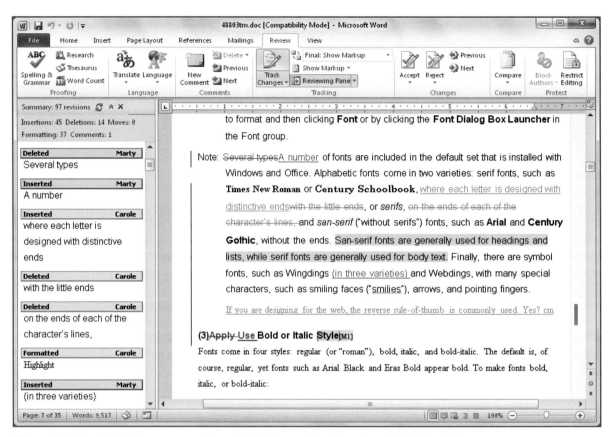

Figure 10-6: The Reviewing pane provides a detailed way of looking at each individual change.

E-MAIL A DOCUMENT FOR REVIEW

Often, when several people are working on a document, they exchange the document using e-mail. Word makes using e-mail with the reviewing process easy. You can both send out a document for review and return it with your changes.

To send out the currently opened document for review:

1. Click **File**, click **Save & Send**, click **Send Using E-mail**, and then click **Send As Attachment**. The E-mail Message window opens with the Word document you want reviewed attached and shown as the subject (see Figure 10-7).

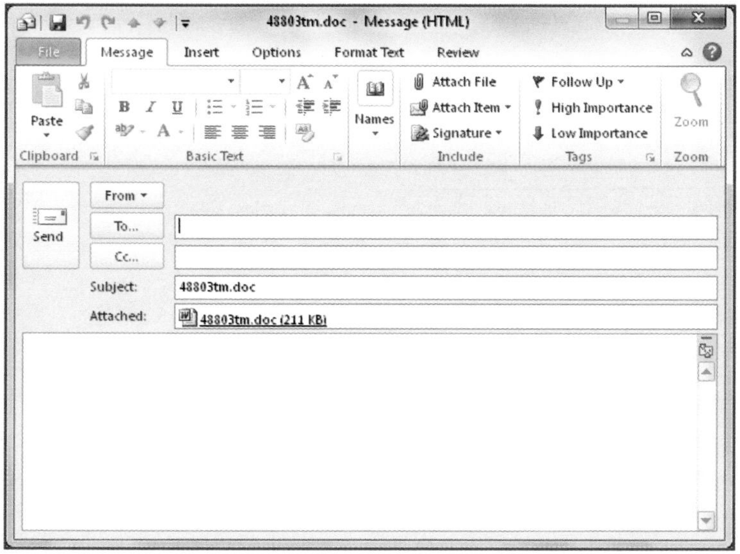

Figure 10-7: When you use the Send Using E-mail option in Word, an e-mail message is opened and the Subject and Attachment lines are filled in for you.

TIP

You can quickly view a comment by pointing the mouse at the comment marker in the text (colored parentheses and your initials) if you have selected the text to which the comment applies. The comment, along with the name of the person who made it and the date and time, will appear above the marker.

NOTE

A comment can be deleted by locating it using the **Next** or **Previous** button on the Review tab Changes group and then clicking **Reject**.

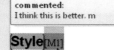

2. Fill in the name of the addressee, plus those who are to get copies, make any desired changes to the Subject line, and add a message. Then, when you are ready, click **Send**.

E-MAIL A REVIEWED DOCUMENT

When a document has been e-mailed to you for review and you have finished making the changes you want, you can e-mail it back in the same way you received it. With the document open in Word:

1. Click **File**, click **Save & Send**, click **Send Using E-mail**, and click **Send As Attachment**. The E-mail Message window opens with the Word document you have reviewed attached and shown as the Subject line.
2. Add the addresses for those who are to receive copies, add a message if desired, make any desired changes to the Subject line and then, when ready, click **Send**.

Add Comments

When you review or edit a document, you may want to make a comment instead of or in addition to making a change. To add a comment:

1. Open your document in Word, display the **Review** tab, and highlight the text to which the comment applies.
2. Click **New Comment** in the Review tab Comments group. An annotation with your initials will appear where the insertion point was in the text. If you have balloons turned on for any purpose, a new balloon will appear where you can type your comment. If you have balloons turned off (a setting of "Never"), the Reviewing pane will open (if it isn't already) and a new comment area will appear.

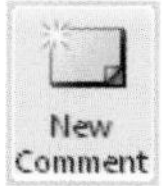

3. Type the comment you want to make (it can be of any length), and then click in the document pane to continue reviewing the document. Your comment will appear in the balloons on the right, as you can see in the top-right example in Figure 10-8, or in the Reviewing pane on the left, as shown in the bottom-left example in Figure 10-8.
4. If you wish, you can close the Reviewing pane by clicking **Reviewing Pane** on the Review tab or clicking **Close** in the upper-right area of the Reviewing pane.

1 2 3 4 5 6 7 8 9 10

Figure 10-8: Comments allow you to explain why you made a change and appear in the balloons (top-right example) or the Reviewing pane (bottom-left example).

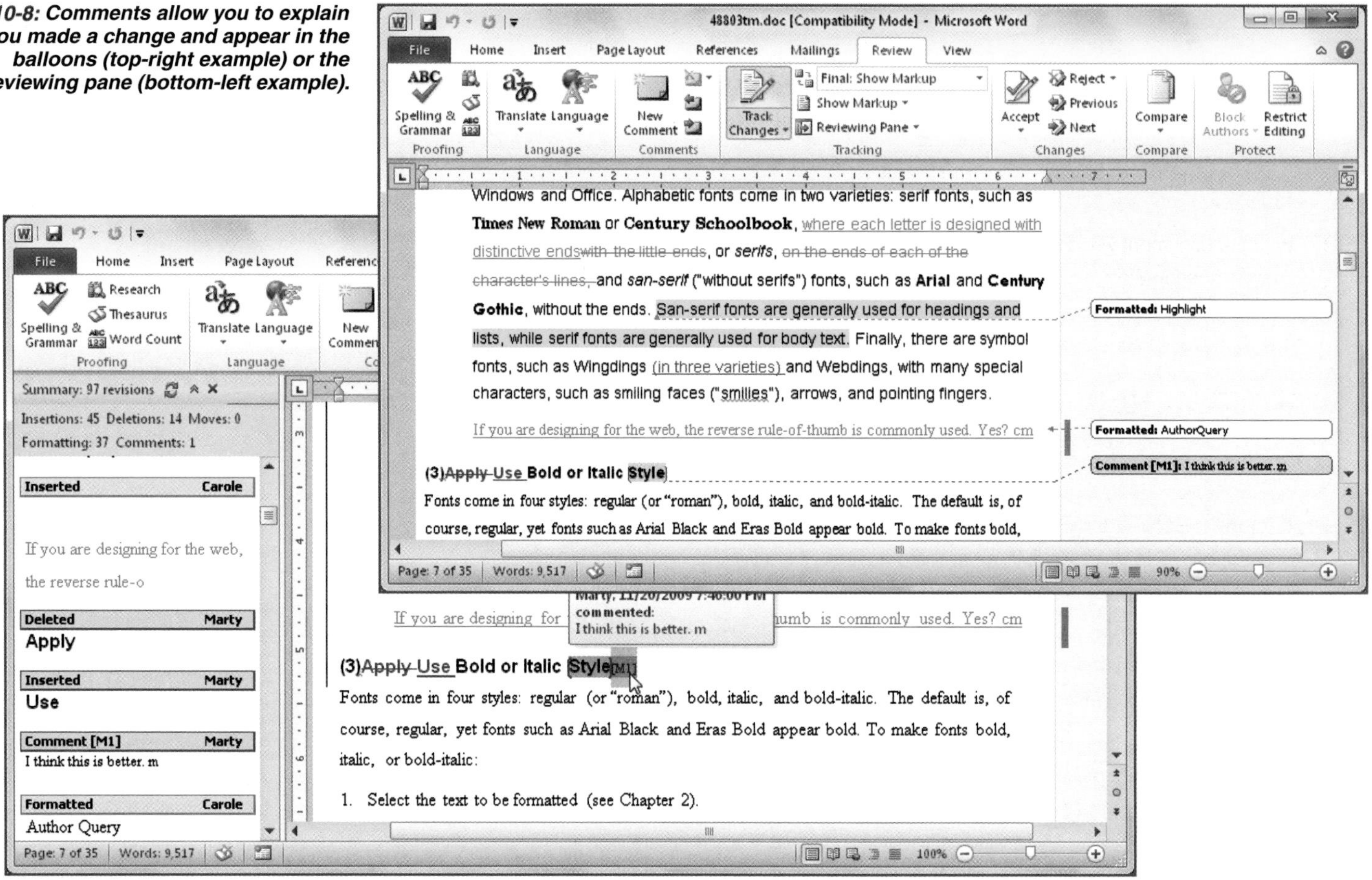

Highlight Objects

As you review and change a document, you may want to highlight some text so you can discuss it in a comment or otherwise call attention to it (see Figure 10-1). You do this using the Highlight tool in the Home tab Font group. You can either select the Highlight tool first and then drag over the text to highlight it, or you can select the text to be highlighted first and then click the Highlight tool.

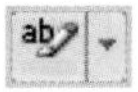

NOTE

On a Tablet PC, you can use the tablet pen to handwrite comments (called "ink comments"). These are similar to the comments entered on a regular PC, except that they are handwritten instead of typed. In addition, you can use the tablet pen to directly mark in the document pane, not just in the comment areas (called "ink annotations"). For example, you might circle an incorrect phrase and write "Fixed?".

SETTING DOCUMENT PROPERTIES

Another way of communicating with several people working on a document is to use a document's Properties area to pass on relevant information (see Figure 10-9). To open and use this area:

1. With the document whose properties you want to change open in Word, click **File**, click **Info**, click **Properties**, and click **Show Document Panel**. The Document Properties section of the Word window appears, as you see in Figure 10-9.

2. Enter the information that you want to communicate into the various fields. None are required, and most are self-explanatory.

3. To view additional properties of the document, click the **Document Properties** down arrow, and click **Advanced Properties**. The Properties dialog box appears.

   The **General** tab tells you where the document is stored and its size and relevant dates. The **Summary** tab repeats some of the information you saw in the Document Properties pane in the Word window. The **Statistics** tab repeats the dates, tells you who last saved the file, and gives you various length statistics. The **Contents** tab repeats the title and may show the headings.

4. The **Custom** tab allows you to attach a value to a category. Click a category in the Name list, click a type of information, and enter the information in the Value text box.

5. Click **OK** when you are done with the Properties dialog box, and then click **Close** to close the Document Properties pane in the Word window.

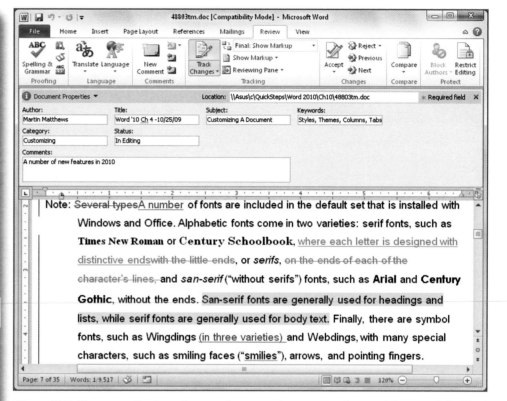

Figure 10-9: The properties for a document are seen in an optional pane at the top of the Word window beneath the ribbon.

The highlighting that is placed on a page can be one of 15 different colors, so unless you want to use the default yellow, you need to select another color.

1. In the Home tab Font group, click the **Highlight** tool down arrow. The highlighting color palette will open.

2. Click the color you want to use. The pointer will turn into a highlighter. Remember: You want whatever color text you are using to show up well on the color you choose (yellow is the most common).

3. Drag over the text you want to highlight if you have not already selected it.

SELECT THE HIGHLIGHT TOOL FIRST

To highlight several sections of text, it is easiest to first select the Highlight tool.

1. With the document you want to highlight open in Word, click the **Highlight** tool in the Review tab Font group. The mouse pointer becomes a highlighter superimposed on the I-beam.

2. Drag over as much and as many separate pieces of text as you want to highlight, also entering comments as needed (you will need to reselect the Highlight tool after you type comments).

3. When you are done with the Highlight tool, you can press **ESC**, click **Highlight**, or click the **Highlight** down arrow in the Review tab Font group and click **Stop Highlighting** to return to the normal I-beam insertion point.

SELECT THE TEXT FIRST

To highlight a single piece of text, it is easiest to first select it.

1. With the document you want to highlight open in Word, drag across the text that you want highlighted.

2. Click the **Highlight** tool in the Review tab Font group. The selected text will be highlighted.

Work with Multiple Documents

As you are going through the reviewing process with several people, it is likely that you will end up with multiple copies of a document. Word gives you a way of comparing these versions.

Save Several Copies of a Document

First, you want to separately save each copy of the document with a unique name, giving you the ability to compare two copies of the document, as explained in the next section.

SAVE A UNIQUE COPY

With the document for which you want to create different versions open in Word, click **File**, click **Save As**, select the format you want to use, select the folder in which you want the file saved, enter a unique name, and click **Save**.

OPEN A DIFFERENT COPY

With a document for which there are multiple copies open in Word, to open another copy, click **File**, click **Open**, select the folder in which the file is stored, select the file, and click **Open**.

Compare Documents

If changes have been made to a copy of a document without using Track Changes, Word has the ability to compare the two and then merge them into a single document, with the differences shown as they would be with Track Changes.

1. In Word, open the first or original document.

2. In the Review tab Compare group, click **Compare** and then click **Compare** again. The Compare Documents dialog box will appear.

3. Click **More** to first select the types of differences you want to see and have reflected in the final document. Second, select whether you want to show changes at the character or word level. Finally, select whether you want the combined changes in the original document, the revised document, or a new document (the default).

4. Select the original document and the revised document you want to compare and merge into the original document, make any changes to the settings that you want, and click **OK**.

5. With the default settings, a four-pane window will open and display the Reviewing pane, the original, the revised, and a compared document, with the changes the revised document makes to the original document, as you can see in Figure 10-10.

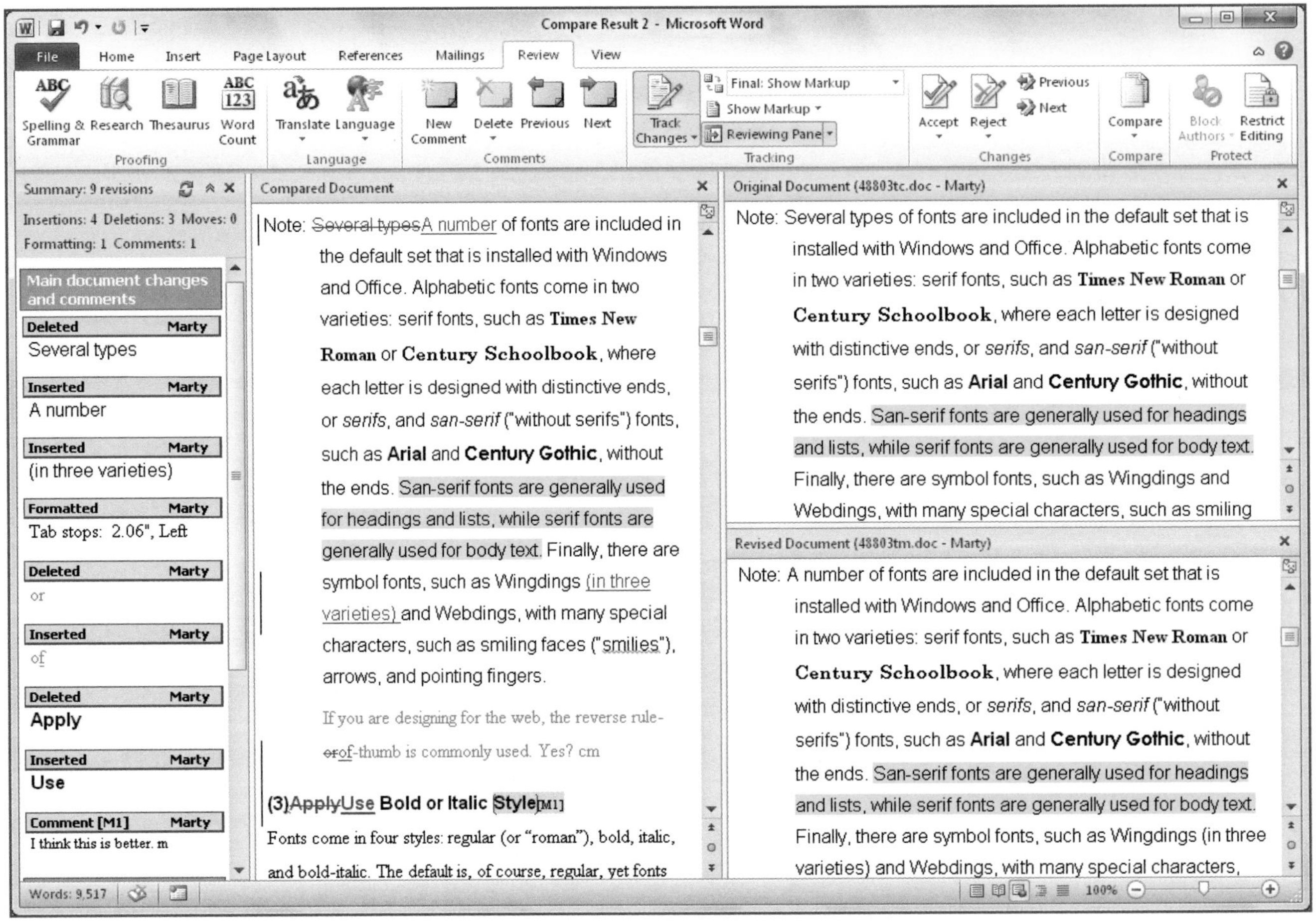

Figure 10-10: In a comparison window in Word, the three panes are synched so that scrolling one scrolls the other two.

NOTE

If you still have Track Changes turned on, Word will ask you if, for the purposes of the conversion, it can consider all the changes accepted.

6. Scroll through the compared document pane, and click **Accept** or **Reject** in the Changes group or use the keyboard shortcuts from the earlier section to accept or reject the changes that have been made.
7. If you want to save the compared document under a new name, click **File**, click **Save As**, select a folder, enter a name, and click **Save**.

character-encoding, 217–218
characters
  count, 115
  formatting text. *See* text formatting
  select within word, 38–39
  space, 61–62
  special, 34–35
charts
  add title, 206
  create, 203–204
  create organizational, 178–180
  determine type of, 204–206
  format items, 208–210
  format text, 210
  select items, 206–207
  understand data series and axes, 208
  work with data table, 210
  work with items, 206–208
Check for Updates, Microsoft Office, 23
Clear Formatting, text, 60
click action, mouse, 8
Clip Art
  add to pictures, 168
  organize clips into collections, 170
Clipboard
  add items, 40
  close, 42
  copy and move text with, 39
  delete items, 41
  open, 39–40
  paste items from, 40
  Redo option, 41–42
  set options, 41
  Undo command, 41–42
Close icon, exit Word, 4
collections, Clip Art, 170
color
  background of Word window, 17

custom themes, 89–90
  fonts, 60
  highlighting, 116, 237
  illustrations, 180–182
  restoring original theme, 91
  text, 182
  themes, 87–88
  Track Changes options, 230
columns, formatting documents into,
  93–94
columns, table
  add, 149
  create tables, 144–145
  remove, 149–150
  select, 147–148
  separators, 157
  set width, 150–151
  sort, 152–154
  split cells into, 159
commands
  add/remove, 14
  add to Quick Access toolbar, 15
  change keyboard shortcuts for, 18
  ribbon containing, 5–7
  tabs displaying, 8–9
comments
  add to document, 235–236
  delete, 235
  handwritten, 236
  quick viewing of, 235
  Track Changes options, 230
compare documents, 239
Compress Pictures, 173
Contact Us, Microsoft Office, 23
Contents tab, document properties, 237
context menu, tables, 147
contextual alternatives, OpenType, 64
contextual tabs, 5

Control Panel, add camera, 169
controls, form, 196–197
Convert Text to Table dialog box, 155–156
Convert to Text, 156
copy
  columns and rows, 154
  formatting, 79
  formulas, 157
  save document as, 53
  text, 39–40
count, characters and words, 115
Create New Document, 221
Create New Style dialog box, 163–164
Create New Theme Colors dialog box, 89–90
Create New Theme Fonts dialog box, 88
Crop tool, pictures, 170–172
Current Folder button, hyperlinks, 219
curves, 175–177
Custom tab, document properties, 237
customization
  bullets and numbers, 74–75
  document. *See* documents, customizing
  with File view, 11–12
  overview of, 10
  print job, 126
  ribbon, 12–14
Customize Keyboard dialog box, 233
cut text, 40

D

data labels, 207–208
data series, charts, 208
data source, mail merge, 132–133, 135
data table, charts, 210
Date & Time, create header or footer, 97
Define New Bullet dialog box, 74–75

delete
  AutoCorrect entry, 108
  cells, rows and columns, 149–150
  chart template, 206
  Clipboard items, 41
  comments, 235
  footnote or endnote, 100
  header or footer, 98–99
  pictures, 43
  section breaks, 93
  styles, 87
  table style, 164
  tables, 157
  text, 42
  Track Changes options, 230
Delivery Address box, print envelope, 128
desktop
  drag picture files to document from,
    168–169
  start Word by creating shortcut, 3
Devices and Printers window, 120, 169–170
diagrams, create, 177–180
Dialog Box Launcher icon, 5–6
directional keys, 33
Display for Review options,
    Track Changes, 230
Document Information panel, 17–18
Document Properties, print, 126–127
Document Views group buttons, 9
documents, 25–54
  add identifying information to, 17–19
  attach envelopes to current, 128–129
  check spelling and grammar, 50–51
  complete and save, 49–53
  copy and move text, 39–41
  create new, 26–30
  delete text, 42

determine where text will appear, 34–36
enter special characters, 34–35
enter text, 34
find and replace text, 45–49
import, 33
insert line or page breaks, 36–37
insert text or type over it, 36
locate existing, 31–33
move around in, 42–45
open existing, 30–33
overview of, 25
printing. *See* printing
saving, 51–53
select text, 37–39
use Office Clipboard, 39–41
use wildcards, 49
documents, customizing
  AutoCorrect. *See* word writing aids
  AutoFormat, 108–110
  building blocks, 110–112
  columns, 93–94
  count characters and words, 115
  different right and left headers, 99–100
  equations, 112–114
  explore thesaurus, 117
  footnotes and endnotes, 99–101
  headers and footers, 96–99
  highlighting, 115–116
  hyphenation, 116–117
  index, 101–102
  outlines, 105–107
  section breaks, 92–93
  styles, 84–90
  table of contents, 102–105
  tabs, 94–96
  understand themes, styles, and
    templates, 84

  view buttons, 90–92, 105–106
.dotx file, 196
double-click action, mouse, 8
double-spacing, 70
Draft view, 10, 106
drag action, mouse, 8
Drawing Tools Format tab, 174, 176–177
drawings
  add objects from other programs, 180–181
  add shapes, 175–176
  apply WordArt, 176
  create, 174–175
  create diagrams, 177–180
  use color effects, 180–182
drop cap, 65
Dynamic Web Programming: A Beginner's Guide
    (Matthews), 225

E

e-Fax, 131
e-mail
  configure with AutoFormat, 109
  create hyperlinks to, 221–223
  of current document for review, 234–235
  of reviewed document, 235
  use to send faxes, 131–132
E-postage properties, 128
edit
  custom theme, 91
  find and replace text, 45–49
  header or footer, 98
  individual letters in mail merge, 139
  moving around, 42–45
  recipient list in mail merge, 138
edit points, curves, 176–177

electronic postage, printing envelope, 128
encoding, Web pages, 217–218
endnotes, 99–100
ENTER key, and overtype mode, 36
enterprise editions, Office 2010, 5
Envelope Options dialog box, 139
envelopes
  merge to, 139–141
  print mailing addresses on, 128–130
Envelopes and Labels dialog box, 128–131
equations, 112–114
Eraser button, 150, 157
Excel, charts, 203–206
exit Word, 4

F

faxes
  send with fax modem, 131–132
  send with online fax service, 131
fields
  form, 197
  merge, 135–136
  set properties, 197–198
File (Backstage) view, 1, 11–12
File tab, ribbon, 7, 12
File view, 7
File window, print options, 123–124
files
  choosing suitable Web formats, 213–214
  graphic formats, 167
  opening Word directly, 33
Files tab, Web Options dialog box, 216–217
fill, for drawings, 182
Find and Replace dialog box, 44–45, 47–48

find and replace text
  with Find and Replace dialog box, 47–48
  navigation pane and, 45–46
  overview of, 45
Find command, 45–47, 49
Find Next command, text, 48
first-line indent
  create, 69
  set tabs with, 95
  set with ruler, 70–71
folder
  find recently used, 33
  store new document in new, 52–53
Font dialog box, 57, 59, 62–64
fonts
  apply bold or italic style, 59
  change size, 59–60
  change theme, 88
  color, 60
  create new set for theme, 88–89
  create with OpenType, 63–64
  customize bullets and numbers, 74–75
  select, 58
  set character spaces, 61
  types of, 59
  underline text, 59–60
  use text effects, 62–63
Fonts tab, Web Options dialog box, 218
footers, add, 96–99
Footnote and Endnote dialog box, 99–100
footnotes
  add, 99–100
  convert to endnotes, 100–101
  delete, 100
formats
  chart items, 208–209
  chart text, 210

  choose Web file, 213–214
  data table for chart, 210
  find highlighted text in document, 116
  find text with Find and Replace, 47
  shape, 182, 184
  table automatically, 162–164
  table content, 157–159
  text effects, 177–178
formatting documents
  add borders and shading, 76–78
  add space between paragraphs, 70–71
  advanced font features, 61–64
  apply character formatting, 57–61
  with AutoFormat, 108–109
  change capitalization, 64–65
  copy formatting, 79
  create drop cap, 65
  indentation, paragraph, 67–68
  line and page breaks, 71–72
  line spacing, 70
  mirror margins, 80
  numbered and bulleted lists, 73–75
  overview of, 55–56
  page orientation, 80
  paper size, 80–81
  paragraph alignment, 66–67
  paragraph spacing, 70–71
  reset to default setting, 69
  split pages, 72–73
  text effects, 62–63
  track inconsistent formatting, 81
  turn on formatting marks, 78
  use dialog box to format page, 78–81
  use ruler for indents, 70–71
forms
  create, 195–198
  modify template, 193–194

use, 198
use Microsoft Form templates, 192–194
formulas
  assemble own, 154
  common terms and concepts, 155–156
  convert to plain text, 157
  copy, 157
  inside brackets, 156
  update after changing cell value, 156
fractions, configure, 109
Freeform tools, 175–176
Full Screen Reading view, 10, 106, 124–125
functions, formulas and, 156

G

Gabriola font, 63–64
General options, Word Options dialog
  box, 19–20
General tab, document properties, 237
Getting Started, Microsoft Office, 23
Go To command, 44–45
Go To Endnote button, 99
Go To Footer button, 97
Go To Footnote button, 99
Go To Header button, 97
gradients, 180–181
grammar checker, 50–51
graphics. *See also* illustrations
  change theme, 89
  file formats accepted by Word, 167
graphs. *See* charts
groups
  create new, 13–14
  of illustrations, 190
  rearranging on ribbon, 12–13
  ribbon and, 5

H

handles, positioning illustrations, 188–190
hanging indents
  create, 69
  defined, 67
  remove, 69
  set tabs with, 95
  set with ruler, 71
headers
  add, 96–99
  configure with AutoFormat, 109
  repeat rows, 157
Help, 20–24
  conduct research, 21
  Microsoft Office, 23
  open, 20–21
  Thesaurus, 22
  translate document, 22–23
  update Word, 23–24
Help icon, 20
Help toolbar, 21
Highlight tool, 236–238
highlights, 115–116, 236–238
Home & Business 2010, Office, 5
Home & Student 2010, Office, 5
Home tab, ribbon, 57–58
horizontal lines, borders, 76–77
HP ink-jet printers, 128
.htm file extension, 213–214
HTML (HyperText Markup Language),
  215–216, 225
HTML, XHTML, and CSS QuickSteps
  (Hart-Davis), 215, 225
http://, hyperlinks, 218
hyperlinks
  configure with AutoFormat, 109

create to e-mail address, 221–222
create to existing file of Web page, 219–220
create to new document, 221
create to place in current document, 220–221
insert, 218–219
understand, 218–219
HyperText Markup Language (HTML),
  215–216, 225
hyphenation
  add, 116–117
  configure with AutoFormat, 109

I

If/Then/Else rule, merge fields, 136–137
illustrations, 165–190
  add caption to pictures, 173
  add objects from other programs, 180–181
  add pictures, 166–170
  add shapes, 175
  add special effects to text, 176–177
  alignment of, 174
  combine by grouping, 190
  create diagram, 177–180
  create drawings, 174–175
  link picture files, 166
  overview of, 165
  position, 185–188
  position "in-line" pictures, 172–174
  reduce picture's file size, 173
  remove unwanted areas, 170–172
  resize and rotate precisely, 184–185
  resize pictures, 167
  take screenshots, 183–184
  understand positioning of, 187
  use color effects, 180–182

illustrations (*cont.*)

use handles and borders to position, 188–190

use Picture Tools Format tab, 170–172

work with, 189–190

work with curves, 175–176

wrap text around picture, 173–174

"in-line" pictures, position, 172–174

indentation

paragraph, 67–69

with ruler, 70–71

small sections of text, 78

tables, 160

index, 101–102

information

add identifying document, 17–19

enter table, 151–152

remove personal document, 222–224

ink comments, 236

inline positioning, illustrations, 187

Insert Cells dialog box, 148

Insert Chart dialog box, 203

Insert Hyperlink dialog box, 218–222

insert mode, text, 36

Insert Picture dialog box, 165–166, 168

Insert Tab Tables group, 145–146

Insert Table dialog box, 145

insertion point

determine where text will appear, 34, 36

insert building blocks, 110–111

move, 44

start document, 27

insertion, Track Changes options, 230

ISO encoding, 217

italic font style, 59, 109

J

justified paragraphs, 66–67

Justify button, 66

K

kerning

achieving professional look with, 62

applying to fonts, 63

keyboard

copying formats with, 79

entering special characters from, 35

move around in document using, 44

moving insertion point with, 34

opening tab or menu with, 8

select chart items using, 207

select text with, 39

keyboard shortcuts

change for specific command, 18

common character, 35

create for reviewing, 233

create special character, 35

move around in table, 152

text formatting, 58–59

L

labels

merge, 141–142

print, 130–131

show chart data, 207–208

landscape, page orientation, 79–80

language

translate whole document, 22

translating word or phrase, 21, 23

language-supported software, 198

layout

changing table size, 147–150

form, 196

select chart items, 206

leaders, set tab, 95–96

left-aligned paragraphs, 66–67

left indentation

change, 67

configure with AutoFormat, 109

move, 67–68

set with ruler, 70

legacy form controls, 197

legend, move chart, 207

ligatures, OpenType, 63

line breaks

insert, 36–37

paragraphs, 71–72

lines

count number of, 115

create horizontal as you type, 76

enhance, 182

selecting text for single, 37

set spacing, 70–71

links, picture files, 166

lists

configure items with AutoFormat, 109

merge with document to create catalog or directory, 132

locations

copying formats to several, 79

going to particular, 44–45

lowercase, 65

OpenType, 63–64
Options dialog box, 222–224, 230
Options, Microsoft Office, 23
ordinals, 109
organizational charts, 178–180
Outline view, 10, 106
outlines
  apply border and shading to tables, 162
  create and use, 105–107
  as indentation, 67
  using for table of contents, 103–104
overtype mode, text, 36

P

page breaks, 36–37, 71–72
page formatting
  copy, 79
  defined, 78
  set margins, 78
  of small sections of text, 78
  track inconsistent, 81
  use Page Setup dialog box, 78–79
Page Setup dialog box, 78–79, 81
pages
  count number in document/portion
    of document, 115
  determining orientation of, 80
  enter line break at end of, 37
paper size, page format and, 80–81
Paragraph dialog box, 67–71
paragraph formatting, 65–78
  add borders and shading, 76–78
  add space between paragraphs, 70–71
  copying, 79
  count number in document/portion of
    document, 115

handle split pages, 72–73
indentation, 67–68
restore to default setting, 69
select text for, 37
set alignment, 66–67
set line and page breaks, 37, 71–72
set line spacing, 70
use numbered and bulleted lists, 73–75
paste preview, 1
paste text, 40–41
personal information, remove from
  Web page, 222
personalize Word, 10
perspective, illustration, 190
phrases, translate, 198
Picture Tools Format tab, 170–172
pictures
  add caption, 173
  add Clip Art, 168
  add directly, 168–170
  browse for, 166–167
  copy, move, delete, 43
  customizing bullets, 74–75
  fill drawing with, 182
  link, 166
  remove unwanted areas from, 170–172
  resize, 167, 173
  specify page size, 80–81
  supported graphic file formats, 167
  wrap text around, 173–174
Pictures tab, Web Options dialog box, 217
pin Word icon, 3–4
point action, mouse, 8
points, font size, 59
portrait orientation, 79, 80
position, character spacing, 62
position illustrations
  absolute positioning, 187–188

alignment, 174, 190
  change how content displays, 185–187
  for "in-line" pictures, 172–174
  move incrementally, 189
  relative to areas in document, 187–188
  set even spacing, 190
  set order of stacked illustrations, 189–190
  understanding, 187
  use handles and borders, 188–190
preferences, set, 19–20
prefix match, Find and Replace dialog box, 47
preview
  merge to envelopes, 140
  merge to labels, 141
  Web page in Word, 222–223
Print Layout view
  defined, 10, 105
  as Print Preview view, 122–124
  repeat header rows, 157
  resize tables by dragging, 149
Print Preview, 122–124
printing, 119–132. *See also* mail merge
  add Quick Print icon, 126
  customize print job, 126–127
  define how document is printed, 121–122
  envelope, 128–129
  faxing, 131–132
  install printer, 119
  labels, 129–130
  overview of, 124–125
  preview what you will print, 122–124
  set up printer, 120
Privacy options, Web pages, 222–224
Professional 2010, Office, 5
Professional Plus 2010, Office, 5
properties
  remove personal information, 222–224
  set column width, 150

search
  for document in Word, 31–32
  find and replace text, 45–49
  Help. *See* Help
  locate existing document, 32–33
section breaks, 37, 92–93
security updates, 24
sentence
  choosing case, 65
  select text for single, 37
separators, column and row, 157
serif fonts, 59
shading
  add, 76–78
  add to tables, 162
shapes
  add to drawings, 175–176
  create diagrams, 178–180
  set gradients, 180–182
SharePoint 2010, 228
SharePoint 2010 QuickSteps
  (McGraw-Hill/Professional), 228
SHIFT key, 64
Show Document Panel, 17
Show/Hide Formatting Marks, 78
Single File Web Page format, 213–214
single-spacing, set line, 70
size
  illustrations, 184–185, 189
  pictures, 167
  table, 147–150
SmartArt, 178–180
sort
  locate existing document with, 32–33
  table data, 151–154
  tables, 152–153
sound-alike words, Find and Replace
  dialog box, 47

source code, create HTML elements, 225
spacing
  add between paragraphs, 70–71
  character, 62
  create between cells, 161
  set line, 70
  between table cells, 162
special characters, 34–35, 47
special effects, add to text, 176–177
special features, 191–210
  create chart, 203–204
  create form, 195–198
  determine chart type, 204–206
  format chart items, 208–210
  format text, 210
  modify template, 193–195
  select chart items, 206–207
  translate entire document, 200–201
  translate selected text, 199–200
  translate word or phrase, 199
  understanding data series and axes, 208
  use Microsoft Form templates, 192–193
  using form, 198
  work with chart items, 206–208
  working with data table, 210
spelling check, 50–51
split pages, format paragraphs, 72–73
splitting table cells, 150, 159–160
Standard 2010, Office, 5
Start menu, 2–3
start Word, 2–4
Starter 2010, Office, 5
static text, 132–133
Statistics tab, document properties, 237
Step by Step Merge Wizard, 134
styles, 84–90
  apply style sets to document, 84–85
  apply table, 162–164

configure with AutoFormat, 109–110
delete document, 87
delete table, 164
identify text with, 84
modify, 85–86
numbered paragraph, 74
restore to default setting, 87
save new Quick Style, 85
set for automatic updates, 86
set table of contents, 102–105
understanding, 84
use themes, 86–90
stylistic sets, OpenType, 64
subdocument commands, table of contents, 104
submenus, 9
suffix match, Find and Replace dialog box, 47
Summary tab, document properties, 237
symbols
  create equation with, 114
  footnote and endnote, 100
  select special characters from, 34–35
  symbol fonts, 59
  use as bullets, 75
syntax, formulas, 155

T

TAB key, 36, 152
table of contents, 102–105
Table Tools Design tab, 146
Table Tools Layout tab, 147–148, 150
tables, 143–164
  add shading, 162
  add spacing between cells, 162
  add styles, 164
  alignment, 160
  border effects, 162

change cell margins, 161
column width and row height, 150–151
configure with AutoFormat, 109
convert to text and text to, 155–156
create, 144–146
enter information, 151–152
format automatically, 162–164
format content, 157–159
formulas for, 154–157
functionality of, 144
merge cells, 158–159
Microsoft Office Word form templates
    based on, 195
move and copy columns, rows and, 154
position, 161
properties, 150, 158–161
remove, 157
remove cells, rows and columns, 149–150
repeat header rows, 157
select rows, columns, cells, 147–148
size, 147–150
sort data, 151–154
split cells, 159–160
tools, 146–147
word wrap, 158
wrap text around, 160–161
Tablet PCs, handwriting comments, 236
tabs
    create new, 13–14
    rearrange on ribbon, 12–13
    ribbon, 5–6, 12
    set using measurements, 95
    set using ruler, 94–95
    set with horizontal ruler, 70–71
    set with leaders, 95–96
    types of, 94
    using table, 146–147
    working with, 8–9

tags
    entries for table of contents, 102–103
    remove Word-specific, in Web pages,
        224–225
taskbar, 3–4
templates
    change default, 90–91
    chart, 205–206
    create, 91
    Microsoft Form, 192–194
    modify form, 193–195
    new document, 91–92
    online, 29–30
    save documents as, 53
    understanding, 84
    from your computer, 26–29
text
    add borders and shading, 77
    add color, 182
    add special effects, 176–177
    convert between tables and, 155–156
    copy formats to separate pieces of, 79
    create diagrams, 178
    create Word Art effect, 176–177
    creating data labels for charts, 208
    creating numbered or bulleted list before
        typing, 74
    enter information into table, 151–152
    find highlighted, 116
    format chart, 210
    highlight document in review, 236–238
    identify with a style, 84
    specify page size, 80–81
    translate entire document, 200–201
    translate selected, 199–200
    translate word or phrase, 199
    views, 9–10
    work with mini toolbar, 9

wrap around pictures, 173–174
wrap around table, 160–161
wrap in cell, 158–159
text box, create equation in, 113–114
text effects, 62–63
text formatting, 57–65
    with advanced font features, 61–64
    apply character formatting, 57–61
    change capitalization, 64–65
    create drop cap, 65
    reset, 60
    select text, 57
    use text effects, 62–63
Theme Effects, 89
themes
    assign to document, 86–87
    change, 87–89
    create custom, 89–90
    understanding, 84
    use, 86–87
Thesaurus feature, 22, 117
three equal signs (===), create borders, 76–77
three hyphens (---), create borders, 76–77
three underscores (___), create borders, 76–77
title
    add axis, 207
    add chart, 206
    save existing Word document as Web page, 213
tOGGLE cASE, capitalization, 65
Tool tabs, ribbon, 12
tools
    add/remove, 14
    rearrange on Quick Access toolbar, 17
    ribbon containing, 5–7
    table, 146–147
Track Changes
    compare documents and, 239–240
    Options dialog box, 230

compare documents, 239
create reviewing shortcuts, 233
highlight objects, 236–238
review changes, 232–235
save several copies, 236–238
save several copies of document, 238–239
set document properties, 237
SharePoint 2010 for major collaboration, 228
Track Changes, 228–232
Word window
changing background color of, 17
exploring, 5–6
ribbon adapting to size of, 7
view buttons in, 44
word writing aids, 107–118
AutoCorrect, 107–108

AutoFormat, 108–110
building blocks, 110–112
count characters and words, 115
equations, 112–114
highlighting, 115–116
hyphenation, 116–117
WordArt effect, 176–177
words
count, 115
translate, 198
words, single
selecting one or more characters, 38–39
selecting text, 37
wrap text
around pictures, 173–174
around table, 160–161

AutoFit option and, 158
change how content displays around
illustration, 185–187
changing in cell, 158–159
www., hyperlinks, 218

X

.xml extension, 214

Z

zoom tools, Print Preview, 123